Leveraging Large Language Models for Quantum-Aware Cybersecurity

Hewa Majeed Zangana
Duhok Polytechnic University, Iraq

Marwan Omar
Illinois Institute of Technology, USA

IGI Global
Scientific Publishing
Publishing Tomorrow's Research Today

Vice President of Editorial	Melissa Wagner
Managing Editor of Acquisitions	Mikaela Felty
Managing Editor of Book Development	Jocelynn Hessler
Production Manager	Mike Brehm
Cover Design	Phillip Shickler

Published in the United States of America by
IGI Global Scientific Publishing
701 East Chocolate Avenue
Hershey, PA, 17033, USA
Tel: 717-533-8845
Fax: 717-533-8661
E-mail: cust@igi-global.com
Website: https://www.igi-global.com

Library of Congress Cataloging-in-Publication Data

CIP Data Pending
ISBN:979-8-3373-1102-9
eISBN:979-8-3373-1104-3

British Cataloguing in Publication Data
A Cataloguing in Publication record for this book is available from the British Library.

Table of Contents

Detailed Table of Contents

The advent of quantum computing poses unprecedented challenges to the security of classical cryptographic systems, driving the need for innovative approaches in cybersecurity. This chapter introduces the concept of quantum-aware cybersecurity, highlighting the pivotal role of large language models (LLMs) in addressing emerging threats. By leveraging LLMs' advanced capabilities in data analysis, threat detection, and adaptive learning, organizations can enhance resilience against quantum-era vulnerabilities. The chapter emphasizes the integration of LLMs with quantum-resistant cryptographic techniques, fostering a secure foundation for the next-generation digital ecosystem. This exploration underscores the urgency of adopting quantum-aware strategies to safeguard critical infrastructures and data integrity.

Quantum computing is rapidly evolving, promising to revolutionize various fields, including cybersecurity. By harnessing the power of quantum mechanics, quantum computers are expected to solve problems that are intractable for classical computers, particularly in areas such as encryption and data security. This chapter explores the fundamental principles of quantum computing and its potential implications for cybersecurity. We discuss the challenges posed by quantum algorithms, including Shor's algorithm and Grover's algorithm, which can break widely-used cryptographic systems like RSA and AES. Furthermore, we examine the transition towards quantum-resistant algorithms, also known as post-quantum cryptography (PQC), and the role of large language models (LLMs) in facilitating the adaptation of cybersecurity strategies to a quantum-enabled future. The chapter concludes with a look at the future of quantum-aware cybersecurity, emphasizing the need for robust, adaptable frameworks to address emerging threats.

The rapid advancement of quantum computing presents both tremendous opportunities and significant challenges for cybersecurity, particularly in the realms of privacy and data protection. Traditional encryption methods face obsolescence in the quantum era, as quantum algorithms like Shor's algorithm can efficiently break widely used cryptographic schemes. Large Language Models (LLMs), with their capacity for processing and analyzing vast amounts of data, have emerged as valuable tools in addressing privacy concerns in quantum computing environments. This chapter explores how LLMs can be leveraged to enhance privacy and data protection by facilitating the development of quantum-resistant cryptographic protocols, automating threat detection, and assisting in the creation of novel security architectures tailored to quantum technologies. By examining the intersection of LLMs and quantum computing, this work highlights their potential to reshape cybersecurity strategies to ensure that data remains secure in a post-quantum world.

The integration of Large Language Models (LLMs) into cybersecurity offers significant potential for enhancing threat detection and incident response, particularly in the context of emerging quantum computing capabilities. As quantum computing threatens to undermine traditional cryptographic systems, there is a pressing need for quantum-aware cybersecurity measures. This chapter explores the application of LLMs in identifying and mitigating threats in a quantum-aware environment. It examines how LLMs can aid in detecting quantum-related vulnerabilities, analyzing quantum-aware attack vectors, and automating incident response protocols. Additionally, the chapter discusses the challenges of adapting LLMs to the quantum landscape, including the need for specialized training datasets and the consideration of quantum-resistant algorithms. Through case studies and theoretical models, this chapter provides a comprehensive view of how LLMs can be leveraged to strengthen cybersecurity in the era of quantum computing.

In the 21st century, there has been a great deal of importance ascribed to international security. A standard procedure used by adversarial states and non-state actors to propagate their continuous and calculated malicious objectives are cyber offenses such as cyber-espionage, hacktivism, cyberwar, as well as other cybercriminal activities (Hwang & Choi, 2021). Even though cyber-attacks were initially thought to be perpetrated by individuals or privately owned organizations, more and more attacks are being orchestrated by nation states, other states or even targeted towards individual organizations. Recent reports have shown that North Korea has an advance cyber warfare capacity, and a substantial number of its workforce is allegedly engaged in the activities of the dark web with a direct support from the government

The rapid rise of cybercrime, fueled by increased reliance on digital systems, underscores the importance of effective digital forensics. This research investigates forensic artifacts within two widely used operating systems, Windows and Linux, to offer a detailed comparison of their impact on forensic practices. Digital forensic artifacts, such as user activity logs, system logs, application data, and volatile memory artifacts, are key sources of evidence that investigators rely on to reconstruct events, identify threats, and secure convictions in cybercrime cases.

The integration of Large Language Models (LLMs) with quantum-enhanced tools is revolutionizing cybersecurity. This chapter explores how these advanced technologies can address critical challenges, including real-time anomaly detection, advanced persistent threats (APTs), and zero-day exploits. By combining LLMs' contextual understanding with the computational power of quantum computing, we propose innovative approaches to strengthen intrusion detection systems, malware analysis, and threat intelligence. The chapter covers automated defense systems, adversarial scenario modeling, and adaptive cybersecurity frameworks that evolve in response to emerging threats. It highlights synergies between LLMs and quantum computing, presenting a dual strategy to detect and mitigate cyber risks more effectively. While discussing technical, ethical, and scalability challenges, the chapter offers practical insights for cybersecurity professionals, equipping them with tools and strategies to defend against increasingly sophisticated threats in a quantum-aware future.

Cybersecurity threats are ever-changing and characterized by more sophisticated attacks including, but not limited to, ransomware, phishing attempts, and Distributed Denial-of-Service (DDoS) attacks. Integration of Artificial Intelligence in cybersecurity is one of the pioneering methods for dealing with the new threats in the digital environment. This article highlights areas where AI technologies improve threat detection, response automation, and risk management. It discusses the challenges, ethical issues, and AI solutions in cybersecurity

Large Language Models (LLMs) have emerged as transformative tools in cybersecurity, offering unprecedented capabilities in automating tasks and providing deep insights into evolving threats. This chapter explores the dual role of LLMs in enhancing cybersecurity—from automating routine operations to generating actionable intelligence. By examining real-world applications, such as threat detection, vulnerability management, and incident response, this chapter highlights the potential of LLMs to mitigate risks while addressing their inherent limitations and ethical concerns. Special attention is given to the interplay between LLMs and quantum-aware cybersecurity, presenting a forward-looking perspective on their integration into complex, next-generation security frameworks.

Adversarial attacks on machine learning models have become a significant concern in cybersecurity, especially with the advent of quantum computing. These attacks aim to manipulate the decision-making process of AI systems, leading to vulnerabilities that can be exploited by malicious actors. As quantum computing promises to revolutionize various industries, it also introduces new challenges for defending against adversarial threats. This chapter explores the impact of quantum computing on adversarial machine learning, examining how quantum algorithms can be both a tool for enhancing attack strategies and a foundation for developing more robust defense mechanisms. It reviews existing defense techniques, such as adversarial training and gradient masking, and discusses the potential for quantum-aware models to counteract these threats.

The intersection of natural language processing (NLP) and cyber threat intelligence (CTI) is gaining momentum as cybersecurity paradigms evolve to address the challenges posed by quantum computing. This chapter explores how advancements in NLP, particularly through the deployment of large language models (LLMs), can be leveraged to enhance CTI in a quantum-aware context. It discusses the capabilities of NLP systems to process vast amounts of threat data, identify patterns, and predict potential risks while considering the implications of quantum technologies on cybersecurity frameworks. Furthermore, the chapter highlights the role of quantum-aware NLP tools in detecting advanced persistent threats, optimizing response strategies, and ensuring the resilience of digital ecosystems in the face of quantum-enabled cyber threats. By integrating LLMs with quantum computing principles, this research provides insights into the future of CTI and its evolution to counteract complex cyber challenges.

Preface

The rapid evolution of quantum computing, coupled with the transformative potential of large language models (LLMs), heralds a new era in cybersecurity. As the quantum threat looms over conventional encryption methods, it is imperative to develop advanced solutions that are both quantum-aware and resilient. *Leveraging Large Language Models for Quantum-Aware Cybersecurity* explores the intersection of these two groundbreaking technologies, presenting strategies to secure digital infrastructures in the face of emerging challenges.

This book brings together leading researchers and practitioners from academia and industry to examine how LLMs can be harnessed to address the complex demands of quantum-aware cybersecurity. By bridging theoretical foundations with practical applications, this volume serves as an essential resource for professionals, students, and researchers invested in the future of cybersecurity. It delves into the technological innovations, ethical considerations, and forward-looking solutions that will define the next generation of secure systems.

Our objectives with this book are to:

- **Deepen Understanding:** Provide a comprehensive exploration of the interplay between LLMs and quantum-aware cybersecurity.
- **Enable Practical Applications:** Highlight how LLMs can be deployed effectively in real-world quantum-resistant cybersecurity scenarios.
- **Encourage Critical Engagement:** Address the ethical and technical challenges to ensure responsible integration of these technologies.
- **Inspire Innovation:** Showcase emerging trends and future directions for research and development at this intersection.

ORGANIZATION OF THE BOOK

The book is structured to offer a coherent narrative, beginning with an introduction to the fundamental concepts and culminating in future possibilities for autonomous defense systems. The chapters are as follows:

Chapter 1: Introduction to Quantum-Aware Cybersecurity: The Need for LLMs
Chapter 2: Understanding Quantum Computing Implications for Cybersecurity
Chapter 3: LLMs for Enhancing Privacy and Data Protection in Quantum Computing Environments
Chapter 4: LLMs for Quantum-Aware Threat Detection and Incident Response
Chapter 5: Nation-State Cyber Attacks on Critical Infrastructure: A Case Study of the 2014 Sony Pictures Hack
Chapter 6: Forensic Artifacts in Operating Systems: Windows vs. Linux
Chapter 7: Applications of LLMs in Quantum-Aware Cybersecurity: Real-Time Anomaly Detection and Threat Intelligence
Chapter 8: Artificial Intelligence-Powered Cybersecurity: The Future of Threat Detection and Response
Chapter 9: Large Language Models in Cybersecurity: From Automation to Intelligence
Chapter 10: Adversarial Attacks and Defense Mechanisms in the Age of Quantum Computing
Chapter 11: Natural Language Processing for Cyber Threat Intelligence in a Quantum World
Chapter 12: The Future of Cybersecurity: Integrating LLMs with Quantum Computing for Autonomous Defense Systems

CONCLUSION

As quantum computing and artificial intelligence continue to redefine the cybersecurity landscape, this book aims to serve as a foundational text and a source of inspiration for ongoing innovation. By exploring the synergies between LLMs and quantum-aware cybersecurity, we hope to equip readers with the knowledge and tools necessary to navigate and shape the future of secure digital ecosystems.

Hewa Majeed Zangana
Duhok Polytechnic University, Iraq

Marwan Omar

Illinois Institute of Technology, USA

Chapter 1
Introduction to Quantum-Aware Cybersecurity:
The Need for LLMs

Hewa Majeed Zangana
https://orcid.org/0000-0001-7909-254X
Duhok Polytechnic University, Iraq

Marwan Omar
Illinois Institute of Technology, USA

ABSTRACT

The advent of quantum computing poses unprecedented challenges to the security of classical cryptographic systems, driving the need for innovative approaches in cybersecurity. This chapter introduces the concept of quantum-aware cybersecurity, highlighting the pivotal role of large language models (LLMs) in addressing emerging threats. By leveraging LLMs' advanced capabilities in data analysis, threat detection, and adaptive learning, organizations can enhance resilience against quantum-era vulnerabilities. The chapter emphasizes the integration of LLMs with quantum-resistant cryptographic techniques, fostering a secure foundation for the next-generation digital ecosystem. This exploration underscores the urgency of adopting quantum-aware strategies to safeguard critical infrastructures and data integrity.

DOI: 10.4018/979-8-3373-1102-9.ch001

1. INTRODUCTION

The rapid advancements in quantum computing present both opportunities and challenges for the cybersecurity landscape. While quantum technologies promise to revolutionize various domains through unparalleled computational power, they also pose significant risks to classical encryption systems, which are foundational to current cybersecurity frameworks. With this backdrop, the integration of Large Language Models (LLMs) into quantum-aware cybersecurity is emerging as a novel paradigm, combining the predictive and analytical prowess of AI with strategies to mitigate quantum threats.

1.1 Quantum Computing: A Double-Edged Sword

Quantum computing introduces an era where classical cryptographic techniques, such as RSA and ECC, are rendered vulnerable due to algorithms like Shor's and Grover's. The quantum threat compels researchers and industry stakeholders to explore quantum-resistant algorithms and frameworks. Sodiya et al. (2024) provide an exhaustive review of the potential impacts of quantum computing on U.S. cybersecurity, emphasizing the urgency of adapting to this paradigm shift.

In parallel, quantum advancements have catalyzed developments in industrial quantum networks (Bush et al., 2021), showcasing opportunities for enhanced communication and computation. However, these advancements also underscore the importance of robust quantum-aware security measures to prevent vulnerabilities in interconnected systems.

To understand the implications of quantum computing on classical cryptography, it is essential to compare the computational approaches of classical and quantum systems. The diagram below illustrates the key differences in their functioning and highlights how quantum algorithms disrupt the foundations of cryptographic systems like RSA and ECC.

Figure 1. Classical vs. quantum computing in cryptography

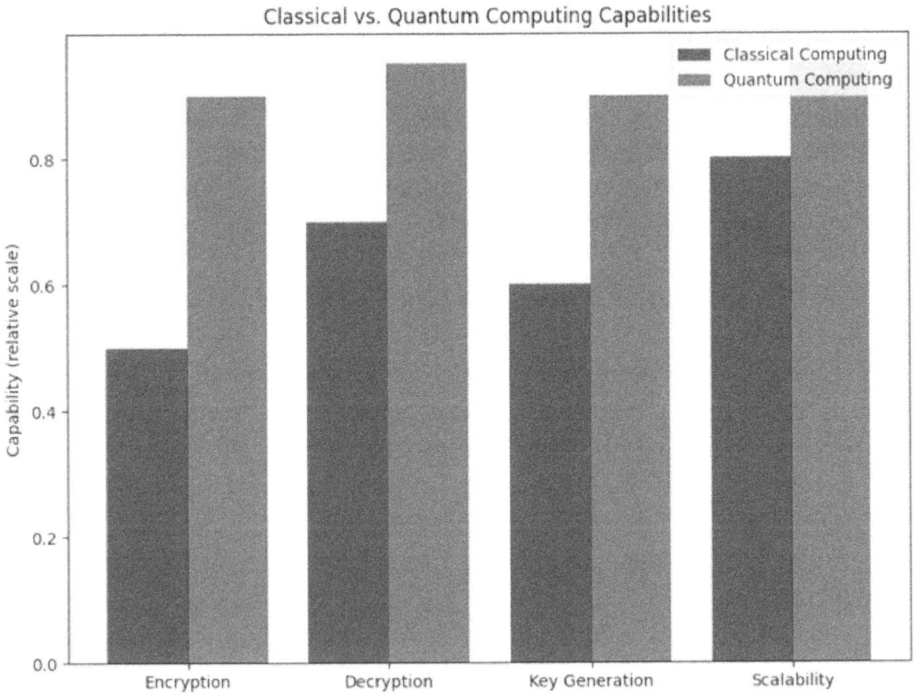

1.2 Large Language Models in Cybersecurity

LLMs, such as OpenAI's GPT and Google's BERT, have proven transformative in analyzing and interpreting vast datasets. Their applications extend from detecting threats in real time to predicting potential vulnerabilities in software systems. According to Gholami and Omar (2023), the efficiency of LLMs can be significantly enhanced through synthetic data, allowing them to learn complex patterns and detect anomalies efficiently.

Furthermore, Jones et al. (2023) demonstrated how machine learning algorithms, combined with cybersecurity strategies, could improve the speed and accuracy of threat detection. Extending this concept to quantum-aware cybersecurity, LLMs can act as intermediaries, bridging traditional systems with quantum-resistant solutions.

1.3 Need for Quantum-Aware Cybersecurity Frameworks

The integration of quantum technologies in critical sectors such as healthcare, finance, and national defense necessitates a reimagining of cybersecurity frameworks. Traditional practices, as discussed by Hamza and Omar (2013), may be inadequate in mitigating risks associated with the abuse and nefarious use of quantum resources. Emerging frameworks, such as quantum-resistant key exchange protocols (Exchange, n.d.), highlight the progress but also reveal the gaps in existing methodologies.

1.4 Role of LLMs in Quantum-Aware Cybersecurity

Leveraging LLMs for quantum-aware cybersecurity involves equipping these models to anticipate and counteract quantum-specific threats. Omar and Zangana (2024) emphasize the need to redefine security paradigms by integrating AI-powered solutions to address evolving threats. Similarly, the contributions of Gholami and Omar (2024) highlight how LLMs, through tailored training, can match or exceed the capabilities of their classical counterparts in identifying vulnerabilities in complex systems.

The fusion of LLMs with quantum-resistant strategies creates a synergistic framework that is both predictive and adaptive. For instance, Huff et al. (2023) explore management practices for mitigating cybersecurity threats, underlining the importance of proactive measures. These principles, when applied in the context of quantum computing, suggest a proactive approach to safeguarding digital assets.

The role of large language models in quantum-aware cybersecurity involves multiple interconnected stages, from data analysis to integrating quantum-resistant strategies. The flowchart below outlines these stages, emphasizing their contribution to adaptive and resilient cybersecurity frameworks.

Figure 2. Role of LLMs in quantum-aware cybersecurity

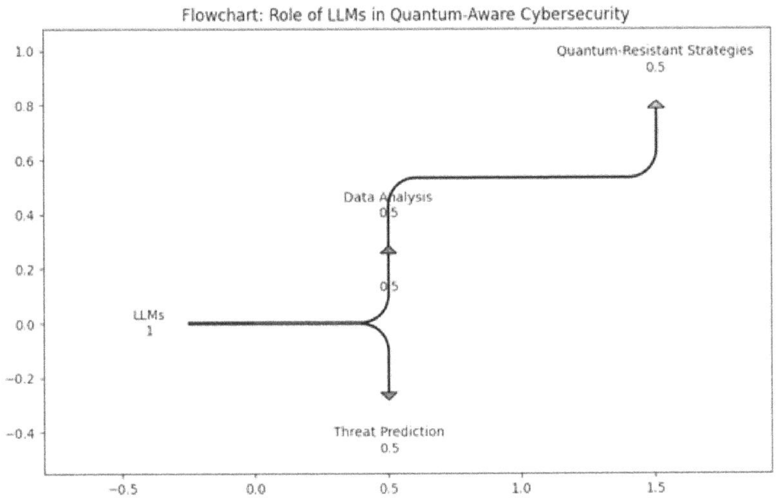

1.5 Future Implications

As quantum computing capabilities grow, so does the urgency for industries and governments to develop quantum-aware cybersecurity solutions. Frameworks like those discussed by Mohamed and Ahmed (2024) in combating man-in-the-middle attacks provide a foundation for developing AI-driven, quantum-resistant solutions.

This chapter establishes the foundational principles of integrating LLMs with quantum-aware cybersecurity, setting the stage for exploring case studies, methodologies, and future directions. By addressing both the opportunities and challenges, it underscores the importance of this integration in safeguarding digital infrastructure against emerging quantum threats.

2. THE EMERGENCE OF QUANTUM COMPUTING AND ITS POTENTIAL IMPACT ON CYBERSECURITY

Quantum computing represents a paradigm shift in computational capabilities, with the potential to solve complex problems that are infeasible for classical systems. This emerging technology has significant implications for cybersecurity, presenting both unprecedented opportunities and formidable challenges.

2.1. Understanding Quantum Computing

Quantum computing leverages the principles of quantum mechanics, including superposition and entanglement, to perform computations at speeds unattainable by classical computers. Unlike traditional binary systems, quantum computers use quantum bits (qubits), which can represent multiple states simultaneously. This allows for massive parallelism in processing tasks (Rahul et al., 2024; Perron et al., 2021). The inherent power of quantum computers has the potential to revolutionize fields like optimization, cryptography, and artificial intelligence (Baseri et al., 2024; Singh, N. B.).

2.2. Opportunities in Enhancing Cybersecurity

Quantum computing could enhance cybersecurity by enabling more robust encryption methods. Quantum key distribution (QKD) systems, for example, offer secure communication channels that rely on the principles of quantum mechanics to prevent eavesdropping (Bush et al., 2021). Additionally, quantum computing's computational power can improve threat detection and response systems, enabling faster analysis of complex datasets (Metawei et al., 2022; Zangana et al., 2025).

2.3. Challenges to Current Cryptographic Standards

The most immediate concern posed by quantum computing is its ability to break widely used cryptographic algorithms, such as RSA and ECC, which underpin modern digital security. Quantum algorithms, such as Shor's algorithm, can factorize large integers exponentially faster than classical algorithms, rendering these encryption methods obsolete (Rahul et al., 2024; Bishwas & Sen, 2024). This necessitates a transition to quantum-resistant cryptographic standards, which is a complex and resource-intensive process (Sodiya et al., 2024; Baseri et al., 2024).

2.4. Implications for Infrastructure and Privacy

Quantum computing could exacerbate vulnerabilities in critical infrastructures, including financial systems, healthcare networks, and defense frameworks. The ability to decrypt sensitive data retroactively poses a significant threat to long-term data privacy (Gholami & Omar, 2023; Mohammed et al., 2018). Organizations must proactively adopt strategies to mitigate these risks, such as deploying quantum-safe cryptographic protocols (How & Cheah, 2023; Zangana et al., 2024).

2.5. Quantum-Resistant Solutions

To address these challenges, the cybersecurity community is exploring quantum-resistant algorithms, which are designed to withstand attacks from quantum computers. Examples include lattice-based cryptography and hash-based signatures (Bishwas & Sen, 2024; Exchange, Q. R. K.). These methods aim to provide a secure foundation for digital communication and data protection in a quantum-enabled world.

2.6. Integration with Artificial Intelligence

The integration of quantum computing with artificial intelligence (AI) presents a dual-edged sword. While quantum-enhanced AI could improve anomaly detection and predictive analytics in cybersecurity, it also raises concerns about adversarial applications, where quantum-powered AI could be used to develop sophisticated cyberattacks (Omar, 2024; Khan et al., 2023). These advancements necessitate robust frameworks for ethical and secure AI deployment (Rahul et al., 2024; Lougovski et al., 2023).

2.7. Global Collaboration and Regulatory Efforts

Addressing the cybersecurity implications of quantum computing requires global collaboration among governments, academia, and industry. International standards for quantum-safe cryptography, such as those promoted by the National Institute of Standards and Technology (NIST), are critical for ensuring secure digital ecosystems (Rahul et al., 2024; Bush et al., 2021). Regulatory bodies must also address the ethical implications of quantum technologies to balance innovation with security (Hamza & Omar, 2013; Omar & Zangana, 2025).

2.8. Future Directions

The path forward involves investing in quantum research, training a quantum-literate workforce, and fostering interdisciplinary collaboration. Embracing quantum technologies responsibly will be key to harnessing their benefits while mitigating associated risks (Seskir, 2019; Huff et al., 2023). As quantum computing transitions from theoretical potential to practical application, it will redefine the cybersecurity landscape in ways that are both exciting and challenging (Omar, 2021; Zangana et al., 2025).

By anticipating the quantum revolution and adapting to its implications, organizations can build resilient cybersecurity frameworks that safeguard against both current and future threats.

3. CHALLENGES IN TRADITIONAL CYBERSECURITY APPROACHES IN THE AGE OF QUANTUM COMPUTING

The evolution of quantum computing represents a profound shift in computational paradigms, offering unprecedented processing power. While this technological leap promises significant benefits, it also threatens the foundations of traditional cybersecurity approaches. This section explores the challenges associated with protecting digital assets in the face of quantum threats.

3.1. Vulnerabilities in Cryptographic Protocols

Traditional cybersecurity heavily relies on cryptographic protocols like RSA, ECC, and AES, which are foundational to secure communications, digital signatures, and data protection. However, the quantum algorithm developed by Shor demonstrates the capability to factorize large integers and solve discrete logarithm problems exponentially faster than classical methods. This poses an existential threat to asymmetric cryptography.

Sodiya et al. (2024) highlight that even widely adopted encryption standards, like RSA-2048, could be rendered obsolete within a decade as quantum computing matures. Similarly, Baseri, Chouhan, and Ghorbani (2024) warn about the need for immediate transition to quantum-resistant algorithms to maintain the security of critical infrastructure.

3.2. Increased Attack Surface

The advent of quantum technologies broadens the attack surface across multiple domains, including financial systems, healthcare, and national security. For example, Mohammed et al. (2018) discuss vulnerabilities in wireless sensor networks, which could be exacerbated by quantum-based attacks. Furthermore, Zangana and Omar (2020) emphasize how smartphone security may also face unique challenges due to quantum-enabled hacking techniques.

3.33. Inefficiency in Detection and Defense Mechanisms

Current cybersecurity frameworks are inadequate in addressing the speed and precision of quantum-enabled attacks. Jones and Omar (2024) propose advanced machine learning methods like GPT-2 Enhanced Attack Detection and Defense (GEADD) as potential solutions. However, implementing such systems across all critical infrastructures remains a logistical and economic challenge.

3.4. Resource Constraints in Transition to Quantum-Resistant Systems

The transition to quantum-resistant cryptography is neither straightforward nor affordable. Perron et al. (2021) outline the technical and educational challenges in integrating quantum computing into existing security infrastructure. These issues are compounded by a lack of skilled professionals trained in quantum-safe protocols (Khan et al., 2023).

3.5. Regulatory and Ethical Implications

Quantum computing's impact extends beyond technical domains, influencing regulatory and ethical considerations. Hamza and Omar (2013) address the issue of abuse and nefarious use of cloud computing, which could be amplified by quantum technology. Additionally, Nguyen et al. (2018) highlight the intersection of net neutrality and security, underscoring the complexity of governance in the quantum era.

3.6. Emerging Threats and Evolving Attack Strategies

Quantum-enabled cyberattacks will likely involve a combination of traditional and quantum-specific techniques. For instance, Mohamed and Ahmed (2024) discuss AI's role in mitigating man-in-the-middle attacks but caution that quantum computing could significantly complicate these defense strategies. Similarly, Ramachandran et al. (2023) demonstrate how advanced resource allocation models could be vulnerable in quantum-enhanced cloud systems.

3.7. Knowledge Gaps in Organizations

Organizations are unprepared for the quantum computing revolution, often lacking both awareness and resources. Huff et al. (2023) emphasize that biotechnology and healthcare sectors are particularly at risk due to their reliance on legacy systems. Wright et al. (2012) also note the inadequacy of existing mobile security applications in addressing advanced threats.

3.8. Incompatibility with Legacy Systems

Many critical infrastructures rely on legacy systems, which are inherently incompatible with quantum-safe technologies. Gholami and Omar (2023, 2024) stress the need for synthetic data and simulation models to evaluate the efficiency of quantum-resistant systems in real-world scenarios. However, adoption is hampered by high costs and technical limitations.

4. THE ROLE OF LARGE LANGUAGE MODELS (LLMS) IN CYBERSECURITY

The rapid advancement of artificial intelligence, particularly Large Language Models (LLMs), has significantly transformed the cybersecurity landscape. These models, such as OpenAI's GPT series and Google's LaMDA, possess advanced natural language processing (NLP) capabilities, enabling their application in threat detection, incident response, and cybersecurity research.

4.1 LLMs in Threat Detection and Prevention

LLMs are increasingly being used to enhance the detection of sophisticated cyber threats, such as phishing, ransomware, and zero-day vulnerabilities. Their ability to process and analyze large volumes of textual data allows for the identification of patterns and anomalies that might signal a potential attack. For instance, Jones and Omar (2024) demonstrated the efficacy of LLM-based methods in detecting zero-day threats through the GPT-2 Enhanced Attack Detection and Defense (GE-ADD) framework. Similarly, Zangana and Omar (2024) explored the role of LLMs in identifying vulnerabilities in software systems, underscoring their importance in preemptive cybersecurity measures.

The incorporation of LLMs into security systems can also facilitate real-time monitoring and response. By leveraging their deep learning architectures, LLMs can parse vast datasets, including logs and network traffic, to identify and classify threats with unprecedented speed and accuracy (Jones et al., 2023).

4.2 Incident Response and Forensics

In the domain of incident response, LLMs can automate the analysis of attack vectors and provide actionable insights for mitigation. Their ability to comprehend and generate human-like text enables them to produce detailed incident reports, assisting cybersecurity teams in understanding the scope and nature of a breach. For example, Mohammed et al. (2018) highlighted the potential of AI-driven systems, such as LLMs, in countering complex attacks like wormholes in wireless sensor networks.

4.3 Enhancing Cybersecurity Research

LLMs have proven invaluable in advancing cybersecurity research by processing large datasets, generating synthetic data, and conducting literature reviews. Gholami and Omar (2023) investigated the efficiency gains of using synthetic data generated by LLMs in training machine learning models, showcasing their role in accelerating innovation. Moreover, the integration of quantum computing concepts with LLMs, as discussed by Sodiya et al. (2024), has opened new frontiers in quantum-resistant cryptography and secure computing.

4.4 Applications in Phishing Detection and Email Security

Phishing remains one of the most pervasive cybersecurity threats. LLMs are particularly effective in identifying phishing attempts by analyzing email content, detecting fraudulent URLs, and flagging suspicious communication patterns. Zangana et al. (2024) delved into the application of LLMs for combating email phishing, emphasizing their ability to unravel deceptive tactics through linguistic and contextual analysis.

4.5 Ethical Considerations and Challenges

Despite their promise, the deployment of LLMs in cybersecurity is not without challenges. Issues such as data privacy, model interpretability, and the potential misuse of LLMs for malicious purposes warrant careful consideration. Wright et al. (2012) pointed to the dual-use nature of such technologies, where the same tools designed for defense could be exploited by attackers.

Furthermore, the reliance on vast datasets raises questions about the ethical handling of sensitive information, as discussed by Hamza and Omar (2013) in the context of cloud computing security. Transparency and compliance with regulatory frameworks are crucial to mitigate these concerns (Omar, 2021).

4.6 Future Directions

The integration of LLMs with emerging technologies like blockchain and quantum computing holds significant potential for cybersecurity. By leveraging their robust NLP capabilities, LLMs can enhance the security of blockchain-based systems and facilitate the development of quantum-resistant algorithms (Rahul et al., 2024; Baseri et al., 2024). Furthermore, their role in educating the next generation of cybersecurity professionals through interactive learning platforms and tailored educational content is worth exploring (Perron et al., 2021).

5. QUANTUM-AWARE CYBERSECURITY: THE NEED FOR A NEW PARADIGM

The emergence of quantum computing has introduced unprecedented opportunities and challenges across various domains, particularly in cybersecurity. As quantum computers edge closer to practical application, their computational capabilities threaten to undermine classical encryption schemes, necessitating a paradigm shift in cybersecurity strategies (Baseri et al., 2024; Sodiya et al., 2024). This section explores the pressing need for quantum-aware cybersecurity and examines frameworks for adapting to this technological upheaval.

5.1 The Quantum Computing Revolution and Its Implications for Cybersecurity

Quantum computers leverage principles of superposition and entanglement, enabling them to perform computations far beyond the reach of classical machines (Bush et al., 2021). Shor's algorithm, for example, can efficiently factorize large integers, rendering RSA encryption vulnerable (Bishwas & Sen, 2024). Similarly, Grover's algorithm threatens symmetric key systems by reducing brute-force attack complexities (Rahul et al., 2024). These advancements demand a transition to quantum-resistant cryptographic solutions to safeguard digital infrastructure.

5.2 Vulnerabilities in Current Cryptographic Systems

Present-day encryption methods rely on computational difficulty as their core security mechanism. Quantum computing disrupts this foundation by significantly reducing the time required to solve these problems (How & Cheah, 2023). For instance, ECC and RSA, which protect global financial systems, secure communications, and digital identities, could become obsolete in a quantum computing era (Block, 2024; Metawei et al., 2022).

Moreover, quantum algorithms' capabilities extend beyond decryption to sophisticated attack mechanisms, potentially accelerating the deployment of advanced persistent threats (Mohamed & Ahmed, 2024). This underlines the urgency to develop new cryptographic standards and protocols that can withstand quantum-powered adversaries.

The emergence of post-quantum cryptography is pivotal in addressing vulnerabilities in current systems. The chart below categorizes these vulnerabilities and quantifies the extent to which quantum-resistant algorithms mitigate risks.

Figure 3. Vulnerabilities addressed by post-quantum cryptography

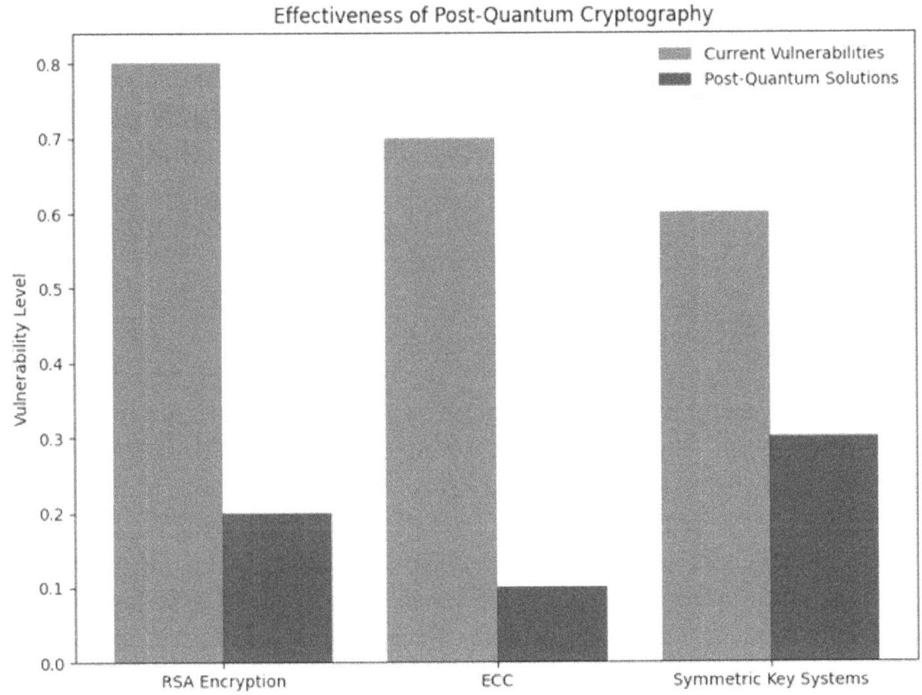

5.3 Transitioning to Post-Quantum Cryptography

Post-quantum cryptography (PQC) focuses on algorithms resistant to quantum attacks, emphasizing lattice-based, hash-based, and multivariate polynomial cryptographic techniques (Lougovski et al., 2023). These algorithms form the basis for securing systems in a quantum-enabled world without relying on the constraints of classical computing (Agrawal & Aggarwal, 2024). Researchers and organizations, including NIST, have accelerated efforts to standardize PQC algorithms, demonstrating a proactive approach to mitigating future threats (Baseri et al., 2024).

5.4 Emerging Paradigms in Quantum-Aware Cybersecurity

Beyond cryptographic solutions, quantum-aware cybersecurity requires holistic frameworks that integrate quantum-enhanced threat detection and response mechanisms. For instance, quantum key distribution (QKD) offers provably secure communication channels leveraging quantum mechanics (Exchange, n.d.). Such innovations redefine security boundaries, offering resilience against eavesdropping and data interception (Zangana & Omar, 2020).

Additionally, the integration of artificial intelligence with quantum computing can enable predictive cybersecurity models, identifying vulnerabilities and attack patterns with unprecedented accuracy (Omar, 2022). Recent advancements in large language models (LLMs) suggest the feasibility of integrating AI-driven insights into quantum-secure systems (Gholami & Omar, 2023).

5.5 Practical and Strategic Challenges

The shift towards quantum-resistant systems faces technical, economic, and organizational challenges. Compatibility issues between existing infrastructure and post-quantum systems necessitate substantial investment in research, development, and implementation (Wright et al., 2012; Perron et al., 2021). Additionally, managing the coexistence of classical and quantum technologies during the transition period will require careful coordination across industries (Khan et al., 2023).

Strategic collaboration between governments, academia, and private sectors will play a pivotal role in addressing these challenges. Initiatives such as the development of quantum-resilient standards, education in quantum technologies, and fostering innovation in quantum software are essential (Perron et al., 2021; Zangana et al., 2024).

5.6 Future Directions

The cybersecurity community must adopt a proactive stance, emphasizing quantum-resilient design, continuous monitoring, and adaptive learning systems. The integration of quantum-safe AI and blockchain technologies into cybersecurity infrastructures is a promising avenue for research and development (Zangana & Omar, 2025). Furthermore, fostering international collaboration will be vital in setting global standards and ensuring equitable access to quantum security technologies (Ramachandran et al., 2023).

5.7 Summary

The advent of quantum computing marks a critical juncture in cybersecurity, demanding a shift from classical defenses to quantum-aware strategies. By embracing innovation and fostering collaboration, organizations and governments can pave the way for a secure digital future, resilient against the transformative power of quantum technologies.

6. APPLICATIONS OF LLMS IN QUANTUM-AWARE CYBERSECURITY

The integration of Large Language Models (LLMs) into quantum-aware cybersecurity frameworks is gaining momentum, driven by their unparalleled ability to process and analyze complex datasets, including those associated with quantum computing threats and opportunities. This section explores how LLMs are being utilized to address the challenges posed by quantum computing in cybersecurity, focusing on areas such as threat detection, cryptographic system analysis, and policy generation.

6.1. Enhancing Threat Detection in Quantum Systems

LLMs, known for their capability to process extensive datasets and uncover patterns, are instrumental in identifying anomalies that signal quantum-based cybersecurity threats. For instance, leveraging the speed and accuracy of LLMs for machine learning in cybersecurity can enhance the detection of zero-day threats in quantum systems (Jones et al., 2023). Furthermore, these models can process telemetry data from quantum devices to identify vulnerabilities that could be exploited by quantum adversaries, a critical task as the landscape of cybersecurity evolves (Omar, 2024).

6.2. Reinforcing Cryptographic Systems

The advent of quantum computing poses significant risks to traditional cryptographic systems due to its potential to break widely used encryption algorithms. LLMs contribute to the development of quantum-resistant cryptography by assisting in analyzing the robustness of new algorithms and simulating potential quantum attacks. For example, the GEADD method, which integrates LLM capabilities with advanced cryptographic analysis, provides a framework for testing system resilience against quantum attacks (Jones & Omar, 2024).

Additionally, LLMs enable automated cryptographic key management by predicting patterns that could compromise keys in quantum-resistant environments, as discussed in the foundational works of Mohammed et al. (2018) and Nguyen et al. (2018).

6.3. Policy Formulation and Compliance Management

Quantum-aware cybersecurity demands a reevaluation of existing policies to account for the unique challenges posed by quantum technologies. LLMs are increasingly utilized to draft policies that address these challenges, ensuring organizations remain compliant with emerging standards. Their ability to analyze extensive regulatory frameworks and propose actionable strategies has been highlighted in works such as Omar and Zangana (2024), which underscore the importance of aligning AI-driven solutions with legal and ethical requirements.

LLMs also assist in identifying gaps in current policies by cross-referencing them with known threats and best practices in quantum computing, as demonstrated in foundational reviews by Hamza and Omar (2013).

6.4. Mitigating Social Engineering and Quantum Deception

As quantum computing advances, adversaries may exploit its capabilities to enhance social engineering attacks. LLMs can counteract such threats by analyzing patterns in communication that may indicate deceptive practices. For example, models trained on phishing datasets can predict and preempt sophisticated email attacks enhanced by quantum capabilities (Zangana & Omar, 2020). This approach aligns with broader efforts to enhance cybersecurity through AI-powered deception detection (Zangana et al., 2024).

6.5. Facilitating Collaboration Between Quantum and Classical Systems

One of the challenges in quantum-aware cybersecurity is bridging the gap between quantum and classical systems. LLMs serve as intermediaries by translating technical details across these domains, facilitating seamless integration and collaboration. They also assist in workforce training, making quantum cybersecurity concepts more accessible, as emphasized by Perron et al. (2021).

6.6. Future Potential in Quantum Cybersecurity Research

Looking forward, the potential of LLMs extends to predicting the trajectory of quantum threats and opportunities. By analyzing emerging trends and academic literature, as highlighted by Gholami and Omar (2024), LLMs can forecast the evolution of quantum cryptography, guiding the development of preemptive defense strategies. Their role in supporting interdisciplinary research, such as that discussed by Singh (2023), further underscores their importance in quantum-aware cybersecurity.

6.7 Summary

The applications of LLMs in quantum-aware cybersecurity are transformative, addressing critical challenges while unlocking new opportunities for innovation. From threat detection to cryptographic analysis and policy development, LLMs provide a robust framework for enhancing security in the quantum era. Continued research and collaboration between quantum and AI experts will be pivotal in realizing the full potential of these technologies.

7. CHALLENGES AND CONSIDERATIONS IN INTEGRATING LLMS WITH QUANTUM-AWARE CYBERSECURITY

The integration of large language models (LLMs) with quantum-aware cybersecurity systems presents unique challenges and considerations. These include computational constraints, model vulnerabilities, ethical dilemmas, and the overarching uncertainty associated with quantum computing. Below is a detailed exploration of these challenges, supported by scholarly references.

7.1. Computational Constraints in Quantum-Enriched Environments

Quantum-aware cybersecurity often demands immense computational resources, which can complicate the deployment of LLMs. Quantum cryptography and error correction require precise calculations, and pairing these with LLMs intensifies computational demand.

For instance, the scalability issues highlighted by Baseri, Chouhan, and Ghorbani (2024) indicate that infrastructure constraints can significantly impede the implementation of quantum-resistant solutions. Moreover, Huff et al. (2023) emphasize that biotechnology industries already face computational bottlenecks when integrating advanced models into cybersecurity frameworks.

7.2. Model Vulnerabilities to Quantum Attacks

LLMs are inherently vulnerable to adversarial attacks. Quantum computing adds another layer of complexity by enabling attackers to exploit weaknesses in traditional cryptographic defenses.

Zangana and Omar (2025) discuss how adversaries might harness quantum algorithms to bypass conventional defenses, rendering standard LLM-based anomaly detection systems ineffective. This aligns with the findings of Gholami and Omar

(2024), who note that LLMs trained on specific datasets may struggle to adapt to rapidly evolving threats posed by quantum systems.

7.3. Ethical and Privacy Concerns

Ethical dilemmas arise when LLMs process sensitive data in quantum-secure frameworks. Nguyen et al. (2018) stress that repealing net neutrality has already exacerbated privacy challenges, making the integration of quantum mechanisms even more complex. The dual-use potential of LLMs for malicious purposes in a quantum-aware ecosystem is a growing concern, as noted by Omar (2022) in discussions about machine learning for cybersecurity.

7.4. Developing Quantum-Resistant Algorithms for LLMs

A key challenge lies in adapting LLM algorithms to work seamlessly with quantum-resistant cryptographic methods. The framework proposed by Bishwas and Sen (2024) for preparing industries against quantum threats underscores the need for specialized algorithmic modifications to ensure resilience. Furthermore, Khan et al. (2023) highlight the lack of agile methodologies in developing quantum software, suggesting that traditional approaches may be insufficient for integrating LLMs with quantum-aware systems.

7.5. Addressing Interoperability Issues

Integrating LLMs with quantum technologies requires seamless interoperability between classical and quantum systems. This often leads to conflicts between traditional protocols and quantum-specific standards. Wright, Dawson Jr., and Omar (2012) stress the necessity of antivirus applications adapted for mobile threats, a challenge paralleled in the broader quantum ecosystem, where traditional solutions may not align with quantum computing standards.

7.6. Data Integrity and Trust

Ensuring the reliability and accuracy of data processed by LLMs in quantum systems is crucial. Mohamed and Ahmed (2024) emphasize the importance of AI in mitigating man-in-the-middle attacks, which could be exacerbated in a quantum environment. Zangana (2024) further explores how blockchain-based timestamping tools might help address data integrity issues, providing potential synergies for LLMs in securing data streams.

7.7. Strategic Planning for Quantum-LLM Integration

Organizations need a robust strategic roadmap for integrating LLMs with quantum-aware cybersecurity systems. The roadmap developed by How and Cheah (2023) suggests a phased approach to address technical, regulatory, and operational challenges. Similarly, Jones et al. (2023) propose that integrating LLMs into cybersecurity should be accompanied by continuous evaluation to adapt to the dynamic threat landscape.

7.8 Summary

The integration of LLMs with quantum-aware cybersecurity offers transformative potential but is fraught with challenges. Addressing computational constraints, enhancing model robustness, and ensuring ethical practices are paramount for successful implementation. By leveraging insights from emerging research, such as those by Omar and Zangana (2025) and Sodiya et al. (2024), the cybersecurity community can develop systems resilient to both classical and quantum threats.

8. FUTURE DIRECTIONS FOR QUANTUM-AWARE CYBERSECURITY

The advent of quantum computing presents a transformative potential for various technological sectors, including cybersecurity. While quantum technologies promise unparalleled computational power, they also introduce significant risks to conventional cryptographic methods. This section explores the future directions for quantum-aware cybersecurity, focusing on research, implementation strategies, and mitigation techniques.

8.1 Adoption of Quantum-Resistant Algorithms

One of the primary challenges in the post-quantum era is the vulnerability of traditional cryptographic systems to quantum-based attacks. Current public-key cryptographic algorithms, such as RSA and ECC, are susceptible to quantum algorithms like Shor's, which can efficiently solve problems underlying these systems (Rahul et al., 2024). To mitigate this, researchers emphasize the adoption of quantum-resistant cryptographic standards, such as those recommended by NIST's post-quantum cryptography (PQC) initiative (Bishwas & Sen, 2024). These algorithms, including lattice-based and code-based systems, aim to sustain the integrity of secure communications in the quantum age.

Furthermore, the strategic framework provided by Bishwas and Sen (2024) outlines industry guidelines for transitioning to quantum-resistant infrastructures, emphasizing preparedness for the quantum threat.

8.2 Hybrid Cryptographic Solutions

A promising short-term approach is the integration of classical and quantum-resistant cryptographic techniques. Hybrid models enable secure communication during the transition to fully quantum-resistant systems (Zangana & Omar, 2025). For instance, combining classical encryption with quantum key distribution (QKD) ensures additional layers of security while addressing immediate vulnerabilities (Bush et al., 2021). Such systems also benefit from the ability to adapt dynamically as quantum technologies evolve.

8.3 Securing Quantum Communication Networks

The future of cybersecurity involves securing quantum communication networks that leverage QKD to provide theoretically unbreakable encryption (Metawei et al., 2022). These networks require robust infrastructure to prevent man-in-the-middle attacks and other vulnerabilities (Mohamed & Ahmed, 2024). Recent advancements suggest that integrating distributed ledger technologies can enhance the transparency and auditability of quantum communications, a perspective explored in Omar (2021).

Additionally, Bush et al. (2021) highlight the role of industrial quantum networks in facilitating secure interconnectivity across industries, addressing scalability and interoperability concerns.

8.4 Development of Quantum-Aware Threat Models

Traditional cybersecurity models require a significant overhaul to address quantum-specific threats. For example, the quantum capabilities to simulate and break machine learning models demand the development of resilient adversarial defenses (Omar, 2024). The DNN Text Classification framework discussed in Omar (2024) demonstrates the application of defensive mechanisms against quantum-enhanced attacks, setting the stage for future innovations.

8.5 Leveraging AI and LLMs in Quantum Contexts

Large Language Models (LLMs) and artificial intelligence (AI) can play pivotal roles in identifying and mitigating quantum-enhanced threats. The integration of LLMs into vulnerability detection and prediction frameworks has shown promise (Zangana & Omar, 2025). These models can proactively identify security gaps in systems transitioning to quantum-resistant architectures, as detailed in Gholami & Omar (2023).

Moreover, AI techniques can support quantum-aware resource allocation, such as the DLTN-LOSP model proposed by Ramachandran et al. (2023), which combines AI-driven logic with enhanced security protocols.

8.6 Policy and Governance for Quantum Security

The rise of quantum computing necessitates comprehensive policies and governance frameworks to ensure responsible and ethical deployment. As Sodiya et al. (2024) argue, quantum technologies pose ethical and operational challenges that require global collaboration. Similarly, How and Cheah (2023) emphasize the need for international regulations to manage the dual-use nature of quantum innovations, balancing opportunities against potential misuse.

Governments and private sectors must also collaborate to establish frameworks for standardizing quantum security practices, a theme echoed in Omar & Zangana (2024).

8.7 Expanding Education and Training

Preparing the workforce for quantum-aware cybersecurity involves expanding education and training programs. Perron et al. (2021) underscore the importance of quantum education in building a talent pool adept at handling quantum systems. This aligns with global efforts to integrate quantum mechanics and cybersecurity into curricula, fostering interdisciplinary expertise.

8.8 Towards a Secure Quantum Future

The journey towards quantum-aware cybersecurity is fraught with challenges but offers unprecedented opportunities for innovation. As highlighted in foundational works such as Zangana et al. (2024), researchers, policymakers, and industry leaders must adopt a proactive approach to quantum threats. Collaboration across sectors and disciplines will be crucial in building robust systems that safeguard against emerging risks.

Through a combination of quantum-resistant cryptography, AI-enhanced defenses, and comprehensive governance, the cybersecurity domain can not only adapt to but also thrive in the quantum era.

Preparing for quantum threats requires a phased approach across industries. The graph below illustrates the projected timeline for adopting quantum-resistant strategies, emphasizing the critical milestones required to ensure preparedness.

Figure 4. Evolution of quantum threat readiness

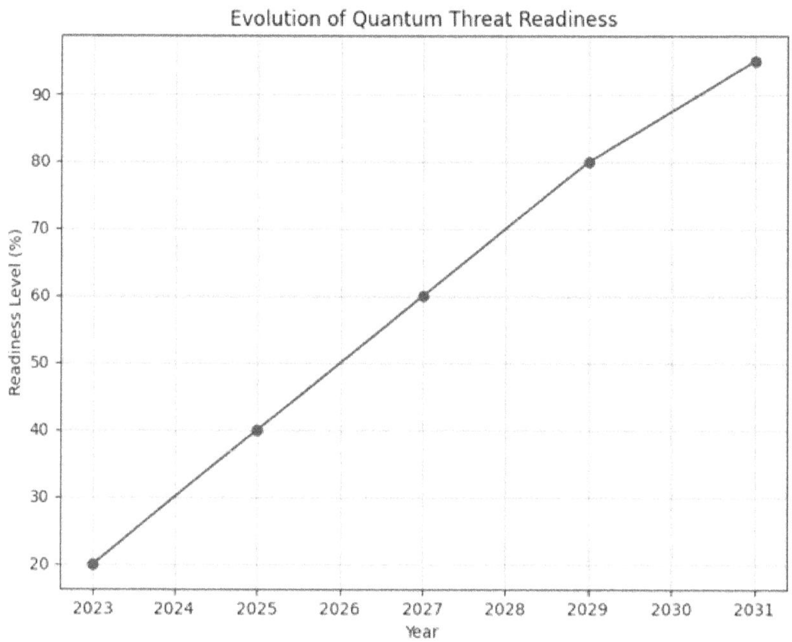

9. CONCLUSION

The advent of quantum computing represents a pivotal shift in the technological landscape, bringing both unprecedented opportunities and significant challenges to the realm of cybersecurity. As quantum systems progress, they promise to solve complex problems far beyond the capabilities of classical computing. However, their potential to break widely-used cryptographic algorithms underscores the urgency for proactive measures in developing quantum-resistant security solutions.

This chapter has explored the intricate interplay between quantum computing and cybersecurity, highlighting the threats posed by quantum-capable adversaries and the ongoing efforts to mitigate them. The integration of quantum-resistant cryptographic protocols and the strategic adoption of hybrid approaches are essential to ensure a seamless transition to a secure post-quantum era. Moreover, leveraging emerging technologies such as AI, blockchain, and large language models can bolster the development of robust defenses, enhancing the resilience of digital infrastructures against both current and future threats.

Looking ahead, fostering collaboration between researchers, industry leaders, and policymakers will be crucial to addressing the multifaceted challenges of quantum-aware cybersecurity. This collective effort must emphasize innovation, scalability, and adaptability to protect critical systems and data in an increasingly interconnected world. By embracing these priorities, the cybersecurity community can effectively safeguard the digital ecosystem while unlocking the transformative potential of quantum technologies.

REFERENCES

Agrawal, K., & Aggarwal, M. Building Efficient Smart Contract for Healthcare 4.0. In *Blockchain for Healthcare 4.0* (pp. 94-123). CRC Press.

AL-Refaey. M. R., Tyagi, A. K., AL-Ghamdi, A. S. A. M., & Kukreja, S. (Eds.). (2024). *Topics in Artificial Intelligence Applied to Industry 4.0*. John Wiley & Sons.

Baseri, Y., Chouhan, V., & Ghorbani, A. (2024). Cybersecurity in the Quantum Era: Assessing the Impact of Quantum Computing on Infrastructure. *arXiv preprint arXiv:2404.10659.*

Bishwas, A. K., & Sen, M. (2024). Strategic Roadmap for Quantum-Resistant Security: A Framework for Preparing Industries for the Quantum Threat. *arXiv preprint arXiv:2411.09995.*

Block, R. S. S. (2024). The 2024 quantum advantage blueprint: Where quantum outpaces classical.

Bush, S. F., Challener, W. A., & Mantelet, G. (2021). A perspective on industrial quantum networks. *AVS Quantum Science*, 3(3), 030501. DOI: 10.1116/5.0051881

Exchange, Q. R. K. Towards a Verifiably Secure Quantum-Resistant Key Exchange in IKEv2.

Gholami, S., & Omar, M. (2023). Does Synthetic Data Make Large Language Models More Efficient? *arXiv preprint arXiv:2310.07830.*

Gholami, S., & Omar, M. (2024). Can a student large language model perform as well as its teacher? In *Innovations, Securities, and Case Studies Across Healthcare, Business, and Technology* (pp. 122-139). IGI Global. DOI: 10.4018/979-8-3693-1906-2.ch007

Hamza, Y. A., & Omar, M. D. (2013). Cloud computing security: Abuse and nefarious use of cloud computing. *International Journal of Computer Engineering Research*, 3(6), 22–27.

How, M. L., & Cheah, S. M. (2023). Business Renaissance: Opportunities and challenges at the dawn of the Quantum Computing Era. *Businesses*, 3(4), 585–605. DOI: 10.3390/businesses3040036

Huff, A. J., Burrell, D. N., Nobles, C., Richardson, K., Wright, J. B., Burton, S. L., Jones, A. J., Springs, D., Omar, M., & Brown-Jackson, K. L. (2023). Management Practices for Mitigating Cybersecurity Threats to Biotechnology Companies, Laboratories, and Healthcare Research Organizations. In *Applied Research Approaches to Technology, Healthcare, and Business* (pp. 1-12). IGI Global.

Jones, R., & Omar, M. (2024). Revolutionizing Cybersecurity: The GPT-2 Enhanced Attack Detection and Defense (GEADD) Method for Zero-Day Threats. *International Journal of Informatics* [INJIISCOM]. *Information System and Computer Engineering*, 5(2), 178–191.

Jones, R., Omar, M., Mohammed, D., Nobles, C., & Dawson, M. (2023). Harnessing the Speed and Accuracy of Machine Learning to Advance Cybersecurity. In *2023 Congress in Computer Science, Computer Engineering, & Applied Computing (CSCE)* (pp. 418-421). IEEE. DOI: 10.1109/CSCE60160.2023.00074

Khan, A. A., Akbar, M. A., Ahmad, A., Fahmideh, M., Shameem, M., Lahtinen, V., . . . Mikkonen, T. (2023, July). Agile practices for quantum software development: practitioners' perspectives. In *2023 IEEE international conference on quantum software (QSW)* (pp. 9-20). IEEE.

Lougovski, P., Parekh, O., Broz, J., Byrd, M., Chembo, Y., de Jong, W. A., . . . Svore, K. M. (2023). *Position Papers for the ASCR Workshop on Basic Research Needs in Quantum Computing and Networking*. USDOE Office of Science (SC), Advanced Scientific Computing Research (ASCR).

Madni, A. F., Shah, M. A., & Al-Naeem, M. (2024). An Investigation of Scalability in EHRs using Healthcare 4.0 and Blockchain. *International Journal of Advanced Computer Science and Applications*, 15(5). Advance online publication. DOI: 10.14569/IJACSA.2024.0150548

Metawei, M. A., Eldeeb, H., Nassar, S. M., & Taher, M. (2022). Quantum Computing Meets Artificial Intelligence: Innovations and Challenges. In *Handbook on Artificial Intelligence-Empowered Applied Software Engineering: VOL. 1: Novel Methodologies to Engineering Smart Software Systems* (pp. 303–338). Springer International Publishing. DOI: 10.1007/978-3-031-08202-3_12

Mohamed, N., & Ahmed, A. A. (2024, June). AI in Combatting Man-in-the-Middle Attacks: A Comprehensive Review. In *2024 15th International Conference on Computing Communication and Networking Technologies (ICCCNT)* (pp. 1-6). IEEE. DOI: 10.1109/ICCCNT61001.2024.10725789

Mohammed, D., Omar, M., & Nguyen, V. (2018). Wireless sensor network security: Approaches to detecting and avoiding wormhole attacks. *Journal of Research in Business. Economics and Management*, 10(2), 1860–1864.

Nguyen, V., Mohammed, D., Omar, M., & Banisakher, M. (2018). The Effects of the FCC Net Neutrality Repeal on Security and Privacy. [IJHIoT]. *International Journal of Hyperconnectivity and the Internet of Things*, 2(2), 21–29. DOI: 10.4018/IJHIoT.2018070102

Omar, M. (2021). New insights into database security: An effective and integrated approach for applying access control mechanisms and cryptographic concepts in Microsoft Access environments.

Omar, M. (2022). *Machine Learning for Cybersecurity: Innovative Deep Learning Solutions*. Springer Brief. https://link.springer.com/book/978303115

Omar, M. (2024). From Attack to Defense: Strengthening DNN Text Classification Against Adversarial Examples. In *Innovations, Securities, and Case Studies Across Healthcare, Business, and Technology* (pp. 174-195). IGI Global.

Omar, M. (2024). Revolutionizing Malware Detection: A Paradigm Shift Through Optimized Convolutional Neural Networks. In *Innovations, Securities, and Case Studies Across Healthcare, Business, and Technology* (pp. 196-220). IGI Global. DOI: 10.4018/979-8-3693-1906-2.ch011

Omar, M., & Zangana, H. M. (Eds.). (2024). *Redefining Security With Cyber AI*. IGI Global., DOI: 10.4018/979-8-3693-6517-5

Omar, M., & Zangana, H. M. (Eds.). (2025). *Application of Large Language Models (LLMs) for Software Vulnerability Detection*. IGI Global., DOI: 10.4018/979-8-3693-9311-6

Perron, J. K., DeLeone, C., Sharif, S., Carter, T., Grossman, J. M., Passante, G., & Sack, J. (2021). Quantum undergraduate education and scientific training. *arXiv preprint arXiv:2109.13850.*

Qualters, I., Taylor, A. J., & Hagberg, A. A. (2019). *IS&T Computing Overview* (No. LA-UR-19-22567). Los Alamos National Lab.(LANL), Los Alamos, NM (United States).

Rahul, R., Geetha, S., Priyatharsini, S., Mehata, K., Sundaresan Perumal, T., Ethiraj, N., & Sendilvelan, S. (2024). Cybersecurity Issues and Challenges in Quantum Computing. *Topics in Artificial Intelligence Applied to Industry*, 4(0), 203–221. DOI: 10.1002/9781394216147.ch11

Ramachandran, D., Naqi, S. M., Perumal, G., & Abbas, Q. (2023). DLTN-LOSP: A Novel Deep-Linear-Transition-Network-Based Resource Allocation Model with the Logic Overhead Security Protocol for Cloud Systems. *Sensors (Basel)*, 23(20), 8448. DOI: 10.3390/s23208448 PMID: 37896541

Seskir, Z. C. (2019). *Current state of quantum information technologies in Turkey* (Master's thesis, Middle East Technical University).

Sodiya, E. O., Umoga, U. J., Amoo, O. O., & Atadoga, A. (2024). Quantum computing and its potential impact on US cybersecurity: A review: Scrutinizing the challenges and opportunities presented by quantum technologies in safeguarding digital assets. *Global Journal of Engineering and Technology Advances, 18*(2), 049-064.

Wright, J., Dawson, M. E.Jr, & Omar, M. (2012). Cyber security and mobile threats: The need for antivirus applications for smartphones. *Journal of Information Systems Technology and Planning*, 5(14), 40–60.

Zangana, H. M. (2024). Exploring Blockchain-Based Timestamping Tools: A Comprehensive Review. *Redefining Security With Cyber AI*, 92-110.

Zangana, H. M. (2024). Exploring the Landscape of Website Vulnerability Scanners: A Comprehensive Review and Comparative Analysis. *Redefining Security With Cyber AI*, 111-129.

Zangana, H. M., Mohammed, A. K., Sallow, A. B., & Sallow, Z. B. (2024). Cybernetic Deception: Unraveling the Layers of Email Phishing Threats. [INJURATECH]. *International Journal of Research and Applied Technology*, 4(1), 35–47.

Zangana, H. M., & Mohammed, D. (2025). Foundations of Large Language Models in Software Vulnerability Detection. In Omar, M., & Zangana, H. (Eds.), *Application of Large Language Models (LLMs) for Software Vulnerability Detection* (pp. 41–74). IGI Global., DOI: 10.4018/979-8-3693-9311-6.ch002

Zangana, H. M., & Omar, M. (2020). Threats, Attacks, and Mitigations of Smartphone Security. *Academic Journal of Nawroz University*, 9(4), 324–332. DOI: 10.25007/ajnu.v9n4a989

Zangana, H. M., & Omar, M. (2025). Harnessing the Power of Large Language Models for Cybersecurity: Applications, Challenges, and Future Directions. In Omar, M., & Zangana, H. (Eds.), *Application of Large Language Models (LLMs) for Software Vulnerability Detection* (pp. 1–40). IGI Global., DOI: 10.4018/979-8-3693-9311-6.ch001

Zangana, H. M., Omar, M., Al-Karaki, J. N., & Mohammed, D. (2024). Comprehensive Review and Analysis of Network Firewall Rule Analyzers: Enhancing Security Posture and Efficiency. *Redefining Security With Cyber AI*, 15-36.

Chapter 2
Understanding Quantum Computing Implications for Cybersecurity

Angel Justo Jones
https://orcid.org/0009-0007-9740-6611
University of Virginia, USA

ABSTRACT

Quantum computing is rapidly evolving, promising to revolutionize various fields, including cybersecurity. By harnessing the power of quantum mechanics, quantum computers are expected to solve problems that are intractable for classical computers, particularly in areas such as encryption and data security. This chapter explores the fundamental principles of quantum computing and its potential implications for cybersecurity. We discuss the challenges posed by quantum algorithms, including Shor's algorithm and Grover's algorithm, which can break widely-used cryptographic systems like RSA and AES. Furthermore, we examine the transition towards quantum-resistant algorithms, also known as post-quantum cryptography (PQC), and the role of large language models (LLMs) in facilitating the adaptation of cybersecurity strategies to a quantum-enabled future. The chapter concludes with a look at the future of quantum-aware cybersecurity, emphasizing the need for robust, adaptable frameworks to address emerging threats.

1. INTRODUCTION

Quantum computing, a field that once seemed to belong to the realm of theoretical science, has rapidly evolved into a powerful tool that promises to revolutionize various industries, including cybersecurity. The fundamental nature of quantum computing,

DOI: 10.4018/979-8-3373-1102-9.ch002

which leverages the principles of quantum mechanics to perform computations that would be impossible or take an impractical amount of time for classical computers, introduces a new paradigm for both protecting and threatening digital assets. As quantum computing becomes increasingly accessible, its impact on cybersecurity is growing more significant, offering both groundbreaking advancements and posing novel risks that need to be managed effectively.

At its core, quantum computing uses quantum bits (qubits) that can exist in multiple states simultaneously, a property known as superposition. Additionally, quantum entanglement allows qubits to be interconnected in a way that enhances computational power exponentially. These properties enable quantum computers to solve complex mathematical problems far more efficiently than their classical counterparts. This is particularly important for encryption algorithms that form the backbone of modern cybersecurity systems. Quantum computers could potentially break widely used encryption schemes, such as RSA and ECC (Elliptic Curve Cryptography), by exploiting their ability to solve factorization and discrete logarithm problems in polynomial time—a feat that classical computers cannot achieve within a reasonable timeframe (Sodiya et al., 2024; Zangana, 2024).

However, while quantum computing presents a potential threat to current cybersecurity systems, it also offers solutions to existing challenges. For example, quantum cryptography and quantum key distribution (QKD) are already being explored as methods to enhance secure communication in a quantum-enabled future (Zangana et al., 2024; Baseri et al., 2024). Moreover, the field of quantum machine learning (QML) shows promise in advancing threat detection, anomaly identification, and response automation, which could augment traditional cybersecurity defenses (Rahul et al., 2024).

In understanding the intersection between quantum computing and cybersecurity, it is essential to examine the implications of quantum technologies on both defense and attack mechanisms. Quantum technologies could be used to develop stronger security protocols, while simultaneously posing challenges to existing cryptographic standards. The concept of quantum-resistant cryptography is already being explored to ensure that cybersecurity infrastructures can withstand quantum threats. This involves the development of new cryptographic algorithms that are resistant to quantum algorithms such as Shor's algorithm, which is capable of efficiently solving the integer factorization problem (Bishwas & Sen, 2024; Khan et al., 2023).

The emergence of quantum computing also necessitates the consideration of how quantum-aware systems, such as those incorporating large language models (LLMs), can enhance cybersecurity operations. LLMs, particularly those trained with a quantum-aware framework, have the potential to revolutionize how cybersecurity teams identify vulnerabilities, respond to threats, and optimize security protocols (Gholami & Omar, 2024; Jones et al., 2023). These models can be trained to recognize quantum-related anomalies in network traffic, enhancing defense mechanisms against quantum-enabled cyberattacks.

The rapid advancement of quantum computing calls for the establishment of a comprehensive cybersecurity strategy that considers both the benefits and risks associated with quantum technologies. This strategy should address the protection of digital assets from quantum-enabled threats, while simultaneously exploiting quantum advancements to enhance the overall resilience of cybersecurity infrastructures.

This chapter explores the implications of quantum computing on cybersecurity, examining its potential to both disrupt and enhance the security landscape. It delves into the challenges presented by quantum technologies and discusses strategies for preparing the cybersecurity industry for the quantum era. Special emphasis is placed on the role of quantum-resistant cryptography, quantum machine learning, and the integration of quantum-aware systems in safeguarding digital environments (Bush et al., 2021; Metawei et al., 2022).

The following sections will provide a deeper understanding of how quantum computing influences cybersecurity and explore emerging technologies and methodologies that can be leveraged to mitigate the risks and capitalize on the opportunities presented by quantum advancements.

2. FOUNDATIONS OF QUANTUM COMPUTING

Quantum computing represents a paradigm shift from classical computation, driven by the principles of quantum mechanics, a branch of physics that studies the behavior of matter and energy at subatomic scales. Unlike classical computers, which process data in binary form (bits as 0s and 1s), quantum computers leverage quantum bits or *qubits*, which can represent 0, 1, or both 0 and 1 simultaneously due to the phenomenon of *superposition*. This ability to exist in multiple states at once enables quantum computers to handle certain types of computations much more efficiently than classical counterparts.

In this section, we will explore the fundamental concepts that underpin quantum computing, including superposition, entanglement, quantum gates, and quantum algorithms. Additionally, we will delve into the potential applications and challenges of quantum computing, particularly in cybersecurity, artificial intelligence (AI), and beyond.

2.1. Superposition and Entanglement

Superposition is one of the most distinctive features of quantum systems. A qubit can exist in a superposition of both 0 and 1, which enables quantum computers to process a vast number of possibilities simultaneously. This property dramatically increases the computational power of quantum systems when compared to classical computers, which are limited to processing one state at a time.

Entanglement, another key concept, refers to the phenomenon where the states of two qubits become intertwined, such that the state of one qubit cannot be described independently of the other, even if they are separated by large distances. This interdependence allows quantum computers to perform operations on multiple qubits in parallel, providing further advantages in terms of computational speed and efficiency.

Understanding the fundamental differences between quantum and classical computing is essential to grasp the implications of quantum technologies on cybersecurity. The diagram below highlights key distinctions between these paradigms, focusing on their computational principles and potential impacts.

Figure 1. Quantum computing vs. classical computing

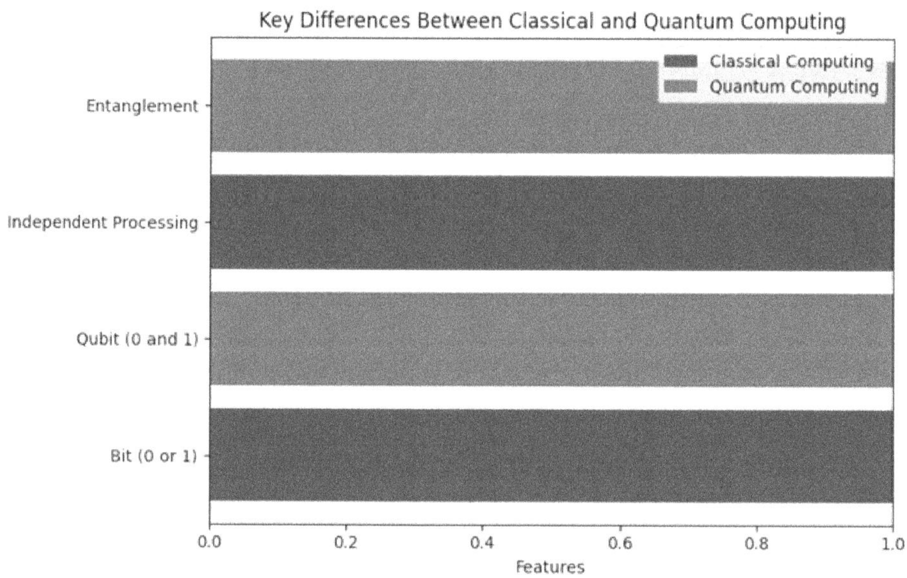

2.2. Quantum Gates and Quantum Circuits

Quantum gates are the building blocks of quantum algorithms, analogous to classical logic gates like AND, OR, and NOT. However, quantum gates manipulate qubits using quantum mechanical principles, enabling operations such as flipping a qubit or entangling two qubits. These gates are represented by matrices and can perform complex operations that are impossible with classical bits.

Quantum circuits are constructed by applying a series of quantum gates to a set of qubits. These circuits are used to perform quantum computations. Unlike classical circuits, quantum circuits rely on quantum phenomena like interference and superposition to solve problems in ways that classical systems cannot match.

2.3. Quantum Algorithms

Quantum algorithms leverage quantum mechanical properties to solve problems more efficiently than classical algorithms. Some of the most well-known quantum algorithms include:

- **Shor's Algorithm**: A quantum algorithm for factoring large numbers exponentially faster than the best-known classical algorithms. This has significant implications for the security of cryptographic systems, as many encryption methods rely on the difficulty of factoring large numbers.
- **Grover's Algorithm**: A quantum algorithm that provides a quadratic speedup for searching through unsorted databases. It has applications in optimization, search problems, and machine learning.

These algorithms represent just a fraction of the potential of quantum computing, with ongoing research uncovering new algorithms that promise to revolutionize fields like optimization, simulation, and cryptography.

2.4. Applications of Quantum Computing

Quantum computing has vast potential across various fields. In cybersecurity, quantum computers could break widely used encryption schemes, such as RSA and ECC, which rely on the difficulty of problems like factoring and discrete logarithms. This has led to the development of *quantum-resistant* encryption methods designed to withstand attacks from quantum computers (Baseri, Chouhan, & Ghorbani, 2024). In AI and machine learning, quantum algorithms may lead to breakthroughs in training efficiency and model accuracy (Gholami & Omar, 2023; Metawei, Eldeeb, Nassar, & Taher, 2022).

In healthcare, quantum computing has the potential to transform drug discovery by simulating complex molecular interactions that are computationally expensive on classical computers (Singh, n.d.). Blockchain technology may also benefit from quantum computing, especially in terms of enhancing security and efficiency (Zangana, 2024).

2.5. Challenges in Quantum Computing

Despite its potential, quantum computing faces several challenges. One of the primary hurdles is *quantum decoherence*, which occurs when qubits lose their quantum properties due to interactions with the external environment. This problem limits the scalability and reliability of quantum systems, making it difficult to maintain qubits in their superposition states long enough to perform meaningful computations.

Moreover, there are significant challenges in developing quantum algorithms that can outperform classical algorithms for practical, real-world applications. Additionally, quantum software development, including the design of error-correcting codes and quantum programming languages, remains in its early stages (Khan et al., 2023).

2.6. The Role of Quantum Computing in Cybersecurity

The rise of quantum computing poses both threats and opportunities in the realm of cybersecurity. On the one hand, quantum computers could break existing cryptographic systems, rendering many current security protocols obsolete (Baseri et al., 2024). On the other hand, quantum computing can enable the development of new, quantum-resistant cryptography techniques (Sodiya, Umoga, Amoo, & Atadoga, 2024). These new techniques will be essential for protecting digital assets in the quantum era.

In response to the potential threat, researchers have been developing *quantum key distribution* (QKD) systems, which use the principles of quantum mechanics to secure communication channels against eavesdropping. These advancements in quantum cryptography will play a critical role in safeguarding sensitive data in a post-quantum world.

2.7. Future Directions and Conclusion

Quantum computing holds immense promise but also presents numerous challenges. As we move into the era of quantum computing, its impact on industries ranging from healthcare to finance to cybersecurity will be profound (Rahul et al.,

2024). For organizations to prepare, it will be essential to invest in quantum research and begin transitioning toward quantum-resistant systems (Bishwas & Sen, 2024).

While quantum computing is still in its early stages, its potential to revolutionize fields like artificial intelligence, cybersecurity, and optimization is undeniable. As quantum technologies continue to evolve, the need for skilled professionals, robust quantum algorithms, and quantum-safe security measures will be more critical than ever (Omar & Zangana, 2024).

By addressing these challenges and harnessing the power of quantum computing, we can unlock new possibilities and drive innovation across a wide range of sectors. With the right investments and research, quantum computing will play a pivotal role in shaping the future of technology.

3. KEY CONCEPTS AND ALGORITHMS IN QUANTUM COMPUTING

Quantum computing represents a transformative paradigm in computation, harnessing the principles of quantum mechanics to process information in fundamentally new ways. Unlike classical computers, which use binary bits to represent data, quantum computers use quantum bits or **qubits**, which can exist in multiple states simultaneously due to **superposition**. This enables quantum systems to perform calculations exponentially faster than classical counterparts in certain problem domains.

3.1 Quantum Superposition and Entanglement

At the heart of quantum computing are two key phenomena: **superposition** and **entanglement**. Superposition allows a qubit to be in a state of both 0 and 1 simultaneously, whereas classical bits can only represent one state at a time. This creates a massive parallelism advantage, enabling quantum computers to explore multiple solution paths simultaneously.

Entanglement, another fundamental concept in quantum mechanics, is a phenomenon where the states of two or more qubits become linked, such that the state of one qubit instantaneously influences the state of the other(s), regardless of the distance between them. This non-local property forms the basis for various quantum algorithms, enabling the transfer of information and the performance of calculations that would be impossible for classical systems.

3.2 Quantum Algorithms

Quantum computing has led to the development of specialized algorithms that exploit quantum phenomena to solve specific types of problems more efficiently than classical algorithms. Here are some of the most notable algorithms:

1. **Shor's Algorithm**: This algorithm provides a quantum solution to integer factorization, which underpins much of modern cryptography, specifically RSA encryption. Shor's algorithm can factor large integers exponentially faster than the best-known classical algorithms, posing potential threats to existing cryptographic systems.
2. **Grover's Algorithm**: Grover's algorithm offers a quantum approach to unstructured search problems. It can search through an unsorted database of NNN items in roughly N\sqrt{N}N operations, whereas classical search algorithms require NNN operations. This makes Grover's algorithm valuable in optimization tasks where brute-force searching is necessary.
3. **Quantum Fourier Transform (QFT)**: The QFT is a quantum algorithm that efficiently computes the discrete Fourier transform, which is central to many applications such as signal processing and solving partial differential equations. The QFT operates exponentially faster than classical counterparts, making it a key tool in quantum computing.
4. **Quantum Approximate Optimization Algorithm (QAOA)**: This is a hybrid quantum-classical algorithm that provides approximate solutions to optimization problems. By leveraging quantum superposition and entanglement, QAOA has shown promise in solving problems in areas such as financial modeling, traffic flow optimization, and machine learning.

Shor's algorithm is a pivotal development in quantum computing, demonstrating its capability to solve integer factorization problems exponentially faster than classical methods. The flowchart below outlines the steps in Shor's algorithm, illustrating its impact on breaking RSA encryption.

Figure 2. Shor's algorithm in cryptography

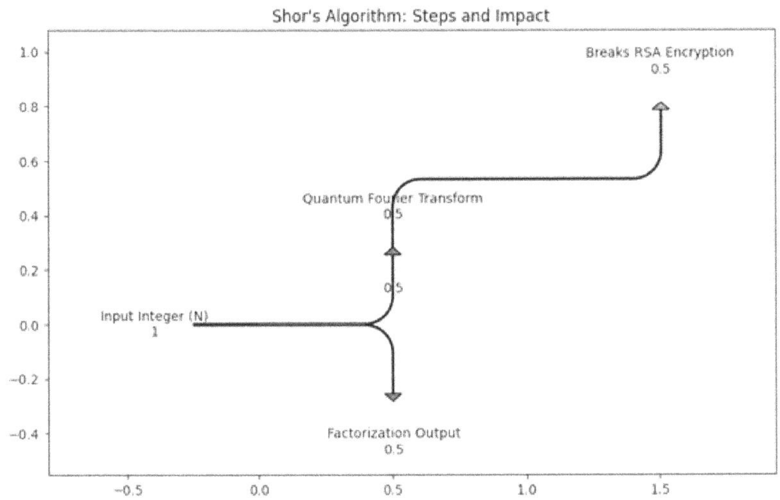

3.3 Quantum Error Correction

One of the significant challenges in quantum computing is the **fragility of quantum states** due to decoherence and noise, which can introduce errors in computations. **Quantum error correction (QEC)** codes are designed to detect and correct these errors without measuring the quantum state directly, which would collapse the superposition. The development of effective QEC is crucial for scaling up quantum computers to a level where they can outperform classical systems in a broad range of practical applications.

3.4 Quantum Hardware and Gate Models

Quantum computers are implemented using various types of quantum hardware, with some of the most common being based on **trapped ions**, **superconducting qubits**, and **topological qubits**. Quantum computers use quantum gates to manipulate qubits in a controlled way, analogous to classical logic gates. However, quantum gates are reversible and operate based on quantum mechanics, allowing them to perform operations such as rotations and entanglements, which are not possible in classical systems.

3.5 Hybrid Quantum-Classical Systems

As quantum computers are still in their developmental stages, hybrid systems that combine classical and quantum computing are emerging as practical solutions. These systems use quantum processors to handle specific subproblems and classical computers for other tasks, leveraging the strengths of both types of systems to solve complex real-world problems more efficiently.

3.6 Applications of Quantum Computing

Quantum computing holds immense promise in fields that require substantial computational power, such as:

- **Cryptography**: With algorithms like Shor's, quantum computing has the potential to break traditional cryptographic systems, but it also opens the door to new forms of quantum-secure cryptography.
- **Optimization**: Quantum computers can significantly improve optimization tasks in logistics, supply chains, and financial markets by efficiently exploring vast solution spaces.
- **Material Science**: Quantum simulations can model molecular interactions at an atomic level, leading to breakthroughs in drug discovery, material science, and energy efficiency.
- **Machine Learning**: Quantum machine learning algorithms, such as QAOA and quantum neural networks, could enhance the speed and accuracy of models in tasks like pattern recognition, data mining, and artificial intelligence.

3.7 Quantum Security Challenges

Quantum computing also presents unique challenges for cybersecurity, especially as it threatens the security of classical encryption schemes. The emergence of quantum computers capable of running Shor's algorithm has led to the development of **quantum-resistant cryptography**, which aims to develop encryption methods that are secure against quantum computing attacks. As quantum technologies continue to evolve, so does the need for robust, quantum-safe cryptographic solutions.

In the context of cybersecurity, the advent of quantum computing calls for a **strategic roadmap for quantum-resistant security** to prepare industries for the quantum era (Bishwas & Sen, 2024; Baseri et al., 2024). As pointed out by Gholami and Omar (2023), the integration of quantum principles in cybersecurity could drive forward the next generation of digital security frameworks.

3.8 Quantum Computing and Industry 4.0

The role of quantum computing in the next industrial revolution (Industry 4.0) is becoming increasingly apparent. As industries adopt quantum technologies, they will need to focus on the development of **quantum software** and quantum hardware integration (Khan et al., 2023). The application of quantum computing to sectors like healthcare, finance, and logistics promises to enhance **resource allocation**, improve **security**, and foster innovation in automated processes (How & Cheah, 2023).

In the realm of **cybersecurity**, the impact of quantum computing on current infrastructures is both promising and challenging. As quantum systems become more accessible, the risk to **traditional security models** and **data privacy** increases, necessitating the exploration of quantum-secure architectures and **quantum-enhanced attack detection models** (Sodiya et al., 2024; Jones et al., 2023). The developments in **quantum networks** and **blockchain** technologies also indicate that the convergence of these fields may offer solutions to some of the pressing challenges in the digital security landscape (Zangana et al., 2024).

3.9 Summary

Quantum computing represents a monumental shift in the computing paradigm, offering both exciting opportunities and complex challenges. Its core principles—superposition, entanglement, and quantum interference—enable algorithms that surpass the capabilities of classical systems in specific domains. However, to unlock the full potential of quantum computing, it is critical to overcome hardware limitations, ensure robust quantum error correction, and establish quantum-resistant security measures to safeguard the future of digital infrastructure. As quantum computing continues to mature, its integration into industries like cybersecurity, healthcare, and finance will shape the trajectory of the next technological revolution.

4. IMPACT OF QUANTUM COMPUTING ON CYBERSECURITY

Quantum computing is poised to revolutionize various fields, and its impact on cybersecurity is a topic of growing concern. As quantum technologies continue to evolve, their capabilities present both significant opportunities and challenges for securing digital systems. This section delves into the potential effects of quantum computing on cybersecurity, exploring the challenges and opportunities it presents, and how organizations can prepare for a quantum-enabled future.

4.1. Quantum Computing and Traditional Cryptography

Traditional cryptographic systems, such as RSA and ECC (Elliptic Curve Cryptography), which form the backbone of modern cybersecurity, are based on the difficulty of certain mathematical problems. For example, RSA relies on the complexity of factoring large prime numbers, while ECC depends on the difficulty of solving discrete logarithms. However, quantum computers, particularly those utilizing Shor's algorithm, have the potential to solve these problems exponentially faster than classical computers (Sodiya et al., 2024). This could render current cryptographic schemes vulnerable to being broken, posing a serious threat to the confidentiality and integrity of data.

The advent of quantum computing threatens to undermine the security of digital assets that depend on these classical encryption techniques. As a result, there is a growing urgency to explore **quantum-resistant cryptography**, which includes developing new algorithms that can withstand quantum computing attacks (Baseri, Chouhan, & Ghorbani, 2024). These new approaches focus on different mathematical foundations that are not susceptible to the speedup provided by quantum algorithms. Researchers are working on lattice-based, code-based, and hash-based cryptography as potential alternatives to classical encryption methods (How & Cheah, 2023).

Quantum computing poses significant risks to traditional cryptographic methods, such as RSA and ECC, by exploiting their reliance on hard mathematical problems. The chart below quantifies these vulnerabilities and compares their resilience to quantum attacks.

Figure 3. Vulnerabilities of classical cryptography

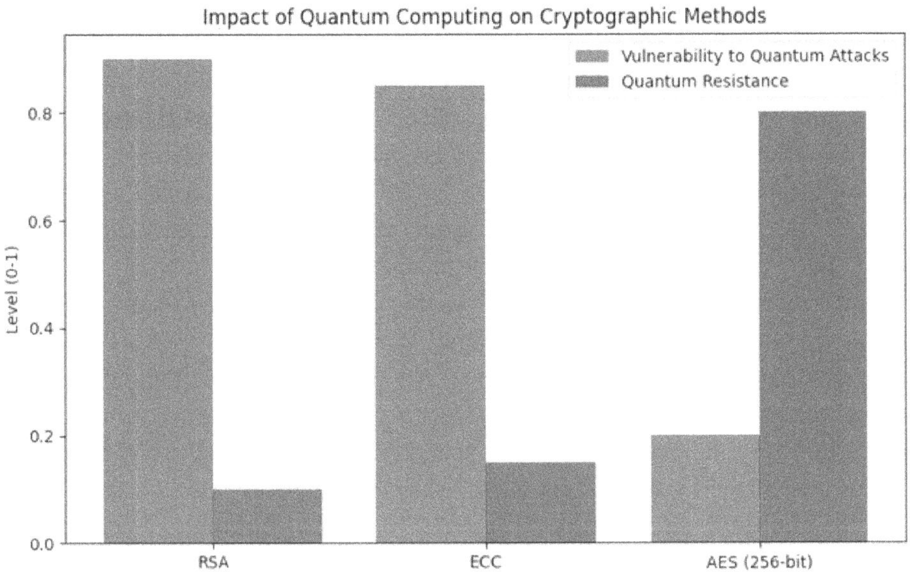

4.2. Post-Quantum Cryptography and Security Infrastructure

As quantum computing advances, the transition to post-quantum cryptography (PQC) becomes imperative. This new class of cryptographic algorithms is designed to protect against the potential threats posed by quantum computers. The **National Institute of Standards and Technology (NIST)** has already initiated a process to standardize PQC algorithms, which will play a key role in future cybersecurity strategies (Sodiya et al., 2024). However, the challenge remains in integrating these new algorithms into existing infrastructure without disrupting current systems and ensuring backward compatibility.

The impact of quantum computing on cybersecurity is not limited to data encryption; it also extends to secure communication protocols, digital signatures, and authentication mechanisms. As organizations prepare for quantum risks, they must assess the vulnerabilities in their current systems and implement a roadmap for adopting quantum-resistant technologies (Rahul et al., 2024). This includes the development of **quantum key distribution (QKD)** technologies, which leverage the principles of quantum mechanics to create unbreakable encryption kcys through quantum entanglement (Bush, Challener, & Mantelet, 2021).

4.3. Quantum Threats and Attack Vectors

In addition to the risks posed to encryption, quantum computing could enable new attack vectors that are not feasible with classical systems. For instance, quantum computers could potentially exploit vulnerabilities in **quantum key exchange** protocols, allowing attackers to intercept encrypted communication in ways that classical computers cannot (Zangana, 2024). This could lead to previously unimaginable threats, such as the cracking of supposedly secure communications or the unauthorized decryption of sensitive information stored in databases.

Moreover, the power of quantum computing can enhance the speed and scale at which cyberattacks are executed. For example, machine learning models that rely on classical computation could be exponentially enhanced with quantum algorithms, leading to more effective cyberattacks on vulnerable systems. Such attacks could include **zero-day vulnerabilities**, where unknown exploits are used to breach systems without prior detection (Jones & Omar, 2024). These attacks could exploit weaknesses in both quantum and classical systems, making it essential for cybersecurity strategies to evolve and integrate quantum-aware defense mechanisms.

4.4. Opportunities in Quantum-Enhanced Cybersecurity

While quantum computing presents several challenges, it also offers promising opportunities for enhancing cybersecurity defenses. **Quantum machine learning** (QML) is one such area that could significantly impact cybersecurity by improving anomaly detection, attack prediction, and defensive strategy development. Quantum algorithms can analyze vast amounts of data at unprecedented speeds, enabling quicker identification of cyber threats and potentially more accurate forecasting of attack vectors (Gholami & Omar, 2024).

Additionally, **quantum-safe authentication** methods could emerge, offering more secure ways to validate users and devices in a quantum world. These methods would be designed to resist the powerful decryption capabilities of quantum computers, providing robust security even as quantum threats become more widespread (Mohammed, Omar, & Nguyen, 2018).

Moreover, the combination of **blockchain technology** with quantum cryptography could lead to the development of highly secure and tamper-resistant systems for various applications, including financial transactions, healthcare data management, and supply chain logistics (Zangana & Mohammed, 2025). Blockchain's inherent decentralization, paired with quantum encryption, could provide a secure infrastructure that is resilient to both classical and quantum-based cyberattacks.

4.5. Preparing for the Quantum Era: Strategic Measures

The shift toward quantum computing necessitates strategic measures to secure infrastructures against emerging quantum threats. Organizations must focus on **quantum literacy** and prepare their cybersecurity teams with the knowledge and tools needed to respond to these challenges. Training in post-quantum cryptography, as well as in quantum-safe protocols and tools, will be essential to ensuring a smooth transition into the quantum era (Khan et al., 2023).

Simultaneously, policy makers and industry leaders must collaborate on establishing regulatory frameworks that guide the adoption of quantum-safe standards and ensure that quantum technologies are developed and implemented responsibly. Industry reports such as those by **The IEEE and NIST** provide detailed guidelines on the future of quantum cybersecurity, and organizations should align their practices with these standards (Zangana, Omar, & Al-Karaki, 2024).

4.6. Summary

The rise of quantum computing introduces both significant risks and remarkable opportunities for the cybersecurity landscape. On one hand, the threat to traditional cryptography could lead to the compromise of data protection mechanisms across industries, from finance to healthcare. On the other hand, quantum technologies offer the potential to enhance cybersecurity through advanced encryption techniques, quantum machine learning, and secure communication methods. The future of cybersecurity in the quantum era will depend on the development of quantum-resistant cryptographic systems, the integration of quantum technologies into cybersecurity frameworks, and proactive measures taken by organizations to adapt to the quantum revolution.

As the impact of quantum computing unfolds, it is crucial for cybersecurity experts to stay ahead of the curve and adopt quantum-aware strategies that safeguard digital assets in an increasingly quantum-driven world. The collaboration between academia, industry, and policy makers will be critical in shaping a secure future in the face of this transformative technology.

5. QUANTUM-AWARE CYBERSECURITY: A NEW PARADIGM

As quantum computing continues to evolve, its implications for cybersecurity are becoming increasingly significant. Quantum computing has the potential to revolutionize the field of cryptography and cybersecurity, both offering groundbreaking opportunities and posing new risks. This section explores the emerging paradigm of quantum-aware cybersecurity, examining its potential impact, challenges, and the strategies required to adapt existing systems to quantum threats.

5.1 The Quantum Threat to Classical Cryptography

One of the most discussed impacts of quantum computing is its ability to break classical encryption algorithms, which form the backbone of current cybersecurity infrastructure. Public-key cryptosystems, such as RSA and ECC (Elliptic Curve Cryptography), rely on the difficulty of mathematical problems—such as factoring large numbers or solving discrete logarithms—that quantum computers can solve exponentially faster than classical computers. This ability threatens to render current cryptographic techniques obsolete. Shor's algorithm, for instance, demonstrates how a sufficiently powerful quantum computer can efficiently factor large integers and compute discrete logarithms, effectively breaking RSA and ECC encryption methods.

The advent of quantum computing brings both challenges and opportunities to the cybersecurity landscape. While it promises to enable faster, more secure methods of data encryption, it also presents a critical challenge: how to transition from existing encryption systems that are vulnerable to quantum attacks to quantum-resistant alternatives. The urgent need for post-quantum cryptography (PQC) has led to extensive research into developing algorithms that can withstand quantum computational power.

5.2 Quantum-Aware Cybersecurity Solutions

Quantum-aware cybersecurity necessitates the development of systems and protocols that are resilient to the computational powers of quantum computers. This transition involves several key approaches:

1. **Post-Quantum Cryptography (PQC)**: PQC refers to cryptographic algorithms that are designed to be secure against the capabilities of quantum computers. These algorithms are being developed by researchers globally to provide secure encryption systems that do not rely on the hardness of problems solvable by quantum algorithms like Shor's algorithm. Standards for PQC are currently being finalized by institutions such as the National Institute of Standards and Technology (NIST), which has already shortlisted several promising algorithms for adoption in future secure communication systems.
2. **Quantum Key Distribution (QKD)**: QKD leverages the principles of quantum mechanics to enable the secure exchange of cryptographic keys. Unlike classical key exchange methods, which are vulnerable to eavesdropping, QKD is based on the quantum properties of light, making it theoretically immune

to interception by quantum computers. However, the integration of QKD into practical cybersecurity systems is still in its early stages, with scalability and cost-effectiveness being significant challenges.

3. **Quantum-Resistant Blockchain**: Blockchain technology, which is fundamentally built on cryptographic principles, is also facing the threat of quantum computing. Quantum computers could potentially break the cryptographic hash functions that secure blockchain networks. Research into quantum-resistant blockchain solutions is focusing on developing new hash functions and consensus algorithms that are immune to quantum attacks (Zangana, 2024). This could ensure the continued reliability of blockchain-based systems in a quantum-enabled future.
4. **Hybrid Quantum-Classical Systems**: Given that quantum computers are not expected to replace classical computers in the near future, hybrid quantum-classical systems are emerging as an important strategy. These systems combine the strengths of quantum computing, such as optimization and machine learning capabilities, with the robust security features of classical computing. This hybrid model allows organizations to leverage quantum technologies while still relying on classical security protocols for critical operations (Gholami & Omar, 2023).

The transition to post-quantum cryptography is crucial for safeguarding digital infrastructures. The timeline below shows projected milestones for adopting quantum-resistant algorithms across industries.

Figure 4. Adoption timeline for post-quantum cryptography

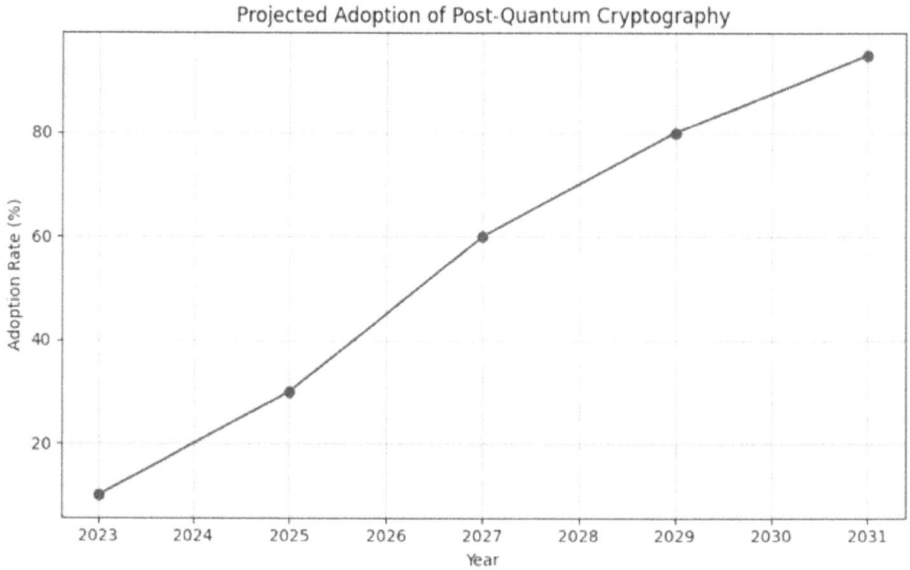

5.3 The Role of AI and Machine Learning in Quantum-Aware Cybersecurity

Artificial intelligence (AI) and machine learning (ML) are already transforming cybersecurity, and their intersection with quantum computing is expected to further enhance their capabilities. AI can help in detecting new types of quantum-enabled threats, automating responses, and improving the efficiency of quantum-resistant algorithms.

For instance, AI-driven cybersecurity systems can identify anomalies and potential threats much faster than traditional methods. As quantum computing becomes more prevalent, integrating AI and quantum computing can enable faster data processing and more accurate predictions about the behavior of quantum-based attacks. Moreover, machine learning models could play a crucial role in optimizing the development of quantum-resistant cryptographic algorithms by analyzing large datasets and testing various algorithms' strengths against quantum attacks (Jones & Omar, 2024).

Furthermore, recent studies suggest that combining machine learning with quantum computing could lead to significant advances in the detection and prevention of zero-day threats, which are typically difficult to identify using classical methods (Jones et al., 2023). The integration of quantum computing into AI-driven cybersecurity systems could provide a new layer of security that is both adaptive and anticipatory in nature.

5.4 Challenges in Quantum-Aware Cybersecurity

Despite the promise of quantum-aware cybersecurity, several challenges remain:

1. **Scalability of Quantum Technologies**: While quantum algorithms and systems are showing potential, building large-scale, fault-tolerant quantum computers is still a major technical hurdle. Current quantum devices are far from being able to break widely used encryption algorithms, but this gap is closing rapidly, making it imperative to prepare for a quantum future (Seskir, 2019).
2. **Cost and Integration**: Transitioning from classical to quantum-resistant systems is costly and complex. For example, implementing post-quantum cryptography requires significant infrastructure changes, including software upgrades and changes in cryptographic protocols. Additionally, the integration of quantum systems into existing cybersecurity frameworks requires expertise in both quantum mechanics and classical security protocols, which may be a barrier to widespread adoption (Baseri et al., 2024).
3. **Lack of Standardization**: There is still no universal standard for quantum-resistant encryption algorithms. While NIST is leading the charge in this area, it will take time before global standards are established and adopted across industries (Perron et al., 2021).
4. **Quantum AI Integration**: Integrating quantum computing with AI in the context of cybersecurity presents its own set of challenges. Quantum AI models are still in the nascent stages, and ensuring their reliability and robustness in the face of sophisticated cyber threats is a critical concern (Rahul et al., 2024).

5.5 The Future of Quantum-Aware Cybersecurity

As we look towards the future, the role of quantum computing in cybersecurity will continue to grow, necessitating the development of quantum-aware cybersecurity practices. The security industry must prepare for the quantum revolution by investing in quantum-resistant technologies, fostering collaboration between quantum researchers and cybersecurity professionals, and focusing on the practical integration of quantum and AI technologies into existing security frameworks.

Given the rapid pace of quantum advancements, cybersecurity professionals must remain vigilant and adaptive, embracing new paradigms that account for both the opportunities and challenges presented by quantum computing. The integration of quantum-aware strategies into cybersecurity will be crucial in maintaining the security and integrity of digital systems in the quantum era.

6. QUANTUM COMPUTING AND MACHINE LEARNING: SYNERGIES AND RISKS FOR CYBERSECURITY

As we enter an era dominated by cutting-edge technologies, quantum computing (QC) and machine learning (ML) stand at the forefront of innovations that promise to reshape industries, including cybersecurity. While these technologies offer immense potential for advancements in security protocols and defenses, they also introduce new risks and challenges that must be addressed for effective cybersecurity.

6.1 The Synergy Between Quantum Computing and Machine Learning

The fusion of quantum computing with machine learning holds the promise of revolutionizing cybersecurity through faster processing capabilities and more efficient data analysis. Quantum computers leverage the principles of quantum mechanics—such as superposition and entanglement—to perform computations that are infeasible for classical computers. Quantum machine learning (QML) can harness the power of quantum algorithms to analyze massive datasets, identify patterns, and optimize decisions at speeds unimaginable with traditional computing. This synergy could enhance threat detection systems, allowing cybersecurity frameworks to respond proactively rather than reactively to potential attacks.

Machine learning algorithms, especially those employing deep learning techniques, have already demonstrated significant promise in anomaly detection, intrusion detection, and predicting vulnerabilities within networks (Jones, Omar, & Dawson, 2023). When combined with quantum computing, ML could achieve unprecedented levels of accuracy and processing speed in identifying new and evolving threats. Quantum-enhanced machine learning algorithms may enable the detection of zero-day vulnerabilities, even in highly complex systems, which is a critical step in ensuring the resilience of digital infrastructures (Jones & Omar, 2024).

Quantum-enhanced ML could also play a pivotal role in secure communications, especially in the context of encryption. Quantum key distribution (QKD) could secure the exchange of information, rendering classical encryption algorithms obsolete in the face of quantum decryption techniques. By integrating QKD into ML-driven cybersecurity tools, organizations could prevent future vulnerabilities that may arise from quantum computing's ability to break current cryptographic standards (Sodiya et al., 2024; Zangana, 2024).

6.2 Risks Associated with Quantum Computing and Machine Learning in Cybersecurity

Despite the enormous potential of QC and ML in cybersecurity, their integration also raises several critical concerns. One of the most pressing issues is the development of quantum-resistant cryptography. While QC can solve certain computational problems exponentially faster than classical computers, it also poses a significant threat to current cryptographic systems, such as RSA and ECC, which rely on the hardness of problems like integer factorization and the discrete logarithm problem. Quantum computers can break these systems using Shor's algorithm, rendering conventional encryption methods obsolete (Baseri, Chouhan, & Ghorbani, 2024).

In response to this threat, researchers are developing quantum-resistant cryptographic algorithms. However, this transition to post-quantum cryptography introduces the risk of vulnerabilities during the interim period when both quantum and classical systems coexist. The rapid pace of technological advancement in QC and the slow adaptation of current systems to quantum resistance could lead to a cybersecurity gap, which malicious actors may exploit (Rahul et al., 2024). Thus, the timeline for quantum-resistant cryptography must be accelerated to stay ahead of emerging threats (Bishwas & Sen, 2024).

Another challenge arises from the potential misuse of quantum computing in adversarial ML attacks. While ML has shown promise in strengthening cybersecurity defenses, it also makes systems vulnerable to attacks where adversaries manipulate ML models to evade detection. Quantum computing could enhance the effectiveness of these attacks, making them harder to detect and mitigate. Quantum-enhanced adversarial machine learning could lead to the creation of highly sophisticated attacks that bypass traditional ML-based security systems (Metawei et al., 2022; Khan et al., 2023).

6.3 Ethical and Privacy Concerns

Quantum computing also raises ethical and privacy concerns that need careful consideration in the context of cybersecurity. One major issue is the challenge of maintaining privacy in a quantum-enabled world. Current encryption techniques, such as symmetric-key encryption, could theoretically remain secure against quantum decryption. However, once quantum computers reach sufficient scale, they may be able to break both symmetric and asymmetric encryption algorithms, leading to the exposure of sensitive personal data on an unprecedented scale (Zangana, Mohammed, & Sallow, 2024).

Further, the integration of quantum computing with ML models presents risks related to data integrity. Quantum machine learning models may rely on massive datasets, which raises concerns about the potential for biased or malicious data inputs. This could result in ML models that are skewed or compromised, leading to inaccurate threat detection or even false positives that may overwhelm security teams (Omar, 2021; Gholami & Omar, 2024). Such vulnerabilities must be mitigated through rigorous validation and testing of quantum-enhanced ML systems.

6.4 Preparing for the Quantum Era in Cybersecurity

To effectively harness the synergies between quantum computing and machine learning, while mitigating the associated risks, a multi-pronged approach to cybersecurity must be adopted. The development of quantum-safe cryptographic protocols is essential to ensuring the security of data in a post-quantum world. Additionally, researchers must focus on advancing quantum machine learning algorithms that not only detect and prevent cybersecurity threats but are also resilient to adversarial attacks and data manipulation (Omar & Zangana, 2024).

Moreover, policymakers and industry leaders must prioritize collaboration to establish global standards for quantum-enhanced cybersecurity practices. This includes setting guidelines for quantum-safe encryption, data privacy, and responsible ML model deployment. Collaborative research efforts, such as those outlined by Lougovski et al. (2023) and Perron et al. (2021), are critical in addressing the technical and ethical challenges posed by QC and ML integration into cybersecurity frameworks.

Finally, as the landscape of quantum computing and machine learning evolves, cybersecurity professionals must stay ahead of these technologies by continually updating their knowledge and practices. Training programs focused on quantum computing, post-quantum cryptography, and quantum machine learning should become integral components of cybersecurity education and workforce development (Bush et al., 2021; Seskir, 2019).

6.5 Summary

The convergence of quantum computing and machine learning presents both a transformative opportunity and a formidable challenge for the field of cybersecurity. While the integration of these technologies promises to enhance threat detection, secure communications, and data analysis, it also raises significant concerns regarding cryptographic security, adversarial attacks, and privacy. By addressing these challenges proactively, the cybersecurity community can leverage the full potential of quantum computing and machine learning while minimizing the associated risks. Ultimately, a balanced and strategic approach will be required to safeguard digital infrastructures in the quantum era.

7. PREPARING FOR QUANTUM-ENABLED CYBERSECURITY: THE ROLE OF LARGE LANGUAGE MODELS

As we stand at the crossroads of the quantum computing revolution, cybersecurity must evolve to address the emerging threats and opportunities that come with these advancements. Quantum-enabled cybersecurity will likely transform digital defenses, bringing with it new challenges such as the vulnerability of current encryption schemes to quantum attacks. However, it also offers the potential for unprecedented improvements in how we detect, mitigate, and respond to these threats. One key technology in this transformation is the integration of Large Language Models (LLMs), which can enhance our understanding and response to cybersecurity issues, especially in the quantum computing era.

7.1 The Need for Quantum-Resistant Security

Quantum computing promises significant advancements in computational power, potentially breaking widely used cryptographic systems such as RSA and ECC that currently secure communications and data. With the advent of quantum computing, existing encryption algorithms could be rendered obsolete, necessitating the development of quantum-resistant security solutions. The transition to quantum-safe cryptography is not just a theoretical concern but a practical need for industries that rely on secure digital infrastructure. Sodiya et al. (2024) explored the implications of quantum technologies in safeguarding digital assets, highlighting both the challenges and opportunities they present. Moreover, Baseri, Chouhan, and Ghorbani (2024) discussed the impact quantum computing will have on cybersecurity infrastructure, stressing the need for robust frameworks that integrate quantum-resistant mechanisms into existing cybersecurity strategies.

7.2 The Role of Large Language Models in Cybersecurity

Large Language Models (LLMs), such as GPT-3 and GPT-4, are gaining prominence as tools in artificial intelligence (AI) for a variety of cybersecurity tasks. These models are particularly useful for analyzing large datasets, recognizing patterns, and making predictions based on vast amounts of information—capabilities that are critical in the evolving cybersecurity landscape. In the context of quantum computing, LLMs can play a key role in identifying vulnerabilities in quantum-resistant algorithms and aiding in the transition to quantum-safe cryptography.

LLMs are not only valuable for their ability to process and analyze textual data but also for their potential to simulate and predict attack vectors that could exploit quantum computing's capabilities. Jones and Omar (2024) demonstrated how GPT-2-enhanced models could be used to detect and defend against zero-day threats, a method that could be adapted to handle threats posed by quantum computing. The ability to predict and understand novel attack strategies is especially important as adversaries exploit quantum-enhanced capabilities to bypass traditional defenses.

Furthermore, LLMs can facilitate the automation of threat detection and response. According to Huff et al. (2023), applying AI-driven models to cybersecurity tasks, such as real-time attack detection, enhances the efficiency and accuracy of threat mitigation in high-risk environments like healthcare and biotechnology. These capabilities will be critical as quantum computing introduces new forms of threats, including those that target quantum communication protocols and quantum cryptography.

7.3 Synthetic Data and Its Impact on LLM Performance

As quantum computing introduces new types of data and attack strategies, LLMs must be trained on large, diverse datasets to remain effective in this new environment. One way to address data scarcity is through the use of synthetic data, which can be generated to simulate various attack scenarios, including those leveraging quantum capabilities. Gholami and Omar (2023) explored the role of synthetic data in improving the efficiency of LLMs, emphasizing how such data can enhance model accuracy by providing diverse and representative examples, particularly in the context of cybersecurity threats.

In the realm of quantum-enabled cybersecurity, synthetic data could simulate quantum-specific attack patterns, allowing LLMs to learn and adapt to new types of vulnerabilities without requiring access to sensitive real-world data. This would enable security professionals to prepare for potential quantum threats while mitigating the risks of data breaches and adversarial manipulation.

7.4 Leveraging LLMs for Quantum-Resistant Security

As quantum computing becomes more prevalent, the importance of LLMs in securing digital infrastructure will only grow. LLMs can be used to test the resilience of existing security protocols against quantum threats by simulating quantum-based attacks and identifying weaknesses in encryption schemes. For instance, LLMs could assist in the development of post-quantum cryptographic algorithms by analyzing large datasets of cryptographic protocols and identifying those most resistant to quantum decryption techniques.

Moreover, LLMs can help organizations transition from classical to quantum-resistant cybersecurity by providing insights into the effectiveness of various cryptographic solutions. As Omar and Zangana (2024) discussed in *Redefining Security with Cyber AI*, the integration of AI tools into cybersecurity frameworks could dramatically improve the ability to adapt to emerging quantum threats. LLMs could continuously analyze network traffic, identify vulnerabilities, and even suggest patches or upgrades to existing systems in real time.

7.5 Challenges and Future Directions

While LLMs offer considerable promise in the quantum-enabled cybersecurity landscape, there are still significant challenges to overcome. Quantum computing is still in its infancy, and there is much uncertainty about how it will interact with existing cybersecurity frameworks. Additionally, the integration of LLMs into cybersecurity workflows requires specialized expertise and the development of new tools to ensure their accuracy and reliability.

Furthermore, the role of synthetic data in training LLMs must be carefully considered, as the generation of realistic data that accurately mimics quantum threats will require substantial research and development. As noted by Zangana (2024), the effectiveness of LLMs depends on the quality and breadth of the data they are trained on, and this is even more critical in the context of emerging quantum technologies. The next steps in this field will involve refining synthetic data generation techniques, improving LLM architectures, and creating more sophisticated frameworks for post-quantum cybersecurity.

In conclusion, the convergence of quantum computing and LLMs presents both challenges and opportunities for the cybersecurity domain. With the rapid advancements in both quantum technologies and AI, the future of cybersecurity will rely heavily on the integration of LLMs to develop quantum-resistant defenses, automate threat detection, and enhance the resilience of digital infrastructures against a new class of quantum-enabled threats.

8. CHALLENGES AND OPPORTUNITIES IN QUANTUM-AWARE CYBERSECURITY

The emerging field of quantum computing promises to revolutionize various industries, including cybersecurity. While quantum computing has the potential to enhance computational capabilities and tackle problems that are intractable for classical computers, it also introduces significant challenges and opportunities for cybersecurity. As quantum technologies evolve, they will inevitably reshape the landscape of digital security. This section explores the main challenges and opportunities quantum computing presents in cybersecurity, focusing on areas such as cryptography, quantum-resistant algorithms, and quantum-based security solutions.

8.1 Challenges in Quantum-Aware Cybersecurity

1. **Quantum-Resistant Cryptography**

One of the most pressing challenges quantum computing poses to cybersecurity is the potential obsolescence of existing cryptographic protocols. Quantum computers can efficiently break many of the cryptographic schemes currently used to secure digital communication. Notably, Shor's algorithm enables quantum computers to solve integer factorization problems exponentially faster than classical computers, which threatens RSA encryption, one of the cornerstones of modern cybersecurity. Similarly, quantum computers can solve discrete logarithm problems, endangering protocols such as Diffie-Hellman and elliptic curve cryptography (ECC). As a result, there is an urgent need for quantum-resistant cryptography. Researchers are exploring lattice-based, code-based, multivariate polynomial, and hash-based cryptographic algorithms as potential candidates for post-quantum encryption (Sodiya et al., 2024; Baseri et al., 2024).

2. **Integration of Quantum and Classical Security Systems**

Integrating quantum and classical security systems presents a significant challenge. Quantum computers can be deployed alongside traditional cybersecurity infrastructures to enhance specific security functions, but their coexistence is complex. Ensuring that both systems operate seamlessly, while also maintaining the security of quantum-enabled assets, requires new frameworks and standards that are still in the development stage (Wright et al., 2012; Zangana et al., 2024). Moreover, transitioning to quantum-resistant systems on a global scale will require substantial coordination across industries, governments, and standards organizations.

3. **Increased Vulnerability to Quantum Attacks**

Quantum computing may expose new attack vectors, such as quantum hacking techniques that exploit quantum algorithms for malicious purposes. For instance, quantum-enhanced attacks could potentially target key exchange protocols, rendering traditional defense mechanisms ineffective. The inherent difficulty in predicting how quantum computers will behave in real-world scenarios means that cybersecurity experts must stay ahead of adversaries, who may use quantum computing for unauthorized access and disruption (Rahul et al., 2024; Seskir, 2019).

4. **Cybersecurity Talent Gap**

As quantum technologies evolve, there is an increasing demand for cybersecurity professionals who understand both quantum computing and cybersecurity principles. This shortage of quantum-aware cybersecurity experts is exacerbating the challenges of preparing for the quantum future. Organizations must invest in education and training to ensure that their cybersecurity workforce can manage quantum-based risks effectively (Khan et al., 2023; Perron et al., 2021).

8.2 Opportunities in Quantum-Aware Cybersecurity

1. **Quantum Key Distribution (QKD)**

Despite the challenges, quantum technologies also offer opportunities for enhancing cybersecurity. Quantum Key Distribution (QKD) is one of the most promising applications in this field. QKD leverages the principles of quantum mechanics to securely exchange cryptographic keys between parties. Unlike classical methods, which rely on mathematical difficulty to ensure security, QKD is theoretically immune to eavesdropping. Any attempt to intercept quantum communication disturbs the quantum state of the transmission, immediately alerting the parties involved to a potential breach. As quantum networks develop, QKD can provide an unprecedented level of security for sensitive data transfers (Lougovski et al., 2023; Block, 2024).

2. **Quantum-Enhanced Machine Learning for Threat Detection**

Quantum computing's ability to process vast amounts of data at high speeds offers opportunities for enhancing machine learning algorithms used in cybersecurity. Quantum-enhanced machine learning models can potentially detect and respond to threats faster and more accurately than classical systems. For instance, quantum algorithms could help improve intrusion detection systems (IDS) and identify anomalies in network traffic with higher precision (Gholami & Omar, 2024). This could significantly improve real-time defense mechanisms against evolving cyber threats.

3. **Accelerating Cryptanalysis and Security Audits**

Quantum computing can also be used for accelerating the cryptanalysis process, enabling organizations to identify weaknesses in their cryptographic systems before malicious actors can exploit them. This proactive approach to security can help mitigate risks associated with vulnerabilities in legacy systems that could be broken by quantum algorithms (Jones et al., 2024). Additionally, quantum tools can be used to conduct more efficient and thorough security audits, identifying potential gaps in existing security protocols (Metawei et al., 2022; Mohammed et al., 2018).

4. **Post-Quantum Cryptographic Standards**

As quantum computing develops, it also opens up an opportunity to redefine global cryptographic standards. Researchers are actively working on the standardization of post-quantum cryptography (PQC), which aims to create algorithms that are resistant to quantum attacks. As these standards are formalized and adopted, organizations will be able to transition to more secure cryptographic solutions that will safeguard their systems from the quantum threat (Bishwas & Sen, 2024; Zangana, 2024). These advancements present an opportunity for both security researchers and industries to collaborate in building resilient cybersecurity infrastructures.

8.3 Summary

Quantum computing introduces both significant challenges and transformative opportunities in the field of cybersecurity. The need for quantum-resistant cryptographic algorithms and the integration of quantum technologies with existing security systems remain major hurdles. However, the potential for quantum-enhanced security solutions such as Quantum Key Distribution, machine learning, and cryptanalysis offers promising avenues for strengthening digital defense mechanisms. The future of cybersecurity will depend on the collaborative efforts of researchers, industry professionals, and policymakers to address these challenges while harnessing the benefits that quantum computing can bring to the field.

9. THE FUTURE OF QUANTUM-AWARE CYBERSECURITY

As we enter a new era dominated by quantum computing, the landscape of cybersecurity is experiencing rapid transformation. Quantum computers possess the potential to break traditional cryptographic systems, leading to significant vulnerabilities in digital infrastructure. This section explores the future of quantum-aware cybersecurity, outlining the emerging challenges, innovative approaches, and the need for adaptive strategies to mitigate quantum threats.

9.1. Quantum Computing's Impact on Cybersecurity

Quantum computing introduces a paradigm shift in computational capabilities, particularly in solving problems that are currently intractable for classical computers. The most concerning threat posed by quantum technology to cybersecurity lies in its ability to break widely used cryptographic algorithms such as RSA and ECC, which form the backbone of many security protocols. Quantum computers use quantum bits (qubits) that can exist in multiple states simultaneously, allowing them to perform parallel computations far beyond the capabilities of classical systems. For example, Shor's algorithm enables a quantum computer to factor large numbers exponentially faster than classical computers, posing a direct risk to public key encryption (Seskir, 2019).

As quantum computing evolves, current cryptographic methods will be rendered obsolete. Thus, the urgent need for quantum-resistant algorithms—often referred to as post-quantum cryptography (PQC)—is becoming a critical area of research. Efforts to develop these algorithms aim to secure data against both quantum and classical computational threats. Researchers like Baseri, Chouhan, and Ghorbani (2024) are exploring how PQC can safeguard digital assets in the face of quantum advancements.

9.2. Quantum-Resistant Cryptography and the Transition

The transition to quantum-resistant cryptography will require a rethinking of many security protocols that are integral to our current systems. Algorithms such as lattice-based encryption, code-based cryptography, and multivariate quadratic equations have emerged as promising candidates for post-quantum security. However, integrating these new cryptographic methods into existing infrastructures presents substantial challenges in terms of both performance and scalability.

For instance, a key concern is the computational overhead that these new quantum-resistant algorithms may introduce. The performance of quantum-resistant algorithms must be evaluated to ensure that they do not hinder the overall efficiency of security systems. Researchers, such as Wright, Dawson, and Omar (2012), highlight that the effectiveness of new cryptographic methods in real-world scenarios needs to be validated through extensive testing and simulations.

The transition from classical to quantum-resistant algorithms also necessitates a comprehensive strategy for public and private sector collaboration. As organizations shift their infrastructure to adopt post-quantum security solutions, the financial, technical, and operational costs may be significant. Therefore, preparing industries for quantum threats requires a strategic roadmap, as outlined by Bishwas and Sen (2024), to ensure a seamless adoption of quantum-resistant technologies.

9.3. Quantum Machine Learning (QML) and Cybersecurity

Quantum Machine Learning (QML) holds great promise in enhancing cybersecurity defenses. By harnessing the unique properties of quantum computing, QML can process and analyze large datasets much more efficiently than classical machine learning techniques. In cybersecurity, this can translate into faster and more accurate threat detection, anomaly detection, and real-time defense mechanisms. Jones et al. (2023) explored the use of machine learning to mitigate cybersecurity threats, and with the advent of quantum computing, these methods can be significantly enhanced.

Quantum-enhanced machine learning algorithms could also aid in the detection of zero-day attacks, which are often difficult to predict and prevent using traditional methods. The potential for quantum computers to handle complex data structures and optimize the detection of cybersecurity risks in real-time makes QML a promising frontier for cybersecurity research and development.

Furthermore, integrating quantum computing with AI-based solutions can lead to more sophisticated, autonomous cybersecurity systems that can adapt and evolve alongside emerging threats. As highlighted by Gholami and Omar (2024), AI and quantum computing together could revolutionize the way security systems respond to attacks by offering an unprecedented level of speed, accuracy, and predictive capabilities.

9.4. Addressing Quantum Threats to Infrastructure and Networks

The deployment of quantum networks, which use quantum entanglement and superposition to transmit data securely, could offer new solutions for securing communication channels. However, the implementation of quantum networks also presents new challenges in terms of ensuring their reliability and scalability. Technologies such as quantum key distribution (QKD) are being developed to establish secure communication channels that are resistant to eavesdropping and hacking.

According to Bush et al. (2021), QKD could become a foundational element of the future quantum-aware cybersecurity framework.

The transition from classical networks to quantum networks requires significant infrastructure updates and the development of new hardware technologies. As Omar and Zangana (2024) suggest, integrating quantum-enhanced security measures into existing systems demands careful consideration of how current digital assets and operations will be impacted.

9.5. Quantum-Safe Infrastructure for Businesses

For businesses, especially those in sectors like healthcare, finance, and biotechnology, quantum threats are becoming an urgent issue. Huff et al. (2023) stress the importance of integrating quantum-safe infrastructure in organizations that rely heavily on sensitive data. Companies will need to incorporate quantum-resistant protocols and strategies as part of their cybersecurity frameworks to remain resilient in the quantum era.

The development of quantum-aware security measures will also involve retraining professionals and adjusting policies to accommodate quantum risks. According to How and Cheah (2023), businesses must prioritize cybersecurity efforts that consider both quantum and classical threats, ensuring that future systems are designed with quantum resilience in mind.

9.6. Cybersecurity Education and Workforce Transformation

As quantum computing becomes more accessible, there will be a growing need for cybersecurity professionals who are well-versed in quantum technologies. The integration of quantum-aware cybersecurity measures into the workforce requires a new generation of trained professionals capable of understanding and addressing quantum-specific risks. Sodiya et al. (2024) highlight that educational institutions must adapt their curriculums to incorporate quantum computing and its implications for cybersecurity, preparing the next generation of experts for the quantum revolution.

Moreover, ongoing research in quantum computing and cybersecurity should be complemented by industry partnerships that promote knowledge sharing and collaboration. As quantum technologies continue to advance, the global workforce must remain agile and prepared to tackle emerging challenges.

9.7 Summary

The future of quantum-aware cybersecurity will undoubtedly be shaped by the intersection of quantum computing, machine learning, and next-generation cryptographic technologies. As quantum capabilities continue to evolve, it is essential to develop quantum-safe infrastructures, integrate quantum-resistant cryptography, and leverage the power of quantum-enhanced machine learning to stay ahead of emerging threats. As Seskir (2019) notes, the coming decades will require a robust global effort to ensure that our digital assets remain secure in the face of quantum disruptions. Thus, preparing for a quantum-powered cybersecurity future will be a complex but critical endeavor for securing both our digital infrastructure and society at large.

10. CONCLUSION

The future of quantum-aware cybersecurity is one of profound transformation, as it brings together cutting-edge technologies like quantum computing and artificial intelligence to create more resilient and adaptive security frameworks. As quantum computing continues to advance, it holds the potential to revolutionize the way we address cybersecurity challenges, particularly in areas such as encryption, threat detection, and data integrity. However, this potential comes with a significant level of uncertainty, as quantum technologies also pose new risks, including the vulnerability of existing cryptographic systems to quantum-based attacks.

To ensure the security of critical infrastructure and sensitive data in the quantum era, it is crucial to develop quantum-resistant encryption algorithms and innovative cybersecurity strategies. These solutions must be able to withstand the computational power of quantum computers while maintaining the high standards of confidentiality, integrity, and availability. Researchers and industry leaders must also focus on building hybrid systems that combine classical and quantum technologies, leveraging the strengths of both to address evolving threats.

Furthermore, collaboration between academia, industry, and government agencies will be essential in accelerating the development of quantum-aware cybersecurity practices. As the threat landscape continues to evolve, it is important to remain proactive, anticipating future risks and preparing systems that are adaptable to new quantum capabilities. Training the next generation of cybersecurity professionals in quantum technologies and their applications will also play a critical role in ensuring a secure digital future.

In conclusion, the intersection of quantum computing and cybersecurity presents both remarkable opportunities and daunting challenges. By addressing these challenges head-on with innovative solutions, industry leaders and researchers can unlock the full potential of quantum technologies while safeguarding the digital world from emerging threats. The journey towards a quantum-secure future will require concerted effort, creativity, and a forward-thinking approach to remain one step ahead of cyber adversaries.

REFERENCES

Agrawal, K., & Aggarwal, M. Building Efficient Smart Contract for Healthcare 4.0. In *Blockchain for Healthcare 4.0* (pp. 94-123). CRC Press.

AL-Refaey. M. R., Tyagi, A. K., AL-Ghamdi, A. S. A. M., & Kukreja, S. (Eds.). (2024). *Topics in Artificial Intelligence Applied to Industry 4.0*. John Wiley & Sons.

Baseri, Y., Chouhan, V., & Ghorbani, A. (2024). Cybersecurity in the Quantum Era: Assessing the Impact of Quantum Computing on Infrastructure. *arXiv preprint arXiv:2404.10659.*

Bishwas, A. K., & Sen, M. (2024). Strategic Roadmap for Quantum-Resistant Security: A Framework for Preparing Industries for the Quantum Threat. *arXiv preprint arXiv:2411.09995.*

Block, R. S. S. (2024). The 2024 quantum advantage blueprint: Where quantum outpaces classical.

Bush, S. F., Challener, W. A., & Mantelet, G. (2021). A perspective on industrial quantum networks. *AVS Quantum Science*, 3(3), 030501. DOI: 10.1116/5.0051881

Exchange, Q. R. K. Towards a Verifiably Secure Quantum-Resistant Key Exchange in IKEv2.

Gholami, S., & Omar, M. (2023). Does Synthetic Data Make Large Language Models More Efficient? *arXiv preprint arXiv:2310.07830.*

Gholami, S., & Omar, M. (2024). Can a student large language model perform as well as its teacher? In *Innovations, Securities, and Case Studies Across Healthcare, Business, and Technology* (pp. 122-139). IGI Global. DOI: 10.4018/979-8-3693-1906-2.ch007

Hamza, Y. A., & Omar, M. D. (2013). Cloud computing security: Abuse and nefarious use of cloud computing. *International Journal of Computer Engineering Research*, 3(6), 22–27.

How, M. L., & Cheah, S. M. (2023). Business Renaissance: Opportunities and challenges at the dawn of the Quantum Computing Era. *Businesses*, 3(4), 585–605. DOI: 10.3390/businesses3040036

Huff, A. J., Burrell, D. N., Nobles, C., Richardson, K., Wright, J. B., Burton, S. L., Jones, A. J., Springs, D., Omar, M., & Brown-Jackson, K. L. (2023). Management Practices for Mitigating Cybersecurity Threats to Biotechnology Companies, Laboratories, and Healthcare Research Organizations. In *Applied Research Approaches to Technology, Healthcare, and Business* (pp. 1-12). IGI Global.

Jones, R., & Omar, M. (2024). Revolutionizing Cybersecurity: The GPT-2 Enhanced Attack Detection and Defense (GEADD) Method for Zero-Day Threats. *International Journal of Informatics* [INJIISCOM]. *Information System and Computer Engineering*, 5(2), 178–191.

Jones, R., Omar, M., Mohammed, D., Nobles, C., & Dawson, M. (2023). Harnessing the Speed and Accuracy of Machine Learning to Advance Cybersecurity. In *2023 Congress in Computer Science, Computer Engineering, & Applied Computing (CSCE)* (pp. 418-421). IEEE. DOI: 10.1109/CSCE60160.2023.00074

Khan, A. A., Akbar, M. A., Ahmad, A., Fahmideh, M., Shameem, M., Lahtinen, V., . . . Mikkonen, T. (2023, July). Agile practices for quantum software development: practitioners' perspectives. In *2023 IEEE international conference on quantum software (QSW)* (pp. 9-20). IEEE.

Lougovski, P., Parekh, O., Broz, J., Byrd, M., Chembo, Y., de Jong, W. A., . . . Svore, K. M. (2023). *Position Papers for the ASCR Workshop on Basic Research Needs in Quantum Computing and Networking*. USDOE Office of Science (SC), Advanced Scientific Computing Research (ASCR).

Madni, A. F., Shah, M. A., & Al-Naeem, M. (2024). An Investigation of Scalability in EHRs using Healthcare 4.0 and Blockchain. *International Journal of Advanced Computer Science and Applications*, 15(5). Advance online publication. DOI: 10.14569/IJACSA.2024.0150548

Metawei, M. A., Eldeeb, H., Nassar, S. M., & Taher, M. (2022). Quantum Computing Meets Artificial Intelligence: Innovations and Challenges. In *Handbook on Artificial Intelligence-Empowered Applied Software Engineering: VOL. 1: Novel Methodologies to Engineering Smart Software Systems* (pp. 303–338). Springer International Publishing. DOI: 10.1007/978-3-031-08202-3_12

Mohamed, N., & Ahmed, A. A. (2024, June). AI in Combatting Man-in-the-Middle Attacks: A Comprehensive Review. In *2024 15th International Conference on Computing Communication and Networking Technologies (ICCCNT)* (pp. 1-6). IEEE. DOI: 10.1109/ICCCNT61001.2024.10725789

Mohammed, D., Omar, M., & Nguyen, V. (2018). Wireless sensor network security: Approaches to detecting and avoiding wormhole attacks. *Journal of Research in Business. Economics and Management*, 10(2), 1860–1864.

Nguyen, V., Mohammed, D., Omar, M., & Banisakher, M. (2018). The Effects of the FCC Net Neutrality Repeal on Security and Privacy. [IJHIoT]. *International Journal of Hyperconnectivity and the Internet of Things*, 2(2), 21–29. DOI: 10.4018/IJHIoT.2018070102

Omar, M. (2021). New insights into database security: An effective and integrated approach for applying access control mechanisms and cryptographic concepts in Microsoft Access environments.

Omar, M. (2022). *Machine Learning for Cybersecurity: Innovative Deep Learning Solutions*. Springer Brief. https://link.springer.com/book/978303115

Omar, M. (2024). From Attack to Defense: Strengthening DNN Text Classification Against Adversarial Examples. In *Innovations, Securities, and Case Studies Across Healthcare, Business, and Technology* (pp. 174-195). IGI Global.

Omar, M. (2024). Revolutionizing Malware Detection: A Paradigm Shift Through Optimized Convolutional Neural Networks. In *Innovations, Securities, and Case Studies Across Healthcare, Business, and Technology* (pp. 196-220). IGI Global. DOI: 10.4018/979-8-3693-1906-2.ch011

Omar, M., & Zangana, H. M. (Eds.). (2024). *Redefining Security With Cyber AI*. IGI Global., DOI: 10.4018/979-8-3693-6517-5

Omar, M., & Zangana, H. M. (Eds.). (2025). *Application of Large Language Models (LLMs) for Software Vulnerability Detection*. IGI Global., DOI: 10.4018/979-8-3693-9311-6

Perron, J. K., DeLeone, C., Sharif, S., Carter, T., Grossman, J. M., Passante, G., & Sack, J. (2021). Quantum undergraduate education and scientific training. *arXiv preprint arXiv:2109.13850.*

Qualters, I., Taylor, A. J., & Hagberg, A. A. (2019). *IS&T Computing Overview* (No. LA-UR-19-22567). Los Alamos National Lab.(LANL), Los Alamos, NM (United States).

Rahul, R., Geetha, S., Priyatharsini, S., Mehata, K., Sundaresan Perumal, T., Ethiraj, N., & Sendilvelan, S. (2024). Cybersecurity Issues and Challenges in Quantum Computing. *Topics in Artificial Intelligence Applied to Industry*, 4(0), 203–221. DOI: 10.1002/9781394216147.ch11

Ramachandran, D., Naqi, S. M., Perumal, G., & Abbas, Q. (2023). DLTN-LOSP: A Novel Deep-Linear-Transition-Network-Based Resource Allocation Model with the Logic Overhead Security Protocol for Cloud Systems. *Sensors (Basel)*, 23(20), 8448. DOI: 10.3390/s23208448 PMID: 37896541

Seskir, Z. C. (2019). *Current state of quantum information technologies in Turkey* (Master's thesis, Middle East Technical University).

Sodiya, E. O., Umoga, U. J., Amoo, O. O., & Atadoga, A. (2024). Quantum computing and its potential impact on US cybersecurity: A review: Scrutinizing the challenges and opportunities presented by quantum technologies in safeguarding digital assets. *Global Journal of Engineering and Technology Advances, 18*(2), 049-064.

Wright, J., Dawson, M. E.Jr, & Omar, M. (2012). Cyber security and mobile threats: The need for antivirus applications for smartphones. *Journal of Information Systems Technology and Planning*, 5(14), 40–60.

Zangana, H. M. (2024). Exploring Blockchain-Based Timestamping Tools: A Comprehensive Review. *Redefining Security With Cyber AI*, 92-110.

Zangana, H. M. (2024). Exploring the Landscape of Website Vulnerability Scanners: A Comprehensive Review and Comparative Analysis. *Redefining Security With Cyber AI*, 111-129.

Zangana, H. M., Mohammed, A. K., Sallow, A. B., & Sallow, Z. B. (2024). Cybernetic Deception: Unraveling the Layers of Email Phishing Threats. [INJURATECH]. *International Journal of Research and Applied Technology*, 4(1), 35–47.

Zangana, H. M., & Mohammed, D. (2025). Foundations of Large Language Models in Software Vulnerability Detection. In Omar, M., & Zangana, H. (Eds.), *Application of Large Language Models (LLMs) for Software Vulnerability Detection* (pp. 41–74). IGI Global., DOI: 10.4018/979-8-3693-9311-6.ch002

Zangana, H. M., & Omar, M. (2020). Threats, Attacks, and Mitigations of Smartphone Security. *Academic Journal of Nawroz University*, 9(4), 324–332. DOI: 10.25007/ajnu.v9n4a989

Zangana, H. M., & Omar, M. (2025). Harnessing the Power of Large Language Models for Cybersecurity: Applications, Challenges, and Future Directions. In Omar, M., & Zangana, H. (Eds.), *Application of Large Language Models (LLMs) for Software Vulnerability Detection* (pp. 1–40). IGI Global., DOI: 10.4018/979-8-3693-9311-6.ch001

Zangana, H. M., Omar, M., Al-Karaki, J. N., & Mohammed, D. (2024). Comprehensive Review and Analysis of Network Firewall Rule Analyzers: Enhancing Security Posture and Efficiency. *Redefining Security With Cyber AI*, 15-36.

Chapter 3
LLMs for Enhancing Privacy and Data Protection in Quantum Computing Environments

Angel Justo Jones
https://orcid.org/0009-0007-9740-6611
University of Virginia, USA

ABSTRACT

The rapid advancement of quantum computing presents both tremendous opportunities and significant challenges for cybersecurity, particularly in the realms of privacy and data protection. Traditional encryption methods face obsolescence in the quantum era, as quantum algorithms like Shor's algorithm can efficiently break widely used cryptographic schemes. Large Language Models (LLMs), with their capacity for processing and analyzing vast amounts of data, have emerged as valuable tools in addressing privacy concerns in quantum computing environments. This chapter explores how LLMs can be leveraged to enhance privacy and data protection by facilitating the development of quantum-resistant cryptographic protocols, automating threat detection, and assisting in the creation of novel security architectures tailored to quantum technologies. By examining the intersection of LLMs and quantum computing, this work highlights their potential to reshape cybersecurity strategies to ensure that data remains secure in a post-quantum world.

DOI: 10.4018/979-8-3373-1102-9.ch003

1. INTRODUCTION

Quantum computing, with its potential to revolutionize computational paradigms, introduces both profound opportunities and complex challenges for cybersecurity, particularly regarding privacy and data protection. As quantum systems evolve, the cryptographic methods that have long safeguarded sensitive data, including symmetric and asymmetric encryption schemes, face obsolescence. The advent of quantum computing threatens to break widely used cryptographic protocols—such as RSA and ECC—due to its ability to solve certain mathematical problems much faster than classical computers, especially using algorithms like Shor's algorithm (Rahul et al., 2024). These shifts in computational power necessitate the development of new approaches for safeguarding data and ensuring privacy in a quantum computing era.

Large Language Models (LLMs), a subset of artificial intelligence (AI), have shown significant promise in addressing cybersecurity challenges. Originally designed for natural language processing tasks, LLMs such as OpenAI's GPT series and Google's BERT have demonstrated remarkable abilities in understanding, generating, and interacting with human language. Recent studies show that these models can be harnessed to detect and mitigate cybersecurity threats, such as zero-day vulnerabilities and malware attacks (Jones et al., 2024; Huff et al., 2023). In particular, LLMs offer unique advantages in quantum computing environments, where traditional security tools may not be applicable (Jones, 2024).

LLMs are also poised to play a crucial role in the development of quantum-resistant cryptographic systems. As quantum algorithms evolve, post-quantum cryptography (PQC) has become important in the research community (Bishwas & Sen, 2024). LLMs, with their capacity to process large volumes of data and model complex patterns, can be leveraged to design and evaluate new cryptographic protocols that withstand the capabilities of quantum computers. Furthermore, they can be used to generate synthetic data for training other AI models, which is particularly beneficial for industries requiring quantum-resilient security systems (Gholami & Omar, 2023).

In addition to cryptography, LLMs can significantly improve privacy protection by enhancing threat detection and incident response capabilities in quantum computing environments. Quantum computing introduces novel attack vectors, such as quantum-enhanced eavesdropping, which could bypass current encryption methods. LLMs, when combined with quantum-specific security protocols, can proactively detect anomalies, identify potential threats, and automate response mechanisms in real-time. Their ability to process and analyze vast datasets enables them to recognize patterns that might be imperceptible to traditional security systems.

The intersection of quantum computing and LLMs in cybersecurity is still an emerging area of research, but it promises to offer innovative solutions to the challenges posed by quantum technologies. As this field develops, it is essential to examine the practical applications, limitations, and potential risks associated with integrating LLMs into quantum-aware cybersecurity frameworks. This chapter explores how LLMs can enhance privacy and data protection in quantum computing environments by focusing on their applications in cryptography, threat detection, and incident response. It also discusses the future directions of research needed to ensure that the evolving landscape of quantum computing does not outpace our ability to secure digital assets.

Quantum computing holds the potential to break traditional encryption. However, through the strategic integration of LLMs, cybersecurity frameworks can adapt to these quantum threats, ensuring that privacy and data protection continue to thrive in this new computational era (Baseri et al., 2024; Sodiya et al., 2024).

2. QUANTUM COMPUTING AND ITS IMPACT ON PRIVACY AND DATA PROTECTION

Quantum computing is a transformative technology that promises to revolutionize many aspects of information processing, including privacy and data protection. The potential of quantum computers to solve problems currently intractable for classical computers has sparked significant interest across various industries, particularly in cybersecurity, encryption, and data privacy. However, the advent of quantum computing also presents a new set of challenges and risks for safeguarding digital assets and sensitive information.

2.1. The Basics of Quantum Computing

At its core, quantum computing leverages the principles of quantum mechanics, including superposition, entanglement, and quantum interference, to perform calculations that would be impossible or take infeasible amounts of time for classical computers. Unlike classical computers, which process information in bits (either 0 or 1), quantum computers use quantum bits, or qubits, which can exist in multiple states simultaneously, allowing for exponentially faster processing power for certain types of problems (Perron et al., 2021; Block, 2024).

One of the most discussed applications of quantum computing is in the realm of cryptography. Classical encryption methods, such as RSA and ECC (Elliptic Curve Cryptography), rely on the difficulty of certain mathematical problems, like factoring large prime numbers, as the foundation of their security. Quantum algorithms, notably Shor's algorithm, have the potential to break these encryption schemes by solving these problems in polynomial time, whereas classical algorithms would require exponential time (Rahul et al., 2024).

2.2. Impact on Privacy and Data Protection

The growing capabilities of quantum computing pose a significant threat to current privacy and data protection mechanisms. Many encryption protocols used today, such as TLS (Transport Layer Security) for securing communications and AES (Advanced Encryption Standard) for data storage, are susceptible to quantum attacks. The ability of quantum computers to efficiently solve problems that classical computers cannot is a double-edged sword—while it holds the promise of unlocking new methods for securing data, it also undermines the very systems that protect sensitive information in today's digital landscape.

For instance, a fully operational quantum computer could potentially decrypt encrypted data that was previously secure, exposing sensitive information such as personal data, financial records, and intellectual property. This threat is particularly acute for data stored for long periods, such as government archives, healthcare records, and corporate trade secrets. As quantum computers become more powerful, the need to develop quantum-resistant cryptography becomes urgent to maintain data confidentiality, integrity, and authenticity (Baseri et al., 2024; Sodiya et al., 2024).

2.3. Quantum-Resistant Cryptography

Researchers are focusing on developing quantum-resistant cryptographic techniques in response to the looming quantum threat. These new methods are designed to withstand attacks from classical and quantum computers. Lattice-based cryptography, hash-based signatures, and multivariate polynomial encryption are some of the leading approaches being explored to secure data in a quantum computing era (Bishwas & Sen, 2024).

The National Institute of Standards and Technology (NIST) has initiated a process to standardize quantum-resistant cryptographic algorithms, intending to identify algorithms that can withstand both classical and quantum attacks. The transition to quantum-resistant encryption will likely be a gradual process, as organizations will need to update their security infrastructure and protocols to adopt these new standards (Omar & Zangana, 2024).

2.4. Data Privacy and Quantum Key Distribution (QKD)

Another promising solution to enhance data privacy in a quantum computing world is Quantum Key Distribution (QKD). QKD leverages the principles of quantum mechanics to create a secure communication channel by using quantum entanglement to transmit cryptographic keys. The security of QKD is based on the fact that any attempt to intercept the key exchange would disturb the quantum state, alerting the communicating parties to the presence of an eavesdropper.

QKD has the potential to revolutionize the way we secure sensitive communications, particularly in industries such as banking, healthcare, and defense, where data privacy is of utmost importance. However, practical implementations of QKD face significant challenges, including the need for specialized hardware, limited transmission distances, and the high cost of deployment (Zangana et al., 2024; Metawei et al., 2022).

2.5. Quantum Computing's Dual Nature: Threat and Opportunity

While quantum computing poses significant privacy and data protection risks, it also offers opportunities to enhance cybersecurity and strengthen data protection systems. For example, quantum algorithms could be used to improve the efficiency of data encryption and decryption processes, providing stronger security mechanisms that are resilient to quantum attacks. Additionally, the advent of quantum computing could lead to the development of more sophisticated methods for detecting and mitigating cyber threats, improving overall cybersecurity (Gholami & Omar, 2023; Jones et al., 2023).

One area where quantum computing can be particularly beneficial is developing more advanced machine learning models for cybersecurity. By leveraging quantum computing's ability to process vast amounts of data in parallel, researchers are exploring how quantum algorithms can enhance anomaly detection, threat analysis, and intrusion detection systems. Combining quantum computing and machine learning could lead to faster and more accurate identification of emerging cyber threats (Rahul et al., 2024).

2.6. Preparing for the Quantum Future

The transition to a quantum-powered future requires governments and businesses to begin planning and implementing quantum-resilient strategies today. The urgency of preparing for the quantum threat cannot be overstated, as the timeline for developing practical quantum computers is rapidly shrinking. Organizations should begin exploring quantum-resistant cryptographic algorithms, invest in quantum-safe hardware, and stay informed about advancements in quantum computing and its potential impact on privacy and data protection (Khan et al., 2023; Hamza & Omar, 2013).

Moreover, industries such as healthcare, finance, and government need to consider the long-term security implications of quantum computing on the data they handle. Collaborative efforts between academia, industry, and government are crucial to maintain privacy and security in the quantum era.

2.7. Conclusion

Quantum computing represents both a threat and an opportunity for the future of privacy and data protection. While the power of quantum computers could break current encryption methods and expose sensitive data, it also opens the door to new, more secure methods for protecting information. To mitigate the risks posed by quantum computing, it is essential to develop quantum-resistant encryption techniques, explore the potential of Quantum Key Distribution, and prepare for the challenges of securing data in the quantum age. As quantum computing evolves, so too must our approaches to safeguarding privacy and data protection in an increasingly complex digital world (Zangana, 2024; Sodiya et al., 2024).

3. LARGE LANGUAGE MODELS (LLMS) IN PRIVACY AND DATA PROTECTION

Large Language Models (LLMs) have transformed various sectors by providing powerful capabilities in natural language processing (NLP). However, their role in privacy and data protection remains a critical area of research and application, as these models can both aid in securing data and present new privacy risks. This section delves into the implications of LLMs on privacy, exploring their applications, the associated risks, and the methods to mitigate these challenges.

3.1 LLMs in Data Privacy Protection

LLMs, by design, handle vast amounts of data, which may include sensitive information. One of their significant roles in privacy protection is the ability to analyze, detect, and prevent data breaches. The use of LLMs in securing personal data within cloud environments has been recognized for enhancing encryption and access control systems (Omar & Zangana, 2024). For example, LLMs can assist in automatically identifying anomalous behaviors or potential data leaks by processing and analyzing patterns in data flows. This capability aligns with emerging strategies in data loss prevention, where LLMs can intelligently classify and respond to threats in real time.

In the context of cloud computing, LLMs can also contribute to security in distributed environments by monitoring and managing data access permissions and ensuring that sensitive data is handled according to compliance standards (Hamza & Omar, 2013). Their natural language understanding allows them to parse complex privacy regulations and offer real-time compliance auditing, thereby reducing human error and enhancing the overall privacy framework of cloud-based services.

Moreover, synthetic data generated by LLMs can be used in the training and testing of privacy-preserving systems. According to Gholami and Omar (2023), synthetic datasets can mirror real-world data without exposing sensitive personal information, providing a safeguard in machine learning systems where privacy concerns are paramount. The use of synthetic data, therefore, ensures that the models do not inadvertently memorize or expose personal details while still learning valuable patterns for security purposes.

3.2 Privacy Risks and Challenges

While LLMs offer substantial benefits in enhancing privacy, they also introduce significant challenges. One of the primary concerns is the potential for these models to inadvertently memorize sensitive data, leading to privacy breaches. For instance, if an LLM is trained on data containing personal information without proper safeguards, it could recall and expose private details in its responses. This phenomenon, often referred to as "model inversion," poses a risk to data privacy (Omar & Zangana, 2025).

Another challenge lies in the ability of LLMs to generate misleading or harmful content, particularly when they are used in cybersecurity applications. As LLMs are deployed in areas like phishing detection and malware analysis, there is a growing concern regarding their susceptibility to adversarial attacks, where malicious actors could exploit the model's weaknesses to bypass security measures. Jones et al. (2023) emphasize that while LLMs can enhance cybersecurity, their vulnerabilities could also be leveraged to deceive automated systems and human operators alike, increasing the sophistication of cyber threats.

In the realm of healthcare and biotechnology, privacy becomes even more critical. Huff et al. (2023) highlight the particular importance of safeguarding patient data when LLMs are used in research and clinical settings. The use of LLMs for generating medical insights must be carefully controlled to prevent any accidental exposure of sensitive health information. This concern is exacerbated by the vast amount of personal data these models are trained on, which, if not properly anonymized, could lead to violations of data protection laws, such as GDPR and HIPAA.

3.3 Mitigating Privacy Risks

To address these concerns, several mitigation strategies have been proposed. One common approach is the integration of differential privacy techniques, which ensure that LLMs do not memorize or expose individual data points. Differential privacy can be implemented during both the training and querying phases of LLM operations, ensuring that any output generated by the model is sufficiently generalized and does not reveal specific details about the data it was trained on (Gholami & Omar, 2024).

Moreover, the implementation of secure data handling practices, such as data encryption and the use of trusted execution environments (TEEs), can safeguard sensitive data in the cloud. These methods, when combined with LLMs, create a layered security approach that protects data both at rest and in transit, mitigating the risks of unauthorized access and data leakage (Jones & Omar, 2024).

Another important aspect is the development of transparent and explainable LLMs. As LLMs are often viewed as "black boxes," their decision-making processes are not always clear to users or developers. Omar (2021) suggests that by improving model transparency and accountability, organizations can build trust with stakeholders and ensure that LLMs are being used ethically and securely in privacy-sensitive applications.

3.4 Ethical Considerations and Regulatory Compliance

As LLMs are increasingly deployed in privacy-critical fields, ethical considerations become crucial. The potential for biased decision-making, particularly in relation to data privacy and security, is a significant concern. LLMs may unintentionally amplify existing biases in the data they are trained on, leading to unfair or discriminatory outcomes. This risk highlights the need for continuous monitoring and fine-tuning of these models, especially when used in sensitive areas like recruitment, finance, or healthcare (Omar & Zangana, 2025).

Regulatory frameworks such as GDPR and the California Consumer Privacy Act (CCPA) provide guidelines on handling personal data, but the rapid evolution of AI technologies often outpaces regulatory updates. This necessitates a collaborative effort between policymakers, researchers, and industry leaders to establish clear guidelines on the ethical use of LLMs in privacy-sensitive applications (Sodiya et al., 2024). Regulatory bodies should focus on creating standards for training and deploying LLMs, particularly in sectors like healthcare and finance, where data privacy is non-negotiable.

3.5 Conclusion

LLMs hold significant promise in enhancing data protection and privacy, but their integration into privacy-sensitive applications must be approached with caution. The benefits, such as improved compliance monitoring and the ability to generate synthetic data, are counterbalanced by the risks, including model inversion and adversarial attacks. By implementing robust privacy-preserving techniques, transparent practices, and ethical considerations, the potential of LLMs to contribute positively to data protection can be realized. Future research must continue to explore innovative ways to mitigate risks while ensuring that LLMs serve their intended purpose of enhancing security and privacy across various domains.

4. LLMS FOR PRIVACY ENHANCEMENT IN QUANTUM COMPUTING ENVIRONMENTS

The intersection of Large Language Models (LLMs) and quantum computing holds transformative potential for enhancing privacy in digital systems. Quantum computing promises to revolutionize information security, but it also introduces new challenges regarding protecting sensitive data. At the same time, LLMs, with their capacity for sophisticated data analysis and understanding, offer innovative solutions to address these challenges. This section explores how LLMs can enhance privacy within quantum computing environments, providing solutions to mitigate emerging security risks.

4.1 Quantum Computing and Privacy Concerns

Quantum computing operates on the principles of quantum mechanics, enabling the processing of vast amounts of data at unprecedented speeds. However, the capabilities of quantum computing also bring substantial risks to traditional privacy mechanisms, particularly in the realms of encryption and secure data transmission. The quantum threat arises from quantum algorithms, like Shor's algorithm, which can break widely used cryptographic protocols such as RSA and ECC (Sodiya et al., 2024). As quantum computing continues to develop, the existing frameworks for securing private information may no longer suffice, necessitating the search for alternative privacy solutions.

The challenges posed by quantum computing include the potential for unauthorized data decryption, even when encrypted using advanced classical algorithms. This creates a pressing need for new cryptographic strategies and mechanisms to ensure that data remains protected even in quantum-enhanced environments. As a result, there is an increasing interest in combining quantum-resistant technologies with artificial intelligence (AI) and machine learning (ML) techniques, particularly LLMs, to maintain data confidentiality and integrity in quantum contexts (Rahul et al., 2024).

This bar chart compares the primary privacy challenges faced by quantum and classical systems, highlighting areas where quantum computing introduces unique vulnerabilities.

Figure 1. Privacy challenges across quantum and classical systems

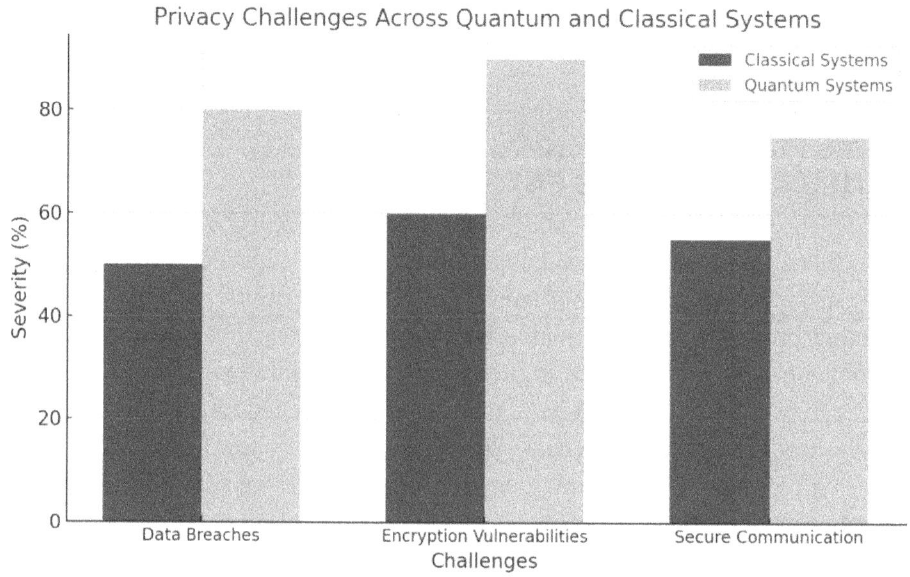

4.2 Role of LLMs in Enhancing Privacy

LLMs have shown great promise in several cybersecurity applications, including anomaly detection, vulnerability scanning, and natural language processing for threat intelligence. When integrated with quantum computing environments, LLMs can play a crucial role in privacy enhancement. By leveraging their ability to understand and generate complex data patterns, LLMs can be employed to identify quantum-specific vulnerabilities and suggest quantum-resistant cryptographic solutions.

One of the most significant ways LLMs can contribute to privacy enhancement is by generating synthetic data. Synthetic data, which AI models generate to replicate real datasets, can be used to simulate quantum computing environments without exposing real private information. This technique is particularly useful in research and development phases, where testing new quantum protocols on sensitive data may not be feasible. According to Gholami and Omar (2023), synthetic data generated by LLMs can effectively reduce the risk of data breaches while developing quantum-based privacy solutions.

LLMs can also be employed to create and refine quantum-resistant encryption algorithms. By processing large datasets containing encrypted and unencrypted information, LLMs can generate insights into potential weaknesses in encryption methods, suggesting improvements that make data more secure in the quantum era. This proactive approach to encryption ensures that privacy mechanisms are resilient to quantum computing threats (Jones & Omar, 2024).

The following flowchart illustrates Large Language Models (LLMs) integration with quantum computing systems for privacy enhancement. It maps out key stages, including data processing, cryptographic model generation, and real-time threat detection.

Figure 2. Integration of LLMs with quantum computing for privacy

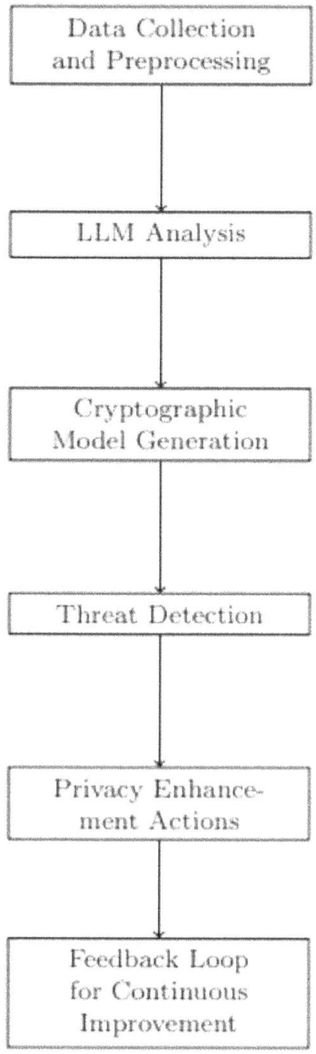

4.3 Integrating Quantum Cryptography with LLMs

Quantum cryptography, particularly quantum key distribution (QKD), has been proposed as a solution to secure communications in the quantum era. However, QKD faces several practical limitations, including scalability and cost. LLMs can complement quantum cryptography by automating the optimization of key management processes. Through natural language understanding and reinforcement learning techniques, LLMs can optimize the generation and distribution of quantum keys, making quantum cryptography more efficient and accessible in real-world applications (Omar, 2021). By reducing human error and streamlining key management, LLMs can enhance the overall privacy of quantum computing environments.

Moreover, as quantum computing advances, LLMs can continuously monitor and assess privacy risks. They can analyze large datasets in real-time to detect anomalies or breaches in privacy protocols, providing an added layer of security. This real-time surveillance capability is essential for adapting to the dynamic nature of quantum computing and its potential impact on privacy (Bishwas & Sen, 2024).

The diagram below outlines a framework for quantum-resistant cryptography enhanced by LLMs, focusing on key generation, threat analysis, and secure communication protocols.

Figure 3. Quantum-Resistant cryptography framework with LLMs

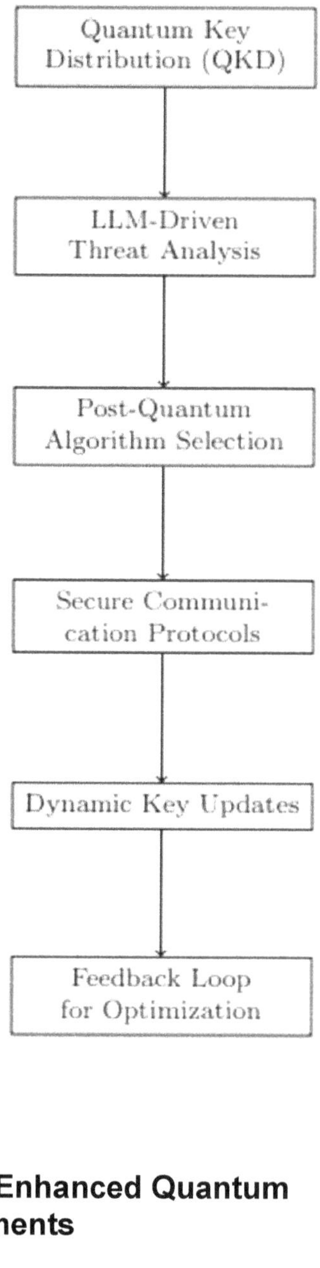

4.4 LLMs in Privacy-Enhanced Quantum Computing Environments

The future of privacy in quantum computing will rely on the seamless integration of quantum-resistant cryptographic solutions, quantum AI, and machine learning algorithms, such as those provided by LLMs. As quantum computing becomes more prevalent, LLMs will be at the forefront of developing adaptive privacy strategies that evolve in response to emerging quantum threats. They can help build frameworks that enhance the privacy of sensitive data, ensuring that quantum computing advancements do not compromise security.

Furthermore, quantum computing's potential to disrupt conventional cybersecurity tools necessitates integrating advanced AI systems like LLMs to predict, detect, and mitigate emerging threats. In healthcare, finance, and government industries, where privacy is paramount, LLMs could provide a dynamic and scalable solution to safeguard digital assets in a quantum-enabled world (How & Cheah, 2023; Zangana, 2024).

The pie chart below showcases the current adoption rates of various quantum-resistant techniques across industries, emphasizing the growing importance of integrating LLMs.

Figure 4. Adoption of quantum-resistant techniques

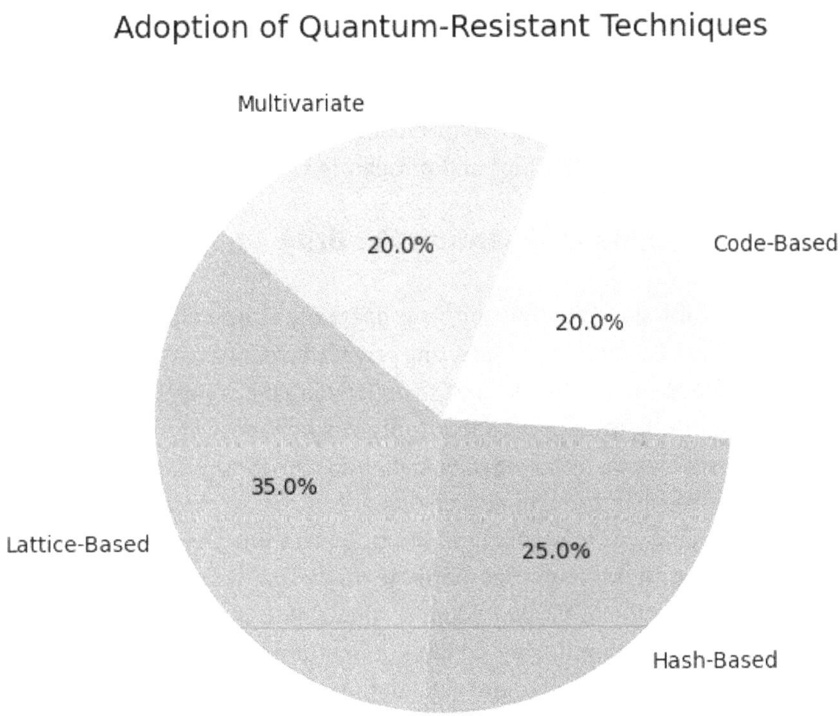

4.5 Conclusion

The synergy between LLMs and quantum computing offers a promising avenue for enhancing privacy in digital systems. As quantum computing poses new threats to traditional encryption and privacy methods, LLMs are essential for developing quantum-resistant solutions. By leveraging their advanced data analysis capabilities, LLMs can help mitigate risks, improve encryption algorithms, and ensure that privacy is maintained despite quantum advancements. As quantum computing technology continues to evolve, integrating LLMs will be critical in safeguarding privacy in this new era.

5. LLMS FOR DETECTING PRIVACY BREACHES IN QUANTUM ENVIRONMENTS

The intersection of large language models (LLMs) and quantum computing presents a promising frontier in cybersecurity, particularly in the context of privacy protection. As quantum environments evolve, the need for advanced detection mechanisms for privacy breaches becomes critical. Traditional cybersecurity measures may not suffice in these quantum environments, necessitating the integration of LLMs for identifying vulnerabilities and mitigating risks.

5.1 The Role of LLMs in Quantum Security

LLMs, known for their proficiency in processing large datasets and learning intricate patterns, can be valuable in detecting privacy breaches within quantum computing contexts. These models are trained to understand the complexity and nuances of language, making them adept at identifying suspicious activities and potential security threats, such as quantum attacks, data breaches, and privacy violations.

Quantum computing introduces new challenges to cybersecurity due to its ability to break classical encryption algorithms through quantum algorithms like Shor's algorithm. As quantum systems become more advanced, there is a pressing need for cybersecurity solutions that can adapt to these new capabilities. In this context, LLMs can assist in monitoring quantum communication protocols, detecting anomalies, and offering predictive insights on potential security threats (Sodiya et al., 2024; Bush et al., 2023).

5.2 Privacy Challenges in Quantum Environments

Quantum computing offers unprecedented computational power, but it also introduces significant privacy concerns. One such challenge is the potential to break current encryption schemes foundational to securing digital privacy. The advent of quantum algorithms capable of decrypting previously secure information highlights the urgency of developing quantum-resistant security solutions (Rahul et al., 2024). This is where LLMs come into play: By leveraging their deep learning capabilities, they can help detect and respond to threats that bypass traditional cryptographic defenses (Jones, 2024).

Furthermore, quantum networks, designed to be more secure through quantum key distribution (QKD), still face vulnerabilities, particularly in applying quantum-resistant cryptography. LLMs can play a crucial role in analyzing these new protocols' effectiveness and identifying weaknesses before they are exploited. Their ability to process vast amounts of data from quantum networks can assist in real-time surveillance of quantum communications and detect anomalies indicative of privacy breaches (Zangana, 2024; Hamza & Omar, 2013).

5.3 Enhancing Quantum Security with LLMs

Combining LLMs and quantum security can lead to enhanced detection and prevention mechanisms for privacy breaches. By integrating LLMs with quantum computing environments, cybersecurity professionals can leverage the models' ability to detect abnormal patterns in quantum data exchanges, flagging potential privacy risks before they materialize into actual breaches. This fusion of artificial intelligence and quantum computing is poised to revolutionize the detection of sophisticated privacy violations, ensuring that sensitive information remains secure even in the most advanced computing paradigms (Gholami & Omar, 2024).

Moreover, LLMs can be used to model and simulate potential attack vectors in quantum environments, testing how various quantum-resistant algorithms might perform under different conditions. This proactive approach to cybersecurity allows for the early identification of privacy vulnerabilities and developing robust countermeasures. The agility of LLMs in adapting to new threats makes them particularly well-suited for quantum environments, where traditional methods may fall short (Jones & Omar, 2024).

5.4 Case Studies and Applications

Real-world applications of LLMs in quantum environments are still emerging, but early studies suggest that these models are already being used in quantum-safe cybersecurity solutions. For example, LLMs have been applied in quantum cryptography to identify weaknesses in key generation processes or in quantum key exchange protocols. These models can process large volumes of transaction data across quantum networks, identifying suspicious patterns that could signal privacy breaches (Zangana & Omar, 2025).

Additionally, LLMs are being explored with machine learning algorithms to enhance quantum threat detection frameworks. By analyzing vast amounts of quantum data, these models can flag anomalies in real-time, allowing cybersecurity teams to take swift action. This integration of LLMs with quantum threat detection systems could significantly reduce response times and improve the overall security posture of quantum networks (Jones et al., 2023).

5.5 Future Directions

As quantum computing technology evolves, so must the methods employed to secure quantum environments. With their ability to process and analyze complex data sets, LLMs will undoubtedly become a critical component of future quantum cybersecurity infrastructures. However, challenges remain, including the need for more robust quantum-safe models and integrating LLMs into quantum computing frameworks (Gholami & Omar, 2023; Block, 2024). Further research is needed to refine these models and enhance their ability to detect and prevent privacy breaches in quantum environments.

By continuing to explore the synergy between LLMs and quantum computing, researchers can pave the way for a more secure quantum future. This will require collaboration across disciplines, including quantum mechanics, machine learning, and cybersecurity, to create integrated solutions that are both effective and scalable in protecting digital privacy in the quantum age (Bishwas & Sen, 2024).

6. AUTOMATED PRIVACY COMPLIANCE AND GOVERNANCE IN QUANTUM SYSTEMS

Integrating quantum computing into various sectors presents both revolutionary opportunities and significant challenges, especially in the domain of privacy compliance and governance. As quantum systems advance, the need for robust mechanisms to ensure privacy protection and adherence to governance standards becomes paramount. This section explores the role of automated privacy compliance systems in quantum environments, emphasizing how these systems can address the privacy challenges of quantum technologies.

6.1. Quantum Computing and Privacy Risks

Quantum computing has the potential to disrupt traditional encryption methods that are foundational to modern cybersecurity. As quantum computers gain the ability to process data exponentially faster than classical computers, they may undermine existing cryptographic protocols, such as RSA and ECC, which are widely used to secure personal and sensitive data. This threat to privacy necessitates the development of new privacy-preserving techniques specifically designed to work in a quantum computing era (Sodiya et al., 2024; Baseri et al., 2024).

In this context, quantum systems introduce new risks that must be managed through automated privacy frameworks. These frameworks must be agile enough to respond to evolving quantum capabilities and their potential to expose previously secure data. For instance, quantum computers could break widely used encryption schemes, making personal data vulnerable to unauthorized access. As a result, the development of quantum-resistant cryptographic algorithms and secure communication protocols is crucial for ensuring the privacy of data in a post-quantum world (Rahul et al., 2024; Jones & Omar, 2024).

6.2. Automated Privacy Compliance in Quantum Systems

Automated privacy compliance systems are designed to ensure that organizations operating within quantum computing environments comply with regulatory frameworks and best practices concerning data protection. These systems can use machine learning and artificial intelligence (AI) to automatically detect and mitigate privacy violations, ensuring that personal and sensitive data is handled according to established privacy laws and governance frameworks, such as the General Data Protection Regulation (GDPR) in the European Union or the California Consumer Privacy Act (CCPA).

In the quantum domain, automated systems can help manage privacy risks by:

- **Real-time Data Monitoring**: AI-driven systems can continuously monitor quantum data processing activities, detecting potential breaches of privacy policies or unauthorized access to sensitive data (Gholami & Omar, 2024). This is especially critical in environments where quantum computers handle vast amounts of data that may be vulnerable to exploitation.

- **Quantum-Resistant Security Protocols**: Automated systems can integrate quantum-resistant cryptographic methods capable of withstanding quantum computers' decryption power. These methods include lattice-based cryptography and post-quantum encryption standards, which are designed to protect data even in the presence of quantum adversaries (Seskir, 2019; Baseri et al., 2024).
- **Auditing and Reporting**: Automated systems can generate detailed audit logs that track data processing, storage, and transmission activities in quantum systems. These logs are essential for compliance with legal and regulatory requirements, enabling organizations to demonstrate their adherence to privacy standards and governance protocols (Zangana & Omar, 2025).

6.3. Challenges in Quantum Privacy Compliance

While the potential for automated privacy compliance systems is significant, several challenges must be addressed to ensure their effective implementation in quantum environments:

- **Scalability**: Quantum systems operate at unprecedented scales, processing large volumes of data at speeds much faster than classical systems. The sheer scale of quantum computations may outpace traditional privacy compliance tools, necessitating the development of scalable and adaptive systems that can manage quantum-specific privacy concerns (Khan et al., 2023).
- **Interoperability with Classical Systems**: Many organizations still rely on classical systems for data storage, processing, and governance. Ensuring that automated privacy systems can work seamlessly across both quantum and classical infrastructures is a critical challenge. Hybrid approaches that combine classical and quantum security measures will likely become a standard shortly (How & Cheah, 2023; Bush et al., 2023).
- **Evolving Legal and Regulatory Frameworks**: The legal landscape surrounding quantum computing is still in its infancy. As quantum technologies develop, privacy laws and regulations must evolve to address new risks and challenges. Automated systems must be flexible enough to adapt to these changing frameworks and ensure compliance across jurisdictions (Hamza & Omar, 2013).

6.4. Future Directions and Opportunities

Looking ahead, the development of automated privacy compliance and governance systems for quantum computing will be crucial in ensuring the secure and ethical use of quantum technologies. Several key areas present opportunities for future research and development:

- **Integration with Blockchain**: Blockchain technology, known for its transparency and immutability, can be leveraged alongside quantum computing to create tamper-proof logs and secure data exchanges. This combination could significantly enhance the effectiveness of automated privacy systems (Zangana et al., 2024).
- **AI-Driven Quantum Privacy Solutions**: Artificial intelligence will play a central role in the development of quantum privacy solutions. By employing machine learning algorithms, automated systems can predict and mitigate potential privacy threats in real time, thus providing proactive privacy protection (Jones et al., 2023; Zangana & Omar, 2025).
- **Post-Quantum Cryptography Research**: Continued research into post-quantum cryptographic algorithms will be essential for building secure quantum environments. Automated privacy systems can play a vital role in deploying and monitoring these algorithms, ensuring that they are implemented correctly and remain effective as quantum computing evolves (Gholami & Omar, 2023; Block, 2024).

This timeline tracks the evolution of privacy mechanisms in quantum computing, focusing on integrating AI, LLMs, and post-quantum cryptography.

Figure 5. Evolution of privacy mechanisms in quantum computing

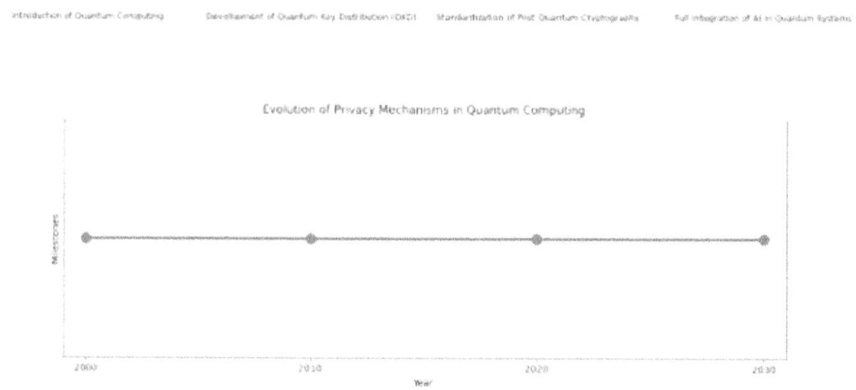

6.5. Conclusion

Automated privacy compliance and governance in quantum systems will be essential for managing the privacy risks associated with quantum computing. By integrating advanced AI and machine learning technologies, quantum-resistant security protocols, and real-time data monitoring, these systems can ensure that organizations remain compliant with privacy laws while mitigating the potential threats posed by quantum computing. The future of privacy compliance in quantum systems will depend on continued innovation in quantum-resistant cryptography, AI-driven privacy tools, and the development of global regulatory frameworks tailored to the unique challenges of the quantum era.

7. CHALLENGES AND LIMITATIONS OF USING LLMS FOR PRIVACY IN QUANTUM ENVIRONMENTS

Integrating large language models (LLMs) in quantum environments offers transformative potential for enhancing data security and privacy. However, this intersection introduces significant challenges and limitations that must be considered carefully. The following explores the critical hurdles when deploying LLMs in quantum environments, particularly concerning privacy.

7.1. Quantum Vulnerabilities to LLMs

Quantum computing has the potential to break many of the cryptographic protocols that currently secure information, which poses a direct threat to the privacy of data processed by LLMs. For instance, quantum algorithms such as Shor's can efficiently factorize large integers, undermining the security of widely used encryption schemes like RSA (Sodiya, Umoga, Amoo, & Atadoga, 2024). This vulnerability can make sensitive data exposed in quantum environments when processed through LLMs susceptible to unauthorized access. Quantum-resistant encryption methods must be integrated with LLMs to maintain privacy and mitigate these risks.

7.2. Data Privacy Concerns in Synthetic Data Generation

One of the proposed benefits of using LLMs is their ability to generate synthetic data, which can be used for privacy-preserving applications, especially when sharing real data might breach privacy (Gholami & Omar, 2023). However, this raises concerns about the privacy implications of synthetic data. If not carefully designed, synthetic datasets can inadvertently contain identifiable patterns that adversaries may exploit using quantum-powered decryption techniques (Gholami & Omar, 2024). Ensuring the complete anonymization of data generated by LLMs becomes challenging, particularly when integrating these models in a quantum context where privacy assurances need to be more robust.

7.3. Scalability of Privacy Measures

Another limitation arises in the scalability of privacy measures when deploying LLMs for privacy in quantum environments. Quantum computing's potential to handle massive amounts of data rapidly could lead to an exponential increase in data processing needs, complicating the deployment of privacy-preserving algorithms (Rahul et al., 2024). As quantum environments scale, ensuring that privacy safeguards—such as encryption and anonymization—remain effective becomes increasingly difficult. The need for quantum-resilient privacy protocols that can scale effectively across large datasets generated and processed by LLMs presents a significant challenge.

7.4. Ethical and Regulatory Challenges

The use of LLMs in quantum environments, especially in sensitive domains like healthcare and finance, brings forth significant ethical and regulatory concerns. The potential for quantum systems to bypass current encryption and privacy laws complicates the establishment of clear privacy standards. Furthermore, the growing use of LLMs to analyze personal data adds another layer of complexity in ensuring compliance with privacy laws such as the GDPR (General Data Protection Regulation) and HIPAA (Health Insurance Portability and Accountability Act) (Omar & Zangana, 2024). The rapid advancement of quantum technology outpaces existing regulatory frameworks, making it difficult to establish legal guidelines for using LLMs in quantum environments.

7.5. Interoperability with Quantum Systems

LLMs were not initially designed to operate within quantum computing environments, which leads to interoperability issues. These models rely heavily on classical computational resources, which might conflict with the principles and architectures of quantum computing (How & Cheah, 2023). A technical challenge is ensuring that LLMs can interface seamlessly with quantum systems while maintaining privacy. Moreover, the requirement for quantum-resistant protocols for such interactions increases the complexity of the integration, as these protocols must be compatible with both quantum and classical systems.

7.6. LLM Training in Quantum Environments

Training LLMs on quantum platforms introduces additional difficulties. Quantum computing could potentially offer improvements in machine learning performance, but current quantum machine learning models are still in their infancy (Khan et al., 2023). The complexity and unpredictability of quantum systems further complicate the ability to train LLMs effectively while ensuring privacy. The need for specialized quantum data architectures to support LLM training without compromising data privacy remains an open research problem (Baseri, Chouhan, & Ghorbani, 2024).

7.7. Resource Intensity and Cost

The resource-intensive nature of quantum computing raises practical concerns about the widespread deployment of LLMs in quantum environments. Quantum computing hardware is still expensive and not widely available, and the energy demands of operating both quantum and classical systems together can be prohibitive (Jones et al., 2023). The cost and resource constraints hinder the ability to scale LLM-based privacy solutions in quantum environments, particularly in sectors where budget constraints limit the adoption of cutting-edge technologies.

7.8. Limitations of Current Privacy-Preserving Techniques

Despite advances in privacy-preserving technologies, there are still limitations when applying these techniques in quantum computing and LLMs. Techniques like differential privacy, which are commonly used in classical environments, face challenges in quantum settings due to the unique nature of quantum information (Sodiya et al., 2024). Preserving privacy in quantum environments requires developing novel cryptographic techniques and privacy-preserving strategies tailored to quantum systems.

7.9. Security of LLMs in Quantum-Enabled Cyber Threats

The future of cybersecurity in the quantum era is filled with new threats and risks, many of which could be exacerbated by the use of LLMs. Quantum computing could potentially create more sophisticated cyberattacks, including advanced zero-day threats, bypassing traditional security measures. LLMs, which are increasingly being utilized in cybersecurity applications, would need to evolve rapidly to handle such quantum-enabled attacks (Jones & Omar, 2024). The ability to defend against quantum-powered attacks while ensuring the privacy of sensitive data processed by LLMs is a major limitation in current systems.

7.10 Conclusion

While integrating LLMs in quantum environments promises to bring substantial benefits in terms of data security and privacy, several challenges need to be addressed. These include ensuring the resilience of LLMs against quantum-enabled cyber threats, safeguarding data privacy in synthetic data generation, scaling privacy-preserving measures, and overcoming interoperability and ethical concerns. As quantum computing evolves, it will be critical to develop specialized protocols and privacy solutions to keep pace with technological advancements and effectively safeguard sensitive information. Addressing these challenges will require collaboration between researchers, practitioners, and policymakers to ensure the privacy and security of data in quantum-enhanced LLM environments.

8. CASE STUDIES AND APPLICATIONS

In the realm of cybersecurity, quantum computing, and AI technologies, various case studies and real-world applications demonstrate the effectiveness and potential of emerging innovations. Below, we explore several key case studies that highlight the application of cutting-edge technologies such as Large Language Models (LLMs), quantum computing, machine learning, and blockchain in enhancing security measures across diverse industries. These applications underscore the significant progress made in securing digital environments while overcoming unique challenges and threats.

8.1. Large Language Models in Cybersecurity: Attack Detection and Defense

One of the most promising applications of Large Language Models (LLMs) in cybersecurity is detecting and defending against zero-day threats. Jones and Omar (2024) introduced the **GPT-2 Enhanced Attack Detection and Defense (GEADD) Method**, which leverages advanced LLMs to identify and mitigate unknown cyber-attacks in real-time. By using natural language processing (NLP) capabilities of the GPT-2 model, GEADD can recognize patterns in data streams that might otherwise go undetected by traditional security measures. This method has significantly reduced false positives while increasing detection speed, providing an essential tool for proactive defense in environments vulnerable to sophisticated cyber-attacks. Applying this method in real-world scenarios, particularly in biotechnology and healthcare sectors, can help protect sensitive research data from exploitation or theft (Huff et al., 2023).

8.2. Quantum Computing for Cybersecurity: Preparing for Quantum Threats

As quantum computing continues to advance, it presents new challenges and cybersecurity opportunities. In a study by Baseri et al. (2024), the potential impacts of quantum computing on infrastructure security were assessed, focusing on the vulnerabilities it could introduce in traditional encryption systems. Quantum computing's ability to break conventional cryptographic techniques such as RSA and ECC has led to the development of quantum-resistant algorithms to safeguard sensitive data against quantum attacks. Researchers like Sodiya et al. (2024) have reviewed quantum computing's potential impact on U.S. cybersecurity, highlighting how industries must prepare for quantum threats by adopting post-quantum cryptography standards.

Case studies on quantum technologies in cybersecurity show promise in ensuring that systems remain secure even in the face of quantum-powered adversaries. For instance, in the healthcare sector, where secure patient data is paramount, quantum cryptography could be deployed to protect electronic health records (EHRs) against unauthorized access in the age of quantum computing. Additionally, Blockchain-based timestamping tools, as explored by Zangana (2024), could be enhanced by quantum-resistant techniques to ensure the integrity and authenticity of digital records in highly regulated industries like healthcare.

8.3. AI-Driven Security for Wireless Networks

AI and machine learning have been instrumental in securing wireless sensor networks (WSNs) from various types of attacks, such as wormhole attacks, which are often used to compromise communication between sensor nodes. Mohammed et al. (2018) developed an AI framework to detect and mitigate wormhole attacks in WSNs. This AI-driven approach helps identify abnormal patterns in network traffic that indicate the presence of these types of attacks. In real-world applications, particularly in military or industrial IoT environments, these AI systems can provide real-time alerts and responses, significantly reducing the risk of system compromise.

Moreover, AI and machine learning models have been shown to enhance traditional network security practices. In particular, machine learning algorithms are becoming indispensable for detecting anomalies in network traffic, which may indicate cyber-attacks. By leveraging these technologies, organizations can respond more efficiently to security breaches, minimizing the damage caused by intrusions.

8.4. Blockchain in Enhancing Security Posture

Blockchain technology has seen increasing use in enhancing security across various domains. Zangana et al. (2024) discussed using blockchain-based timestamping tools to protect digital assets and ensure data integrity. Blockchain can provide a decentralized, transparent record of events in sectors where data authenticity is crucial, such as finance and healthcare. Blockchain's decentralized nature ensures that once a record is created, it cannot be altered, making it an invaluable tool for securing transactions, digital identities, and records.

In addition, blockchain is being applied to secure cloud computing environments, addressing concerns related to data privacy and integrity. Hamza and Omar (2013) highlighted the need for secure cloud computing frameworks, particularly in preventing cloud platform abuse and nefarious use. By integrating blockchain for data verification, users can ensure that their information remains secure from unauthorized access or tampering.

8.5. Machine Learning for Threat Detection in Cybersecurity

Machine learning (ML) technologies have increasingly been utilized for automating the detection and response to cyber threats. As explored by Jones et al. (2023), integrating machine learning in cybersecurity helps accelerate the real-time detection of vulnerabilities and attacks. When trained on vast datasets of previous security incidents, ML algorithms can accurately identify potential threats and vulnerabilities. This application is particularly valuable in environments where quick response times are critical, such as financial institutions or military organizations.

In practice, ML models are being deployed to secure software development processes by detecting flaws in code before they can be exploited. For instance, the Application of Large Language Models for Software Vulnerability Detection (Omar & Zangana, 2025) explores how LLMs are used to automatically detect vulnerabilities in source code, drastically reducing the time spent on manual code audits and increasing the security of software products.

8.6. Cybersecurity and Mobile Threats

Mobile cybersecurity has become a pressing concern as smartphones and mobile applications have become essential tools for communication, banking, and social networking. In their work on mobile security, Wright et al. (2012) emphasized the need for antivirus applications to protect smartphones from emerging threats such as malware, ransomware, and phishing attacks. In practice, mobile security solutions, often powered by AI, can now detect suspicious activity in real-time, protecting users from a wide array of cyber threats. The integration of AI-based security tools on smartphones not only protects sensitive personal information but also ensures secure transactions and communication.

8.7. AI and Quantum Computing Integration in Cybersecurity

The fusion of AI and quantum computing has the potential to revolutionize cybersecurity. As explored by Bush et al. (2023), quantum computing could offer unprecedented power in breaking encryption, but when combined with AI, it could also provide innovative solutions to securing digital environments. For example, AI can be used to predict potential quantum attacks, while quantum computing itself can develop unbreakable encryption methods that safeguard data against future threats. The challenge lies in ensuring that the cybersecurity frameworks of today are adaptable enough to incorporate these emerging technologies.

8.8 Conclusion

These case studies demonstrate the transformative impact of quantum computing, AI, LLMs, and blockchain on cybersecurity. As these technologies evolve, they offer new ways to address traditional security challenges and provide enhanced protection against the next generation of cyber threats. Integrating these technologies in real-world applications has already shown significant improvements in attack detection, data integrity, and the overall security posture of critical systems. However, it remains essential to continue researching and refining these technologies to stay ahead of emerging threats in an increasingly interconnected world. The ongoing efforts to combine quantum computing with AI, blockchain with quantum-resistance features, and machine learning with traditional security measures are set to redefine the future of cybersecurity.

9. FUTURE DIRECTIONS AND INNOVATIONS

The evolution of cybersecurity in the age of quantum computing, artificial intelligence (AI), and large language models (LLMs) presents a multitude of challenges and opportunities. As new technologies such as quantum computing and AI continue to reshape the cybersecurity landscape, the industry is witnessing significant advancements in threat detection, vulnerability management, and defense mechanisms. This section explores some promising future directions and innovations in these areas, highlighting how emerging technologies will drive the next wave of cybersecurity advancements.

9.1. Quantum Computing and Cybersecurity

Quantum computing is expected to have a profound impact on cybersecurity. With its potential to solve problems that are currently intractable for classical computers, quantum technology introduces both significant opportunities and risks. One of the most anticipated breakthroughs is quantum-resistant cryptography. As quantum computers become more powerful, they could break widely used encryption methods, rendering many current security protocols obsolete (Sodiya, Umoga, Amoo, & Atadoga, 2024; Baseri, Chouhan, & Ghorbani, 2024). Researchers are focused on developing quantum-safe algorithms that can withstand quantum attacks, including lattice-based encryption schemes and post-quantum cryptography solutions (Bush, Challener, & Mantelet, 2021).

In addition to cryptography, quantum technologies will enable more sophisticated intrusion detection systems. Quantum-enhanced machine learning (ML) could lead to more accurate anomaly detection in real-time, improving early threat detection and response times. As Jones et al. (2023) discussed, integrating quantum computing with existing cybersecurity infrastructures could help overcome some of the limitations of classical methods, such as the inability to detect subtle, complex attack patterns.

9.2. Artificial Intelligence and Machine Learning

AI and ML have already begun to revolutionize cybersecurity, and their role will only grow stronger in the coming years. AI-powered systems are expected to enhance threat detection by analyzing large volumes of data at speeds and accuracy levels that humans and traditional systems cannot achieve. For instance, AI can enable predictive analytics to identify and neutralize threats before they materialize, as demonstrated by the GPT-2 Enhanced Attack Detection and Defense (GEADD) method for zero-day threats (Jones & Omar, 2024). Furthermore, LLMs, such as those discussed by Gholami and Omar (2024), will continue to improve as they are trained on vast datasets, making them invaluable tools in cybersecurity applications, including vulnerability detection and malware analysis.

Integrating LLMs with AI models has already shown promise in automating cybersecurity tasks, reducing response times, and improving decision-making in threat mitigation strategies. As these models evolve, we can expect them to take on more complex roles, such as automating security policy management and continuously adapting to new cyberattacks. Furthermore, LLMs' ability to simulate and predict attacker behaviors could aid in proactive defense strategies, enhancing organizations' resilience against cyberattacks.

9.3. AI-Driven Security Protocols

Another promising innovation lies in the development of AI-driven security protocols. By leveraging deep learning and neural networks, AI systems can be used to optimize security measures in real-time, responding to emerging threats with unprecedented speed. For example, research by Huff et al. (2023) highlights the potential of AI in the biotechnology and healthcare sectors, where AI-based protocols can mitigate cyber threats that target sensitive research data and patient information. Such protocols could evolve to incorporate advanced techniques like adversarial training, making them more robust against evolving attack vectors.

Moreover, AI's ability to understand and process complex attack patterns means that organizations can expect more adaptive, dynamic security systems. As the complexity of cyberattacks increases, AI will become integral in orchestrating multi-layered defense strategies that incorporate threat intelligence, behavioral analytics, and automated countermeasures.

9.4. Large Language Models in Software Vulnerability Detection

LLMs are proving to be highly effective in detecting vulnerabilities in software systems. These models can be trained to understand code structures and identify potential vulnerabilities, automating tasks that would otherwise require manual inspection by cybersecurity professionals. As LLMs are refined and scaled, their ability to identify zero-day vulnerabilities and obscure attack surfaces will improve, leading to faster identification and patching of security flaws (Zangana & Omar, 2025).

The future of vulnerability detection will likely involve a hybrid approach, combining LLMs with traditional static and dynamic analysis tools. This integration could lead to developing real-time vulnerability detection systems capable of adapting to new attack methods, ensuring that organizations stay ahead of attackers. Additionally, LLM-based tools can be used to suggest potential fixes for vulnerabilities, further automating the vulnerability management lifecycle.

9.5. Blockchain and Cybersecurity

Blockchain technology, often associated with cryptocurrency, is also poised to significantly impact cybersecurity. The inherent characteristics of blockchain—decentralization, immutability, and transparency—can be leveraged to enhance data security, particularly in sensitive applications such as healthcare, finance, and supply chain management. As Zangana (2024) highlighted, blockchain can be used for secure timestamping, identity verification, and audit trails, ensuring that sensitive data remains tamper-proof and traceable.

Blockchain-based timestamping tools for securing software updates and patches is another potential growth area (Zangana, 2024). By recording every modification to a software system securely and verifiable, blockchain could help organizations ensure that their software is always up to date and free from tampering. Furthermore, blockchain's role in secure smart contracts and decentralized authentication could play a key part in preventing fraud and unauthorized access in distributed systems (Agrawal & Aggarwal, 2024).

9.6. Quantum-Resistant Security Infrastructure

As quantum computing becomes more practical, industries must implement quantum-resistant security infrastructures. This includes cryptographic solutions and specialized hardware capable of withstanding quantum attacks. Researchers are exploring quantum key distribution (QKD) to securely exchange encryption keys, ensuring that even quantum computers cannot intercept or decrypt communications (Block, 2024).

Another area of interest is quantum network security, which could enable the creation of ultra-secure communication channels based on quantum entanglement. These channels would be immune to traditional interception techniques, providing a new layer of protection for sensitive data in transit (Lougovski et al., 2023).

9.7. Hybrid Security Models

In the near future, cybersecurity will likely evolve toward hybrid models that integrate multiple technologies to create more robust defense mechanisms. Combining quantum computing, AI, and blockchain will enable organizations to create layered security architectures that can withstand various cyber threats. The use of AI for real-time decision-making, combined with quantum-resistant cryptographic protocols and blockchain-based validation methods, offers a promising approach for defending against both classical and quantum-enabled threats.

As digital systems become more complex, these hybrid models will provide a more flexible, adaptable defense strategy, capable of responding to emerging threats across various environments. The successful integration of these technologies will require collaboration between researchers, industry leaders, and governments to establish best practices and standards for securing digital assets in the quantum era.

9.8 Summary

The future of cybersecurity lies at the intersection of quantum computing, AI, LLMs, and blockchain technologies. As these innovations continue to evolve, they will change the landscape of threat detection and mitigation and introduce new paradigms for securing digital systems. Embracing these advancements while addressing their challenges will be key to ensuring the protection of critical infrastructure and sensitive data in an increasingly interconnected world.

10. CONCLUSION

The future of cybersecurity and its intersection with advanced technologies such as Artificial Intelligence (AI), Quantum Computing, and Large Language Models (LLMs) presents exciting opportunities and challenges. As the digital landscape evolves, so must the tools and methodologies designed to secure it. Integrating LLMs into cybersecurity practices can revolutionize how organizations detect and respond to threats, enhancing both efficiency and accuracy. At the same time, the rise of quantum computing introduces new vulnerabilities but also promises to reshape encryption methods and security protocols to adapt to quantum threats.

The continuous advancement in AI technologies, particularly in cybersecurity, points to an era where automated systems can predict, identify, and mitigate risks with unprecedented speed and precision. However, this also highlights the importance of developing robust ethical considerations and accountability frameworks in AI-driven systems. Furthermore, as quantum technologies mature, the necessity for quantum-resistant security mechanisms will become increasingly critical, prompting industries and governments alike to prepare for the challenges posed by quantum computing.

Looking ahead, ongoing research and innovation will be key to addressing the emerging risks and harnessing the full potential of these groundbreaking technologies. Collaboration across disciplines, industries, and borders will play a crucial role in shaping the future of secure digital ecosystems. As we move toward a more interconnected world, the continued evolution of cybersecurity strategies, alongside the responsible development of AI and quantum technologies, will be essential in safeguarding data, privacy, and trust in the digital age.

In conclusion, while the path forward is filled with complexity, it is also rich with opportunities for innovation. By staying at the forefront of these developments and adapting to the ever-changing threat landscape, the next generation of cybersecurity solutions will not only meet the challenges of today but also anticipate and prepare for tomorrow's threats. The convergence of AI, quantum computing, and cybersecurity promises a more secure, resilient, and sustainable digital future.

REFERENCES

Agrawal, K., & Aggarwal, M. Building Efficient Smart Contract for Healthcare 4.0. In *Blockchain for Healthcare 4.0* (pp. 94-123). CRC Press.

AL-Refaey. M. R., Tyagi, A. K., AL-Ghamdi, A. S. A. M., & Kukreja, S. (Eds.). (2024). *Topics in Artificial Intelligence Applied to Industry 4.0*. John Wiley & Sons.

Baseri, Y., Chouhan, V., & Ghorbani, A. (2024). Cybersecurity in the Quantum Era: Assessing the Impact of Quantum Computing on Infrastructure. *arXiv preprint arXiv:2404.10659.*

Bishwas, A. K., & Sen, M. (2024). Strategic Roadmap for Quantum-Resistant Security: A Framework for Preparing Industries for the Quantum Threat. *arXiv preprint arXiv:2411.09995.*

Block, R. S. S. (2024). The 2024 quantum advantage blueprint: Where quantum outpaces classical.

Bush, S. F., Challener, W. A., & Mantelet, G. (2021). A perspective on industrial quantum networks. *AVS Quantum Science*, 3(3), 030501. DOI: 10.1116/5.0051881

Exchange, Q. R. K. Towards a Verifiably Secure Quantum-Resistant Key Exchange in IKEv2.

Gholami, S., & Omar, M. (2023). Does Synthetic Data Make Large Language Models More Efficient? *arXiv preprint arXiv:2310.07830.*

Gholami, S., & Omar, M. (2024). Can a student large language model perform as well as its teacher? In *Innovations, Securities, and Case Studies Across Healthcare, Business, and Technology* (pp. 122-139). IGI Global. DOI: 10.4018/979-8-3693-1906-2.ch007

Hamza, Y. A., & Omar, M. D. (2013). Cloud computing security: Abuse and nefarious use of cloud computing. *International Journal of Computer Engineering Research*, 3(6), 22–27.

How, M. L., & Cheah, S. M. (2023). Business Renaissance: Opportunities and challenges at the dawn of the Quantum Computing Era. *Businesses*, 3(4), 585–605. DOI: 10.3390/businesses3040036

Huff, A. J., Burrell, D. N., Nobles, C., Richardson, K., Wright, J. B., Burton, S. L., Jones, A. J., Springs, D., Omar, M., & Brown-Jackson, K. L. (2023). Management Practices for Mitigating Cybersecurity Threats to Biotechnology Companies, Laboratories, and Healthcare Research Organizations. In *Applied Research Approaches to Technology, Healthcare, and Business* (pp. 1-12). IGI Global.

Jones, A. J. (2024). Integration of LLMs With Traditional Security Tools. *Application of Large Language Models (LLMs) for Software Vulnerability Detection*, 295.

Jones, R., & Omar, M. (2024). Revolutionizing Cybersecurity: The GPT-2 Enhanced Attack Detection and Defense (GEADD) Method for Zero-Day Threats. *International Journal of Informatics* [INJIISCOM]. *Information System and Computer Engineering*, 5(2), 178–191.

Jones, R., Omar, M., Mohammed, D., Nobles, C., & Dawson, M. (2023). Harnessing the Speed and Accuracy of Machine Learning to Advance Cybersecurity. In *2023 Congress in Computer Science, Computer Engineering, & Applied Computing (CSCE)* (pp. 418-421). IEEE. DOI: 10.1109/CSCE60160.2023.00074

Khan, A. A., Akbar, M. A., Ahmad, A., Fahmideh, M., Shameem, M., Lahtinen, V., . . . Mikkonen, T. (2023, July). Agile practices for quantum software development: practitioners' perspectives. In *2023 IEEE international conference on quantum software (QSW)* (pp. 9-20). IEEE.

Lougovski, P., Parekh, O., Broz, J., Byrd, M., Chembo, Y., de Jong, W. A., . . . Svore, K. M. (2023). *Position Papers for the ASCR Workshop on Basic Research Needs in Quantum Computing and Networking*. USDOE Office of Science (SC), Advanced Scientific Computing Research (ASCR).

Madni, A. F., Shah, M. A., & Al-Naeem, M. (2024). An Investigation of Scalability in EHRs using Healthcare 4.0 and Blockchain. *International Journal of Advanced Computer Science and Applications*, 15(5). Advance online publication. DOI: 10.14569/IJACSA.2024.0150548

Metawei, M. A., Eldeeb, H., Nassar, S. M., & Taher, M. (2022). Quantum Computing Meets Artificial Intelligence: Innovations and Challenges. In *Handbook on Artificial Intelligence-Empowered Applied Software Engineering: VOL. 1: Novel Methodologies to Engineering Smart Software Systems* (pp. 303–338). Springer International Publishing. DOI: 10.1007/978-3-031-08202-3_12

Mohamed, N., & Ahmed, A. A. (2024, June). AI in Combatting Man-in-the-Middle Attacks: A Comprehensive Review. In *2024 15th International Conference on Computing Communication and Networking Technologies (ICCCNT)* (pp. 1-6). IEEE. DOI: 10.1109/ICCCNT61001.2024.10725789

Mohammed, D., Omar, M., & Nguyen, V. (2018). Wireless sensor network security: Approaches to detecting and avoiding wormhole attacks. *Journal of Research in Business. Economics and Management*, 10(2), 1860–1864.

Nguyen, V., Mohammed, D., Omar, M., & Banisakher, M. (2018). The Effects of the FCC Net Neutrality Repeal on Security and Privacy. [IJHIoT]. *International Journal of Hyperconnectivity and the Internet of Things*, 2(2), 21–29. DOI: 10.4018/IJHIoT.2018070102

Omar, M. (2021). New insights into database security: An effective and integrated approach for applying access control mechanisms and cryptographic concepts in Microsoft Access environments.

Omar, M. (2022). *Machine Learning for Cybersecurity: Innovative Deep Learning Solutions*. Springer Brief. https://link.springer.com/book/978303115

Omar, M. (2024). From Attack to Defense: Strengthening DNN Text Classification Against Adversarial Examples. In *Innovations, Securities, and Case Studies Across Healthcare, Business, and Technology* (pp. 174-195). IGI Global.

Omar, M. (2024). Revolutionizing Malware Detection: A Paradigm Shift Through Optimized Convolutional Neural Networks. In *Innovations, Securities, and Case Studies Across Healthcare, Business, and Technology* (pp. 196-220). IGI Global. DOI: 10.4018/979-8-3693-1906-2.ch011

Omar, M., & Zangana, H. M. (Eds.). (2024). *Redefining Security With Cyber AI*. IGI Global., DOI: 10.4018/979-8-3693-6517-5

Omar, M., & Zangana, H. M. (Eds.). (2025). *Application of Large Language Models (LLMs) for Software Vulnerability Detection*. IGI Global., DOI: 10.4018/979-8-3693-9311-6

Perron, J. K., DeLeone, C., Sharif, S., Carter, T., Grossman, J. M., Passante, G., & Sack, J. (2021). Quantum undergraduate education and scientific training. *arXiv preprint arXiv:2109.13850.*

Qualters, I., Taylor, A. J., & Hagberg, A. A. (2019). *IS&T Computing Overview* (No. LA-UR-19-22567). Los Alamos National Lab.(LANL), Los Alamos, NM (United States).

Rahul, R., Geetha, S., Priyatharsini, S., Mehata, K., Sundaresan Perumal, T., Ethiraj, N., & Sendilvelan, S. (2024). Cybersecurity Issues and Challenges in Quantum Computing. *Topics in Artificial Intelligence Applied to Industry*, 4(0), 203–221. DOI: 10.1002/9781394216147.ch11

Ramachandran, D., Naqi, S. M., Perumal, G., & Abbas, Q. (2023). DLTN-LOSP: A Novel Deep-Linear-Transition-Network-Based Resource Allocation Model with the Logic Overhead Security Protocol for Cloud Systems. *Sensors (Basel)*, 23(20), 8448. DOI: 10.3390/s23208448 PMID: 37896541

Seskir, Z. C. (2019). *Current state of quantum information technologies in Turkey* (Master's thesis, Middle East Technical University).

Singh, N. B. *Quantum Mechanics in Drug Discovery*. NB Singh.

Sodiya, E. O., Umoga, U. J., Amoo, O. O., & Atadoga, A. (2024). Quantum computing and its potential impact on U.S. cybersecurity: A review: Scrutinizing the challenges and opportunities presented by quantum technologies in safeguarding digital assets. *Global Journal of Engineering and Technology Advances, 18*(2), 049-064.

Wright, J., Dawson, M. E.Jr, & Omar, M. (2012). Cyber security and mobile threats: The need for antivirus applications for smartphones. *Journal of Information Systems Technology and Planning*, 5(14), 40–60.

Zangana, H. M. (2024). Exploring Blockchain-Based Timestamping Tools: A Comprehensive Review. *Redefining Security With Cyber AI*, 92-110.

Zangana, H. M. (2024). Exploring the Landscape of Website Vulnerability Scanners: A Comprehensive Review and Comparative Analysis. *Redefining Security With Cyber AI*, 111-129.

Zangana, H. M., Mohammed, A. K., Sallow, A. B., & Sallow, Z. B. (2024). Cybernetic Deception: Unraveling the Layers of Email Phishing Threats. [INJURATECH]. *International Journal of Research and Applied Technology*, 4(1), 35–47.

Zangana, H. M., & Mohammed, D. (2025). Foundations of Large Language Models in Software Vulnerability Detection. In Omar, M., & Zangana, H. (Eds.), *Application of Large Language Models (LLMs) for Software Vulnerability Detection* (pp. 41–74). IGI Global., DOI: 10.4018/979-8-3693-9311-6.ch002

Zangana, H. M., & Omar, M. (2020). Threats, Attacks, and Mitigations of Smartphone Security. *Academic Journal of Nawroz University*, 9(4), 324–332. DOI: 10.25007/ajnu.v9n4a989

Zangana, H. M., & Omar, M. (2025). Harnessing the Power of Large Language Models for Cybersecurity: Applications, Challenges, and Future Directions. In Omar, M., & Zangana, H. (Eds.), *Application of Large Language Models (LLMs) for Software Vulnerability Detection* (pp. 1–40). IGI Global., DOI: 10.4018/979-8-3693-9311-6.ch001

Zangana, H. M., Omar, M., Al-Karaki, J. N., & Mohammed, D. (2024). Comprehensive Review and Analysis of Network Firewall Rule Analyzers: Enhancing Security Posture and Efficiency. *Redefining Security With Cyber AI*, 15-36.

Chapter 4

LLMs for Quantum-Aware Threat Detection and Incident Response

Luay Albtosh
https://orcid.org/0009-0009-0338-9123
Capitol Technology University, USA & Houston Community College, USA

ABSTRACT

The integration of Large Language Models (LLMs) into cybersecurity offers significant potential for enhancing threat detection and incident response, particularly in the context of emerging quantum computing capabilities. As quantum computing threatens to undermine traditional cryptographic systems, there is a pressing need for quantum-aware cybersecurity measures. This chapter explores the application of LLMs in identifying and mitigating threats in a quantum-aware environment. It examines how LLMs can aid in detecting quantum-related vulnerabilities, analyzing quantum-aware attack vectors, and automating incident response protocols. Additionally, the chapter discusses the challenges of adapting LLMs to the quantum landscape, including the need for specialized training datasets and the consideration of quantum-resistant algorithms. Through case studies and theoretical models, this chapter provides a comprehensive view of how LLMs can be leveraged to strengthen cybersecurity in the era of quantum computing.

1. INTRODUCTION

As quantum computing continues to evolve, its potential to revolutionize the fields of cryptography and cybersecurity is becoming increasingly apparent. Quantum computing's ability to process vast amounts of data and perform complex calculations

DOI: 10.4018/979-8-3373-1102-9.ch004

at unprecedented speeds introduces both opportunities and challenges in securing digital assets. Traditional security measures, particularly cryptographic protocols that form the backbone of modern cybersecurity systems, are vulnerable to quantum computing's capabilities (Sodiya et al., 2024). This vulnerability underscores the need for quantum-aware cybersecurity systems, which can detect, mitigate, and respond to threats in environments where quantum computing may be actively utilized by malicious actors.

In this context, Large Language Models (LLMs), which have shown exceptional capabilities in natural language processing (NLP), are emerging as powerful tools for enhancing cybersecurity frameworks. LLMs, such as OpenAI's GPT models, are capable of processing and analyzing massive datasets to detect anomalous patterns, predict attack vectors, and generate responses in real-time. Their application in cybersecurity, particularly in threat detection and incident response, is of significant interest due to their ability to learn from vast datasets and adapt to emerging cyber threats. Furthermore, as quantum computing becomes more accessible, LLMs must be adapted to understand quantum-aware attack vectors and integrate quantum-resistant mechanisms into their models.

The potential for LLMs in quantum-aware cybersecurity is multifaceted. For instance, LLMs can aid in the identification of quantum-related vulnerabilities, such as those posed by quantum key distribution (QKD) and the vulnerability of current encryption algorithms to quantum attacks (Rahul et al., 2024). By training LLMs on quantum-specific datasets, researchers can develop systems that are capable of predicting and mitigating these novel types of attacks before they impact critical systems.

Moreover, the integration of LLMs into quantum-aware cybersecurity systems can facilitate more efficient incident response. LLMs can analyze attack logs, identify patterns indicative of a quantum-enhanced cyberattack, and autonomously trigger countermeasures. This ability is particularly important for detecting zero-day threats, which are notoriously difficult to identify using traditional security measures (Jones & Omar, 2024). LLMs' capacity to understand the context of a cyberattack, whether quantum-related or not, makes them an invaluable tool in minimizing damage and restoring system integrity swiftly.

However, the adoption of LLMs in quantum-aware threat detection and incident response is not without challenges. One of the main hurdles is the need for specialized training datasets that can represent both classical and quantum-aware cybersecurity threats (Gholami & Omar, 2024). While LLMs excel at identifying patterns in large datasets, they are only as good as the data on which they are trained. Quantum-specific datasets are still in their infancy, and significant efforts are required to develop data that accurately represents the evolving landscape of quantum cyber threats. Additionally, LLMs must incorporate quantum-resistant algorithms to ensure that they remain effective in the face of quantum-enhanced attacks.

This chapter delves into the role of LLMs in quantum-aware threat detection and incident response. It discusses the potential benefits and challenges of integrating LLMs into cybersecurity systems, particularly in the context of quantum computing. Through a review of current research and case studies, we explore how LLMs can be utilized to safeguard critical infrastructures from emerging quantum threats. Finally, we examine the future of quantum-aware cybersecurity, considering both the promises and the limitations of LLMs in this rapidly evolving field.

2. UNDERSTANDING QUANTUM-AWARE THREATS

As quantum computing continues to evolve, it has introduced new paradigms for cybersecurity, creating a need to reevaluate existing threat models. Quantum computing's unique properties, such as quantum superposition and entanglement, have the potential to challenge current cryptographic systems and introduce novel threats that can undermine data security. As quantum computers advance, the industry must develop quantum-aware security strategies that consider the implications of these emerging technologies.

2.1 Quantum Computing and Its Impact on Cybersecurity

Quantum computing promises to revolutionize industries by offering exponential increases in processing power for specific problem types. However, with this power comes the risk of vulnerabilities in traditional cryptographic systems, such as RSA and ECC, which rely on the computational difficulty of factoring large numbers or solving discrete logarithms. Quantum computers, through algorithms like Shor's algorithm, can solve these problems exponentially faster than classical computers, rendering current encryption schemes obsolete (How & Cheah, 2023). This shift in computational capabilities necessitates a fundamental rethinking of cybersecurity frameworks, as quantum-aware threats become a central concern in securing digital infrastructures.

In the quantum era, attacks that were previously infeasible due to computational complexity could become practical. For example, quantum-enabled adversaries could break widely used public-key cryptosystems with ease, thereby compromising data privacy and integrity. This highlights the importance of developing quantum-resistant encryption methods, which can withstand the capabilities of quantum computers. These methods include lattice-based cryptography, hash-based signatures, and code-based cryptosystems, all of which are being researched as part of the post-quantum cryptography initiative (Sodiya et al., 2024).

2.2 Quantum-Aware Threats in Critical Infrastructure

Critical infrastructure, such as financial systems, healthcare, and telecommunications, is particularly vulnerable to quantum-aware threats. As quantum computing evolves, the potential for exploiting weaknesses in these sectors increases. For instance, quantum-enabled cyberattacks could target sensitive health data stored on cloud platforms, which are currently protected by classical cryptography (Hamza & Omar, 2013). The threat to sensitive data storage is not just theoretical; it is an emerging risk as quantum computing capabilities grow.

Moreover, industries reliant on artificial intelligence (AI) and machine learning (ML) for cybersecurity will need to adapt their models to incorporate quantum-resistant algorithms. Research suggests that quantum computing could enhance the accuracy and speed of AI/ML-driven threat detection systems, but it also presents the risk of adversaries using quantum computers to overcome these defenses (Gholami & Omar, 2024). Quantum computing could offer attackers unprecedented computational power, enabling faster exploitation of vulnerabilities that AI-based systems are currently designed to detect and mitigate (Jones & Omar, 2024).

The chart below highlights the vulnerabilities in traditional and quantum-aware systems, emphasizing the increased risk posed by quantum computing in critical sectors like healthcare, finance, and telecommunications.

Figure 1. Vulnerabilities in quantum and classical systems

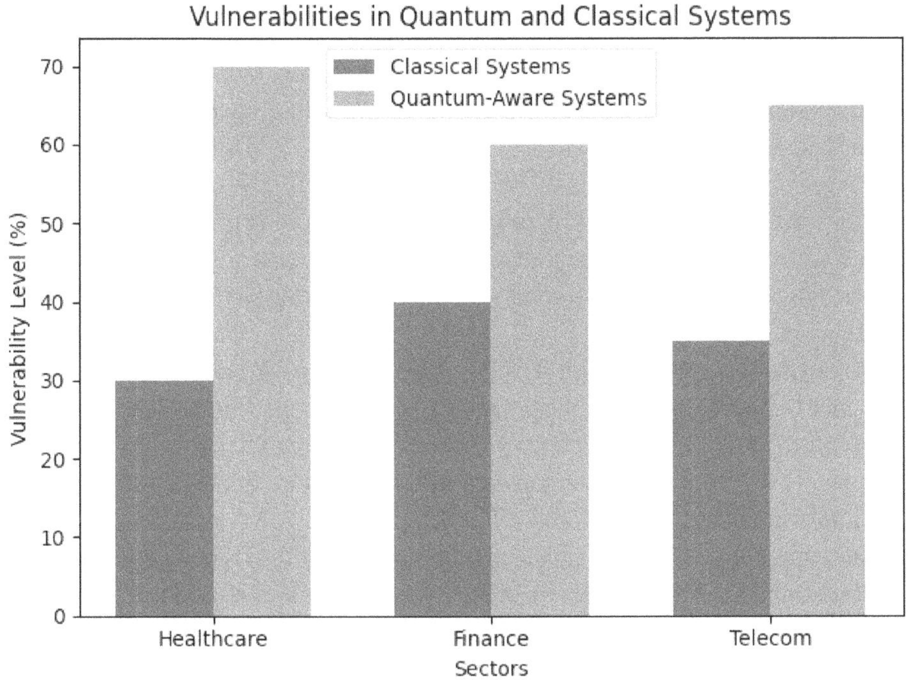

2.3 Quantum Security Frameworks: A New Paradigm

Addressing quantum-aware threats requires the development of new security frameworks that incorporate quantum-resilient technologies. A key area of focus is the secure generation and management of cryptographic keys in the post-quantum era. While traditional methods of key exchange rely on the difficulty of solving mathematical problems, quantum computers can efficiently break these mechanisms. Therefore, organizations must transition to quantum-resistant protocols to safeguard the exchange of cryptographic keys and the integrity of digital communications (Baseri et al., 2024).

The application of blockchain technology in the context of quantum-resilient security has also gained attention. Blockchain systems, which currently rely on cryptographic algorithms vulnerable to quantum attacks, could be enhanced with quantum-resistant protocols. This integration is vital in securing transactions and maintaining the trustworthiness of blockchain networks in a post-quantum world (Zangana, 2024).

2.4 Preparing for Quantum-Aware Threats: Mitigation Strategies

Given the rising threats posed by quantum computing, organizations must take proactive steps to secure their systems and infrastructure against quantum-aware threats. These steps include:

1. **Adopting Post-Quantum Cryptography**: Transitioning to encryption methods that are resistant to quantum attacks is essential. Lattice-based cryptographic schemes, for instance, are seen as a promising solution in the post-quantum era (Rahul et al., 2024).
2. **Quantum Key Distribution (QKD)**: Implementing QKD is another promising avenue for securing communications in a quantum-enabled future. This technology leverages the principles of quantum mechanics to create secure communication channels that cannot be intercepted without detection (Block, 2024).
3. **Quantum-Resilient AI Models**: The development of AI models that can withstand quantum computing attacks will be critical in the fight against quantum-aware threats. These models must incorporate quantum-resistant techniques to detect and mitigate threats in real-time (Jones et al., 2023).
4. **Collaborative Efforts and Standards**: Governments, academia, and private organizations must collaborate to establish global standards for quantum-resistant security technologies. The NIST post-quantum cryptography project, for example, is working towards the standardization of quantum-resistant algorithms to ensure that cryptographic systems can withstand quantum threats (Bishwas & Sen, 2024).

The following pie chart shows the current adoption rates of quantum-resistant techniques, reflecting trends across industries preparing for the quantum era.

Figure 2. Quantum-Resistant techniques adoption

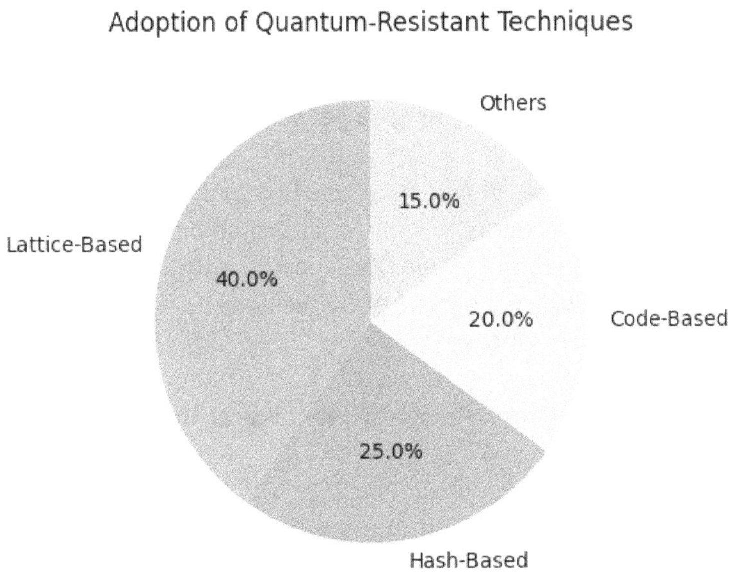

2.5 Conclusion

As quantum computing continues to develop, its implications for cybersecurity are profound. Quantum-aware threats are no longer a distant concern but a reality that must be addressed now to ensure the continued security of critical infrastructures and sensitive data. By understanding the potential risks and preparing with quantum-resistant technologies and strategies, organizations can safeguard themselves against the emerging quantum threats of the future.

3. LARGE LANGUAGE MODELS: CAPABILITIES AND APPLICATIONS IN CYBERSECURITY

Large Language Models (LLMs), such as OpenAI's GPT series, have revolutionized various domains through their capacity to understand and generate human-like text. This transformative capability stems from their ability to process vast amounts of data and generate insightful responses. In cybersecurity, LLMs are proving to be invaluable tools due to their ability to detect and mitigate threats, automate responses, and optimize security protocols. This section discusses the capabilities of LLMs, particularly in the realm of cybersecurity, and highlights their applications across different cybersecurity challenges.

3.1 Capabilities of Large Language Models in Cybersecurity

LLMs are sophisticated AI systems trained on massive datasets, which allow them to learn intricate patterns in text, code, and communication. This enables LLMs to perform various tasks essential for cybersecurity, such as natural language understanding, anomaly detection, and threat intelligence. Their capabilities can be classified into several core areas:

1. **Natural Language Processing (NLP) for Threat Intelligence**

LLMs excel in processing natural language, which is a critical asset in cybersecurity. For instance, cybersecurity professionals often rely on threat reports, alerts, and other text-heavy sources to monitor and detect vulnerabilities. LLMs can analyze these documents to identify emerging threats, detect unusual patterns, and even correlate information from different sources (Zangana & Omar, 2025). By synthesizing vast amounts of text data, LLMs provide timely insights into the latest attack techniques, helping security teams stay ahead of potential risks (Gholami & Omar, 2024).

2. **Malware Detection and Analysis**

Malware detection is one of the key areas where LLMs have shown promise. By analyzing code snippets or system behavior described in textual form, LLMs can assist in detecting malicious activities, including zero-day attacks. In particular, they can be employed to process large datasets of malware reports and source code to classify and detect new types of malware that may otherwise evade traditional detection methods (Omar & Zangana, 2025).

3. **Automating Security Responses**

One of the most impactful uses of LLMs in cybersecurity is in automating responses to security incidents. By leveraging their ability to generate text, LLMs can draft response plans, suggest remediation actions, and even generate alerts that notify security professionals of potential breaches. This automation is particularly useful for mitigating the time lag between the identification of a threat and the implementation of a solution (Jones et al., 2023). Furthermore, LLMs can be integrated into security orchestration tools to create self-healing systems capable of responding to attacks in real time (Jones & Omar, 2024).

4. **Vulnerability Detection and Software Security**

LLMs can assist in identifying software vulnerabilities by analyzing code repositories, system logs, and other related documentation. Their ability to parse through large volumes of code enables them to identify subtle security flaws that might be missed by traditional static analysis tools. This application is particularly important in the context of software development and maintenance, where vulnerabilities can be difficult to detect manually (Omar & Zangana, 2025).

3.2 Applications of LLMs in Cybersecurity

1. **Threat Detection and Defense Mechanisms**

LLMs have been instrumental in enhancing threat detection systems. Their ability to understand the context within logs and security alerts allows them to identify potential threats more accurately. For example, LLMs can process security logs in real-time, detecting anomalies that signify potential threats such as intrusions, data exfiltration, or unauthorized access. The GPT-2 enhanced attack detection and defense method (Jones & Omar, 2024) leverages the power of LLMs to defend against zero-day threats by predicting new attack vectors based on patterns identified in previous incidents.

2. **Phishing Detection and Prevention**

Phishing remains one of the most prevalent attack methods, with cybercriminals continually evolving their tactics. LLMs are effective in recognizing phishing attempts by analyzing email content, URLs, and metadata. By training on vast datasets containing phishing emails, LLMs can detect patterns in language and structure that are indicative of phishing attempts, significantly reducing the risk of human error in identifying fraudulent communications (Zangana, 2024).

3. **Enhancing Vulnerability Management Systems**

In vulnerability management, LLMs contribute by automating the scanning, identification, and prioritization of vulnerabilities. The integration of LLMs with vulnerability scanners allows these systems to process large amounts of data from different sources, including CVE (Common Vulnerabilities and Exposures) databases, and prioritize patches or mitigation strategies based on potential impact (Omar & Zangana, 2024). This application reduces the workload on cybersecurity teams and ensures that high-priority vulnerabilities are addressed promptly.

4. **Adaptive Security Protocols**

LLMs can enhance security protocols by dynamically adapting them to new threats. Through continuous learning from new data, LLMs are capable of adjusting security configurations, firewalls, and intrusion detection systems (IDS) to mitigate novel attack techniques. The ability of LLMs to learn from emerging threats allows them to adjust defensive strategies in real-time, ensuring that organizations remain protected even as cyber threats evolve (Omar, 2022).

5. **Quantum-Resistant Security**

As quantum computing poses new challenges to cybersecurity, LLMs play a role in preparing for the post-quantum era. LLMs can assist in developing quantum-resistant cryptographic protocols by analyzing large datasets of cryptographic algorithms and identifying vulnerabilities that quantum computers might exploit. This capability is crucial as industries begin to adopt quantum-safe strategies to future-proof their cybersecurity frameworks (Sodiya et al., 2024).

6. **Cybersecurity for IoT and Cloud Computing**

The rise of Internet of Things (IoT) devices and cloud computing infrastructure presents new security challenges. LLMs are particularly adept at securing IoT networks by analyzing communication patterns and detecting anomalies in data streams that could indicate attacks such as man-in-the-middle or denial-of-service attacks (Mohammed et al., 2018). Additionally, LLMs can assist in cloud security by identifying misconfigurations and access control flaws that could be exploited by attackers (Hamza & Omar, 2013).

3.3 Challenges and Future Directions

Despite their immense potential, LLMs in cybersecurity face several challenges. One significant hurdle is the requirement for high-quality, domain-specific training data. As cybersecurity is an ever-evolving field, LLMs need continuous updates and retraining to remain effective. Additionally, LLMs' reliance on large datasets makes them susceptible to biases, which could affect their accuracy and fairness in threat detection (Gholami & Omar, 2023).

Another challenge is the interpretability of LLM-based decisions. While LLMs are powerful, their "black-box" nature can make it difficult for security professionals to understand how a decision was reached, raising concerns about trust and accountability. Therefore, there is a need for more transparent models that can explain their reasoning process in a way that is understandable to human users (Omar & Zangana, 2025).

Looking forward, the integration of LLMs with other advanced technologies such as quantum computing (Bush et al., 2021) and blockchain (Zangana & Omar, 2025) holds great promise. Combining these technologies with LLMs could lead to the development of even more robust and adaptive cybersecurity solutions capable of defending against both classical and quantum threats.

3.4 Conclusion

The capabilities of Large Language Models in cybersecurity are vast, ranging from threat detection to vulnerability management and beyond. By leveraging their natural language understanding, pattern recognition, and automation capabilities, LLMs offer transformative solutions to the challenges faced by cybersecurity professionals today. However, challenges such as data quality, model interpretability, and the need for continuous updates remain. The future of LLMs in cybersecurity will likely see greater integration with emerging technologies, driving innovations in defense mechanisms and improving overall security posture.

4. LLMS FOR QUANTUM-AWARE THREAT DETECTION

The integration of Large Language Models (LLMs) with quantum-aware threat detection systems represents a forward-thinking approach to enhancing cybersecurity in the emerging quantum computing era. This synergy is essential as quantum computing poses both challenges and opportunities for digital security, necessitating innovative solutions that leverage both quantum technology and artificial intelligence (AI). This section delves into how LLMs, with their natural language processing (NLP) capabilities, can be employed for threat detection in a quantum-aware environment, discussing the challenges and opportunities within this rapidly evolving domain.

4.1. Quantum Computing and Cybersecurity: A Paradigm Shift

Quantum computing promises to revolutionize fields such as cryptography, data processing, and optimization. However, it also introduces significant security risks due to its potential to break traditional encryption schemes used to safeguard sensitive information (Sodiya et al., 2024; Baseri et al., 2024). In this context, cybersecurity systems must evolve to defend against quantum-enhanced attacks that could compromise the integrity of conventional cryptographic methods. One promising area of defense is the use of AI, particularly LLMs, which have demonstrated impressive capabilities in detecting and mitigating threats in classical computing environments (Jones et al., 2023; Wright et al., 2012).

4.2. Quantum-Aware Threat Detection Using LLMs

LLMs are increasingly being recognized for their potential to detect complex cybersecurity threats, such as zero-day exploits, malware, and phishing attempts, by analyzing vast amounts of unstructured data (Jones & Omar, 2024). These models are trained to process and understand natural language, enabling them to discern patterns and anomalies in text-based data, such as logs, emails, and network traffic. When integrated into a quantum-aware threat detection system, LLMs can be enhanced to identify threats that may exploit the computational advantages of quantum technologies.

Quantum-aware threat detection involves monitoring for vulnerabilities that could be exposed by quantum computing's power, such as weaknesses in current cryptographic systems. LLMs, when fed with quantum-specific threat intelligence, can analyze quantum computing algorithms and protocols to detect anomalies that indicate potential security breaches. For instance, LLMs can be trained to understand quantum encryption algorithms like quantum key distribution (QKD) and monitor for discrepancies or malicious attempts to exploit these mechanisms.

To provide a clear understanding of the process involved in quantum-aware threat detection using LLMs, the following flowchart outlines the key steps in identifying and mitigating quantum-enhanced vulnerabilities.

Figure 3. Quantum-Aware threat detection framework

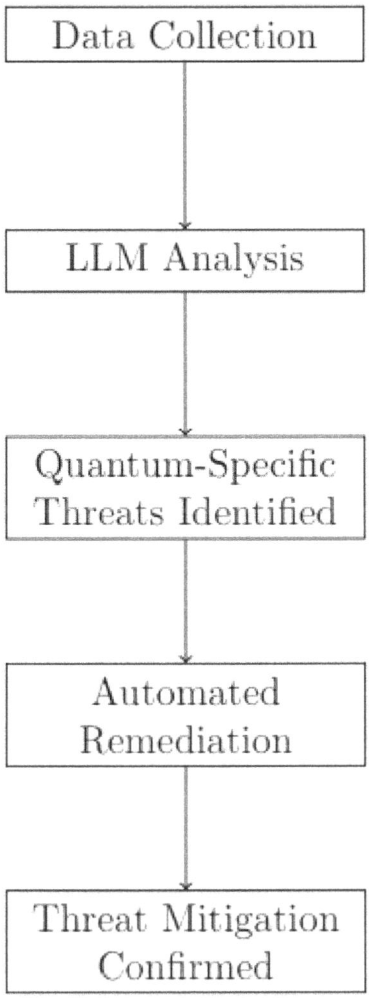

4.3. Leveraging Synthetic Data for Efficient Model Training

One of the key challenges in applying LLMs to quantum-aware threat detection is the need for large and diverse datasets for training these models. Given the relatively new emergence of quantum threats, acquiring real-world quantum-aware cybersecurity data is difficult. This is where synthetic data generation comes into play. According to Gholami and Omar (2023), synthetic data can be used to simulate quantum-based attacks and defenses, providing a valuable resource for training

LLMs. By generating realistic data that mimics potential quantum vulnerabilities and attacks, researchers can enhance the predictive capabilities of LLMs in identifying quantum-aware threats before they manifest in the real world.

4.4. Quantum-Resistant Machine Learning

As quantum computing develops, it is crucial to consider quantum-resistant machine learning techniques that can maintain their effectiveness even in the presence of quantum-enhanced adversaries. LLMs, traditionally trained on classical computing systems, will need to adapt to quantum algorithms that might undermine their performance (Rahul et al., 2024). Researchers are exploring methods to make machine learning models, including LLMs, more resilient to quantum attacks. This involves the integration of quantum-resistant cryptography and algorithms that are robust to quantum computing threats (Bishwas & Sen, 2024).

Moreover, LLMs could benefit from quantum machine learning (QML) techniques, where quantum computing resources are utilized to train AI models more efficiently, enabling the rapid identification of previously unseen patterns in large-scale cybersecurity datasets (Metawei et al., 2022). These advancements could lead to the development of more robust cybersecurity systems that are capable of defending against quantum-enabled adversaries.

4.5. Applications in Zero-Day Threat Detection

One of the most promising applications of LLMs in quantum-aware threat detection is in the area of zero-day threat detection. Zero-day attacks exploit vulnerabilities that are unknown to the security community, making them particularly challenging to detect using traditional methods (Jones et al., 2023). LLMs, with their ability to learn from vast quantities of unstructured data and identify novel attack vectors, could provide a much-needed defense mechanism. By analyzing quantum-specific vulnerabilities and learning to recognize quantum-enhanced exploitation techniques, LLMs could be pivotal in detecting zero-day threats in quantum computing environments.

Jones and Omar (2024) introduced a GPT-2-enhanced method, the GEADD, specifically designed to detect zero-day attacks in cybersecurity systems. Integrating this method with quantum-aware data streams could improve its detection capabilities, allowing the system to identify novel quantum-based threats before they cause harm.

4.6. The Future of LLMs in Quantum-Aware Cybersecurity

As quantum technologies mature, it is essential for cybersecurity frameworks to evolve in tandem. LLMs, with their scalability and adaptability, offer a promising solution for tackling the challenges posed by quantum computing in cybersecurity. Their ability to process and analyze vast amounts of data can help identify quantum-specific vulnerabilities and provide early warnings of potential quantum attacks. However, for LLMs to be effective in this domain, they must be trained on quantum-aware datasets and incorporate quantum-resistant techniques to ensure their resilience against future threats (Gholami & Omar, 2024).

As quantum computing continues to evolve, there will be an increasing need for collaborative efforts between researchers in quantum computing, cybersecurity, and AI to develop effective strategies for quantum-aware threat detection. This multidisciplinary approach will help bridge the gap between emerging quantum technologies and traditional cybersecurity systems, ensuring that organizations are well-equipped to defend against both classical and quantum-enhanced cyber threats (Khan et al., 2023).

4.7. Conclusion

LLMs represent a powerful tool in the fight against emerging quantum-aware cybersecurity threats. By leveraging their ability to process large volumes of data and detect complex patterns, LLMs can play a critical role in identifying and mitigating quantum-enhanced vulnerabilities. As quantum computing continues to evolve, the integration of LLMs into cybersecurity systems will be essential for ensuring the security of digital assets in a quantum-enabled future.

5. LLMS FOR QUANTUM-AWARE INCIDENT RESPONSE

As quantum computing continues to evolve, its implications for cybersecurity, particularly incident response, are becoming increasingly critical. Large Language Models (LLMs) have shown promise in enhancing various facets of cybersecurity, but their integration with quantum computing introduces both opportunities and challenges that require innovative strategies. This section explores the role of LLMs in quantum-aware incident response, focusing on their ability to assist in detecting, mitigating, and responding to cyber threats in a quantum computing environment.

5.1 The Intersection of Quantum Computing and Cybersecurity

Quantum computing introduces computational capabilities that far exceed those of classical computers, posing both opportunities and threats to cybersecurity. Quantum algorithms, particularly those related to factorization and simulation, threaten the security foundations of current encryption schemes. For instance, Shor's algorithm has the potential to break widely used cryptographic methods like RSA, leaving networks vulnerable to quantum-powered attacks (Baseri et al., 2024). On the other hand, quantum computing can also enhance cybersecurity by enabling new cryptographic techniques, such as quantum key distribution (QKD), which can make communications more secure.

However, with the rapid development of quantum technologies, there is a pressing need to rethink incident response strategies. As threats evolve, LLMs—already proven in cybersecurity tasks such as malware detection and attack prediction (Jones et al., 2023)—could play a pivotal role in developing quantum-aware security protocols. These models, when integrated with quantum-resistant strategies, could potentially enhance the detection and mitigation of quantum-enabled cyberattacks, such as those targeting the integrity of data and communications.

5.2 Quantum-Aware Incident Response: A New Paradigm

Traditional incident response strategies, while effective in the classical realm, may not suffice in the face of quantum-enhanced cyber threats. LLMs can bridge this gap by providing dynamic, context-aware responses to quantum-based incidents. The ability of LLMs to process vast amounts of unstructured data, generate hypotheses, and recommend responses in real-time makes them particularly suited to quantum-aware incident response.

LLMs can assist in several critical areas, including:

1. **Threat Detection and Attribution**

Quantum computing offers novel attack vectors, such as the potential to break current encryption systems or launch more sophisticated denial-of-service (DoS) attacks. LLMs, with their ability to analyze large datasets, could be trained to recognize quantum-specific attack patterns. For example, as quantum computing progresses, network traffic may exhibit new anomalies that classical systems might miss. LLMs can analyze and correlate these anomalies, alerting security teams to potential threats faster than traditional systems (Gholami & Omar, 2023).

2. **Quantum-Resistant Security Protocols**

Developing quantum-resistant algorithms is essential for ensuring the security of sensitive data and communications in a post-quantum world. LLMs can play a role in optimizing the deployment of quantum-safe cryptographic protocols, such as lattice-based cryptography (Rahul et al., 2024). By analyzing existing frameworks, LLMs can recommend adaptive changes to security protocols that take into account the unique properties of quantum computers. Additionally, as quantum-resistant technologies evolve, LLMs can aid in the automated generation of patches and updates to mitigate new vulnerabilities.

3. **Automated Response and Remediation**

The ability to automatically respond to cyber threats is a key feature of modern incident response. LLMs, when trained on quantum-specific attack scenarios, can generate response strategies that are optimized for quantum-enhanced environments. These models can not only detect a breach but also provide guidance on the immediate steps to contain the threat, including isolating quantum-powered attack vectors, securing vulnerable data, and initiating rollback protocols (Gholami & Omar, 2024). Moreover, LLMs can be used to automate the reporting and documentation of incidents, ensuring compliance with emerging quantum-era regulations.

The diagram below illustrates the incident response workflow driven by LLMs, detailing how they process data, detect anomalies, and suggest remediation strategies in real time.

Figure 4. LLM-Driven incident response workflow

4. **Simulation and Prediction of Quantum Threats**

One of the most exciting aspects of quantum computing is its potential to simulate complex systems far more efficiently than classical computers. LLMs, when paired with quantum simulators, can be used to predict potential attack vectors in a quantum-enhanced landscape. These predictive capabilities could enable proactive defense strategies, where security teams are alerted to threats before they manifest. For instance, using quantum simulators, LLMs can anticipate the impact of various quantum attacks on critical infrastructures and suggest preemptive measures to mitigate risks (Bishwas & Sen, 2024).

5.3 Challenges in Integrating LLMs with Quantum-Aware Incident Response

While LLMs offer significant promise, there are several challenges to integrating them effectively into quantum-aware incident response systems:

1. **Training Data and Quantum Knowledge**

One of the primary challenges is the lack of sufficient training data that integrates both quantum computing and cybersecurity concepts. Most LLMs, like GPT models, are trained on classical data, and their quantum-awareness is limited. For LLMs to be truly effective in the quantum space, they must be trained on datasets that include quantum-specific vulnerabilities, attack strategies, and defensive measures. This requires collaboration between quantum scientists and cybersecurity experts to curate relevant datasets (Sodiya et al., 2024).

2. **Scalability and Computational Demands**

The integration of quantum computing with LLMs can lead to significant computational challenges. Quantum algorithms are notoriously difficult to simulate classically, and even if quantum computers become available, the computational resources needed to scale LLMs for quantum-aware tasks could be enormous (Bush et al., 2023). Researchers like Lougovski et al. (2023) highlight that quantum networks may require new infrastructure capable of handling the unique demands of LLMs in quantum environments.

3. **Quantum-Resistant Algorithms**

Another challenge is the rapid evolution of quantum-resistant algorithms, which may outpace the ability of current LLMs to adapt. As quantum computing research progresses, the field of quantum-resilient cybersecurity is also evolving, with new cryptographic techniques constantly being proposed. LLMs need to be agile enough to incorporate these developments into their decision-making processes. This necessitates continuous retraining and updating of LLMs to keep pace with the evolving threat landscape (Jones et al., 2024).

5.4 Future Directions

As the quantum computing landscape evolves, the synergy between LLMs and quantum-aware incident response will become increasingly important. Future research should focus on developing hybrid models that combine the predictive capabilities of quantum simulators with the data-processing power of LLMs. Furthermore, efforts should be made to enhance the integration of quantum-safe algorithms into the incident response protocols facilitated by LLMs, ensuring that security systems are ready for the quantum age.

In summary, LLMs hold significant promise for transforming incident response strategies in a quantum-aware world. Their ability to detect, analyze, and respond to quantum-enhanced threats positions them as key tools in safeguarding digital assets. However, realizing this potential requires overcoming technical challenges, including the need for quantum-aware training datasets and scalable computational models. As quantum technologies continue to mature, the role of LLMs in cybersecurity will undoubtedly expand, offering new solutions to emerging threats in a post-quantum world.

6. TRAINING LLMS FOR QUANTUM-AWARE CYBERSECURITY

As the cybersecurity landscape evolves, so too do the threats posed by increasingly sophisticated attacks, many of which leverage emerging technologies such as quantum computing. Large Language Models (LLMs) have shown great promise in tackling complex problems within cybersecurity, and incorporating quantum-aware considerations into their training can offer significant advantages in preparing them for future challenges. This section delves into the processes, methodologies, and significance of training LLMs for quantum-aware cybersecurity, emphasizing the intersection of AI, quantum technologies, and secure computing.

6.1 The Role of Quantum Computing in Cybersecurity

Quantum computing represents a paradigm shift in computational power, with the potential to break traditional cryptographic algorithms and challenge the security protocols that underpin the current digital infrastructure. While quantum computing promises breakthroughs in various fields, its impact on cybersecurity is twofold: on one hand, it introduces powerful tools for optimizing security measures; on the other, it poses existential threats to classical encryption schemes (Sodiya et al., 2024; Rahul et al., 2024). Understanding this duality is crucial for developing quantum-aware systems that are capable of not only anticipating quantum-enabled threats but also leveraging quantum resources to enhance security.

6.2 The Convergence of LLMs and Quantum Computing

LLMs, such as GPT models, have revolutionized the field of natural language processing (NLP) by demonstrating remarkable capabilities in text generation, understanding, and decision-making tasks. Their application to cybersecurity is becoming increasingly relevant, especially in the context of detecting and mitigating cyber threats (Jones et al., 2023; Zangana & Omar, 2025). However, to remain resilient in the quantum era, these models need to be trained with an understanding of the unique characteristics and vulnerabilities introduced by quantum computing.

Quantum-aware training of LLMs involves integrating quantum principles into the data preparation, feature extraction, and model design processes. For instance, one approach is to simulate quantum-based attacks or leverage quantum-enhanced data structures for training LLMs on tasks such as anomaly detection, pattern recognition, and predictive modeling in cybersecurity (Gholami & Omar, 2024). By incorporating quantum algorithms, LLMs can learn to identify patterns or predict vulnerabilities that are not readily apparent under classical conditions.

6.3 Data Representation and Quantum-Aware Features

A key challenge in training LLMs for quantum-aware cybersecurity is the representation of quantum data. Classical data representation methods may not adequately capture the quantum properties that could inform security risk assessment, such as quantum entanglement or superposition. To address this, innovative data encoding techniques, such as quantum-inspired feature maps, can be employed. These techniques use quantum mechanics principles to create more nuanced representations of data, which can improve the model's ability to predict and mitigate quantum-enabled threats (Rahul et al., 2024).

Moreover, synthetic data plays a critical role in training these models efficiently. Researchers have explored how synthetic data, particularly in the context of quantum simulations, can augment the training process by providing large, diverse datasets that encompass a wide range of quantum-induced anomalies (Gholami & Omar, 2023). This enables LLMs to generalize better and adapt to unseen quantum-enabled attacks during real-world deployment.

6.4 Quantum-Specific Threat Detection

One of the most crucial applications of quantum-aware LLMs is the detection and mitigation of quantum-specific threats. As quantum computing advances, cyber threats such as quantum-enhanced phishing attacks, quantum key distribution vulnerabilities, and quantum-resistant cryptographic breaks will become more common. By training LLMs to recognize these threats, organizations can build more proactive defenses (Jones & Omar, 2024; Baseri et al., 2024). For example, LLMs can be trained to detect quantum-enhanced malware by analyzing code patterns that may exploit vulnerabilities in quantum-optimized cryptography.

The GEADD (GPT-2 Enhanced Attack Detection and Defense) method is a notable example of using LLMs to enhance cybersecurity defenses. It utilizes a GPT-2-based model that can be fine-tuned for zero-day threat detection, a critical area in quantum-aware cybersecurity, where novel attack vectors could be introduced rapidly due to the accelerated power of quantum systems (Jones & Omar, 2024).

6.5 Challenges in Training Quantum-Aware LLMs

While the potential of quantum-aware LLMs is immense, several challenges must be addressed in their training. Quantum-aware training demands high computational resources due to the need to simulate quantum effects and model complex quantum systems. Additionally, there is a dearth of sufficiently large and well-labeled quantum-specific cybersecurity datasets. This limitation makes it difficult to build robust models that can generalize well across diverse quantum scenarios (Zangana & Omar, 2024).

Another significant challenge is the integration of quantum computing with existing cybersecurity infrastructures. Many of the current models used in cybersecurity are built on classical systems and require substantial modification to incorporate quantum principles. Therefore, researchers must develop hybrid quantum-classical systems that leverage both technologies effectively to enhance the overall security posture (Bishwas & Sen, 2024).

6.6 Future Directions and Research Opportunities

The intersection of quantum computing, cybersecurity, and LLMs offers exciting avenues for future research. One area that warrants further investigation is the development of quantum-resilient machine learning algorithms that can operate effectively even in a post-quantum world. Researchers like Sodiya et al. (2024) and Baseri et al. (2024) have highlighted the need for a strategic roadmap to integrate quantum-resistant mechanisms into machine learning workflows, a crucial step in ensuring that LLMs remain effective in detecting and mitigating future quantum-based cybersecurity threats.

Furthermore, the application of quantum computing in enhancing the capabilities of LLMs for threat prediction, data encryption, and secure communication protocols could lead to the creation of more advanced and resilient cybersecurity systems. As quantum technologies continue to mature, the synergy between quantum-aware LLMs and quantum security measures will become an essential aspect of next-generation cybersecurity defenses (Lougovski et al., 2023; Wright et al., 2012).

The timeline below summarizes the major milestones in the development of post-quantum cryptography, highlighting key advancements and their implications for quantum-aware cybersecurity.

Figure 5. Development of post-quantum cryptography

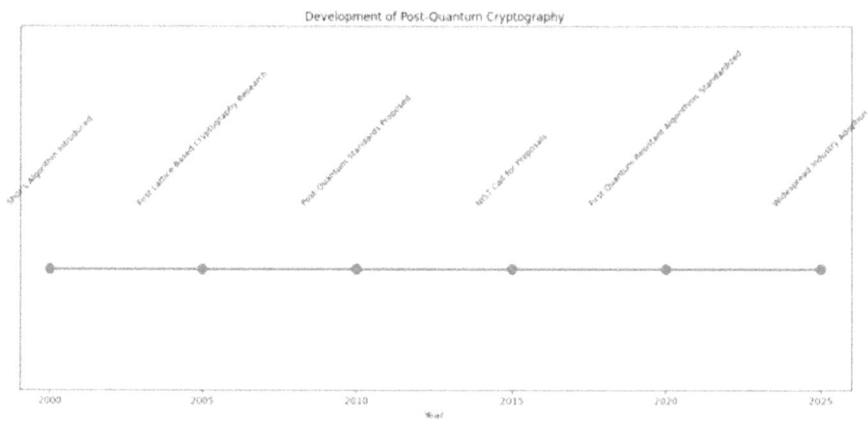

6.7 Conclusion

Training LLMs for quantum-aware cybersecurity presents a unique challenge but also a significant opportunity to future-proof digital defense systems against quantum-enabled threats. By integrating quantum principles into the training process and leveraging synthetic data and advanced quantum simulation techniques, LLMs can be equipped to identify, analyze, and mitigate emerging cybersecurity risks in the quantum era. As quantum computing continues to evolve, the development of quantum-aware LLMs will be critical for maintaining the integrity and security of digital infrastructures across industries.

7. CHALLENGES IN USING LLMS FOR QUANTUM-AWARE CYBERSECURITY

As quantum computing emerges as a disruptive force in the field of cybersecurity, the integration of Large Language Models (LLMs) to address quantum-aware threats presents both promising opportunities and formidable challenges. While LLMs have demonstrated remarkable capabilities in traditional cybersecurity contexts, their adaptation to the quantum computing era requires overcoming several technical, conceptual, and ethical hurdles.

7.1. Quantum Threats and Algorithmic Compatibility

One of the primary challenges in using LLMs for quantum-aware cybersecurity is the incompatibility of classical cryptographic algorithms with quantum computing. Quantum computers are expected to break many of the current cryptographic systems that form the backbone of cybersecurity protocols (Baseri, Chouhan, & Ghorbani, 2024; Sodiya et al., 2024). This shift introduces a need for LLMs to be capable of recognizing and defending against new, quantum-resistant algorithms. Existing LLMs, which are primarily trained on classical data, may not be equipped to deal with the complexity and unpredictability of quantum computing techniques that could be leveraged by attackers (Rahul et al., 2024). Training LLMs to identify quantum-specific vulnerabilities, such as those in post-quantum cryptography or quantum key distribution (QKD), will require significant adaptation of their learning algorithms and data sets.

7.2. Data Availability and Quantum-Specific Training

Another significant hurdle is the limited availability of quantum-specific datasets. LLMs require large volumes of data to learn effectively, and most cybersecurity data available today is based on classical computing models. As quantum computing technologies evolve, new datasets that reflect quantum cryptographic structures and quantum network threats will need to be generated. However, the scarcity of these quantum-specific datasets presents a substantial challenge to training LLMs for quantum-aware tasks (Gholami & Omar, 2024). As the quantum field is still in its nascent stages, much of the data necessary for such training may not yet be available, limiting the ability of LLMs to generalize across quantum-enabled attack vectors.

7.3. Complexity in Model Interpretation and Trustworthiness

LLMs have gained attention due to their power in recognizing patterns and making predictions based on vast amounts of input data. However, their "black-box" nature poses a significant challenge in the context of cybersecurity, particularly when applied to quantum-aware threats. In traditional cybersecurity, the traceability and interpretability of model decisions are crucial for understanding why a particular defense mechanism was deployed or why an attack was detected. In quantum cybersecurity, where potential vulnerabilities may involve advanced quantum states and behaviors, the opacity of LLM decision-making could undermine trust in their recommendations and responses (Omar & Zangana, 2024). Addressing this concern will require developing methods to enhance the explainability of LLMs, ensuring they provide interpretable and actionable insights for quantum cybersecurity practitioners.

7.4. Scalability Issues in Quantum Computing Environments

Quantum computing environments often involve complex and highly scalable architectures that operate in fundamentally different ways from classical systems. Adapting LLMs to work efficiently in these environments presents scalability challenges, particularly in terms of computational resources. Quantum systems require specialized hardware and software that are not yet widely accessible, and integrating LLMs into such systems could introduce significant performance bottlenecks. This issue is compounded by the fact that quantum computing is still in the research and development phase, with significant challenges in scaling quantum hardware for practical applications in cybersecurity (Block, 2024). Furthermore, the computational power required to train LLMs may exceed the capabilities of quantum systems, leading to inefficiencies or the need for hybrid models that combine classical and quantum computational resources.

7.5. Adapting to Emerging Quantum Threats

Quantum computing will not only enhance the capabilities of attackers but may also lead to entirely new classes of threats that are difficult to predict. The ability of quantum computers to solve problems that are infeasible for classical computers, such as factoring large numbers or simulating quantum systems, opens up new avenues for attack, such as the breaking of asymmetric cryptography or vulnerabilities in quantum-enabled IoT devices (Jones et al., 2023). LLMs used in cybersecurity will need to be continually updated and retrained to detect and mitigate these emerging quantum threats. The rapid pace of quantum advancements makes it challenging to maintain the relevance and effectiveness of LLM models in real-time threat detection and defense.

7.6. Ethical and Regulatory Concerns

The ethical implications of using LLMs in quantum-aware cybersecurity are substantial. As quantum computing makes current encryption methods obsolete, it will force industries to adopt new post-quantum security protocols. This transition will require careful attention to the regulatory landscape and potential legal implications of using AI models to enforce new security protocols. Additionally, quantum-aware LLMs may inadvertently amplify biases in their predictions, especially in contexts where quantum systems are used in critical infrastructure or sensitive personal data (Gholami & Omar, 2023). The challenges of maintaining fairness and equity in AI-driven security measures must be addressed to ensure that LLMs do not unintentionally harm certain user groups or create new vulnerabilities.

7.7. Integrating Quantum and Classical Cybersecurity Systems

Lastly, the integration of LLMs with quantum-aware cybersecurity systems poses a significant challenge due to the hybrid nature of quantum and classical computing environments. Quantum systems, still emerging and developing, will have to coexist with classical systems for the foreseeable future. LLMs will need to be capable of working across both quantum and classical platforms, ensuring that security measures are consistent, effective, and able to detect hybrid threats that involve both paradigms. This dual requirement introduces challenges in terms of the flexibility, adaptability, and interoperability of LLM models, which must evolve to address the intersection of these two complex technologies (How & Cheah, 2023).

7.8 Conclusion

The integration of Large Language Models into quantum-aware cybersecurity is fraught with challenges, from data limitations and model interpretability to scalability and the emergence of new threats. As quantum technologies continue to evolve, addressing these challenges will be crucial for ensuring that LLMs can effectively contribute to securing digital assets in a quantum-enabled future. Only through targeted research, enhanced model training, and the development of new tools will we be able to harness the power of LLMs in the quantum era of cybersecurity.

8. CASE STUDIES AND APPLICATIONS

The integration of cybersecurity strategies and technologies in real-world settings offers valuable insights into the challenges and opportunities within the digital landscape. Case studies and applications of advanced systems, including Large Language Models (LLMs), cloud computing, quantum computing, and deep learning, reveal the transformative potential of these innovations in addressing contemporary security threats. The following cases highlight the practical application of these emerging technologies in fields such as biotechnology, mobile security, software vulnerability detection, and healthcare.

8.1. Biotechnology and Healthcare Cybersecurity

Biotechnology and healthcare sectors face unique cybersecurity threats due to their reliance on sensitive data, including genetic information and patient records. A notable case study by Huff et al. (2023) explores management practices for mitigating cybersecurity risks in biotechnology companies, laboratories, and healthcare research organizations. The study emphasizes the importance of adopting robust security frameworks, including the integration of AI-driven threat detection systems, to safeguard proprietary data and protect against cyberattacks. Machine learning models, particularly those powered by LLMs, are also being employed for early detection of potential vulnerabilities in healthcare networks (Jones et al., 2023).

In another case, the work by Omar and Zangana (2024) discusses the growing adoption of blockchain technology in healthcare for secure data sharing and timestamping. By ensuring data integrity and reducing the risk of cyberattacks, blockchain applications can enhance trust and security in healthcare data systems.

8.2. Cloud Computing Security

Cloud computing has become a foundational technology for businesses and government entities, but it also introduces significant security challenges. Hamza and Omar (2013) provided a comprehensive analysis of cloud computing security, particularly focusing on the misuse and potential threats posed by malicious actors exploiting cloud services for nefarious purposes. These challenges have led to the development of cloud-specific security protocols, including the use of AI and machine learning for real-time monitoring and threat mitigation. Gholami and Omar (2023) further expanded this by investigating how synthetic data can improve the efficiency of large language models (LLMs) in detecting abnormal patterns within cloud environments, thereby enhancing cloud security.

The cloud's distributed nature, combined with quantum computing's potential, is also becoming a focal point for cybersecurity experts. The rise of quantum computing necessitates the development of quantum-resistant encryption mechanisms, with applications in both cloud and edge computing environments (Sodiya et al., 2024). This is especially relevant for businesses leveraging cloud services to store sensitive information, where quantum security could offer new protection strategies (Baseri et al., 2024).

8.3. Quantum Computing and Cybersecurity

Quantum computing is poised to revolutionize various fields, including cybersecurity. As quantum technologies advance, so too does the need for quantum-resistant security solutions. A key challenge in quantum cybersecurity is the vulnerability of traditional encryption methods, which could be easily broken by sufficiently advanced quantum computers. Wright, Dawson Jr., and Omar (2012) highlighted the significance of quantum-resistant algorithms in securing data, particularly for mobile devices. As quantum computing evolves, organizations must adapt their cybersecurity frameworks to mitigate the risks of quantum-enabled attacks.

Zangana et al. (2024) discuss the transformative potential of quantum computing in network security, particularly in enhancing the efficiency and effectiveness of network firewalls and intrusion detection systems. The application of quantum algorithms in these areas could substantially reduce the time required to detect and respond to cyber threats, potentially leading to a paradigm shift in cybersecurity strategies. These developments underscore the importance of preparing for the challenges posed by quantum computing and ensuring that security measures are adaptable to the new technological landscape.

8.4. Large Language Models (LLMs) for Vulnerability Detection

LLMs, such as GPT-based models, are increasingly used in cybersecurity for vulnerability detection and attack prevention. A case study by Jones and Omar (2024) demonstrated the effectiveness of the GPT-2 Enhanced Attack Detection and Defense (GEADD) method in identifying zero-day threats. The model's ability to process vast amounts of unstructured data, including threat reports and security advisories, enables it to detect previously unknown vulnerabilities and suggest defensive measures.

In the context of software vulnerability detection, Omar and Zangana (2025) explored how LLMs could revolutionize the detection and mitigation of security flaws in code. By leveraging these models, software developers can automate the identification of potential security vulnerabilities, reducing the time and effort required for manual code reviews. Furthermore, Gholami and Omar (2024) examined how LLMs could be utilized to generate synthetic data for training more robust models capable of detecting complex security threats in real-time environments.

8.5. Mobile Device Security

The growing reliance on smartphones and mobile devices in both personal and professional settings has raised concerns regarding mobile security. In their research, Zangana and Omar (2020) analyzed the evolving threat landscape for mobile devices, focusing on common attacks such as phishing and malware. They proposed a range of preventive measures, including the use of AI-powered antivirus applications for smartphones, which have the potential to detect and neutralize threats in real time.

In a related case study, Wright, Dawson Jr., and Omar (2012) highlighted the need for effective antivirus solutions tailored to mobile devices, as traditional security measures often fail to address the unique threats posed by mobile platforms. With the integration of deep learning algorithms into mobile security applications, these systems can offer enhanced detection and defense capabilities against new and emerging mobile threats.

8.6. Cybersecurity in Quantum Computing Era

The shift toward quantum computing poses significant challenges to cybersecurity, as many existing encryption protocols are vulnerable to quantum-enabled attacks. Baseri et al. (2024) explored the impact of quantum computing on cybersecurity infrastructures and highlighted the need for new security protocols that are resistant to quantum attacks. The development of quantum-resistant encryption algorithms will be critical in safeguarding sensitive data in industries such as finance, healthcare, and government, where data integrity and confidentiality are paramount.

Similarly, Sodiya et al. (2024) provided a detailed examination of the potential implications of quantum computing for US cybersecurity, discussing both the challenges and opportunities presented by quantum technologies. They emphasized the importance of preparing industries for the quantum threat by developing robust security frameworks that can withstand future quantum-enabled attacks.

8.7 Conclusion

The case studies and applications presented in this section underscore the critical role of emerging technologies, such as LLMs, quantum computing, and AI-driven solutions, in enhancing cybersecurity measures across various sectors. As digital threats evolve, organizations must adopt innovative security frameworks that incorporate these advanced technologies to stay ahead of potential risks. The integration of LLMs for vulnerability detection, the development of quantum-resistant encryption, and the continued exploration of AI for cloud and mobile security will undoubtedly shape the future of cybersecurity, providing more resilient and adaptive systems to combat an increasingly sophisticated threat landscape.

9. FUTURE DIRECTIONS AND INNOVATIONS

The future of cybersecurity, particularly in the context of large language models (LLMs) and quantum computing, is poised for dramatic advancements. Several emerging trends and technological innovations suggest that we are on the brink of a new era where AI, quantum technologies, and machine learning (ML) will redefine the security landscape. This section explores some of the key areas of future development, particularly focusing on how these technologies will impact cybersecurity, vulnerability detection, and threat mitigation.

9.1. Integration of Quantum Computing and Cybersecurity

Quantum computing has the potential to disrupt the current landscape of cybersecurity, presenting both challenges and opportunities. As quantum computers become more powerful, they could potentially break existing encryption methods that are vital for protecting sensitive information. This has led to the development of quantum-resistant encryption protocols, which will be critical for securing data in a post-quantum world. Several studies, such as those by Baseri et al. (2024) and Seskir (2019), emphasize the need for quantum-secure cryptographic systems that can withstand the power of quantum attacks. Additionally, emerging quantum technologies may enable more efficient algorithms for detecting vulnerabilities and managing security protocols in cloud and networked environments (Bush et al., 2023; Khan et al., 2023).

Moreover, quantum computing could also enhance the speed and accuracy of machine learning algorithms in detecting and mitigating cyber threats. The exploration of quantum machine learning (QML) holds significant promise for advancing the capabilities of AI-driven cybersecurity systems. By harnessing the computational power of quantum systems, cybersecurity tools could analyze large datasets more effectively, leading to faster detection of zero-day vulnerabilities and more accurate threat predictions (How & Cheah, 2023; Zangana & Omar, 2025).

9.2. Large Language Models (LLMs) in Vulnerability Detection and Threat Mitigation

Large language models have shown significant promise in the field of cybersecurity, particularly for tasks such as threat intelligence, attack detection, and vulnerability analysis. With their ability to understand and process natural language, LLMs can be employed to parse through vast amounts of cybersecurity data, including logs, reports, and real-time threat feeds, to identify patterns indicative of cyberattacks. As noted by Omar (2024) and Jones et al. (2024), LLMs can significantly enhance the speed and efficiency of detecting novel threats by analyzing textual data for emerging vulnerabilities, phishing attempts, or other types of attacks.

One of the most exciting directions for LLMs in cybersecurity is the ability to create models that are fine-tuned for specific tasks, such as detecting vulnerabilities in software or identifying anomalous network behaviors. As demonstrated in recent work by Gholami and Omar (2023), LLMs trained on synthetic data can outperform traditional models in certain scenarios, particularly when dealing with large volumes of cybersecurity data. This opens up new avenues for training specialized LLMs to detect vulnerabilities in real-time, a critical need for organizations dealing with constantly evolving threats.

Additionally, integrating LLMs with other AI and machine learning techniques could lead to more robust systems for both attack detection and defense. LLMs can enhance traditional threat modeling techniques by incorporating contextual knowledge from across various domains, improving their ability to detect sophisticated attacks that might otherwise evade detection. For instance, the GPT-2 enhanced attack detection method developed by Jones and Omar (2024) demonstrates how LLMs can be leveraged to detect zero-day threats, thus enabling a proactive defense strategy rather than relying solely on reactive measures.

9.3. Cybersecurity in the Era of Blockchain and AI

Blockchain technology is gaining traction as a secure and transparent method for verifying transactions and maintaining data integrity, which can be highly beneficial in cybersecurity. Zangana (2024) and Sodiya et al. (2024) highlight the potential of blockchain-based systems for enhancing security in critical areas such as identity management, access control, and secure communications. One promising area is the use of blockchain-based timestamping tools, which provide verifiable proof of the integrity of data. Blockchain's decentralized nature also reduces the risks associated with single points of failure, making it an attractive solution for securing cloud environments and distributed systems (Zangana & Omar, 2024).

Moreover, the integration of blockchain with AI models like LLMs could provide an added layer of security. For instance, blockchain could be used to verify the integrity of machine learning models, ensuring that they remain tamper-proof and operate as intended. This is particularly important in adversarial machine learning, where attackers attempt to manipulate or poison training data to compromise AI systems. The combination of AI and blockchain could help mitigate these risks by providing decentralized verification mechanisms (Zangana et al., 2024; Gholami & Omar, 2024).

9.4. Synthetic Data and its Impact on Cybersecurity Models

Another key area of future development in cybersecurity is the use of synthetic data. As Gholami and Omar (2023) suggest, synthetic data can be used to train large language models in scenarios where real data might be scarce or sensitive. This is particularly important in cybersecurity, where access to real-world attack data is often limited due to privacy and ethical concerns. Synthetic data allows researchers and practitioners to simulate various attack scenarios, enabling the development of more robust models for threat detection and vulnerability assessment.

Furthermore, synthetic data can help enhance the efficiency of LLMs by providing a broader range of examples for training. As LLMs become more adept at understanding complex cybersecurity problems, they could be used to simulate potential threats and attack vectors, helping organizations better prepare for future security challenges. This approach also enables the creation of more diverse datasets, which is crucial for developing AI models that can generalize across different types of attacks (Gholami & Omar, 2024).

9.5. The Role of Machine Learning in Enhancing Malware Detection

Machine learning continues to play a pivotal role in the detection and mitigation of malware. By leveraging advanced techniques such as deep learning, machine learning models can identify previously unknown malware strains by analyzing their behavior rather than relying on signatures alone. As highlighted by Omar (2024), the development of optimized convolutional neural networks (CNNs) for malware detection represents a significant step forward in cybersecurity. These models can analyze large volumes of data in real-time, enabling faster and more accurate detection of malware, which is critical for mitigating the risks of cyberattacks.

Moreover, the integration of quantum computing with machine learning for malware detection could lead to even more powerful solutions. Quantum-enhanced ML models could potentially provide faster analysis and more accurate predictions, further improving the efficiency of cybersecurity systems. This is a developing area of research, and as quantum computing capabilities improve, it could play a major role in reshaping how cybersecurity professionals approach malware detection and defense (Omar, 2024; Baseri et al., 2024).

9.6 Summary

As cybersecurity continues to evolve, the integration of quantum computing, AI, and machine learning presents numerous opportunities to address current and future challenges. The convergence of these technologies will enable faster, more accurate threat detection, improve vulnerability management, and provide more robust defenses against a wide range of cyberattacks. By embracing these innovations and continuing research in fields like synthetic data, blockchain, and quantum-resistant encryption, cybersecurity professionals will be better equipped to safeguard digital assets in an increasingly complex and interconnected world. Future developments in these areas will undoubtedly shape the next generation of cybersecurity strategies and technologies.

10. CONCLUSION

The landscape of cybersecurity continues to evolve at a rapid pace, driven by advancements in technology, artificial intelligence, and emerging fields like quantum computing. As organizations face increasingly sophisticated threats, the need for innovative approaches to protect digital infrastructures becomes more critical. The integration of machine learning, deep learning, and large language models (LLMs) is reshaping the way we understand and defend against cyber threats. These technologies are not only enhancing the speed and accuracy of attack detection but are also empowering systems to anticipate and mitigate risks proactively.

One of the most promising developments in cybersecurity is the application of quantum computing. While still in its infancy, quantum technology holds the potential to revolutionize encryption methods and security protocols. It promises to offer unprecedented computational power, which could render current security mechanisms obsolete. However, it also introduces new challenges, particularly in the form of quantum-resistant security measures. Researchers are working diligently to address these challenges, exploring solutions like quantum-resistant cryptography and novel defense mechanisms tailored to the quantum era.

Moreover, the growing adoption of AI-driven tools, such as those using deep neural networks (DNNs), has the potential to significantly enhance threat detection and response times. These tools can analyze vast amounts of data, identify patterns, and detect anomalies faster than traditional systems. As a result, organizations can respond to threats more quickly, reducing the risk of data breaches and minimizing the impact of attacks.

As we look to the future, the focus should be on developing more robust, scalable, and adaptive security systems that can handle the complexities of modern digital environments. This includes integrating AI with quantum technologies and improving the resilience of machine learning models against adversarial attacks. The challenge will be to stay ahead of increasingly sophisticated cyber threats while balancing the need for privacy, usability, and efficiency in these systems.

Ultimately, the future of cybersecurity will be defined by collaboration across multiple domains—AI, quantum computing, and cybersecurity. By combining expertise from these areas, we can create more effective, adaptive, and secure systems that will be capable of protecting against both present and future threats. The key will be staying agile and continuously innovating to address the evolving nature of cyber risks.

REFERENCES

Agrawal, K., & Aggarwal, M. Building Efficient Smart Contract for Healthcare 4.0. In *Blockchain for Healthcare 4.0* (pp. 94-123). CRC Press.

AL-Refaey. M. R., Tyagi, A. K., AL-Ghamdi, A. S. A. M., & Kukreja, S. (Eds.). (2024). *Topics in Artificial Intelligence Applied to Industry 4.0*. John Wiley & Sons.

Baseri, Y., Chouhan, V., & Ghorbani, A. (2024). Cybersecurity in the Quantum Era: Assessing the Impact of Quantum Computing on Infrastructure. *arXiv preprint arXiv:2404.10659*.

Bishwas, A. K., & Sen, M. (2024). Strategic Roadmap for Quantum-Resistant Security: A Framework for Preparing Industries for the Quantum Threat. *arXiv preprint arXiv:2411.09995*.

Block, R. S. S. (2024). The 2024 quantum advantage blueprint: Where quantum outpaces classical.

Bush, S. F., Challener, W. A., & Mantelet, G. (2021). A perspective on industrial quantum networks. *AVS Quantum Science*, 3(3), 030501. DOI: 10.1116/5.0051881

Exchange, Q. R. K. Towards a Verifiably Secure Quantum-Resistant Key Exchange in IKEv2.

Gholami, S., & Omar, M. (2023). Does Synthetic Data Make Large Language Models More Efficient? *arXiv preprint arXiv:2310.07830*.

Gholami, S., & Omar, M. (2024). Can a student large language model perform as well as its teacher? In *Innovations, Securities, and Case Studies Across Healthcare, Business, and Technology* (pp. 122-139). IGI Global. DOI: 10.4018/979-8-3693-1906-2.ch007

Hamza, Y. A., & Omar, M. D. (2013). Cloud computing security: Abuse and nefarious use of cloud computing. *International Journal of Computer Engineering Research*, 3(6), 22–27.

How, M. L., & Cheah, S. M. (2023). Business Renaissance: Opportunities and challenges at the dawn of the Quantum Computing Era. *Businesses*, 3(4), 585–605. DOI: 10.3390/businesses3040036

Huff, A. J., Burrell, D. N., Nobles, C., Richardson, K., Wright, J. B., Burton, S. L., Jones, A. J., Springs, D., Omar, M., & Brown-Jackson, K. L. (2023). Management Practices for Mitigating Cybersecurity Threats to Biotechnology Companies, Laboratories, and Healthcare Research Organizations. In *Applied Research Approaches to Technology, Healthcare, and Business* (pp. 1-12). IGI Global.

Jones, R., & Omar, M. (2024). Revolutionizing Cybersecurity: The GPT-2 Enhanced Attack Detection and Defense (GEADD) Method for Zero-Day Threats. *International Journal of Informatics* [INJIISCOM]. *Information System and Computer Engineering*, 5(2), 178–191.

Jones, R., Omar, M., Mohammed, D., Nobles, C., & Dawson, M. (2023). Harnessing the Speed and Accuracy of Machine Learning to Advance Cybersecurity. In *2023 Congress in Computer Science, Computer Engineering, & Applied Computing (CSCE)* (pp. 418-421). IEEE. DOI: 10.1109/CSCE60160.2023.00074

Khan, A. A., Akbar, M. A., Ahmad, A., Fahmideh, M., Shameem, M., Lahtinen, V., . . . Mikkonen, T. (2023, July). Agile practices for quantum software development: practitioners' perspectives. In *2023 IEEE international conference on quantum software (QSW)* (pp. 9-20). IEEE.

Lougovski, P., Parekh, O., Broz, J., Byrd, M., Chembo, Y., de Jong, W. A., . . . Svore, K. M. (2023). *Position Papers for the ASCR Workshop on Basic Research Needs in Quantum Computing and Networking*. USDOE Office of Science (SC), Advanced Scientific Computing Research (ASCR).

Madni, A. F., Shah, M. A., & Al-Naeem, M. (2024). An Investigation of Scalability in EHRs using Healthcare 4.0 and Blockchain. *International Journal of Advanced Computer Science and Applications*, 15(5). Advance online publication. DOI: 10.14569/IJACSA.2024.0150548

Metawei, M. A., Eldeeb, H., Nassar, S. M., & Taher, M. (2022). Quantum Computing Meets Artificial Intelligence: Innovations and Challenges. In *Handbook on Artificial Intelligence-Empowered Applied Software Engineering: VOL. 1: Novel Methodologies to Engineering Smart Software Systems* (pp. 303–338). Springer International Publishing. DOI: 10.1007/978-3-031-08202-3_12

Mohamed, N., & Ahmed, A. A. (2024, June). AI in Combatting Man-in-the-Middle Attacks: A Comprehensive Review. In *2024 15th International Conference on Computing Communication and Networking Technologies (ICCCNT)* (pp. 1-6). IEEE. DOI: 10.1109/ICCCNT61001.2024.10725789

Mohammed, D., Omar, M., & Nguyen, V. (2018). Wireless sensor network security: Approaches to detecting and avoiding wormhole attacks. *Journal of Research in Business. Economics and Management*, 10(2), 1860–1864.

Nguyen, V., Mohammed, D., Omar, M., & Banisakher, M. (2018). The Effects of the FCC Net Neutrality Repeal on Security and Privacy. [IJHIoT]. *International Journal of Hyperconnectivity and the Internet of Things*, 2(2), 21–29. DOI: 10.4018/IJHIoT.2018070102

Omar, M. (2021). New insights into database security: An effective and integrated approach for applying access control mechanisms and cryptographic concepts in Microsoft Access environments.

Omar, M. (2022). *Machine Learning for Cybersecurity: Innovative Deep Learning Solutions*. Springer Brief. https://link.springer.com/book/978303115

Omar, M. (2024). From Attack to Defense: Strengthening DNN Text Classification Against Adversarial Examples. In *Innovations, Securities, and Case Studies Across Healthcare, Business, and Technology* (pp. 174-195). IGI Global.

Omar, M. (2024). Revolutionizing Malware Detection: A Paradigm Shift Through Optimized Convolutional Neural Networks. In *Innovations, Securities, and Case Studies Across Healthcare, Business, and Technology* (pp. 196-220). IGI Global. DOI: 10.4018/979-8-3693-1906-2.ch011

Omar, M., & Zangana, H. M. (Eds.). (2024). *Redefining Security With Cyber AI*. IGI Global., DOI: 10.4018/979-8-3693-6517-5

Omar, M., & Zangana, H. M. (Eds.). (2025). *Application of Large Language Models (LLMs) for Software Vulnerability Detection*. IGI Global., DOI: 10.4018/979-8-3693-9311-6

Perron, J. K., DeLeone, C., Sharif, S., Carter, T., Grossman, J. M., Passante, G., & Sack, J. (2021). Quantum undergraduate education and scientific training. *arXiv preprint arXiv:2109.13850.*

Qualters, I., Taylor, A. J., & Hagberg, A. A. (2019). *IS&T Computing Overview* (No. LA-UR-19-22567). Los Alamos National Lab.(LANL), Los Alamos, NM (United States).

Rahul, R., Geetha, S., Priyatharsini, S., Mehata, K., Sundaresan Perumal, T., Ethiraj, N., & Sendilvelan, S. (2024). Cybersecurity Issues and Challenges in Quantum Computing. *Topics in Artificial Intelligence Applied to Industry*, 4(0), 203–221. DOI: 10.1002/9781394216147.ch11

Ramachandran, D., Naqi, S. M., Perumal, G., & Abbas, Q. (2023). DLTN-LOSP: A Novel Deep-Linear-Transition-Network-Based Resource Allocation Model with the Logic Overhead Security Protocol for Cloud Systems. *Sensors (Basel)*, 23(20), 8448. DOI: 10.3390/s23208448 PMID: 37896541

Seskir, Z. C. (2019). *Current state of quantum information technologies in Turkey* (Master's thesis, Middle East Technical University).

Singh, N. B. *Quantum Mechanics in Drug Discovery*. NB Singh.

Sodiya, E. O., Umoga, U. J., Amoo, O. O., & Atadoga, A. (2024). Quantum computing and its potential impact on US cybersecurity: A review: Scrutinizing the challenges and opportunities presented by quantum technologies in safeguarding digital assets. *Global Journal of Engineering and Technology Advances, 18*(2), 049-064.

Wright, J., Dawson, M. E.Jr, & Omar, M. (2012). Cyber security and mobile threats: The need for antivirus applications for smartphones. *Journal of Information Systems Technology and Planning*, 5(14), 40–60.

Zangana, H. M. (2024). Exploring Blockchain-Based Timestamping Tools: A Comprehensive Review. *Redefining Security With Cyber AI*, 92-110.

Zangana, H. M. (2024). Exploring the Landscape of Website Vulnerability Scanners: A Comprehensive Review and Comparative Analysis. *Redefining Security With Cyber AI*, 111-129.

Zangana, H. M., Mohammed, A. K., Sallow, A. B., & Sallow, Z. B. (2024). Cybernetic Deception: Unraveling the Layers of Email Phishing Threats. [INJURATECH]. *International Journal of Research and Applied Technology*, 4(1), 35–47.

Zangana, H. M., & Mohammed, D. (2025). Foundations of Large Language Models in Software Vulnerability Detection. In Omar, M., & Zangana, H. (Eds.), *Application of Large Language Models (LLMs) for Software Vulnerability Detection* (pp. 41–74). IGI Global., DOI: 10.4018/979-8-3693-9311-6.ch002

Zangana, H. M., & Omar, M. (2020). Threats, Attacks, and Mitigations of Smartphone Security. *Academic Journal of Nawroz University*, 9(4), 324–332. DOI: 10.25007/ajnu.v9n4a989

Zangana, H. M., & Omar, M. (2025). Harnessing the Power of Large Language Models for Cybersecurity: Applications, Challenges, and Future Directions. In Omar, M., & Zangana, H. (Eds.), *Application of Large Language Models (LLMs) for Software Vulnerability Detection* (pp. 1–40). IGI Global., DOI: 10.4018/979-8-3693-9311-6.ch001

Zangana, H. M., Omar, M., Al-Karaki, J. N., & Mohammed, D. (2024). Comprehensive Review and Analysis of Network Firewall Rule Analyzers: Enhancing Security Posture and Efficiency. *Redefining Security With Cyber AI*, 15-36.

Chapter 5
Nation-State Cyber Attacks on Critical Infrastructure:
A Case Study and Analysis of the 2014 Sony Pictures Hack by North Korea

Ngozi Tracy Aleke
https://orcid.org/0009-0005-2328-5680
Illinois Institute of Technology, USA

Ivan Livingstone Zziwa
Illinois Institute of Technology, USA

Kwame Opoku-Appiah
Illinois Institute of Technology, USA

ABSTRACT

In the 21st century, there has been a great deal of importance ascribed to international security. A standard procedure used by adversarial states and non-state actors to propagate their continuous and calculated malicious objectives are cyber offenses such as cyber-espionage, hacktivism, cyberwar, as well as other cybercriminal activities (Hwang & Choi, 2021). Even though cyber-attacks were initially thought to be perpetrated by individuals or privately owned organizations, more and more attacks are being orchestrated by nation states, other states or even targeted towards individual organizations. Recent reports have shown that North Korea has an advance cyber warfare capacity, and a substantial number of its workforce is allegedly

DOI: 10.4018/979-8-3373-1102-9.ch005

engaged in the activities of the dark web with a direct support from the government

OVERVIEW OF NATION-STATE SPONSORED CYBERATTACKS

In the 21st century, there has been a great deal of importance ascribed to international security. A standard procedure used by adversarial states and non-state actors to propagate their continuous and calculated malicious objectives are cyber offenses such as cyber-espionage, hacktivism, cyberwar, as well as other cybercriminal activities (Hwang & Choi, 2021). Even though cyber-attacks were initially thought to be perpetrated by individuals or privately owned organizations, more and more attacks are being orchestrated by nation states, other states or even targeted towards individual organizations. Recent reports have shown that North Korea has an advance cyber warfare capacity, and a substantial number of its workforce is allegedly engaged in the activities of the dark web with a direct support from the government (Kshetri, 2014).

Even though the general population in North Korea has limited access to advanced internet infrastructure, the nation has developed a highly skilled cyber arsenal that it has use to carry out cyberattacks on other nations (Hwang & Choi, 2021). For example, in 2009, North Korean hackers, using servers in Austria, Germany, Georgia, and the U.S., lunched an attack in South Korea, shutting down computers in the nation's presidential palace at Seoul for days. Also on July 4, 2009, North Korea also targeted U.S. government servers, including the Treasury Department and the Secret Service. Similarly Distributed Denial of Service (DDoS) attacks in 2011 affected South Korean government and bank websites. In 2012, a traditional South Korean newspaper outlet, JoongAng Daily, was hacked. A series of cyberattacks followed on March 20, 2013, when North Korea launched malware attacks on South Korean banks and broadcast stations, deactivating 48,000 computers and disabling networks within the organizations. Despite this, North Korea denied involvement and attempted to hide their digital footprint. In March 2013, North Korean hackers also targeted ATMs in Seoul, using malware called Dark Seoul, which was designed to bypass antivirus software. Similar attacks were reported against South Korea's presidential palace, military websites, and U.S. institutions like the Treasury Department and the Federal Trade Commission (Hwang & Choi, 2021).

Definition And Characteristics of Nation-State Cyberattacks

Definition

A nation-state cyberattack or a nation-state-sponsored cyberattack refers to a cyberattack carried out by a state-sponsored actor against another government's critical infrastructure, individuals, or organization (Lundbohm, 2017). An actor can have various goals for the attack, it could be for espionage, disruption, or destruction of the other states' infrastructures – an act of war, or even a way of sending a political message can be some of the reasons some states carry out these attacks. Even though the need for critical infrastructure protection has always been a watchword in the United States way before the event of 9/11, the 9/11 conspiracy has played a key role in the awareness of the possibility of an attack of such magnitude without the traditional forms of warfare. According to the congressional testimony of John A. Serabian Jr., before the Joint Economic Committee on Cyber Threats and the U.S. Economy, he noted that "the attack the experts say cannot happen or that terrorists are not interested in pursuing is simply an attack that hasn't happened yet."

More recently, reports have shown that foreign nations back and finance well-organized cyber warfare against other states (Schmitt,2010). An attack on a nation's critical infrastructure could be highly disruptive if the target is unprepared, and this may even become worse if the actors implore various techniques in carrying out the attack (Billo & Chang, 2004). An attack targeted towards the finance, transportation, communication, power, and educational sector or any other infrastructure of a State would at the least lead to disruption of the daily life of citizens, causing chaos and confusion in the nation-state (Billo & Chang, 2004).

Characteristics

A nation-sponsored cyber-attack, unlike an attack engineered by an individual or a group, is usually very sophisticated and targeted. The Nation State actor is backed by the state and has a license to hack. These actors work for the Nations targeting other nations, organizations, or even private individuals to either gain access to valuable information or intelligence or create internationally significant incidents that will influence the targeted nation or even the world at large. Nation-state actors operate with little fear of legal consequences, as they are unlikely to face arrest in their own country for their actions. These individuals often have strong ties to their nation's military, intelligence agencies, or state control systems, and possess advanced technical expertise.

Alternatively, some Nation-State actors are selected for their specific skills in areas such as language, social media, or cultural knowledge, enabling them to engage in espionage, propaganda, or disinformation campaigns. They benefit from the full support and resources of their government, receiving directives from government officials or military personnel. Nation-state actors also influence other cybercriminals, sharing new tactics, insights, and attack methods that are often adopted by others.

The Role of Geopolitical Tensions in Cyber Warfare

Geopolitical tension plays a critical role in cyber warfare (Khan, 2022). Tension between major political powers breeds escalation of warfare into a new domain where cyberattacks are used as both a weapon of disruption of critical infrastructures and an instrument for espionage. These attacks would ordinarily threaten a nation's security and even global peace (Ribeiro, 2024). State-sponsored actors and politically motivated groups are increasingly targeting critical infrastructures such as Operational Technology (OT) and Industrial Control Systems (ICS) to disrupt critical services like power, water, and transportation (Lehto, 2022). Once isolated, these systems are now interconnected with information technology networks, exposing vulnerabilities and expanding the attack surface. This shift has made strengthening cyber defenses a priority for both nations and organizations. Some techniques that most cyber attackers use include supply chain compromises, living-off-the-land techniques, and zero-day exploits. These techniques help them to bypass traditional security measures (Ribeiro, 2024). Aside from the fact that These attacks result in disruptions to the operations of the victims, they also pose a great deal of risks to public safety and economic stability. The rise of geopolitical tensions among nation-states has necessitated the need for stronger cybersecurity strategies to protect critical infrastructure. The need for nations to build a robust critical infrastructure that is resilient to attacks, engage in stricter cybersecurity protocols, and foster international collaboration to counter cyber threats cannot be overemphasized.

Ribeiro (2024) references Paul Veeneman, a cybersecurity risk management expert, who remarked on the heightened targeting of critical infrastructure during the Russian Ukrainian war. Veeneman observed that cyberattacks have evolved, with ransomware now encompassing extortion and data theft. The introduction of artificial intelligence and machine learning has further advanced these attacks, making them harder to detect (Ozkan-Ozay, et, al.,2024). This sophistication in cyber warfare tactics has been demonstrated in several high-profile incidents, including the 2014 cyberattack on Sony Pictures Entertainment, where North Korea employed advanced malware to infiltrate and cripple the company's network in retaliation for a politically controversial film.

BACKGROUND ON THE SONY PICTURES HACK

Timeline of Events Leading Up to the Attack

Figure 1.

https://www.smh.com.au/technology/sony-to-pay-up-to-11-million-as-part-of-hacking-lawsuit-settlement-20151021-gkecoy.html

The 2014 cyberattack on Sony Pictures was one of the most prominent cyber incidents of the decade, targeting a major Hollywood studio. The attack began in late November when Sony Pictures Entertainment staff were abruptly logged out of the company's networks and computers. A message appeared on their screens from a group calling itself the "Guardians of Peace" (GOP), which threatened further action if Sony did not cancel the release of The Interview, a comedy depicting the assassination of North Korean leader Kim Jong-un.

The attackers infiltrated Sony's system through spear-phishing emails sent to employees, exploiting this method to bypass security measures. The chain of events leading to the attack began in June 2014, when Sony released the trailer for The Interview ahead of its planned October release, triggering controversy and eventually escalating to a full-scale cyberattack

Summary of Key Events in the Sony Hack Timeline

November 24, 2014: Initial Breach

- GOP (Guardians of Peace) breached Sony's network using advanced malware undetected by antivirus software.
- The breach caused significant system disruptions, forcing Sony to temporarily shut down operations.
- Stolen data included unreleased movies, personal employee information, private emails, and sensitive company data.
- GOP demanded Sony cancel the distribution of *The Interview* to prevent further leaks.

November 28, 2014: Public Disclosure

- News of the Sony hack surfaced in the media, with speculation about North Korea's involvement.
- North Korea denied responsibility.

December 16, 2014: Threat Escalation

- GOP explicitly referenced *The Interview* and used violent language, threatening physical harm to theaters screening the film.
- The FBI launched an official investigation, and Sony canceled the film's release.

December 19, 2014: Government Reaction

- President Obama criticized Sony's decision to cancel the release, stating it rewarded cybercriminals' behavior.
- The U.S. Department of Homeland Security found no evidence to substantiate GOP's threats of physical harm.

December 23-25, 2014: Film Release

- Sony reversed its decision and announced the film's release.
- *The Interview* premiered in over 300 independent theaters and was released on video-on-demand platforms like YouTube and Google Play after major theater chains declined to screen it.

Figure 2. Timeline of event surrounding 2014 Sony Cyber Attack

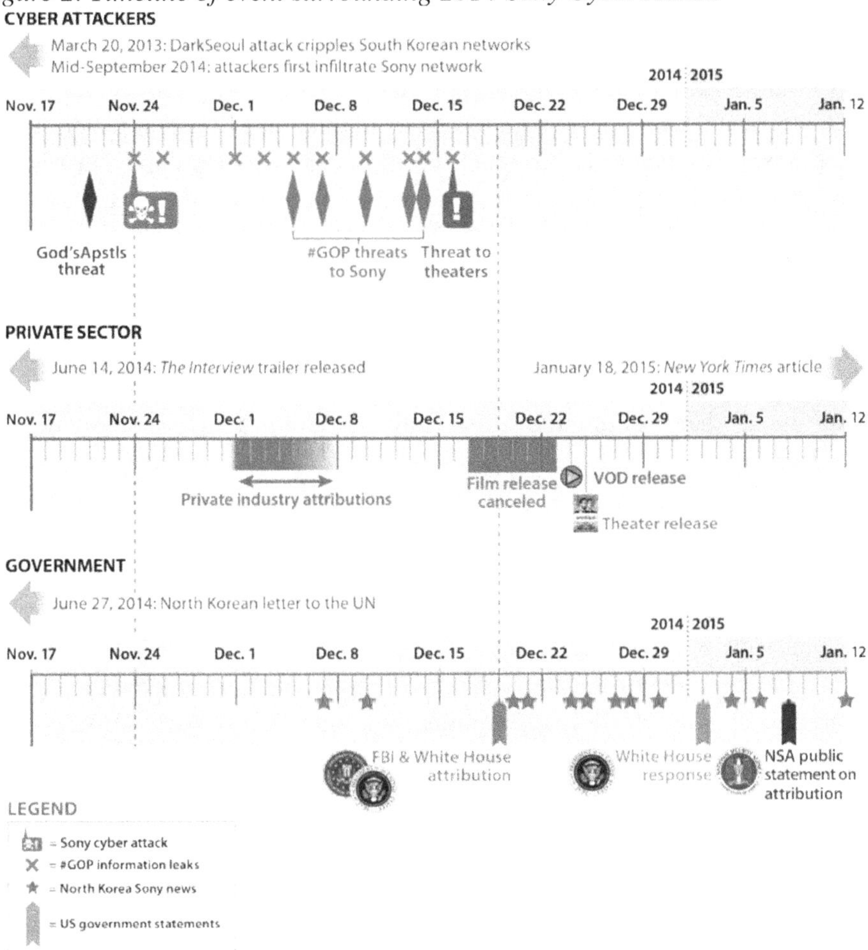

https://www.jhuapl.edu/sites/default/files/2022-12/SonyNightmareBeforeChristmas.pdf

Attribution to North Korea (Guardians of Peace)

There wasn't clear information as to whether North Korea was involved in the Sony Pictures hack at first, for example, stakeholders were blamed on hacktivists or internal personnel who had grudges to bear. But the scope, together with the peculiar threats referring to The Interview, raised investigators' suspicions about the state of the actor's involvement. In June 2014, days after the film's first trailer was released, the North Korean government released a statement threatening "a merciless countermeasure" for the film, which it deemed not only offensive but "the most blatant act of terrorism and war (Sean et al., 2022; Reuters, 2014). The U. S. government formally accused the North Korean government of the cyberattack on Sony Pictures Entertainment on December 19, 2014, backed with evidence that linked the tools and tactics used by the hackers to those used in other cyberattacks that were previously connected to other North Korean cyber groups, namely the Lazarus Group (FBI, 2014). Also, some of the malware used in the attack seems to have been written in Korean giving grounds for authority to conclude that that was enough circumstantial evidence to link the attacks to the North Koreans.

The group known as Guardians of Peace was blamed for the attack (Ellen et al., 2018). The cast of the film that satirized the assassination of Kim Jong-un was considered an insult to the regime hence the hack reminded Hollywood and Western governments that insulting the North Korean leader has serious consequences (Davis, 2015).

The Role of the Movie "The Interview" as a Catalyst for the Attack

The Interview is a comedy film produced by Seth Rogen and James Franco, based on a plot centered on the assassination of the North Korean Supreme Leader Kim Jong-un. Most North Koreans thought the production of such a film was an act of aggression and a cultural invasion of their country. And their supreme leader (Kang, 2015).

Amidst the rising controversy surrounding the release, Sony chose to postpone the movie's release date, and the company also went ahead to carry out some post-production edits, specifically toning down the violent representation of Kim Jong-un's death (Kang, 2015). This latter moves by Sony necessitated the rescheduling of the release date of the film to December 25, 2014. Nevertheless, these recent edits were not considered to be enough, as different North Korean officials demanded that the film be canceled in its entirety. Shortly after the trailer of the edit was released, North Korea voiced its disapproval, with its UN ambassador condemning the film as an "act of war" due to its depiction of Kim Jong-un's assassination.

Broader Implications of the Sony Attack for Critical Sectors like Media, Finance, and Energy.

The FBI on December 12, 2014, officially linked the Sony attack to North Korea. Accordingly, the FBI noted that "North Korea's actions were intended to inflict significant harm on a U.S. business and suppress the right of American citizens to express themselves. Such acts of intimidation fall outside the bounds of acceptable state behavior. The FBI takes seriously any attempt — whether through cyber-enabled means, threats of violence, or otherwise—to undermine the economic and social prosperity of our citizens," (Federal Bureau of Investigation, 2014). Additionally, United States President Barack Obama, suggested that there was a clear connect the Sony attack with other attackers attempting to do the same thing in the future by attempting to attack the critical infrastructure of the United States. He further noted that American society cannot indulge a dictator in some place imposing censorship on the United States (Verton, 2014). Even if it can be argued that the Sony hack did not directly affect the critical infrastructure of the United States as Sony and not the US bore the loss, the attack however, demonstrated the lengths an aggrieved nation-state would go to achieve its aim and objectives in this case stopping the release of a movie.

It is often argued that North Korea opted for cyber terrorism and that the Sony Hack was the beginning of that, to suppress what was considered an insult to the country's leadership. The attack broke the stereotype that high-profile hackers and cybercriminals are persons of Japanese or Chinese origin who are technically competent to breach security and create havoc. The attack also showed that cultural and political provocations are potentially lethal to global security and can lead to highly organized cyberattacks on Governments (Weaver, 2015).

METHODS AND TOOLS USED BY THE ATTACKERS

Methods

The primary vector of attack in the Sony hack was Spear-Phishing. The attackers sent out what appeared to be legitimate emails from Facebook, Google and Apple to specifically target Sony employees who had broad access to the company's networks. Several Sony employees fell victim to suspicious emails that contained hyperlinks to deceptive websites that were crafted by the hackers impersonating a legitimate site. Once these links were clicked on, the attackers gained access to several sensitive information from those employees, and this opened the door for more sophisticated attacks. Although, it's unclear as to what exact spear-phishing emails allowed the hackers to get the exact credentials to infiltrate Sony's system, but the fact that phishing was used as the primary point of infiltration cannot be disputed.

Figure 3. Target spear phishing attack model

Techtarget.com

Tools

After the hackers got access to Sony's systems, they infiltrated their system with a destructive malware called "Wiper". Wiper exploited Microsoft's Windows network file sharing and management features. The "Wiper" malware propagated once it had its way inside Sony's network and was able to shut down network services. The Wiper malware created a link between Sony's network, and the hackers were able to steal protected information and destroy data on their systems.

Figure 4. How do hackers infiltrate your data?

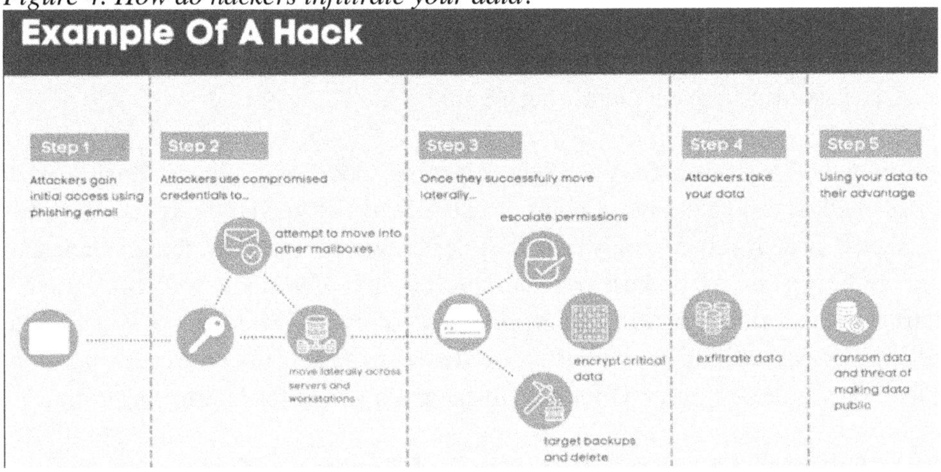

https://www.axiom.tech/how-do-hackers-infiltrate-your-data-a-guide-to-understanding-their-process-and-how-to-ensure-proper-data-breach-prevention/

Another malware also used in the Sony attack, which is known as the Server Message Block (SMB) worm tool, was made up of several features and capabilities such as a "Listening Implant, Proxy Tool, Lightweight Backdoor, Destructive Hard Drive Tool, and Destructive Target Cleaning Tool". This malware was so sophisticated to the extent that, it spread to and infiltrated other computers on the same network as the infected computer, brute-forces login mechanisms, and tried to have full control over the affected systems, send logs and other critical system information back to the attacker's command and control (C2) computer, causing havoc, and self-destroy when there's a need to do so.

Exploited Vulnerabilities in Sony's Infrastructure

- The main vulnerability that led to the compromise of Sony's system was Human negligence or lack of proper security training of employees, or simply put, the attackers exploited the weakest link of security, thus, Humans.
- Sony also didn't employ basic security measures that could have served as contingencies in case of human security failure. From the leaked documents, security steps such as multi-factor authentication (MFA) were not in place for critical aspects of Sony's systems which allowed the attackers to gain access to their network with just login credentials and no additional security verifications.
- Also, the SMB worm tool was able to spread across Sony's network and was able to bypass login mechanisms using brute-force, which simply im-

plies how Sony employs weaker passwords on their systems. From one of the leaked documents, it was revealed that the word "password" was used to sign 3 certificates which shows how Sony was less cautious about using strong passwords to protect their infrastructure.

From the SMB worm tool, a "Lightweight backdoor" was utilized which served as a backdoor listener, or as a point of entrance which the attackers use to come inside the system and go at any time they desire, which also gives them remote access to the system. All of these were possible because of a "not so well-configured" Intrusion Detection System (IDS) by Sony. A poorly configured or lack of IDS in network or system infrastructure leaves systems on the network prone to infiltration and allows attackers to get a foot hold inside the network for future exploitation.

Data Exfiltration, and Destruction of Company Data

A. Data Exfiltration

The attackers exfiltrated Sony's network using different approaches of spear-phishing emails as well as exploiting vulnerabilities in the company's systems. After the attackers got access to Sony's systems, they employed different kinds of malware which were able to self-replicate and spread across various systems on the network giving them access to substantial amount of sensitive and private data. Such data included unreleased movies, internal communications, and personal information

Figure 5. Data exfiltration diagram

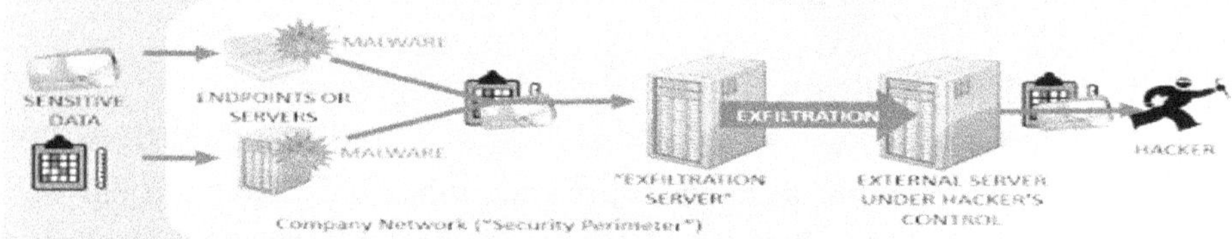

- **Unreleased Movies:** Five unreleased movies were stolen and leaked to the public before their official release, which caused monetary damage to Sony as well as their reputation.
- **Internal Communications:** A significant number of internal emails and documents were accessed and leaked to the public. The contents of some of these documents were so sensitive it led to a major backlash from the public

on how Sony executives treat their employees resulting in the resignation of some of Sony's top executives.

- **Personal Information:** Several private employee information including but not limited to social security numbers, salary information, and addresses was made public. Public access to this information was a significant threat to employee safety and privacy.

B. Destruction of Data

The hack on Sony resulted in about three-quarters of the company's servers and ample amounts of data being erased. The malware the attackers used comprised of different components which could steal and delete data and render computers unusable by directly manipulating and destroying hard drive data past recovery. The Sony hackers also utilized a Destructive Target Cleaning Tool which was a component of the attack malware, this tool's main motive was to render Sony's computers inoperable by overwriting their Master Boot Record (MBR) which is responsible for loading the operating systems needed by the computers to function. So, in simple terms, "no running operating system, no functioning computers". This disrupted Sony's business operations resulting in the loss of over $15 million in operational revenue.

LESSONS FOR INDUSTRIES DEPENDENT ON DIGITAL INFRASTRUCTURE

In the aftermath of the Sony hack, one of the major lessons learnt from the attack is that basic security measures cannot be ignored in an organization (Young, 202). Simple security steps such as utilizing various forms of threat detection software such as patch management tools, endpoint detection systems and monitoring infrastructures could have played a critical role in adverting the intrusion and breach. Organizations, whether public or private, are encouraged to install email filters and firewalls to detect and minimize cybercriminals' access to their network.

Sensitive information and intellectual properties are expected to be properly always secured (Samuelson, 1999). One of the major ruins related to the Sony incident was the company's failure to adequately safeguard its most sensitive data. Some of the best practice recommended by cybersecurity practitioners includes encryption, imbibing the need-to-know policy (Vegh, 2018), requiring employees to use a multi-factor authentication password system before accessing sensitive data, etc. Private organizations should always be on alert as they can be cut up in political conflict between nation-states. Depending on a company's operations, an organization should always be prepared for the likelihood of being a target of attack by a foreign nation (Garrick, 2004).

A takeaway from the Sony attack highlighted the need for companies to proactively create strong public relations tactics to manage the aftermath of high-profile digital breaches. Beyond legal liabilities and the negative press Sony experienced due to its security lapses, the company also dealt with the damaging effects of weeks of sensitive information being out in the open.

GEOPOLITICAL TENSIONS FROM NATION-STATE-SPONSORED CYBERATTACKS: IMPLICATIONS FOR INTERNATIONAL RELATIONS

Nation-state-sponsored cyberattacks have become a potent instrument of geopolitical strategy, influencing international relations and exacerbating tensions among states. These attacks often serve as tools for espionage, disruption, and retaliation, leaving significant political, economic, and social consequences in their wake. A detailed examination of the implications of such cyber operations underscores their transformative impact on global diplomacy, security, and stability.

Erosion of Trust Between Nations

Cyberattacks attributed to nation-states often undermine trust between countries, complicating diplomatic relations. For instance:

- The U.S. government's response to the **2014 Sony Pictures hack**, particularly the FBI's attribution of the attack to North Korea, was swift but controversial. While the FBI publicly identified North Korea as the perpetrator, cybersecurity experts questioned the reliability of the evidence, arguing that links to malware and IP addresses were insufficient proof and could have been misdirected by the hackers. Critics emphasized the need for more concrete evidence to substantiate claims of North Korean involvement. In retaliation, the U.S. imposed economic sanctions on North Korean officials, further isolating the regime. However, the attack highlighted the challenges of responding to cyber warfare within the existing diplomatic and military frameworks. Unlike conventional warfare, cyberattacks operate in a legally ambiguous global context, complicating efforts to deter or address them. The incident underscored the need for new deterrence strategies and defense mechanisms in cyberspace. The Sony hack also escalated tensions between Washington and Pyongyang, showcasing North Korea's asymmetric warfare strategy and its ability to target Western interests in cyberspace. A criminal complaint later implicated Park Jin Hyok, a member of the Lazarus Group, in the Sony hack and other high-profile attacks, including the Bangladesh Bank heist and the WannaCry ransomware attack. These actions exposed significant vulnerabilities across various sectors, highlighting the persistent global threat of state-sponsored cyberattacks.

- In the same vein, the 2020 **SolarWinds hack**, attributed to Russian intelligence, infiltrated U.S. government agencies and private organizations, eroding U.S.-Russia relations. The attack underscored vulnerabilities in supply chain security and fueled ongoing accusations of Russian interference in Western systems. The White House (April 15, 2021)
- Also, China's cyber-espionage campaigns, such as the **Microsoft Exchange Server hack in 2021**, prompted U.S. allies to publicly condemn Beijing, heightening tensions between China and Western nations. The White House (July 19, 2021)

The Role of Nation-Sponsored Cyberattacks in Political Retaliation and Global Power Dynamics

Cyberattacks sponsored by a nation such as Sony Pictures are today's political sabotage. Unlike conventional war, the North Koreans chose to retaliate against the perceived slights against its leadership by cyber attacking a U. S. corporation to cause it an economic loss and tarnish its reputation. Cyber warfare enables a country. manipulate the entire global network through other means beyond its traditional military and economic capabilities (Kshetri, 2016). For example, North Korea uses cyberattacks, such as cryptocurrency thefts, to bypass economic sanctions and fund its nuclear program, further complicating international efforts to curb Pyongyang's ambitions.

The Sony attack rightly explains the evolution of cyber warfare into a strategic element of warfare policy where nation-states employ it as an instrument both as an act of pressure and as a form of vengeance. Cyberattack actors can achieve effecting interstate coercion, manipulating critical infrastructures, and subverting political rivals using covert operations that do not necessarily involve traditional warfare. Sony's cyber-attack is an example of how states are using technology to tackle political enemies which is a factor that complicates international order and law (Davis, 2015). Similarly, Iran's ongoing cyber campaigns targeting critical infrastructure in the U.S. and Israel have led to retaliatory cyber operations, intensifying hostilities and raising concerns about broader regional instability (CISA, FBI October 2024 fact sheet).

Diplomatic Responses and International Efforts to Mitigate State-Sponsored Cyber Threats

As a result of the hack at Sony, the societies of the world were given the task of establishing new strategies for international relations and the law to address the issue of state cyber terrorism. Closely related to the issue of countermeasures the absence of well-defined international customary law or conventions regarding cyber warfare hinders collective action against threat actors such as North Korea. Even in the case of the USA imposing sanctions for human rights violation, there were not many efforts for international condemnation, partly because of issues such as attribution and the messy nature of geopolitics when dealing with a pariah state like North Korea (Lewis, 2015).

To this end, the Sony attack occasioned calls for a more united front and formation of international intelligence-sharing, public-benefit partnerships, diplomats, and other relevant entities (Perlroth, 2014). The case also caused debate on whether private companies can protect themselves from cyber warfare spearheaded by the state, especially in the event of state-sponsored cyber-attacks such as the one on Sony (Weaver, 2015).

Recommendations for Addressing Geopolitical Tensions

To mitigate the destabilizing effects of nation-state-sponsored cyberattacks, the international community must adopt comprehensive strategies:

a. **Strengthening Multilateral Cooperation:** Enhanced collaboration among nations through forums like the United Nations and NATO can establish clearer norms and coordinated responses to cyber threats.
b. **Developing Cyber Deterrence Strategies:** Nations must balance defensive measures with offensive capabilities to deter adversaries from launching cyberattacks.
c. **Promoting Public-Private Partnerships:** Governments should work closely with the private sector to improve threat intelligence sharing and bolster critical infrastructure defenses.
d. **Enforcing Accountability:** Imposing sanctions, indictments, and other consequences for state-sponsored cyber actors can deter future aggression and uphold international norms.

POST-ATTACK MITIGATION AND CYBERSECURITY LESSONS FOR ORGANIZATIONS

Post-Attack Mitigation

Although Sony had an ineffective security implementation across their systems, they had a post-attack mitigation plan to minimize the impact of attacks across the organization's networks. One of the earlier steps taken by the organization was to temporarily shut down the PlayStation Network and Priority services, enhancing security measures across its network, while consulting with external security firms to triage the incident and investigate thoroughly. After the incident was made known to the public, Sony offered its affected users Identity Protection Services, access to complimentary content, and a year of no-charge credit monitoring to help monitor and safeguard against impersonation and identity fraud which is not uncommon after a hack or data breach.

Network and Database administrators in Sony worked hard to restore from backups which enabled them to continue with normal business operations a few days after the attack. They also investigated the root cause of the network leaks and blocked every hole enhancing security measures across the network.

Recommendations for Future Cyber Defense Strategies

The U.S. Government Accountability Office in its High-Risk Series (2021) highlighted four major cybersecurity challenges faced by both government and other organizations and suggested 10 associated critical actions that both the government and other organizations must take to fight against these challenges. (see figure 6)

Establishing a comprehensive cybersecurity strategy and performing effective oversight	Securing federal systems and information	Protecting cyber critical infrastructure	Protecting privacy and sensitive data
1 Develop and execute a more comprehensive federal strategy for national cybersecurity and global cyberspace.	5 Improve implementation of government- wide cybersecurity initiatives.	8 Strengthen the federal role in protecting the cybersecurity of critical infrastructure (e.g., electricity grid and telecommunications networks).	9 Improve federal efforts to protect privacy and sensitive data.
2 Mitigate global supply chain risks (e.g., installation of malicious software or hardware).	6 Address weaknesses in federal agency information security programs.		10 Appropriately limit the collection and use of personal information and ensure that it is obtained with appropriate knowledge or consent.
3 Address cybersecurity workforce management challenges.	7 Enhance the federal response to cyber incidents.		
4 Ensure the security of emerging technologies (e.g., artificial intelligence and Internet of Things).			

Source: GAO analysis. | GAO-21-288

A major criticism of Sony in the wake of the attack was that the company's failure to prioritize cyber security measures was the major cause of the data loss (Sean et al., 2021). Experts opined that the case would have been different if sensitive information were properly encrypted or stored on a separate server (Chen et al., 2023).

Some of these industry best practices are included.

a. Patch Management: one of the vulnerabilities state actors' exploits is patches (Wilusz, et, al., 2022). An unpatched vulnerability will create room for nefarious actors to gain access to an organization's network system. As little as promptly administering patches and their update can play a great role in bridging the gap that threat actors could exploit to take advantage of an organization. organizations need to implement security policies from the ground up of the organizations' business modeling and not integrate piece-by-piece security features which are mostly prone to basic attacks because of a weaker security foundation (Sigholm, 2013).
b. Endpoint Security: organizations are encouraged to use reputable endpoint security solutions on all devices they use (Zayed, 2016), including mobile devices (Souppaya & Scarfone, 2013), as this will help to protect the organizations' devices from malware and other threat intrusion (Kadrich, 2007).

c. Email Filtering: The need to develop an email and document retention policy can't be taken for granted (Gradwell, 2015), as several private and damaging email communications between top executives about employees were leaked in the Sony attack, and most of these emails were so old, they wouldn't have still existed on their systems if there was an email retention policy in place. On the other hand, phishing is one of the most common attack vectors used by attackers to gain access to an organization's network (Alkhalil, et al., 2021). Email security solutions such as filtering and spam detection systems can help identify and block a malicious email before its delivery to a target (Karim, et, al., 2019).
d. Account Security and Access Control: By far one of the most important measures an organization can take (Das, 2020), the use of multi-factor authentication and access to a document on a need-to-know basis make a system more secure and may discourage attacks (Vegh, 2018).
e. Employee sensitization: humans are usually considered to be the weak link in any organization (Pieters, 2013). Even when an organization has engaged in all best practices, if proper employee or personnel education is not carried out, the attack cannot be averted (Colwill, 2009).

Figure 7. Cyberattack mitigation

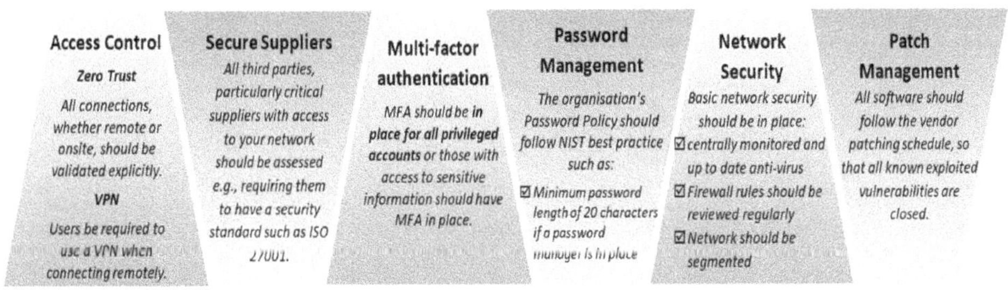

Nation-State Cyber Attacks Impact – Smarttech247

In conclusion, as Choi (2021) puts it, having technical expertise is crucial for effectively preventing and responding to cyber-attacks across all levels of cybersecurity roles. While recommendations for government agencies provide frameworks for mitigating cyber threats, they often assume that employees possess foundational technical skills, such as system patching and data backup management. Without these competencies, even well-designed strategies may fail to achieve their intended impact. Tom Fanning, the Chair of the CISA Cybersecurity Advisory Committee (2023) in commentary on the attack on Colonial Pipeline, opined that cyber risks needed to be normalized for the public with the recognition that cyber-attacks are a reality for the foreseeable future. He further noted that society cannot completely prevent attacks from happening, but what we can do is minimize the impact of those risks by building resilience in our infrastructure and our society. Nations to look no further than the Ukrainian society for an example of the power of societal resilience.

These changes are not easy, but we must hold every person accountable for the lessons learned from every cybersecurity attack we have experienced. Society must also decide whether to make the choices that will lead us to a more secure, resilient, and prosperous future or to allow inaction to dictate a future in which national security and the way of life of its people hang in the balance. We have proven that it can be done but only if we act now.

REFERENCES

Aaron, W. C., Irekponor, O., Aleke, N. T., Yeboah, L., & Joseph, J. E. (2024). Machine learning techniques for enhancing security in financial technology systems.

Aleke, N. T. (2025). Combatting Deepfakes: Ethical Frameworks and Technological Solutions for Preserving Integrity in Digital Media. In Omar, M., & Zangana, H. (Eds.), *Application of Large Language Models (LLMs) for Software Vulnerability Detection* (pp. 375–412). IGI Global Scientific Publishing., DOI: 10.4018/979-8-3693-9311-6.ch010

Alkhalil, Z., Hewage, C., Nawaf, L., & Khan, I. (2021). Phishing attacks: A recent comprehensive study and a new anatomy. *Frontiers of Computer Science*, 3, 563060. DOI: 10.3389/fcomp.2021.563060

Bea Systems. (2024) https://www.baesystems.com/en/digital/feature/the-nation-state-actor#:~:text=The%20Nation%20State%20Actor%20will%20use%20social%20engineering%20to%20target,their%20victim%20in%20doing%20so. Retrieved September 10, 2024

Billo, C., & Chang, W. (2004). *Cyber warfare. An Analysis of the means and motivations of selected nation-states.* ISTS.

Choi, K. S. (2021). The driving force behind cybercrime: Cyber resilience and cyber criminology. [References]. *Journal of Contemporary Criminal Justice*, 37(3), 1–3. DOI: 10.1177/10439862211001631

CISA. (2023). America's Cyber Defense Agency, National Coordinator for Critical Infrastructure Security and Resilience. The Attack on Colonial Pipeline: What We've Learned & What We've Done Over the Past Two Years. https://www.cisa.gov/news-events/news/attack-colonial-pipeline-what-weve-learned-what-weve-done-over-past-two-years

CISA & FBI Fact Sheet. (2024). How to Protect against Iranian Targeting of Accounts Associated with National Political Organizations. October 2024 https://www.cisa.gov/sites/default/files/2024-10/cisa-fbi-protecting-against-irgc-phishing-508c.pdf Retrieved November 28, 2024

Colwill, C. (2009). Human factors in information security: The insider threat–Who can you trust these days? *Information Security Technical Report*, 14(4), 186–196. DOI: 10.1016/j.istr.2010.04.004

Das, S. (2020). *A risk-reduction-based incentivization model for human-centered multi-factor authentication.* Indiana University.

De Tomas Colatin, S. (2021, June 9). Sony Pictures Entertainment attack (2014). Cyber Law Wiki. https://cyberlaw.ccdcoe.org/wiki/Sony_Pictures_Entertainment_attack_(2014)

Ellen Nakashima. "US Attributes Cyberattack on Sony to North Korea," (December 19, 2014), accessed December 10, 2018, https://www. washingtonpost.com/world/national-security/us-attributes-sony-attack-to-north-korea/2014/12/19/fc3aec60-8790-11e4-a702-fa31ff4ae98e_ story.html?utm_term=.831d67544d1f Ellen Nakashima, Craig Timberg, and Andrea Peterson, "Sony Pictures Hack Appears to be Linked to North Korea, Investigators Say," Washington Post, December 3, 2014, accessed November 25, 2024, https://www.washingtonpost.com/world/national-security/hack-at-sony-pictures-appears-linked-to-north-korea/2014/12/03/6c3c7e3e-7b25-11e4-b821-503cc7efed9e_story.html?utm_term=.a21e2ffc8b96

, F. M. (2018). North Korea—South Korea. American Psychological Association EBooks, 121–133. https://doi.org/DOI: 10.1037/0000089-008

FBI. (2014) Update on Sony Investigation https://www.fbi.gov/news/press-releases/update-on-sony-investigation

FBI. (2014). *North Korea Cyber Intrusion*. Federal Bureau of Investigation.

FBI and North Korea Respond to Sony Hack: December 19 and 21, 2014. (2015). CQ Press EBooks, 637–644. https://doi.org/DOI: 10.4135/9781483380506.n69

Framework Security. (2024, June 28). The Sony Pictures breach: A deep dive into a landmark cyberattack. Framework Security. https://www.frameworksec.com/post/the-sony-pictures-breach-a-deep-dive-into-a-landmark-cyber-attack

Heeren-Moon, E. (2023). Risk, reputation and responsibility: Cybersecurity and centralized data in United States civilian federal agencies. *Telecommunications Policy*, 47(2), 102502.

Garrick, B. J., Hall, J. E., Kilger, M., McDonald, J. C., O'Toole, T., Probst, P. S., & Zebroski, E. L. (2004). Confronting the risks of terrorism: Making the right decisions. *Reliability Engineering & System Safety*, 86(2), 129–176. DOI: 10.1016/j.ress.2004.04.003

Gradwell, M. (2015). Retention of email records in New Zealand tertiary institutions (Doctoral dissertation, Open Access the Herenga Waka-Victoria University of Wellington).

Haggard & Lindsay (2015), "North Korea and the Sony Hack: Exporting Instability Through Cyberspace

Hwang & Choi. (2021).. . *International Journal of Cybersecurity Intelligence and Cybercrime*, 4(2), 4–24.

Kadrich, M. (2007). *Endpoint security*. Addison-Wesley Professional.

Karim, A., Azam, S., Shanmugam, B., Kannoorpatti, K., & Alazab, M. (2019). A comprehensive survey for intelligent spam email detection. *IEEE Access : Practical Innovations, Open Solutions*, 7, 168261–168295. DOI: 10.1109/ACCESS.2019.2954791

Khan, K., Su, C. W., Umar, M., & Zhang, W. (2022). Geopolitics of technology: A new battleground? *Technological and Economic Development of Economy*, 28(2), 442–462. DOI: 10.3846/tede.2022.16028

Kshetri, N. (2014). Cyberwarfare in the Korean Peninsula: Asymmetries and strategic responses. *East Asia (Piscataway, N.J.)*, 31(3), 183–201. DOI: 10.1007/s12140-014-9215-1

Lehto, M. (2022). Cyber-attacks against critical infrastructure. In *Cyber security: Critical infrastructure protection* (pp. 3–42). Springer International Publishing. DOI: 10.1007/978-3-030-91293-2_1

Lundbohm, E. (2017). Understanding nation-state attacks. *Network Security*, 2017(10), 5–8. DOI: 10.1016/S1353-4858(17)30101-0

Mazzarella, J. (2015, January 6). The SONY HACK — What happened, how did it happen…. What did we learn? IT News. https://blogs.umb.edu/itnews/2015/01/06/the-sony-hack/

Ozkan-Ozay, M., Akin, E., Aslan, Ö., Kosunalp, S., Iliev, T., Stoyanov, I., & Beloev, I. (2024). A Comprehensive Survey: Evaluating the Efficiency of Artificial Intelligence and Machine Learning Techniques on Cyber Security Solutions. IEEE Access.

Pieters, W. (2013, December). Defining" the weakest link" comparative security in complex systems of systems. In 2013 IEEE 5th International conference on cloud computing technology and science (Vol. 2, pp. 39-44). IEEE.

Q., Xing, L., & Zhou, C. (2019). Probabilistic modeling and analysis of sequential cyber-attacks. Engineering Reports, 1(4). https://doi.org/DOI: 10.1002/eng2.12065

Ribeiro, A. (2024). Growing convergence of geopolitics and cyber warfare continue to threaten OT and ICS environments in 2024. Industrial Cyber, February 18, 2024 https://industrialcyber.co/features/growing-convergence-of-geopolitics-and-cyber-warfare-continue-to-threaten-ot-and-ics-environments-in-2024/#:~:text=Geopolitical%20tensions%20between%20major%20powers,infrastructure%20and%20industrial%20sectors%20worldwide. Retrieved September 12, 2024

Samuelson, P. (1999). Privacy as intellectual property. *Stanford Law Review*, 52(5), 1125. DOI: 10.2307/1229511 PMID: 11503653

Schmitt, M. N. (2010). Cyber operations in international law: The use of force, collective security, self-defense, and armed conflicts. In Proceedings of a workshop on deterring cyberattacks: Informing strategies and developing options for US policy (Vol. 151, pp. 163-64). Washington, DC: National Academies Press.

Chen, L., Drannbauer, E., Ademoroti, A., & Williams, D. H. How Plausible is North Korea's Involvement in the Sony Pictures Hack? A Comprehensive Analysis.

Sigholm, J. (2013). Non-state actors in cyberspace operations. *Journal of Military Studies*, 4(1), 1–37. DOI: 10.1515/jms-2016-0184

Souppaya, M., & Scarfone, K. (2013). Guidelines for managing the security of mobile devices in the enterprise. NIST special publication, 800(124), 124-800.

, T., & Jenkins, T. (2017). An Act of War? The Interview Affair, the Sony Hack, and the Hollywood–Washington Power Nexus Today. Journal of American Studies, 53(1), 1–27. https://doi.org/DOI: 10.1017/S0021875817000512

ROOM, B. (2021). The United States, joined by allies and partners, attributes malicious cyber activity and irresponsible state behavior to the People's Republic of China.

Vegh, L. (2018, February). Cyber-physical systems security through multi-factor authentication and data analytics. In *2018 IEEE International Conference on Industrial Technology (ICIT)* (pp. 1369-1374). IEEE. DOI: 10.1109/ICIT.2018.8352379

Verton, D. (2014) The Sony hack and its larger implications for cybersecurity. Fedscoop December 19, 2014. https://fedscoop.com/sony-hack-matters/ Retrieved September 12, 2024

Wilusz, D., Sadowczyk, D., Wójtowicz, A., & Tasiemski, L. (2022). Long Tail of Security Vulnerabilities and Nation-State APT Actors. *Proceedings Book*, 25(26th), 3.

Young, K. (2021). Cyber Case Study: Sony Pictures Entertainment Hack. Coverlink Insurance November 8, 2021. https://coverlink.com/case-study/sony-pictures-entertainment-hack/ Retrieved September 12, 2024.

Zayed, K. (2016). Information security awareness: Managing web, mobile, and endpoint security; overcoming the challenges of bring your own device. *International Journal of Teaching and Case Studies*, 7(3-4), 271–288. DOI: 10.1504/IJTCS.2016.080929

KEY TERMS AND DEFINITIONS

Brute Force: A method of attempting to gain unauthorized access by systematically trying every possible combination of credentials until the correct one is found.

Data Exfiltration: The unauthorized transfer of data from a computer or network, often carried out by cybercriminals after infiltrating a system.

Data Infiltration: Unauthorized access to a network or system by attackers to gain access to sensitive data.

Destructive Hard Drive: A tool or malware designed to corrupt or erase data stored on a computer's hard drive, often used to disrupt operations or cover the attacker's tracks.

Destructive Target Cleaning: The process of systematically erasing or corrupting data on a targeted system to render it unusable, often as part of a cyberattack.

Hyperlink: A clickable text or graphic in a digital document or webpage that directs the user to another location, file, or webpage when clicked.

Intrusion Detection System (IDS): A cybersecurity tool designed to monitor network traffic or system activities for malicious activities or policy violations, alerting administrators to potential threats.

Lightweight Backdoor: A minimalistic malicious tool that allows attackers to maintain unauthorized access to a system while avoiding detection.

Listening Implant: A malicious program or tool installed on a compromised system to monitor activity, collect data, or relay information back to attackers.

Malware: Malicious software designed to infiltrate, damage, or disrupt computer systems. Common types of malwares include viruses, ransomware, spyware, and trojans.

Master Boot Record (MBR): A section of a hard drive containing essential information about disk partitions and the system's boot process, often targeted by malware to disrupt or control the system's startup.

Multi-Factor Authentication (MFA): A security mechanism requiring two or more verification methods, such as a password, biometric scan, or authentication code, to access a system or account.

Proxy Tool: Software used by attackers to relay communication between a compromised system and their command-and-control servers, masking their identity and location.

Server Message Block (SMB): A network protocol used for sharing files, printers, and communication between devices within a network. Attackers often exploit SMB vulnerabilities for unauthorized access.

Spear Phishing: A targeted cyberattack where attackers send deceptive emails appearing to be from trusted sources to specific individuals or organizations, aiming to steal sensitive information such as login credentials or financial data.

Wiper: A type of malware designed to destroy data on a targeted system, often rendering it irrecoverable and causing significant operational disruption.

Chapter 6
Forensic Artifacts in Operating Systems Windows vs. Linux

Noble Antwi
https://orcid.org/0009-0000-5123-5051
Illinois Institute of Technology, USA

ABSTRACT

The rapid rise of cybercrime, fueled by increased reliance on digital systems, underscores the importance of effective digital forensics. This research investigates forensic artifacts within two widely used operating systems, Windows and Linux, to offer a detailed comparison of their impact on forensic practices. Digital forensic artifacts, such as user activity logs, system logs, application data, and volatile memory artifacts, are key sources of evidence that investigators rely on to reconstruct events, identify threats, and secure convictions in cybercrime cases.

INTRODUCTION

Background and Significance

The increasing reliance on digital devices has led to a rise in cybercrimes and security breaches. With around 17 billion Internet of Things (IoT) devices globally, translating to an average of four devices per person, there is an urgent need for effective cybersecurity measures to address the evolving threats (Lueth, 2020). Computer forensics involves recovering and examining digital data from various devices, ensuring that evidence is preserved in a legally admissible manner (Slonopas, 2024). This field is critical for cases of identity theft, hacking, and cyberterrorism,

DOI: 10.4018/979-8-3373-1102-9.ch006

where digital information is vital. Operating systems, like Windows and Linux, are central to digital forensics, serving as the main platforms for generating and storing forensic artifacts essential for investigations (Messier, 2015). This research compares the forensic artifacts in Windows and Linux, aiming to enhance digital forensic practices and improve outcomes in cybercrime investigations.

Timeline of Important Developments in Digital Forensics

The image below is a diagrammatic representation highlighting key milestones in the evolution of digital forensics, with a focus on developments related to Windows and Linux:

Figure 1. Overview of digital forensics process

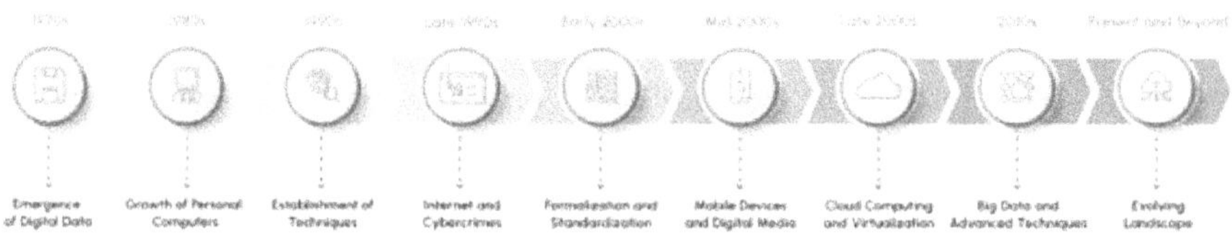

Note. Adapted from What is Digital Forensics?, August 31, 2023 (https://www.oxygenforensics.com/en/resources/what-is-digital-forensics/). Copyright 2023 by Oxygen Forensics.

Scope of the Research

This research examines forensic artifacts essential for digital investigations in Windows and Linux operating systems. The scope will include artifacts related to user activity (such as browser history, recently accessed files), system logs (event logs, system logs), application logs and volatile memory analysis (RAM information). In exploring these areas, the research will provide a comprehensive understanding of how forensic artifacts contribute to investigations in both environments (Adelstein, 2006). Figure 2 below is a conceptual Framework of Digital Forensics in Windows and Linux Environments

Figure 2. Conceptual framework of digital forensics in Windows and Linux environments

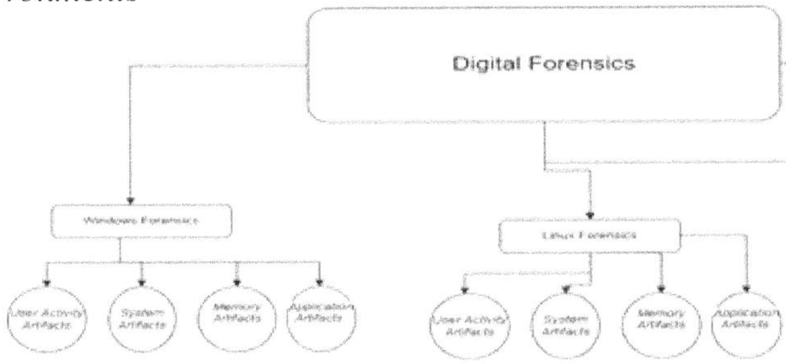

LITERATURE REVIEW

Digital forensics plays a critical role in combating cybercrime by examining data from digital devices to uncover evidence. Over time, it has grown from simple file system analysis to more advanced domains such as memory, network, cloud, and mobile forensics (Abulaish & Alam, 2023). On Windows systems, valuable forensic artifacts like Event Logs, Prefetch files, and the Registry reveal user activity and system events (Casey, 2011). These logs aid investigators in tracing actions, creating timelines, and reconstructing events, although specialized tools are often needed to manage challenges like encryption or fragmentation (Moskvichev & Dolgachev, 2020). In Linux environments, forensic logs, including those stored in /var/log, and bash history offer critical insights into user activities and system behavior, but the open-source architecture requires more advanced manual handling (Adelstein, 2006a). Relevant logs include of:

- /var/log/auth.log: Records authentication attempts, sudo use, and unauthorized access.
- /var/log/syslog: General system messages, including daemon activities.
- /var/log/kern.log: Kernel-related messages, including hardware errors.
- /var/log/messages: System-wide messages from many services.
- ~/.bash_history: Stores commands run in shell, although trivial to change.
- /var/log/audit/audit.log: Detailed system-level event logs, provided auditd is enabled.

These logs help in detecting security incidents, unauthorized access, and system failures. However, Linux's open-source nature means logs can be easily manipulated, and manual handling is often needed to correlate data across various sources. Investigators should also check for log rotation and file integrity, as these logs may not be kept or can be altered by attackers.

Windows and Linux forensic approaches vary significantly. Windows, with its user-friendly design and built-in tools such as Volume Shadow Copies and Prefetch files, simplifies data recovery and application usage tracking, but offers limited customization due to its closed-source nature (Hacker Noob Tips, 2024). Conversely, Linux's decentralized, open-source system allows greater flexibility but demands more ability, particularly in retrieving artifacts from various directories like /var/log (Ligh, Case, Levy, & Walters, 2014). Despite these differences, both operating systems generate essential artifacts for forensic analysis, which are crucial for finding malware, user actions, and system behaviors (Easttom, 2021).

However, there are still significant gaps in these studies, particularly those on multi-platform investigations across both Windows and Linux environments (Carrier, 2005). The increasing complexity of hybrid cloud systems, on top of the anti-forensic feature of encryption and obfuscation techniques limits the extraction and analysis of forensic data (Quick & Choo, 2018). This, therefore, requires more research on cross-platform forensic tools and techniques that will enable investigators to conduct more effective investigations across a variety of computing platforms (Garfinkel, 2010; Altheide & Carvey, 2011).

As shown in Table 1, researchers have made significant strides in understanding the forensic artifacts available in both Windows and Linux systems. These studies provide a foundation for the comparative analysis conducted in this research.

Table 1. Summary of key studies in Windows and Linux forensics

Author(s) & Year	Study Focus	Key Findings	Relevance to Current Study
Casey (2011)	Windows forensic artifacts	Event Logs, Prefetch files, and Registry provide valuable user activity data	Highlights importance of system logs in Windows forensics
Adelstein (2006)	Linux forensic artifacts	/var/log files and bash history offer critical insights into user activities	Emphasizes the significance of log files in Linux forensics
Ligh et al. (2014)	Memory forensics in Windows and Linux	Volatile memory analysis reveals active processes, network connections, and loaded modules	Demonstrates the value of memory forensics in both OS

continued on following page

Table 1. Continued

Author(s) & Year	Study Focus	Key Findings	Relevance to Current Study
Easttom (2021)	Comparative analysis of Windows and Linux artifacts	Both OS generate essential artifacts for forensic analysis, crucial for finding malware, user actions, and system behaviors	Provides foundation for comparative analysis in current study
Quick & Choo (2018)	Challenges in multi-platform investigations	Increasing complexity of hybrid cloud infrastructures and use of encryption complicate retrieval of forensic data	Shows gaps in current forensic methodologies

Additional Insights

Cloud Forensics

The rise of cloud computing has introduced new challenges and opportunities for digital forensics. Cloud environments are dynamic and distributed, making data acquisition and preservation more complex. Investigators must deal with issues such as data jurisdiction, multi-tenancy, and the volatility of cloud data. Tools and techniques for cloud forensics are evolving to address these challenges, focusing on getting data from virtual machines, storage services, and network logs (Ruan et al., 2011).

Mobile Forensics

With the proliferation of smartphones and tablets, mobile forensics has become a crucial area of focus. Mobile devices store a wealth of personal information, including call logs, messages, location data, and app usage. Extracting and analyzing this data requires specialized tools and techniques, as mobile operating systems like iOS and Android have unique security features and data structures (Zdziarski, 2012).

Network Forensics

Network forensics involves capturing, recording, and analyzing network traffic to detect and investigate security incidents. This field has grown in importance with the increasing prevalence of network-based attacks. Tools like Wireshark and Snort are commonly used to monitor network traffic, find suspicious activities, and trace the origins of attacks (Jansen & Ayers, 2007).

OVERVIEW OF WINDOWS AND LINUX OPERATING SYSTEMS

Operating systems (OS) are crucial in managing hardware, software, and providing services to user applications. Windows and Linux, two of the most widely used OS, are key in digital forensic investigations due to their distinct architectures, user bases, and the forensic artifacts they generate. This section offers an overview of both systems and their impact on forensic investigations.

Windows Operating System

Windows is a popular operating system found in many homes and businesses due to its user-friendly design and compatibility with a wide range of software. Its structure is modular, making up key elements like the kernel, device drivers, and the user interface, all of which contribute to how the system is used effectively. According to Carpenter (2011), Windows includes various security features, such as user account control and built-in firewalls, which are essential for protecting against unauthorized access. In the context of digital forensics, Windows generates many artifacts, including event logs, registry entries, and metadata from files. These artifacts are crucial for gaining insights during forensic analysis. Therefore, becoming proficient in Windows is important for anyone pursuing a career in Information Technology, requiring both dedicated learning and practical experience.

Linux Operating System

Linux is a popular open-source operating system created by Linus Torvalds in 1991. (History of Linux - GeeksforGeeks) It is derived from Unix and is recognized for its reliability, security, and adaptability. As a free, Unix-like system, Linux has garnered a significant following among users worldwide. It adheres to the POSIX standard, enabling features like multitasking, virtual memory, shared libraries, and efficient memory management, which are comparable to those in commercial operating systems. A defining characteristic of Linux is its open-source nature; its source code is available for free under the GNU General Public License (GPL), allowing users to share, change, and distribute the software without restrictions (Balakrishnan, 1999). A notable feature of Linux is its modular structure, consisting of a core kernel along with various user-space applications and libraries. This design enables customization for different uses, whether for desktops, servers, or embedded systems (Silberschatz, Galvin, & Gagne, 2018). Linux runs on a wide array of hardware, from personal computers to mobile devices, and serves as the basis for many other systems, including Android. Its strong security measures, such as user permissions and access controls, make it a preferred choice for servers and critical applications (Nemeth, Snyder, Hein, & Whaley, 2017). Additionally, the collaborative nature of its development encourages innovation, with contributions from developers globally, ensuring it stays current with technological advancements (Silberschatz et al., 2018)

FORENSIC ARTIFACTS IN WINDOWS

Forensic artifacts in Windows are critical to understanding user behavior and system events. These artifacts include remnants of user activity, application generated artifacts, system-generated logs, and memory data, which forensic analysts rely on to reconstruct actions and show potential security incidents (Easttom et al., 2024)

User Activity Artifacts

Javed et al. (2024) indicated that, user activity artifacts in Windows forensics provide insights into the actions performed by users on a system. These artifacts include browser history, recent documents, and registry entries. For instance, the analysis of Tor browser artifacts can reveal user activity through registry and storage forensics. Additionally, web browser forensics can retrieve artifacts from popular browsers like Google Chrome and Mozilla Firefox, offering a comprehensive view of user activities (Nelson, Shukla, & Smith, 2020).

System Artifacts

System artifacts are created by the operating system and include elements like event logs, swap files, and system restore points. These artifacts can provide insights into system activities, user logins, and how applications are used. By proving a framework for analyzing Windows system artifacts, investigators can extract and visualize this data more effectively, which aids in examining system-generated information. For instance, event logs can show evidence of logins, authentication processes, and actions taken with elevated privileges (Hashim & Sutherland, 2011). Additionally, Windows systems produce various other forensic artifacts, such as prefetch files, application compatibility caches (Shim Cache), jump lists, and most recently used (MRU) lists, along with UserAssist entries, browser history, cache data, and details about network connections. These artifacts help forensic investigators piece together user actions, program runs, and significant system events, which is essential for reconstructing incidents and spotting potential security threats (Security Ninja, 2016).

Memory Artifacts

Memory artifacts refer to transient data held in a computer's RAM, including details about active processes, network connections, and loaded modules (Mistry & Dahiya, 2019). By examining these artifacts, investigators can gain essential insights into the system's status at a particular moment. Techniques like signature-based volatile memory forensics help find key elements such as private browsing histories, user credentials, and signs of malware. Moreover, memory forensics can reveal active processes and potential threats contained in memory dumps, which are crucial for forensic investigations (Harlan & Peterson, 2020; Casey, 2011). This approach provides valuable information that can support casework and enhance understanding of security incidents.

Application Artifacts

Application artifacts are generated by software applications installed on the system. These artifacts can include configuration files, log files, and user data. For example, forensic analysis of cloud storage applications on Windows 10 can reveal artifacts left by these applications, even after their deletion. Furthermore, web browser forensics can compare artifacts recovered from different browsers, including private-browsing modes, to show user activities (Hashim & Sutherland, 2011)

FORENSIC ARTIFACTS IN LINUX

Linux, being an open-source operating system, offers a unique set of artifacts that differ from those found in other operating systems like Windows. While Linux artifacts are stored differently than in Windows systems, they offer valuable insights into security incidents and user actions. These artifacts can be categorized into user activity artifacts, system artifacts, memory artifacts, and application artifacts. Understanding and analyzing these artifacts is essential for effective forensic investigations in Linux environments (Reddy, 2019)

User Activity Artifacts

User activity artifacts in Linux are crucial for tracking what users have done on the system. Key places to find this data include user directories, like /home/username, which house the .bash_history file that records terminal commands. This file provides insights into the commands and scripts executed by the user. Additionally, logs in the /var/log/ directory, such as lastlog and syslog, offer timestamps for user logins and system events, including sudo command usage. These logs are important for creating timelines of user interactions. Temporary files in directories like /tmp and /var/tmp can also hold remnants of user activities that may serve as valuable forensic evidence (Magnetic Forensics, 2024).

System Artifacts

System artifacts in Linux include automatically generated files and logs that provide insights into operating system processes and configuration changes. A major source is the syslog found in /var/log/syslog, which records various system events, including boot processes, hardware interactions, and errors (Magnetic Forensics, 2024). The dmesg command shows messages from the kernel ring buffer, capturing hardware interactions and startup events, which can help diagnose hardware issues or unexpected reboots (McKay, 2023). Additionally, cron job schedules in /etc/crontab inform about automated tasks, such as when scripts run. Analyzing these cron jobs can reveal any malicious tasks that may have been added (Oliveira, 2022). Another critical source of information is the /etc/passwd and /etc/shadow files. The /etc/passwd file has basic user account details, such as usernames and home directories, while the /etc/shadow file holds encrypted passwords and password expiration information. Access to the /etc/shadow file is limited to root users, which enhances security. These files are essential for identifying authorized users and detecting any unauthorized account activities (Linuxize, 2019).

Memory Artifacts

Memory forensics in Linux systems focuses on examining volatile memory to show and analyze complex cyber-attacks. Techniques like signature-based detection are key for spotting malicious activity within memory. By investigating memory artifacts such as processes, network connections, and loaded modules, forensic analysts can reveal hidden malware and gain insights into cyber threats' behavior. Tools specifically designed for Linux help thorough forensic analysis, supporting the maintenance of system integrity and security. This method is crucial not only for detecting malware but also for understanding its effects on the system, thus offering a detailed perspective on incidents. As highlighted by researchers like Mistry and Dahiya (2019) and Singh and Vigna (2021), these techniques are vital in addressing the challenges posed by increasingly advanced cyber threats.

Application Artifacts

Linux applications generate their own forensic artifacts, including configuration files, logs, and caches. These artifacts can provide evidence of how users interacted with specific applications and what actions were performed. For example, web browsers like Firefox and Chrome, widely used on Linux systems, store history files, cookies, and cached data within user directories such as /home/username/.mozilla/firefox (Nelson, Shukla, & Smith, 2019).

For forensic purposes, email applications like Thunderbird store email content and metadata in .mbox or .eml formats within user directories, offering insight into communications sent or received on the system (Ghafarian, 2019). According to Gangwar (2022), server applications, such as Apache or Nginx, store logs in /var/log/apache2 or /var/log/nginx, which can reveal web server access logs and errors, crucial for tracking attacks or misconfigurations. Database applications like MySQL or PostgreSQL also generate logs that can be examined to trace queries executed by users or attackers, providing evidence of data access or manipulation (Nikkel, 2021).

COMPARATIVE ANALYSIS: WINDOWS VS. LINUX FORENSIC ARTIFACTS

A comprehensive grasp of the similarities and differences in forensic artifacts between Windows and Linux systems is crucial for digital investigations. Both platforms generate artifacts that reflect user interactions, system activities, and application usage. However, their organization, storage locations, and accessibility vary considerably. Analyzing these forensic artifacts will focus on file systems, log files, user activities, volatile memory, and the privacy and security protocols specific to Windows and Linux environments. This examination enables forensic investigators to efficiently navigate and interpret evidence from each system. Recognizing these differences is essential for effective data recovery and incident response, improving the effectiveness of digital forensic practices (Easttom et al., 2024; Domingues et al., 2019).

File System Artifacts

File system artifacts play a crucial role in forensic investigations. Windows employs the New Technology File System (NTFS), featuring a Master File Table (MFT) that logs extensive details about files, including creation, modification, and deletion timestamps (Nelson, Shukla, & Smith, 2019). NTFS's rich metadata aids investigators in reconstructing file histories and activities. Moreover, Windows automatically generates backups, such as Volume Shadow Copies, which are beneficial for recovering deleted files (Microsoft Learn, 2024). In contrast, Linux uses file systems like ext4 and XFS, with ext4 being the predominant choice for general server operations. Ext4 offers enhanced security features, such as security labels for directories, making it suitable for environments requiring strict access controls. However, it lacks support for parallel I/O, which is crucial for efficiently managing large files—a strength of XFS. XFS is fine-tuned for large file storage and retrieval, particularly in settings like media servers or extensive databases. Both ext4 and XFS utilize journaling to aid recovery from crashes, though XFS also incorporates additional backup and recovery capabilities that ext4 does not provide (Pure Storage, 2024).

File System Artifacts: Real-World Applications

File system artifacts in both Windows and Linux serve as foundational elements in forensic investigations, revealing critical information about user actions and system events. However, their accessibility and utility differ significantly, influencing the investigative approach.

For instance, a corporate insider threat investigation highlighted the utility of Windows Prefetch files, which recorded details of unauthorized FTP client usage to exfiltrate sensitive data. The investigator analyzed the Prefetch files alongside AmCache, which provided metadata, including the executable's SHA-1 hash and first execution time. Figure 3 is an illustrative example of Pre-fetch file

Figure 3. Prefetch files

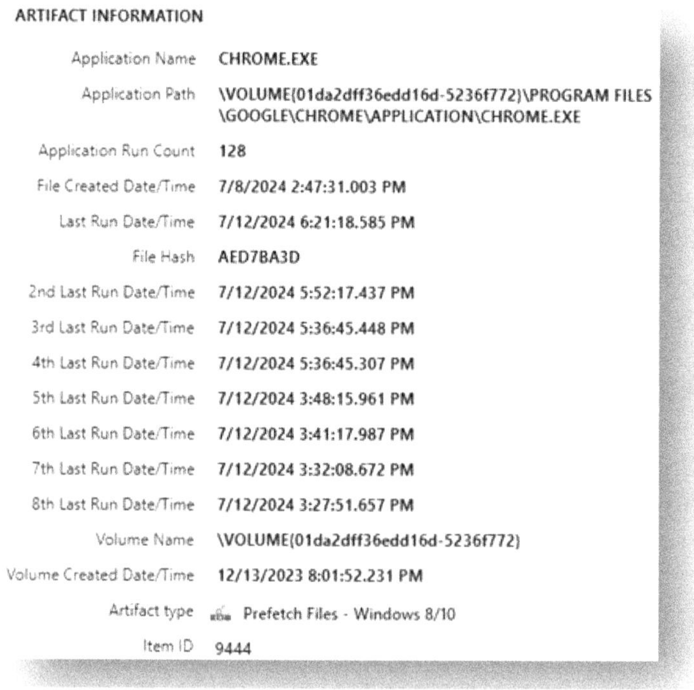

This corroborated findings from PowerShell logs, revealing script execution linked to unauthorized data transfers (Magnet Forensics, 2024a). Such centralized artifact storage in Windows simplifies forensic workflows, enabling faster and more comprehensive evidence gathering.

In contrast, Linux's open-source architecture provides flexibility but demands manual efforts for artifact correlation. A breach involving a compromised Linux server demonstrated this challenge. Investigators used The Sleuth Kit (TSK) to recover deleted files and identified unauthorized edits to the /var/log/auth.log file. The figure 4 below illustrates a section of the auth,log file

Figure 4. Section of auth.log

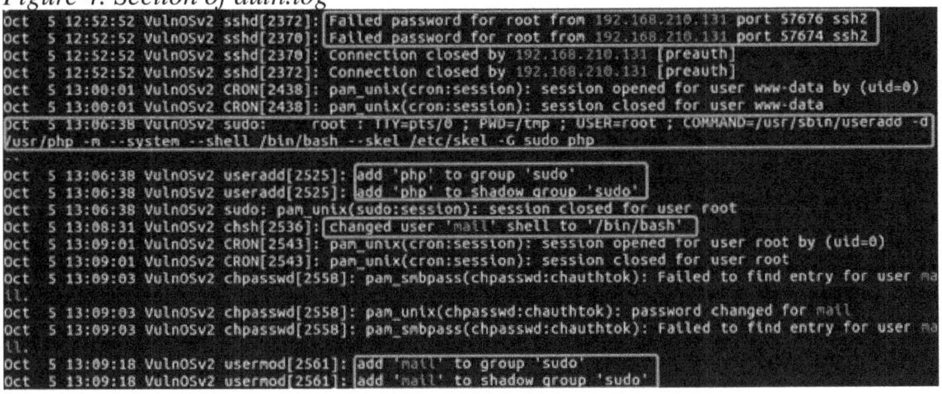

```
Oct  5 12:52:52 VulnOSv2 sshd[2372]: Failed password for root from 192.168.210.131 port 57676 ssh2
Oct  5 12:52:52 VulnOSv2 sshd[2370]: Failed password for root from 192.168.210.131 port 57674 ssh2
Oct  5 12:52:52 VulnOSv2 sshd[2370]: Connection closed by 192.168.210.131 [preauth]
Oct  5 12:52:52 VulnOSv2 sshd[2372]: Connection closed by 192.168.210.131 [preauth]
Oct  5 13:00:01 VulnOSv2 CRON[2438]: pam_unix(cron:session): session opened for user www-data by (uid=0)
Oct  5 13:00:01 VulnOSv2 CRON[2438]: pam_unix(cron:session): session closed for user www-data
Oct  5 13:06:38 VulnOSv2 sudo:     root : TTY=pts/0 ; PWD=/tmp ; USER=root ; COMMAND=/usr/sbin/useradd -d
/usr/php -m --system --shell /bin/bash --skel /etc/skel -G sudo php
--
Oct  5 13:06:38 VulnOSv2 useradd[2525]: add 'php' to group 'sudo'
Oct  5 13:06:38 VulnOSv2 useradd[2525]: add 'php' to shadow group 'sudo'
Oct  5 13:06:38 VulnOSv2 sudo: pam_unix(sudo:session): session closed for user root
Oct  5 13:08:31 VulnOSv2 chsh[2536]: changed user 'mail' shell to '/bin/bash'
Oct  5 13:09:01 VulnOSv2 CRON[2543]: pam_unix(cron:session): session opened for user root by (uid=0)
Oct  5 13:09:01 VulnOSv2 CRON[2543]: pam_unix(cron:session): session closed for user root
Oct  5 13:09:03 VulnOSv2 chpasswd[2558]: pam_smbpass(chpasswd:chauthtok): Failed to find entry for user ma
il.
Oct  5 13:09:03 VulnOSv2 chpasswd[2558]: pam_unix(chpasswd:chauthtok): password changed for mail
Oct  5 13:09:03 VulnOSv2 chpasswd[2558]: pam_smbpass(chpasswd:chauthtok): Failed to find entry for user ma
il.
Oct  5 13:09:18 VulnOSv2 usermod[2561]: add 'mail' to group 'sudo'
Oct  5 13:09:18 VulnOSv2 usermod[2561]: add 'mail' to shadow group 'sudo'
```

This log traced a brute-force attack, followed by successful root access. Further analysis of the .bash_history file revealed the commands executed by the attacker to escalate privileges and create malicious scripts (Forensic Focus, 2024). This case underscores Linux's reliance on dispersed yet highly informative file system artifacts.

These examples illustrate the nuanced approaches needed for each platform: Windows' structured centralization aids rapid investigation, while Linux's manual log correlation provides deeper, albeit slower, insights (Reyes, 2007).

LOG FILES AND USER ACTIVITY

Log files and user activity records are essential for monitoring user interactions and system events. In Windows, log data is primarily housed in the Event Viewer, particularly within directories like C:\Windows\System32\winevt\Logs. These logs document a variety of system activities, including login attempts, application errors, and security warnings. Windows also generates Prefetch files that keep track of executed programs and their timestamps, offering valuable insights into user behavior (Ligh et al., 2014). Conversely, Linux organizes its logs in the /var/log/ directory. Key files include auth.log, which captures user authentication attempts, and syslog, which logs general system events. Additionally, user commands are recorded in .bash_history within each user's home directory, providing a direct account of command-line usage. This functionality is like Windows' Prefetch files but is more focused on documenting command-line activities (Casey, 2011).

Log Files and User Activity: Investigative Insights

Windows Log Analysis: Tracking Insider Threats

In a data theft case, Windows Event Logs proved invaluable for tracking user activity and system changes. The forensic team used the Security Log to show unauthorized RDP sessions, and the System Log revealed privilege escalations during the same period. USB device activity, extracted from the USBSTOR registry key, confirmed that an external drive was connected, likely used for transferring sensitive files. Prefetch and AmCache artifacts further corroborated the findings by indicating the execution of unauthorized applications, creating a detailed timeline of events (SANS Institute, 2024).

Linux Log Analysis: Reconstructing Attacker Actions

A separate investigation on a Linux server involved analyzing /var/log/syslog to track system events. Investigators noted anomalies in daemon activities, correlating them with suspicious user logins recorded in /var/log/auth.log. Using command-line tools, they examined .bash_history to show actions taken by the attacker, such as downloading malicious files and attempting privilege escalations. The logs offered a granular view of the attack timeline, despite being dispersed across multiple locations (Forensic Focus, 2024).

VOLATILE MEMORY ARTIFACTS

Volatile memory, or RAM, holds vital temporary data such as active processes, open network connections, and cached files, which are crucial for forensic investigations. In Windows, tools like Volatility and Rekall are commonly employed to capture and analyze memory dumps, revealing insights into processes, threads, and network activities now of acquisition (Adams & McDonough, 2022). These memory artifacts can uncover malware, encryption keys, and session information for users who are currently active (Ligh et al., 2014). While Linux memory forensics shares similarities with its Windows counterpart, it poses unique challenges due to its modular architecture. Tools like LiME are used for memory capture, but analyzing these artifacts requires a deeper understanding of Linux processes and structure (Palhière, 2020). Linux memory artifacts can offer insights into running processes, socket connections, and loaded kernel modules, which are essential for detecting rootkits or malware that may exist solely in memory.

Table 2 provides a comparative overview of key forensic artifacts in Windows and Linux systems, highlighting their distinct characteristics and tools used for analysis. Table 2 further illustrates the similarities and differences between these operating systems in terms of forensic artifact generation and analysis.

Table 2. Comparative analysis of forensic artifacts in Windows and Linux systems

Aspect	Windows	Linux
File System	NTFS with Master File Table (MFT)	ext4 and XFS
File System Features	Rich metadata, Volume Shadow Copies	Enhanced security (ext4), Fine-tuned for large files (XFS)
Log Files Location	Event Viewer (C:\Windows\System32\winevt\Logs)	/var/log/ directory
User Activity Tracking	Prefetch files, Event logs	auth.log, syslog, .bash_history
Memory Analysis Tools	Volatility, Rekall	LiME (Linux Memory Extractor), Volatility
Memory Artifact Types	Processes, threads, network activities	Running processes, socket connections, loaded kernel modules
Application Artifacts	Configuration files, log files, user data in AppData folders	Configuration files in /etc, logs in /var/log, user data in home directories

Memory Forensics in a Real-Life Scenario

In a recent case, a major healthcare provider experienced a sophisticated cyber-attack involving fileless malware. This type of malware is particularly challenging because it doesn't leave traditional file traces on the system, making it difficult to detect with standard antivirus software. The IT security team turned to volatile memory forensics to uncover the attack.

Using the Volatility framework, they captured and analyzed the memory dump from an infected system. The analysis revealed the presence of fileless malware, which had been using legitimate system processes to execute its payload and communicate with external command-and-control servers. By examining the memory, the team was able to identify the malware's behavior, including the processes it injected into, the network connections it established, and the data it attempted to exfiltrate. The figure 4 below Illustrates the memory acquisition and analysis process.

Figure 5. Memory acquisitiona and analysis

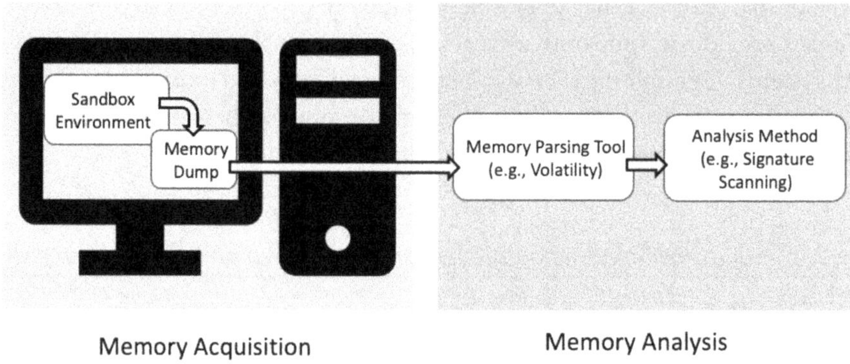

This investigation was crucial in understanding the full scope of the attack. The insights gained from the memory analysis allowed the healthcare provider to implement more effective security measures, such as enhanced monitoring of system processes and network traffic, to prevent similar attacks in the future. This case highlights the importance of volatile memory forensics in detecting and mitigating advanced cyber threats that evade traditional detection methods (Nyholm et al., 2022).

FORENSIC TOOLS FOR WINDOWS AND LINUX

Forensic investigations often require specialized tools that can extract, analyze, and preserve digital evidence from both Windows and Linux systems. The effectiveness of these tools depends on the operating system and the type of artifacts being investigated. This section provides an overview of commonly used forensic tools for Windows and Linux, detailing their features and strengths in specific scenarios.

Windows Forensic Tools

Windows forensic tools are designed to handle the complexities of the Windows operating system, including its proprietary file systems (NTFS) and the wide array of user activity and system logs generated. One of the most widely used tools for Windows forensic investigations is FTK Imager, which allows investigators to create forensic images of disks and volumes, preserving the integrity of evidence while enabling detailed analysis. FTK Imager is particularly effective for recovering deleted files and metadata, offering a comprehensive view of user activity. Another powerful tool is EnCase Forensic, which is highly regarded for its ability to analyze Windows-specific artifacts such as registry files, Prefetch data, and event logs.

EnCase's advanced filtering capabilities help forensic professionals quickly sift through large datasets to find relevant artifacts. Volatility, a memory analysis tool, is invaluable for investigating Windows volatile memory. It extracts data related to running processes, network connections, and open files, making it possible to uncover malware and rootkits existing in memory. Additionally, X-Ways Forensics offers a comprehensive suite of tools for disk analysis, file carving, and metadata extraction, with a strong focus on Windows systems. Another tool worth noting Parabens E3, which I have come to love due to its ease of use, also takes away the heavy load from the investigator by doing most of the analysis. These tools collectively provide forensic investigators with the ability to extract detailed information from Windows environments, often focusing on user activity, file system analysis, and memory forensics (Casey, 2019).

Linux Forensic Tools

Linux systems require specialized forensic tools to effectively analyze diverse file systems. The Sleuth Kit (TSK) is a robust framework for analyzing file systems such as ext4 and XFS, enabling investigators to recover deleted files and track file metadata (Carvey & Altheide, 2011). Paired with TSK, Autopsy provides a user-friendly graphical interface that simplifies the processes of file recovery, keyword searches, and metadata analysis, making it an essential tool for forensic investigations.

For memory analysis, LiME (Linux Memory Extractor) is designed to capture the contents of volatile memory, helping find rootkits and other malicious software that may not leave traces on disk (Carvey & Altheide, 2011). Additionally, foremost serves as a file carver that can recover deleted files based on their headers, while tools like Chkrootkit and Rootkit Hunter focus specifically on detecting rootkits within Linux environments (Carvey & Altheide, 2011).

Table 3 provides a comparative overview of forensic tools commonly used in Windows and Linux environments, highlighting their primary functions and key features

Table 3. Comparison of forensic tools for Windows and Linux systems

Feature	Windows Tools	Linux Tools
Disk Imaging	FTK Imager	dd, dcfldd
File System Analysis	EnCase Forensic, X-Ways Forensics	The Sleuth Kit (TSK), Autopsy
Memory Analysis	Volatility	LiME (Linux Memory Extractor)
File Recovery	FTK Imager, EnCase Forensic	Foremost, Scalpel
Malware Detection	Windows Defender, Volatility	Chkrootkit, Rootkit Hunter

continued on following page

Table 3. Continued

Feature	Windows Tools	Linux Tools
User Interface	Mostly GUI-based	Command-line and GUI options
Artifact Analysis	Registry Explorer, Event Log Explorer	Log2Timeline, Plaso
Network Forensics	Wireshark, NetworkMiner	Wireshark, Tcpdump
All-in-One Solution	EnCase Forensic, Parabens E3	SIFT Workstation

It is however worth noting that most of these tool's work in both systems in retrieving forensics artifacts.

IMPACTS OF EMERGING TECHNOLOGIES ON DIGITAL FORENSICS

The rapid evolution of technology has significantly transformed the landscape of digital forensics. This section examines how emerging trends, particularly cloud computing, the Internet of Things (IoT), and Artificial Intelligence (AI), are reshaping forensic practices and presenting new challenges and opportunities for investigators.

Cloud Computing

Cloud computing has fundamentally altered the way digital evidence is stored, accessed, and analyzed. Traditional forensic methods often rely on physical access to storage media and are no longer sufficient in cloud environments. Investigators now face challenges related to data sovereignty, remote evidence collection, and the distributed nature of cloud storage (O'Shaughnessy & Keane, 2017). One of the primary challenges in cloud forensics is the lack of physical access to servers. As Brittain notes, "Gone, for the most part, are the days when the forensics investigator could pop out the hard drive of an on-premises server for a forensic image and simply analyze it for clues on what happened" (Lawton, 2023). This shift necessitates innovative approaches to evidence acquisition and analysis. To address these challenges, forensic investigators must:

1. Develop new tools and techniques for remote data acquisition
2. Collaborate closely with cloud service providers
3. Understand the legal implications of cross-jurisdictional investigations

Despite these challenges, cloud computing also offers opportunities. The vast computing resources available in the cloud can be used to process large volumes of data more efficiently than ever before (Lawton, 2023).

Internet of Things (IoT)

The proliferation of IoT devices has expanded the scope of digital forensics beyond traditional computers and smartphones. These devices, ranging from smart home assistants to wearable technology, generate vast amounts of data that can be crucial in investigations' devices can serve as "digital witnesses," capturing traces of activities that could be immensely helpful during forensic investigations (Cognixia, 2020). For example:

- Smart home devices may record audio or video evidence
- Wearable devices can provide location data and biometric information
- Connected vehicles can offer insights into a suspect's movements

However, IoT forensics also presents unique challenges:

1. Device heterogeneity: The wide variety of IoT devices and protocols complicates evidence collection and analysis.
2. Data volatility: Many IoT devices have limited storage, potentially leading to the loss of critical evidence.
3. Encryption: Increasing use of encryption in IoT communications can hinder investigators' ability to access and interpret data.

Artificial Intelligence (AI)

AI and machine learning are revolutionizing digital forensics by enhancing the efficiency and accuracy of investigations. These technologies can automate many aspects of the forensic process, from data collection to analysis. Key applications of AI in digital forensics include:

1. Pattern recognition: AI can identify patterns and anomalies in large datasets that human investigators might miss.
2. Image and video analysis: Advanced AI algorithms can enhance and authenticate visual evidence, aiding in tasks such as facial recognition and object detection.
3. Natural language processing: AI can analyze text-based communications to identify relevant information and patterns.

As noted by Cornerstone Discovery (n.d.), "AI technologies help specialists investigate cyber-crimes quickly by sifting through the unstructured forensics data investigators collected." This capability is particularly valuable given the increasing volume and complexity of digital evidence. However, the use of AI in forensics also raises concerns:

1. Reliability: AI systems may produce false positives or inaccurate conclusions, necessitating human oversight.
2. Explainability: The "black box" nature of some AI algorithms can make it challenging to explain findings in court.
3. Legal and ethical considerations: The use of AI in forensics raises questions about privacy and the admissibility of AI-generated evidence.

While emerging technologies present significant challenges to traditional forensic practices, they also offer powerful new tools for investigators. As the digital landscape continues to evolve, forensic professionals must adapt their methods and embrace modern technologies to still be effective in their work. To illustrate the future trends about the rise in these technologies, table 4 below summarizes what has been written above and more.

Table 4. Impact of new technology on digital forensics

Trend/Technology	Description	Impact on Digital Forensics
AI and Machine Learning	Automated data analysis, pattern recognition	Faster processing of large datasets, improved anomaly detection
Cloud Forensics	Analysis of data from cloud platforms	Challenges in data retrieval, opportunities for remote access
IoT Forensics	Extracting data from interconnected devices	Expanded scope of evidence sources, new analytical challenges
Blockchain Forensics	Tracing transactions on blockchain networks	Enhanced cryptocurrency crime investigations
Big Data Analytics	Processing and analyzing massive datasets	Improved pattern detection in complex data structures
Automated Forensic Tools	Streamlining repetitive tasks	Reduced investigation time, focus on complex analysis
VR and AR	Immersive training and evidence visualization	Enhanced forensic training and crime scene analysis
Quantum Computing	Solving complex cryptographic problems	Potential for faster data decryption and advanced simulations

continued on following page

Table 4. Continued

Trend/Technology	Description	Impact on Digital Forensics
Advanced Image/Video Processing	Enhancing and authenticating visual evidence	Improved recovery and analysis of digital media
Forensic Readiness	Proactive preparation for investigations	Faster response to incidents, reduced investigation costs

BEST PRACTICES IN FORENSIC INVESTIGATIONS OF WINDOWS AND LINUX

In digital forensic investigations, adhering to best practices is essential to ensure the integrity and reliability of the evidence collected. This section outlines the best practices for getting, preserving, analyzing, and documenting forensic artifacts in both Windows and Linux environments.

Acquisition of Artifacts

Acquisition of the artifacts is that very first crucial step in the forensic process. It involves creating bit-for-bit copies of storage media to preserve original data. For both Windows and Linux systems, the use of write-blockers is paramount to ensure no alteration of original data in the acquisition process (Cybrary, 2020). Windows investigators may use specific tools such as FTK Imager or EnCase to capture disk images that include most file systems and related artifacts (Carvey & Altheide, 2011). In the Linux environment, dd and dcfldd are the common tools used; these tools are versatile and powerful in data acquisition. The chain of custody must be meticulously kept; everything done by the process of acquisition must be well documented to keep the integrity of the evidence. For best acquisitions, the guidelines below will help in doing that:

1. Use write-blockers:
    - For Windows: Employ hardware write-blockers for physical drives
    - For Linux: Use software write-blocking techniques like mounting drives as read-only
2. Create forensic images:
    - Windows: Use FTK Imager or EnCase
    - Linux: Utilize dd or dcfldd commands
3. Verify image integrity:

    - Calculate and document hash values (MD5 and SHA-256) for all acquired images
    - Use tools like HashMyFiles for Windows or sha256sum for Linux
4. Document the acquisition process:
    - Record hardware details, tool versions, and command-line arguments used
    - Note any error messages or unusual occurrences during acquisition
5. Maintain chain of custody:
    - Use tamper-evident bags for physical evidence
    - Log all accesses to the evidence, including date, time, and reason for access

Preservation and Analysis

The data should be preserved after getting the artifacts so that tampering or loss of the data can be avoided. The data must be stored in access-controlled environments; forensic images should be verified with hash functions (for example, MD5 or SHA-1) for checking the integrity of the data (Sammons, 2014). When the analysis is done, each operating system should have its corresponding forensic tools. While in the Windows systems, Autopsy and X1 Social Discovery tools can be used in the extraction and analysis of user activities and the system logs, most forensic analyses carried out on a Linux-based system are done using command-line tools, for example, Plaso or SIFT Workstation (which is a work stations comprising of several tools developed by SANS institute), enabling deep analysis of log files and system configurations. Original artifacts must not be changed by following a non-intrusive analytical approach. Analysts must work with copies of the raw data to avoid unintentional changes. To simplify things, the steps below will serve as a guiding principle for proper preservation of evidence

1. Work on copies of forensic images:
    - Never analyze original evidence directly
    - Create working copies for analysis, preserving the master copy
2. Use right analysis tools:
    - Windows: Autopsy, X-Ways Forensics, or EnCase
    - Linux: The Sleuth Kit (TSK), Autopsy, or SIFT Workstation
3. Document all analysis steps:
    - Maintain a detailed log of all commands and actions performed
    - Record timestamps for each significant finding
4. Employ data carving techniques:
    - Use tools like Scalpel or Foremost to recover deleted files

- Document file signatures and carving parameters used

5. Analyze volatile data:
    - For Windows: Use Volatility or Rekall for memory analysis
    - For Linux: Employ LiME (Linux Memory Extractor) followed by Volatility
6. Examine system-specific artifacts:
    - Windows: Analyze Registry hives, Event Logs, and Prefetch files
    - Linux: Investigate /var/log files, bash history, and systemd journal logs

Reporting and Documentation

Effective reporting and documentation are essential components of any forensic investigation. Reports must clearly outline the procedures followed during acquisition, analysis, and findings to be understandable to non-technical stakeholders (Easttom, 2021). Key elements include a structured format that begins with an executive summary, clear articulation of findings, use of visual aids for complex data, and thorough documentation of challenges faced, and decisions made. Adhering to these best practices enhances the credibility of findings, ensuring that forensic investigations are conducted systematically and reliably, which is crucial in legal contexts.

Figure 5 illustrates the best practices in digital forensic investigations for Windows and Linux systems, highlighting the four key stages: acquisition of artifacts, preservation, analysis, and reporting and documentation.

Figure 6. Best practices in digital forensic investigations for Windows and Linux systems

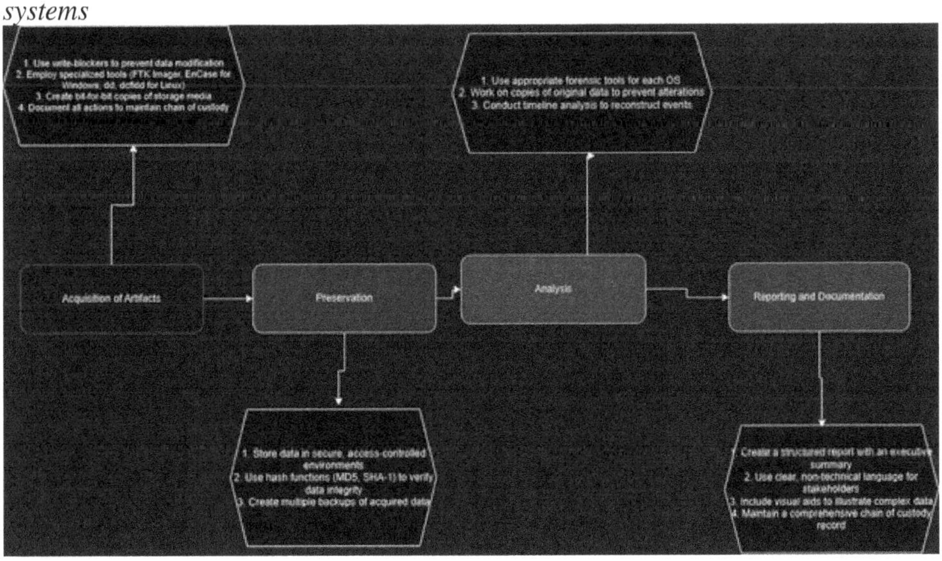

For a standardized and well structure documentation, enhance reporting practices with these actionable steps:

1. Structure your report:
    - Executive summary
    - Methodology
    - Findings
    - Analysis
    - Conclusions
    - Appendices (for technical details)
2. Use clear, concise language:
    - Avoid technical jargon when possible
    - Define necessary technical terms
3. Include visual aids:
    - Use screenshots, diagrams, and charts to illustrate complex concepts
    - Create timelines of noteworthy events
4. Detail your methodology:
    - List all tools used, including version numbers
    - Explain why specific techniques were chosen
5. Address potential challenges:
    - Discuss any limitations in the investigation
    - Explain how encrypted or inaccessible data was handled
6. Provide a findings summary:
    - Use bullet points for key discoveries
    - Relate findings to the initial investigation objectives
7. Include recommendations:
    - Suggest further areas of investigation if applicable
    - Provide actionable steps for remediation or improvement
8. Peer review:
    - Have another forensic analyst review the report for accuracy and clarity
    - Address any feedback before finalizing the report

REAL-WORLD APPLICATIONS OF DIGITAL FORENSICS

Digital forensics has proven to be an invaluable tool in solving complex criminal cases, providing critical evidence that can lead to the identification and prosecution of perpetrators. Here are some notable real-world examples where digital forensics played a crucial role:

The BTK Serial Killer

Dennis Rader, infamously known as the BTK (Bind, Torture, Kill) killer, terrorized Wichita, Kansas, for over three decades, committing ten murders between 1974 and 1991. Despite many investigations, Rader managed to evade capture for years. However, in 2004, he reignited his communication with the police and media, sending a floppy disk to the authorities. Rader believed the disk was untraceable, but digital forensics experts were able to recover deleted data from it. This data led them to a computer at a local church, where Rader was a congregation president. The metadata on the disk contained the name "Dennis" and the church's location, which ultimately led to Rader's arrest and conviction. This case highlights the power of digital forensics in uncovering hidden evidence and solving cold cases (TickTechTold, 2023).

The Boston Marathon Bombing

On April 15, 2013, two bombs exploded near the finish line of the Boston Marathon, resulting in three deaths and hundreds of injuries. The attack sent shockwaves across the nation, and a massive search ensued. Digital forensics played a pivotal role in this investigation. Investigators analyzed surveillance footage, cellphone data, and social media activity to piece together the events leading up to the bombing. By meticulously examining these digital traces, they were able to identify the suspects, Tamerlan and Dzhokhar Tsarnaev. The analysis of their digital footprints provided crucial insights into their planning and execution of the attack, ultimately leading to their capture. This case underscores the importance of digital forensics in modern counter-terrorism efforts (TickTechTold, 2023).

Catching the Catfish

In a more personal but equally significant case, a woman named Sarah was deceived by a man she met online, who went by the name "Chris." Over time, Sarah grew suspicious of "Chris" and hired a private investigator to uncover the truth. The investigator used digital forensics tools to analyze the images and messages sent by "Chris." By examining metadata and tracing the IP address, the investigator discovered that "Chris" was a catfish using a fake identity. This revelation helped

Sarah move on from the deception and highlighted the role of digital forensics in protecting individuals from online fraud and identity theft (TickTechTold, 2023).

These cases illustrate the significant impact of digital forensics in solving crimes and protecting individuals. By uncovering critical evidence hidden within digital data, forensic experts can provide law enforcement with the tools needed to bring criminals to justice.

CONCLUSION

The field of digital forensics is constantly evolving with the development of technology. This research explored essential aspects of forensic analysis in both Windows and Linux environments, with emphasis on the critical processes of artifact acquisition, preservation, and examination. Significant differences were found between the two operating systems. Windows provides most of the user activity artifacts, system logs, and registry entries that help in understanding user activities. On the other hand, Linux systems are quite potent with their command-line utilities and log files, although they often require a higher level of technical ability to extract and analyze data efficiently. Best practices in forensic investigations should be followed to keep the integrity of evidence intact.

Proper acquisition techniques, such as the use of write-blockers and specialized tools, will ensure that data is not altered. This evidence must be preserved in secure, access-controlled environments to avoid tampering or loss; hash functions should be used to set up the integrity of forensic images. This analysis must be done using the right tools specific to each operating system; all should be non-intrusive and work with replicas of the original data. Forensic analysts ensure their investigations are well-organized and reliable, following these standards, which affects the credibility of results.

REFERENCES

Adelstein, F. (2006). Live forensics: Diagnosing your system without killing it first. *Communications of the ACM*, 49(2), 63–66. DOI: 10.1145/1113034.1113070

Adelstein, F. (2018). Live forensics: Diagnosing your system without killing it first. *Communications of the ACM*, 49(2), 63–66. DOI: 10.1145/1113034.1113070

Balakrishnan, S. (1999). The Linux operating system. *Resonance*, 4(4), 64–72. DOI: 10.1007/BF02838342

Balasubramaniyan, V. A., Poonguzhali, E., & Anbalagan, G. (2020). System of collection and analysis event log from sources under control of Windows operating system. *Semantic Scholar*. https://www.semanticscholar.org/paper/40ff547a0b5472801516df565eef00636427cb7c

Carpenter, T. (2012). *Microsoft Windows Operating System Essentials*. John Wiley & Sons.

Carrier, B., & Spafford, E. H. (2004). An event-based digital forensic investigation framework. *Digital Investigation*, 1(1), 2–12.

Carvey, H., & Altheide, C. (2011). *Digital forensics with open source tools*. Elsevier.

Cognixia. (2020, January 22). How can IoT help digital forensics? *Cognixia*. https://www.cognixia.com/blog/how-can-iot-help-digital-forensics/

Cornerstone Discovery. (n.d.). The future is now — The impact of AI on digital forensics. Retrieved November 25, 2024, from https://cornerstonediscovery.com/the-future-is-now-the-impact-of-ai-on-digital-forensics/

Cybrary. (2020, January 21). *Write blockers: A central part of a forensic analyst's toolbox*.

Cybrary. https://www.cybrary.it/blog/write-blockers-central-part-forensic-analysts- toolbox

Domingues, P., Frade, M., Andrade, L. M., & Silva, J. V. (2019). Digital forensic artifacts of the Your Phone application in Windows 10. *Digital Investigation*, 30, 32–42. DOI: 10.1016/j.diin.2019.06.003

Easttom, C., Butler, W., Phelan, J., Bhagavatula, R. S., Steuber, S., Rodriguez, K., & Naseer, Z. (2024). *Windows Forensics: Understand Analysis Techniques for Your Windows*. Springer Nature. DOI: 10.1007/979-8-8688-0193-8

Forensic Focus. (2024). A Linux forensics starter case study. https://www.forensicfocus.com/articles/a-linux-forensics-starter-case-study/

Gangwar, M. (2022, August 3). NGINX access logs and error logs. DigitalOcean. h ttps://www.digitalocean.com/community/tutorials/nginx-access-logs-error-logs

Garfinkel, S. L. (2010). Digital forensics research: The next 10 years. *Digital Investigation*, 7, S64–S73. DOI: 10.1016/j.diin.2010.05.009

Ghafarian, A. (2019). Capabilities of Email Forensic Tools. In *Intelligent Computing:Proceedings of the 2019 Computing Conference,* Volume 2 (pp. 514-528). Springer I nternational Publishing.

Hacker Noob Tips. (2024). Windows forensics: Techniques for analyzing Windows artifacts. Hackernoob.tips

Hashim, N., & Sutherland, I. (2011). An architecture for the forensic analysis of Windows system artifacts. In *Digital forensics and cyber crime: Second International ICST Conference, ICDF2C 2010, Abu Dhabi, United Arab Emirates, October 4-6, 2010, revised selected papers 2* (pp. 120-128). Springer Berlin Heidelberg. https://doi.org/DOI: 10.1007/978-3-642-19513-6_10

Javed, M. S., Sajjad, S. M., Mehmood, D., Mansoor, K., Iqbal, Z., Kazim, M., & Muhammad, Z. (2024). Analyzing Tor browser artifacts for enhanced web forensics, anonymity, cybersecurity, and privacy in Windows-based systems. *Information (Basel)*, 15(8), 495. DOI: 10.3390/info15080495

Lawton, S. (2023, October 17). How the cloud changed digital forensics investigations. *Dark Reading*. https://www.darkreading.com/cloud-security/how-the-cloud-changed-digital-forensics-investigations

Ligh, M. H., Case, A., Levy, J., & Walters, A. (2014). *The Art of Memory Forensics: Detecting Malware and Threats in Windows, Linux, and Mac Memory*. Wiley. Easttom, C. (2021). *Digital forensics, investigation, and response* (4th ed.). Jones & Bartlett Learning. Carrier, B. (2005). *File system forensic analysis*. Addison-Wesley Professional. Casey, E. (2011). *Digital evidence and computer crime: Forensic science, computers, and the internet*. Academic press.

Linuxize. (2019). Understanding the /etc/shadow File. Linuxize. https://linuxize.com/post/etc-shadow-file/

Lueth, K. L. (2020, November 19). *State of the IoT 2020: 12 billion IoT connections, surpassing non-IoT for the first time.* IoT Analytics. https://iot-analytics.com/state-of-the-iot-2020-12-billion-iot-connections-surpassing-non-iot-for-the-first-time/

Magnet Forensics. (2024a). ShimCache vs AmCache: Key Windows forensic artifacts. https://www.magnetforensics.com/blog/shimcache-vs-amcache-key-windows-forensic-artifacts/

McKay, D. (2023, November 13). How to use the dmesg command on Linux. *How to Geek*. https://www.howtogeek.com/449335/how-to-use-the-dmesg-command-on-linux/

Messier, R. (2015). *Operating System Forensics* (1st ed.). Syngress.

Microsoft. (2024). Volume Shadow Copy Service (VSS). *Microsoft Learn*. https://learn.microsoft.com/en-us/windows-server/storage/file-server/volume-shadow-copy-service

Mistry, N. R., & Dahiya, M. S. (2019). Signature based volatile memory forensics: A detection-based approach for analyzing sophisticated cyber attacks. *International Journal of Information Technology : an Official Journal of Bharati Vidyapeeth's Institute of Computer Applications and Management*, 11(3), 583–589. DOI: 10.1007/s41870-018-0263-4

Moskvichev, A. D., & Dolgachev, M. V. (2020). System of collection and analysis event log from sources under control of Windows operating system. *2020 International Multi-Conference on Industrial Engineering and Modern Technologies. FarEastCon*, 2020, 1–5. Advance online publication. DOI: 10.1109/FarEastCon50210.2020.9271520

Moskvichev, A. D., & Dolgachev, M. V. (2020). System of collection and analysis event log from sources under control of Windows operating system. *2020 International Multi-Conference on Industrial Engineering and Modern Technologies (FarEastCon)*. https://doi.org/DOI: 10.1109/FarEastCon50210.2020.9271520

Nelson, B., Phillips, A., & Steuart, C. (2015). *Guide to computer forensics and investigations* (5th ed.). Cengage Learning.

Nelson, R., Shukla, A., & Smith, C. (2020). Web browser forensics in Google Chrome, Mozilla Firefox, and the Tor Browser Bundle. In Zhang, X., & Choo, K. K. (Eds.), *Digital forensic education* (Vol. 61, pp. 29–50). Springer., DOI: 10.1007/978-3-030-23547-5_12

Nemeth, E., Snyder, G., Hein, T. R., & Whaley, B. (2017). *UNIX and Linux System Administration Handbook* (5th ed.). Pearson Education.

Nikkel, B. (2021). *Practical Linux Forensics: A Guide for Digital Investigators*. No Starch Press.

Nyholm, H., Monteith, K., Lyles, S., Gallegos, M., DeSantis, M., Donaldson, J., & Taylor, C. (2022). The Evolution of Volatile Memory Forensics. *Journal of Cybersecurity and Privacy*, 2(3), 556–572. DOI: 10.3390/jcp2030028

O'Shaughnessy, S., & Keane, A. (2017). Impact of cloud computing on digital forensic investigations. In *Advances in Digital Forensics IX* (pp. 291–303). Springer Berlin Heidelberg.

Oliveira, A. (2022, December 15). How to schedule jobs using the Linux 'cron' utility. *Red Hat*. https://www.redhat.com/sysadmin/linux-cron-command

Oxygen Forensics. (2023, August 31). What is digital forensics? *Oxygen Forensics*. https://www.oxygenforensics.com/en/resources/what-is-digital-forensics/

Palhière, A. (2020, December 5). *SharkyCTF - EZDump writeups / Linux forensics introduction*. Synacktiv. https://www.synacktiv.com/en/publications/sharkyctf-ezdump-writeups-linux- forensics-introduction.html

Pure Storage. (2024, January 24). *XFS vs. Ext4: Which Linux file system is better?* Pure Storage. https://blog.purestorage.com/purely-educational/xfs-vs-ext4-which-linux-file-system-is- better/

Quick, D., & Choo, K. K. R. (2018). Big forensic data reduction: Digital forensic images and electronic evidence. *Cluster Computing*, 21(2), 1277–1297. DOI: 10.1007/s10586-016-0553-1

Quick, D., & Choo, K. K. R. (2018). Big forensic data reduction: Digital forensic images and electronic evidence. *Cluster Computing*, 21(2), 1277–1297. DOI: 10.1007/s10586-016-0553-1

Reddy, N. (2019). *Practical cyber forensics*. Apress. Magnet Forensics. (2024, September 23). 7 essential Linux forensics artifacts every investigator should know. https://www.magnetforensics.com/blog/linux-forensics-artifacts-every-investigator-should-know/

Roussev, V. (2016). Digital forensic science: Issues, methods, and challenges. *Synthesis Lectures on Information Security, Privacy, &. Trust*, 8(5), 1–155.

Ruan, K., Carthy, J., Kechadi, T., & Crosbie, M. (2011). Cloud forensics: An overview. In *Advances in Digital Forensics VII* (pp. 35-46). https://doi.org/DOI: 10.1007/978-3-642-24212-0_3

Sammons, J. (2014). *The basics of digital forensics: the primer for getting started in digital forensics*. Syngress.

SANS Institute. (2024). FOR500: Windows forensic analysis. https://www.sans.org/cyber-security-courses/windows-forensic-analysis/

Security Ninja. (2016, June 22). Understanding critical Windows artifacts and their relevance during an investigation: Artifacts. *Infosec Institute*. https://www.infosecinstitute.com/resources/digital-forensics/understanding-critical-windows-artifacts-and-their-relevance-during-investigation-part-2/

Silberschatz, A., Galvin, P. B., & Gagne, G. (2018). *Operating System Concepts* (10th ed.). John Wiley & Sons, Inc.

Singh, B., & Vigna, G. (2021, March 25). *Memory forensics for virtualized hosts*. VMware. https://blogs.vmware.com/security/2021/03/memory-forensics-for-virtualized-hosts.html

Slonopas, A. (2024, March 3). *What is digital forensics? A closer examination of the field*. Information Technology Blog | American Public University. https://www.apu.apus.edu/area-of-study/information-technology/resources/what-is-digital-forensics/

TickTechTold. (2023). 7 real-life cases solved using digital forensics. https://www.ticktechtold.com/cases-using-digital-forensics/

Zdziarski, J. (2012). *The iOS Hacker's Handbook*. Wiley.

Chapter 7
Applications of LLMs in Quantum-Aware Cybersecurity Leveraging LLMs for Real-Time Anomaly Detection and Threat Intelligence

Soby T. Ajimon
Amity Institute of Forensic Sciences, Amity University, Noida, India

Sachil Kumar
https://orcid.org/0000-0002-2681-3937
Amity Institute of Forensic Sciences, Amity University, Noida, India

ABSTRACT

The integration of Large Language Models (LLMs) with quantum-enhanced tools is revolutionizing cybersecurity. This chapter explores how these advanced technologies can address critical challenges, including real-time anomaly detection, advanced persistent threats (APTs), and zero-day exploits. By combining LLMs' contextual understanding with the computational power of quantum computing, we propose innovative approaches to strengthen intrusion detection systems, malware analysis, and threat intelligence. The chapter covers automated defense systems, adversarial scenario modeling, and adaptive cybersecurity frameworks that evolve in response to emerging threats. It highlights synergies between LLMs and quantum computing, presenting a dual strategy to detect and mitigate cyber risks more effectively. While discussing technical, ethical, and scalability challenges, the chapter offers practical

DOI: 10.4018/979-8-3373-1102-9.ch007

insights for cybersecurity professionals, equipping them with tools and strategies to defend against increasingly sophisticated threats in a quantum-aware future.

INTRODUCTION

The increasing complexity of digitalization in modern society has led to a rise in sophisticated cyber-attacks, creating a pressing need for novel cybersecurity strategies and methodologies. Among the most transformative innovations in this field are the integration of Large Language Models (LLMs) and quantum technologies. LLMs, empowered by artificial intelligence (AI), have demonstrated exceptional capabilities in natural language understanding, anomaly detection, and automation, positioning them as invaluable tools for detecting and preventing cybersecurity threats. Concurrently, quantum computing offers the potential to solve previously intractable computational problems, particularly in encryption and cryptographic attacks, where classical systems are currently unable to cope.

The convergence of LLMs and quantum technologies signifies a paradigm shift in cybersecurity, providing groundbreaking solutions for combating advanced threats, zero-day exploits, and encrypted communications analysis. LLMs, known for their prowess in handling large datasets, can be effectively deployed for real-time threat intelligence with smaller models, while larger models enable fully automated forensics and deep anomaly detection. Quantum computing adds an additional layer of security, offering quantum-safe cryptography and the ability to detect anomalies at unprecedented scales.

This chapter explores the foundational principles behind the integration of LLMs and quantum technologies within cybersecurity applications. It addresses critical challenges, including anomaly detection, threat intelligence, intrusion detection systems, and adversarial model construction. By investigating the intersection of AI and quantum computing, this chapter provides insights into how these technologies can shape the next generation of automated defense systems, improve threat detection, and build more robust cybersecurity environments. It also discusses the technical, ethical, and scalability issues associated with their convergence, emphasizing the evolving cybersecurity skillset needed to tackle these novel threats.

Ultimately, the chapter offers a holistic perspective on how AI and quantum computing can revolutionize cybersecurity practices in the near future, providing a roadmap for integrating these disruptive technologies into the defense strategies of tomorrow.

LLMs and Quantum-Aware Cybersecurity

Large Language Models (LLMs) and quantum-aware cybersecurity are two technologies that will help us tackle the challenges of the digital and quantum eras. LLMs like GPT-4 are great at processing large amounts of text data and producing coherent results, making them a valuable tool for improving cybersecurity. They have been useful in many applications, including vulnerability detection, threat intelligence, secure code generation, and automated code repair. Domain-specific tuning approaches like continuous pre-training and supervised fine-tuning allow LLMs to be adapted to cybersecurity-specific datasets (Faruk et al., 2022; Zhang et al., 2024). For example, secure coding benchmarks have shown how LLMs reduce vulnerabilities and produce safer code. But there are still issues like removing biases in LLM-generated outputs and ensuring robustness against adversarial attacks (Zhang et al., 2024).

Quantum-aware cybersecurity addresses the dual role of quantum computing as a threat and an intermediary in cybersecurity. Quantum computers are a threat to traditional cryptography methods like RSA and ECC by exploiting mathematical shortcuts like Shor's algorithm. This has led to the creation of quantum-resistant cryptography like lattice-based and code-based approaches. NIST has been promoting the standardization of these approaches (Faruk et al., 2022). Quantum technologies solve cybersecurity-related optimization problems like secure communication protocols and cryptographic agility (Faruk et al., 2022).

LLMs also play a role in quantum computing research, particularly in quantum circuit design and optimization. Advanced approaches like Variational Quantum Algorithms (VQAs) benefit from LLM's ability to design efficient quantum systems. Researchers have used LLMs to create tools like Quantum GPT-Guided Architecture Search (QGAS) to improve the efficiency and correctness of quantum algorithm designs (Liang et al., 2023). This integration accelerates research in quantum chemistry and finance and allows for more expressive and effective quantum algorithms.

The convergence of LLMs and quantum-aware cybersecurity highlights the importance of interdisciplinary approaches. Together these technologies form a framework to negotiate the vulnerabilities of the classical-to-quantum transition. They optimize resources for better cybersecurity, which is a big step towards securing both digital and quantum infrastructures (Faruk et al., 2022; Zhang et al., 2024; Liang et al., 2023).

The Convergence of AI and Quantum Technologies in Cybersecurity

The combined use of artificial intelligence (AI) and quantum technologies in digital security is one of the developments in the area of digital security. When coupled with the data mining and pattern recognition capabilities of artificial intelligence, the increased utility of quantum computing creates new and potent solutions for information security in the networked world (Bhosale et al., 2023). Quantum computers, powered by the principles of superposition and entanglement, have speed and efficiency superiority, enabling them to quickly decrypt classical cryptographic schemes. Quantum-resistant cryptography (QRC) is essential to safeguard sensitive communications given the high risks involved (Rosch-Grace & Straub, 2024; Faruk et al., 2024).

Quantum Key Distribution (QKD) demonstrates the feasibility of using quantum mechanics to ensure the security of communications while preserving information content integrity and confidentiality, even in the presence of eavesdropping. The application of AI enhances cybersecurity by enabling predictive analytics of cyberattacks, anomaly detection, and real-time countermeasures. Quantum-enhanced machine learning (QEML)-based algorithms accelerate workflows on massive datasets and detect complex cyberattacks, such as advanced persistent threats (APTs) (Faruk et al., 2024).

Moreover, the hybridization of AI and quantum intelligence lays the foundation for new encryption algorithms and secure multiparty computation. These interfaces are critical for emerging fields such as secure cloud computing and blockchain technology. However, this integration is still in its early stages, requiring a multidisciplinary effort to bridge knowledge gaps among AI scientists, quantum physicists, and cybersecurity engineers. Quantum technology is revolutionizing both defensive and offensive techniques in cybersecurity.

Figure 1. AI and quantum technologies in cybersecurity foundations of LLMS and quantum technologies

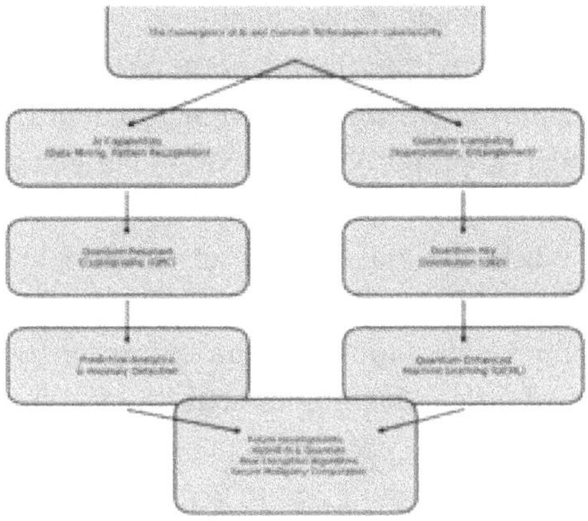

The junction of Large Language Models (LLMs) and quantum technologies are an increasingly lively research area in contemporary computer science. LLMs especially generative pre-trained transformers (GPT) have demonstrated phenomenal abilities in the natural language processing (NLP) area and have been employed in several NLP applications including text generation, translation, and summarization. These architectures are the ones based on the transformers, a recurrent neural network with attention capabilities that allow parallelized processing of the input sequence and long-order representation learning in a data (Vaswani et al., 2017). Having received mass text corpus pre-training, they acquire general text patterns and text structures, which may be further fine-tuned for specific task activities (e.g., sentiment analysis or medical text generation) (Moradi et al., 2024).

On the other hand, quantum technologies rely on lower and upper quantum mechanics effects (superposition or entanglement), which cannot be used by traditional computers, for information processing. Quantum computing based on the elementary unit, the qubit, has the potential to lead to extremely rapid computation of some tasks, such as the factorization of large numbers and modelling of quantum systems. Noise and decoherence in quantum devices restrict state simulation, as well as optimization, thereby raising the need for noise-resilient algorithms (Zhou et al., 2024).

The complexity and size to which systems that are of the interdisciplinary concern belong pose a great obstacle. LLM [e. g., GPT - 4 models have more than 1 trillion parameters, and these have to be trained and then fine-tuned on a high computational infrastructure. Just as the scalability of quantum systems increases with the number of qubits, the algorithms in quantum system simulation and control have to become increasingly complex. Since there is an increasing number of quantum bits, traditional approaches of simulating quantum systems are computationally expensive from the point of view of resource. Thus, concourse with these simulations, machine learning approaches such as LLMs are under investigation (Liang et al., 2023).

There is interest in LLMs within the quantum computing community as a tool for optimization of quantum architectural design. Quantum circuits, the brain of a quantum algorithm, must be properly singly parameterized and the gates must behave in an optimal way for superior performance. LLMs such as GPT are leveraged to create and search for effective quantum ansatz form, which are the basis of the algorithms, for example, the Variational Quantum Eigensolver (VQE) (Liang et al., 2023). These models can be used to search through extensive and intricate design spaces, to generate novel circuit topologies with the use of the existing quantum circuit information and thereby to accelerate the search for desirable solutions.

Furthermore, the possibility of LLMs to parse sequence information, and to build upon a substantial dataset are both highly suited to quantum simulation, where the evolution of quantum states can be computationally demanding. LLMs can be trained to predict quantum states, as a function of the quantum circuit features, from an accurate description of the relation between output state and quantum circuit features. In this interaction, more accurate simulation of quantum systems can be performed, which may have lower time and computational cost than simulation on the physical quantum computers (Zhou et al., 2024).

While their potential is transparent, there are limitations. In the example case, LLMs remain most useful for point tasks and require a fair amount of training data, which can be very difficult to achieve in quantum research. Hardware constraints of quantum computing, such as decoherence and error rates, pose a significant challenge in integration of LLMs without additional noise-robust schemes (Moradi et al., 2024) and LLMs with noise calls for further rigorous validation as errors can result in failures of the physical processes. Despite the reality that such challenges do exist, the merger of LLMs and quantum technologies is an ongoing process and it is anticipated that this hybridising will produce substantial breakthroughs not only theoretically, but also at the practical level of quantum computation applications, approaching the limit of computing power.

Understanding LLMs and Their Capabilities

Large Language Models (LLMs) are a major inflection point in AI and natural language processing (NLP). These models, based on large data sets and with complex architectures (e.g., transformers), not only perform well on the interpretation and generation of human-like writing. Their key capabilities are natural language understanding, language generation, natural language reasoning, therefore they can be applied to a diversified set of applications.

LLM models are trained to model language in a highly intricate fashion in an entirely unsupervised fashion. Compared to conventional models, they have the capacity to learn not only the tasks, but also how to move through the whole process, from task specific to domain-general use. This is achieved by pre-training over data-sets and fine-tuning over individual tasks, which are thus context-adaptable (Danish, 2024; Ali & Kostakos, 2023).

Their primary competencies include: Their primary competencies include:

- **Natural Language Understanding (NLU):** Visualizing, decoding visual scene representations, inferring a (latent) meaning, and understanding language context in a deep and flexible way are capabilities of LLMs. Predictively, they have demonstrated high effectiveness in tasks including text classification, sentiment analysis, and semantic search. (Ali & Kostakos, 2023).
- **Natural Language Generation (NLG):** models generate grammatically correct, semantically significant, and factually consistent language. They can also be trained to write narratives, to summarize text, and to write in an imaginative way (such as articles and code) with minimal or no user instructions (Ali & Kostakos, 2023).
- **Multimodal learning:** Advanced LLMs enable multimodal learning by processing and creating content from several data kinds, including as text, graphics, and audio. In principle, this interface can also be applied to, e.g., image captioning, multimodality reasoning (Ali & Kostakos, 2023; Ferrag et al., 2024).
- **Few-Shot and Zero-Shot Learning:** LLMs can complete tasks without considerable domain-specific instruction. They can generalize with essentially no dependence on task instances, thus with a reduced requirement for labelled data sets (Ferrag et al., 2024).
- **Logical Reasoning and Decision-Making:** Today, thanks to the advent of LLMs, it is possible to perform logic-based reasoning, problem-solving with multiple steps, and assist in decision making, issues with direct implications for real-world applications, such as threat identification in the field of cybersecurity (Xu et al., 2024; Danish, 2024).
- **Logical Reasoning and Decision-Making:** Nowadays, LTMs are able to execute logical reasoning, multi-step problem solving and decision support (Ali & Kostakos, 2023) a task that has direct application to, for instance, cybersecurity (threat) identification.

- **Cyber defence:** LLMs can perform knowledge transfer across domains, therefore being useful to cyber defence, diagnostic in medicine, or review of law (Ferrag et al., 2024).
- **Enhanced Scalability and Generalization:** The ability to handle large-scale heterogeneous data sets allows for generalization across languages, cultures, and domains, extending the scope of their applications in inter-national and multi-disciplinary problems (Ferrag et al., 2024).

Principles of Quantum Computing and Its Application to Cybersecurity

Quantum computing is revolutionizing paradigm that can be used to compute beyond the scope of classical systems by employing quantum mechanics. The key components of quantum computing are quantum bits (qubits), which can be in any superposition of multiple states of a qubit and are coupled to each other by entanglement, so that parallelism or computational speedup is possible. In contrast to conventional computer architectures, where data is manipulated using bits (0s and 1s), Quantum Computing (QC) utilizes quantum bits (qubits) to solve elaborately complex problems at incredibly fast speeds (Dini & Saponara, 2023; Alam et al., 2024).

In cybersecurity, quantum computing is a promise and a threat. The evolution of quantum algorithms (in particular, the Shor's and the Grover's algorithms) has a strong impact on modern cryptographic protocols. Shor's algorithm can efficiently factorize both large integers and pose a threat to the RSA encryption system and analogous public-key cryptosystems, whereas Grover's algorithm speeds up brute-force attacks against common symmetric key cryptosystems by offering quadratic speedups (Dini & Saponara, 2023; Alam et al., 2024).

These threats are alleviated by post-quantum cryptography, one of the key research subjects. These cryptographic techniques have been developed to be quantum proof and at the same time, usable with classical digital systems. Examples include lattice-based, code-based, and multivariate polynomial cryptography methods which are other promising approaches for resisting quantum-based attacks (Dini & Saponara, 2023; Alam et al., 2024).

Beyond risks, quantum computing offers significant opportunities in cybersecurity. Based on quantum mechanics, Quantum Key Distribution (QKD) offers unconditionally secure communication such that the existence of an eavesdropper can be detected by the no-cloning theorem. Security protocols, e.g., BB84 enable covert sharing of encryption keys and therefore fundamentally changed the possibility for secure communication and data privacy (Dini & Saponara, 2023).

Quantum computing applications towards cybersecurity include the new level of data security architecture, real-time detection of attacks, and in general, the rugged network architecture. As examples quantum-enhanced ML models are being proposed for an intrusion detection in cybersecurity with significantly improved accuracy and better robustness against those continuously changing threats. In addition, quantum algorithms allow to optimize network flow and the immediate location of faults in large scale systems (Dini & Saponara, 2023).

Despite the great promise of quantum computing, its applicability to cybersecurity is restricted by scalability, the necessity of error correction and high price of quantum hardware. Co-research of quantum physicists and cybersecurity specialists continues to be important for the solution of these problems and for the exploitation to the fullest extent of the dual nature of quantum technology (Dini & Saponara, 2023; Alam et al., 2024).

This synergistic influence of quantum computing as a force and a platform states a stream of the existing reformers of quantum-resistant cryptography and the creation of new cybersecurity-based structures. Maturing of quantum technologies will become a necessity for them to be integrated in the general paradigm of cybersecurity strategies for the protection of digital infrastructures against next generation threats.

Integrating LLMs with Quantum Technologies

The intersection of large language models (LLMs) and quantum technologies offers a potential way to upscale quantum computing applications. Transformer-based deep learning, a subset of deep learning offers great promise for the design, optimization, and solution process of quantum architectures. LLMs offer much promise in areas where they are useful, such as the design of quantum circuits, which are fundamental to the success of quantum algorithms (for example, Variational Quantum Eigensolvers (VQEs) (Liang et al., 2023).

Integration, in a general sense, is supported by the application of LLMs to chart and refine ansatz architectures, the essential building blocks of quantum algorithms. These architectures define the topology of quantum circuits, and therefore they manage the efficiency and the quality of the quantum circuits. LLMs can scan large datasets defined on a quantum circuit, regularize them, and propose a path toward optimizing them, that in turn results in more efficient quantum circuits (Liang et al., 2023). Moreover, LLMs help to explore the search spaces of quantum architectures by once generating high-fidelity and by repeatedly refines them with the use of feedback (Liang et al., 2023).

In addition, with LLMs, it is also possible to decrease computational requirements by providing initial parameter guesses and to accelerate quantum circuits by exploiting machine learning approaches. This interaction between analytic machine learning models and quantum computing hardware provides a hybrid approach to optimization of a quantum computation with hardware noise and error correction free (Liang et al., 2023).

Although current capacity of LLMs to understand quantum physics problem is not yet advanced enough to support self-service, the capacity of LLMs to exploit large dataset and assist the design of quantum circuits has indeed been beneficial to the quantum computing community (Liang et al., 2023). Such an integration is anticipated to mature and extend the capabilities of quantum technologies to larger and more stable systems.

REAL-TIME ANOMALY DETECTION AND THREAT DETECTION

Real-time anomaly/threat detection is a key feature of cybersecurity. These approaches are based on algorithms that make use of deep knowledge, and have the ability to identify anomalous behaviour in systems and networks, and in general predict future risk ahead of time. Unlike traditional security, which is based on static rules or known signatures, real-time detection employs dynamic models such as machine learning or predictive analytics, allowing the system to absorb new threat information as it becomes available.

In problem domains, those questions are about deviating from the normal pattern, such as network traffic or system behaviour. For instance, algorithms (e.g., neural networks) could be used to annotate and warn for anomalous behaviour (e.g., suspicious logins/data exfiltration) at a trade-off between speed and sensitivity. Additionally, predictive models for historical, in-situ and real-time data are also presented to identify zero-day attacks, a new type of threat activity (Danish, 2024).

A further layer of threat detection is provided by classifying flagged anomalies and taking the right decision. It has many systems, for example Intrusion Detection System (IDS), which uses on-line data to detect and counter an attack, for instance a malicious access to and/or data theft from a system. In particular, for the subject of automotive cybersecurity, it has been shown the effectiveness of use of the IDS to monitor communications with the Controller Area Network (CAN) bus and the effectiveness of neural network-based anomaly detectors for example, to recognize anomalies and to interpret attacks (Dini & Saponara, 2023).

These technologies are of highest significance for today's cyber security, with greater mean response times and a smaller mean false positive rate. The capacity of organizations to shift from a reactive security model to an increasingly proactive model by integrating real-time threat detection logic into the organizations' designs is a powerful adaptation to state of the art and constantly changing cyber-attacks.

Enhancing Anomaly Detection with LLMs

Figure 2. Application of LLMs in threat detection

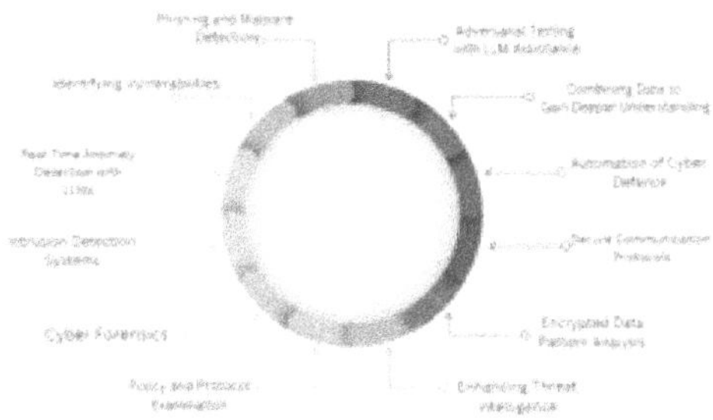

The use of Large Language Models (LLMs) for real-time anomaly and threat detection has great transformative potential in cyber security. By effectively combining natural language understanding and reasoning, LLMs leverage their power to identify and tackle complex cybersecurity problems across a wide range of applications, including intrusion detection, malware analysis, and network security.

Real-Time Anomaly Detection with LLMs

Anomaly detection in real time consists in detecting deviation from normal behaviour patterns, which can result in performance problems or security breaches. LLMs with deep contextual knowledge are becoming more and more employed for this task. The ability to ingest and process non-structured and structured data allows the logging, analysis, and processing of logs, system events and telemetry data done in real-time. For example, LLMs are mixed with machine learning classifiers (e.g., Random Forests) in the infrastructure HuntGPT to successfully classify anomalies while harnessing explanation mechanisms (e.g., SHAP, LIME) to gain on the model's explainability (Hassanin & Moustafa, 2024; Tseng, Lee, & Wang, 2024)

Fine-tuning of LLMs on domain-specific datasets greatly improves their ability to recognize and interpret anomalous behaviours e.g., denial-of-service (DoS) attacks, unauthorized access, and anomalous data flows. The use of models such as GPT-4 and related architectures for anomaly detection in systems has exhibited improvement in detection accuracy and generalized performance in a variety of different network settings (Tseng et al., 2024; Serketzis et al., 2019).

Identifying Vulnerabilities

When trained on domain-specific data, LLMs are very powerful to detect vulnerabilities in the software code. Using code repositories, error logs, and known vulnerability databases as inputs, LLMs can track down defects in the code that might be prey to attackers. They can also suggest potential fixes or patches, automating the remediation process. This helps reduce the time it takes to identify and patch vulnerabilities, particularly for complex systems that would otherwise require manual review (Serketzis et al., 2019).

LLMs can also be used to interpret security policies and the configurations to detect holes in software defences and to harden systems against known exploit methods. Automatic generation of patches consolidates threat management workflows, and enables organizations to rapidly reduce the risks.

Phishing and Malware Detection

Phishing attacks know to use sophisticated language patterns to trick targets. LLMs are adept at analysing textual content in emails, social media messages, and websites to detect these subtle, deceptive cues. They may also be able to detect phishing attempts by looking for indicators of malicious behaviour e.g., suspicious URLs, deceptive text, and phishing campaign. LLMs may also classify malware from the textual descriptions of its behaviour, find malicious code patterns, and find harmful domains from analysis of DNS queries and metadata (Serketzis et al., 2019).

The ability of LLMs to identify harmful domains and malware families based on a large corpus of data ensures that emerging threats, including zero-day attacks, can be detected early. At the same time that it is done in real time, the dynamic detection of the detection window shortens the period of vulnerability between the discovery of a threat and its response (Hassanin & Moustafa, 2024).

Intrusion Detection Systems (IDS)

LLMs improve Intrusion Detection Systems (IDS) through the examination of network traffic and the detection of subtle, multi-step attack patterns often multi-stage, that involve sophisticated coordinated attack behaviour at multiple stages of an attack. They can detect attempts to use system weaknesses in different ways, including sideways traversing through a network, privilege escalation, and exfiltration of confidential information. LLMs are able to associate information from sources other than logs and system outputs that one might find in an intrusion detection system (IDS), such as in an intrusion detection system (IDS) or in a general-purpose machine learning system, which it is possible to deduce an attack that might have been overlooked by a typical signature-based IDS (Tseng et al., 2024; Serketzis et al., 2019).

Through the use of real-time analysis, LLMs can categorize network traffic, identify anomalous activity and support near real-time response. This capability to identify attacks at an early stage of their development cycle is important for preventing major security incidents around a national scale.

Cyber Forensics

In the field of cyber forensics, LLMs assist by analysing and filtering logs to reconstruct attack timelines and identify the sources of breaches. They can correlate information from diverse log sources—such as firewall logs, application logs, and system event logs—making it easier to trace back to the origin of the attack. By understanding the context and content of log data, LLMs can provide a detailed account of the methods used in an attack, the scope of the damage, and potential areas still at risk (Tseng et al., 2024).

These powers render LLMs extremely powerful in post-incident analysis as providing cybersecurity teams not only a way to recover from intrusion, but also to make their defences more robust by learning how attackers work around the existing security infrastructure (Serketzis et al., 2019).

Policy and Protocol Examination

Similarly, LLMs can be applied to determine the success of cybersecurity policies and protocols. By analysing security guidelines and comparing them with the latest threat intelligence, LLMs can assess the overall compliance of systems and networks to security standards. They are particularly useful in scrutinizing protocols like TLS/SSL, helping to identify flaws that could lead to vulnerabilities, such as improper key management or encryption weaknesses.

On top of detecting weaknesses, LLMs can also be used to give insight into the most effective way to secure communication procedures and ensure the robustness of systems in the face of man-in-the-middle (MITM) attacks, data interception or access (Serketzis et al., 2019).

Enhancing Threat Intelligence

LLMs are able to ingest and analyse large volumes of threat intelligence information such as indicators of compromise (IoCs) and threat actor tactics, techniques and procedures (TTPs). They are able to detect patterns for threat intelligence feeds and predict the new attack paths. Combining historical attack data with real-time data allows LLMs to predict potential attacks and adapt defences in advance (Tseng et al., 2024).

The predictive power of these methods is most useful in areas with constantly changing threat environments, including financial and health services, where novel attack approaches constantly arise (Tseng et al., 2024).

Encrypted Data Pattern Analysis

LLMs equipped with quantum-enhanced capabilities are capable of detecting harmful activities in encrypted communications. They can also compute high-dimensional data and extract hidden patterns, which could lead to detection of malicious behaviours. Using quantum-enhanced correlation techniques, LLMs can scale to analyse encrypted traffic, making it easier to identify data exfiltration, or espionage of sensitive information over secure communication channels (Hassanin & Moustafa, 2024).

This ability to detect threats in encrypted data enhances the security of modern communication systems, ensuring that sensitive information remains protected while still being monitored for potential threats (Hassanin & Moustafa, 2024).

Secure Communication Protocols

LLMs can be used to perform and improve the cyber security protocols, providing protection against a constantly changing cyber threat. Protocol validity which includes the ability to assess the robustness of protocols such as TLS/SSL can be assessed and potential vulnerabilities which can be exploited can be identified by attackers. In addition, they can also support resilience optimization via the use of quantum cryptography methods in order to safeguard secret information against any of the best possible adversary attack types.

Automation of Cyber Defence

LLMs enable the automatization of threat response activities, thereby greatly decreasing the time taken to respond to security events. Through simulating different types of attacks, LLMs can perform tests to test system defences and optimize the security protocols in order to better safeguard the system. Automating through LLMs can also react to novel threats in real time by keeping organizations one step ahead of the next attack phenomenon (Serketzis et al., 2019; Tseng et al., 2024).

Combining Data to Gain Deeper Understanding

Using LLMs, it is possible to develop realistic cybersecurity training situations. For instance, phishing attacks and data breach simulations. These scenarios are of great value in training security teams to identify and to handle threats well. Through the synthesis of data from multiple sources, LLMs can produce a holistic simulation for example, bring realistic attack models, and can hence be used to great effect in training and preparedness (Tseng et al., 2024).

Adversarial Testing with LLM Assistance

LLMs play a critical role in adversarial testing, where they simulate potential attacks to evaluate the robustness of security systems. Using simulations of multi-vector and sophisticated persistent threats, LLMs assist with locating weaknesses in defence systems prior to exploitation by actual attackers. This adaptive strategy has the positive effect of strengthening system resilience, guaranteeing that cybersecurity actions function well under different threat scenarios (Serketzis et al., 2019).

Through the use of LLMs, it is possible to enhance the cybersecurity of organisations, leading to faster and more robust identification of threats, as well as improved preparedness for and response to cyberattacks.

Quantum-Enhanced Detection of APTs and Zero-Day Vulnerabilities

Advanced-Persistent-Threats (APTs) and zero-day-vulnerabilities are difficult issues in cybersecurity. APTs comprise sophisticated stealthy hacking methods, which are aimed to obtain unauthorized access to a network for as long as possible, with the attacker remaining undetected. In particular, a zero-day vulnerability is a flaw in the software that the software developer is not aware of, therefore very attractive to an attacker who can take advantage of it even before a patch is introduced.

Quantum computing holds the promise of detecting and deterring such dangers in an entirely new way. Because its capability lies at the top end of high-performance, complex calculation at super-human speeds, it can be used to facilitate inquiry into previously unattainable volumes of data that in turn allow us to build models with greater precision at detecting patterns and anomalies, which subsequently allow effective detection and process to attacks such as APT and zero-day exploitation and so on. Quantum algorithms are powerful and can be used to perform machine learning tasks to quickly scan and process network traffic looking for anomalous behaviour indicative of an ongoing or imminent attack (Gade Reddy, 2020).

Moreover, principles of quantum mechanics, superposition and entanglement lead to the development of high advanced technological cryptographic techniques. These approaches can also be applied in order to increase the security systems which safeguard against compromising data in the network. For example, quantum key distribution (QKD) is capable of establishing secure channels that are untouchable from eavesdroppers, and as such the channel is protected from APTs data leaks and zero-day attacks (Althobaiti Dohler, 2020).

A hybrid Quantum-classical models are also there to reflect the benefit that quantum computing can provide while using existing tools in cybersecurity. These models may enhance the effectiveness of threat detection, and at the same time, reduce the number of false positives, the system feature with the traditional security evaluation procedure (Suryotrisongko Musashi, 2022).

Continuous research and development activities in order to exploit fully the capability of quantum-enhanced detection in order to fully harness them still play a significant role to upgrade the current cybersecurity framework. With the advent of quantum technology, a new age in the war on cybercrime will begin and this accordingly illustrates the relevance of a head start in the prevention of APT and zero-day attacks, as a small part of an expanding digital sky of activities.

Threat Intelligence and Cyber Forensics

Threat Intelligence (TI) and Cyber Forensics have an important role in building the resilience of an organization against cyber-attacks. TI is the gathering, analysis and sharing of understanding of how cyber threats are developing and being used to be tackle to the best of defence and responses as quickly as possible. This is relevant to accessing information about the victims of exploitation, how to apply techniques used and speculate as to what, in the form of this Deep neural network (DNN) which represents an extension of machine learning (ML), is such a novel branch of ML which has been demonstrably successful for several complex tasks

On the other hand, Cyber Forensics will be defined as the techniques and practices involved in the collection, the safeguarding, and the evaluation of digital agents and/ or data resulting from cyber incidents. Its goal is to collect data related to a cyber event, which allows a responsive measure in the context of an incident/ a response to an incident as well as civil litigation.

The synergy between Threat Intelligence and Cyber forensics drives the creation of Digital Forensic Readiness (DFR), which refers to the process of the organization becoming more ready to plan and manage response to cybersecurity incidents. By embedding the actionable intelligence in forensic operations, the amount of data to be investigated can be pruned during security investigations, and thus the effectiveness and the success of security investigation can be strengthened for the detection of security incidents. The practical consequence of this fusion is the reduction of time and budget in a forensic process, and the detailed inquiry into the remote past (Serketzis et al., 2019).

AUTOMATING THREAT INTELLIGENCE WITH LLMS

Automation of threat intelligence based on Large Language Models (LLM) is a promising step forward to improve the rate and accuracy of threat detection and analysis in cyber security. Large language models (LLMs) are engineered for big data analytics across unstructured data, providing organizations with a novel means to manage the cyber threat landscape.

Data Collection and Preprocessing

Automating the data acquisition and preprocessing is one of the key use cases of LLMs for threat intelligence. LLMs can also be exploited to integrate information from different sources, e.g., threat reports, blogs, or microblogging sites. The capacity of an automated system to operate with this facility removes the need for collection of specific relevant data and works the analysts to release the requirement for data entry to an advanced analysis level. By natural language processing (NLP) techniques, LLMs can be used to segment and filter data based on topic and importance so that security personnel are notified of the most important information (Alam et al., 2024).

Threat Analysis

LLMs show their great strength in large data sets processing to identify patterns and anomalies that can serve as clues for threats. They are able to parse and understand data to identify evolutions in the distribution of malware, phishing, or into other malicious activities such as to compromise victims on social media. These automated analytics can enhance situational awareness by enabling security teams to detect and deflect evolving threats earlier and perform so in a preventive fashion. As the context (semantics) can also be analysed by LLMs, the analysis that is supported by the LLMs is deeper than the analysis that is possible with a conventional method, and therefore is more effective at identification of threats (Hassanin & Moustafa, 2024).

Report Generation

Another important application is automated threat report generation. LLMs can be used to integrate information over sources and generate comprehensive, from inequivalent, reports that use available intelligence on threats and risks. These reports can include an abundance of data including case specifics, historical data and predictive analysis, all of which are presented in a structured format to be easily comprehensible by decision makers. This automation, in addition to the time saving benefits for cybersecurity practitioners, also provides consistency in reporting and clarity (Tseng et al., 2024).

Knowledge Base Creation

Knowledge bases of past events wisdom are also facilitated by agents of LLMs. Leveraging historical data, LLMs are capable of detecting trends and generating suggestions for how to tackle future prevention policies. This continuous learning loop allows the organizations to learn from attempt experiences and, consequently, enhance their risk perceptions (Hassanin Moustafa, 2024).

Investigating Encrypted Communications and Digital Forensics

Due to the extensive deployment of encryption technologies, a number of very challenging situations are being presented to the field of digital forensics, and therefore, criminal investigations. Criminals use encryption to facilitate the following of illegal activity, and therefore, "There is a significant need for forensic practitioners to innovate with a view to extracting the encrypted data. Effective strategies include the use of aids to locate unencrypted versions, social engineering to obtain passphrases, and the use of techniques to guess these passphrases (Casey, 2002).

Digital forensics becomes increasingly complex as encryption algorithms evolve. But for forensic practitioners, technical encryption itself is not enough to know, but also understand the legal consequences of technical encryption of an item. Although law regarding privacy and access to data sets out the bounds of investigations, forensic practitioners are collectively tackling the task of working within legal constraints regarding examination of encryption information (Demming Baugh, 1997).

As encrypted communication becomes a pervasive, diverse threat environment across a spectrum of criminal activity from organized crime to terrorism, there is evidence suggesting the need for continuous evolution of forensic instruments and methods in response (Casey, 2002). Further, it is of crucial importance that police personnel be informed on the reasons and the limitations of storing information, on the regulatory force of encryption (Biryukov, Shamir, Wagner, 2000).

In fact, the research within the encrypted communications has been essentially a task needing an innovative approach of technical know-how, legal understanding, and the out-of-the-box thinking, with the aim of bringing to life complete digital forensic investigations.

Leveraging Quantum Technologies in Threat Intelligence

Quantum computing offers the promise for transformative changes to the cyber security landscape e.g., through computationally feasible tasks. As the complexity and sophistication of cyber-attacks rise, existing detection mechanisms are overwhelmed with volume and complexity of data. On the other hand, the exploitation of superior processing capacity and more efficient algorithms will be unavoidable for the effective cyber threat intelligence and cyber threat deterrence of quantum technology.

QUANTUM COMPUTING AND CYBERSECURITY

Computational Power: Quantum computers leverage effects of quantum mechanics to produce more computationally complex problems that can be solved exponentially faster than by any contemporary electronic device. This framework of integration, applied to large datasets, which are the first step toward finding "unknown knowns" i.e., potential cyber-attack (Ladd et al., 2010).

Advanced Algorithms such as Quantum Support Vector Machines (QSVM) or Quantum Neural networks (QNN) are promising for security domain applications, e.g., security analytics and threat detection. These algorithms work on very large amounts of data more effectively, and hence enhance either the accuracy of detection of malware and ransomware or the detection of APTs (Biamonte et al., 2017).

Enhancements in Threat Intelligence

Real-time Threat Detection: An increase in processing speed i.e., in which quantum computing can be used to crunch the numbers comes about in the context of the refinement of anomaly detection and faster response to threats. Reduced latency for threat analysis enables organizations to respond more rapidly to cyberattacks that threaten the possibility (Schuld Petruccione, 2018).

Pattern Recognition: Quantum technologies excel in pattern recognition tasks. What is understood is that, when convincingly identifying anomalies (in data streams and in system behaviour), the probability of being able to identify and prevent such an incident becomes high.

Implications for Cybersecurity Landscape

Improved Security Posture: Organizations using quantum technologies to perform threat intelligence will be in a position to leverage a more robust underpinning, under a better defence against adversary attacks. The combination of quantum computing features in existing cybersecurity technology increases both the accuracy and number of threat detections. The existence of this ability is especially relevant to industries such as finance, healthcare, and military that have high costs of failure, as well as high costs of breaches.

Long-term Benefits: For the reasons that quantum computing is capable of offering not just performance at a speed that can be made constant over a long period of time as a source of competitive benefit to the employment activities of the cyber criminals ahead, there is a career advantage for companies venturing into the development of the next generation cyberspace. Proactive immersion into this evolving technological domain will allow organisations to better protect themselves against emerging cybercrimes.

Intrusion Detection Systems (IDS) and Malware Classification

Signature-based (i.e., attack patterns) and anomaly-based (i.e., the base traffic is learned and anomalies are detected). Machine learning algorithms are routinely exploited to enhance the sensitivity and detection capability of an IDS in a way that it automatically incorporates new attack models without additional cost, which updates periodically according to modified pattern (Kumar et al., 2023).

Malware classification is one of the main indicators in cyber security system which can be leveraged for classification of different types (e.g., viruses, worms), its subtypes, etc. In particular classification from the detail up to actual, specific countermeasures in respect of specific threat and so on. Machine learning (ML) models have in fact been shown to be able to perform such classification automatically so that prediction are uniformly more accurate and false positives are minimized (Sajid et al., 2024).

Improving IDS with LLMs

Embedding Large Language Models (LLMs) in Intrusion Detection Systems (IDS) has the capacity to change the landscape of cybersecurity by dramatically improving the detection power and efficiency of operations. LLMs, which are strong at working with and extracting from large text data sets can play a key role in detecting patterns and anomalies that signify cyber threats.

Advanced Pattern Recognition

Deep Learning Approaches: Current architectures of LLMs (e.g., GPT, BERT) base their capabilities on deep learning, that is, the ability to learn complex patterns from huge data pools with heterogeneous sources, such as network traffic or IoT log files (Kheddar et al., 2023). These models are particularly capable of incorporating context, and therefore, are more susceptible of incorporating history and/or to evaluate the deviations from the normal behaviour in order to better detect anomalies.

Enhanced Contextual Understanding

Real-time Analysis: The use of LLMs for contextualizing security events has been demonstrated, where the association strength between network regions is computed (Kheddar et al., 2023). This is realised through the capability of computerised systems to distinguish between positive and negative behaviour and this is practical in real-time intrusion detection in dynamic environments.

Transfer Learning for Optimization

Selective Transfer Learning: By selectively transferring learning from LLMs, it is possible to transfer learned information from pre-trained models to novel cybersecurity applications, i.e., the case of limited data sets (Kheddar et al., 2023). This versatility permits to maintain a good performance over a large context, allowing the robustness of IDS to be transferred to a much greater extent.

Addressing Adversarial Threats

Collaborative Defence Mechanisms: The future of LLMs will involve even further integration of online threat intelligence across domains. With this integration, another thing that it will achieve will be increased levels of adversarial robustness, and thus the IDS would be capable of detecting even more sophisticated adversaries with high effectiveness (Kheddar et al., 2023). Furthermore, the synergetic integration ensembles of specialized LLMs are able to increase detection accuracy and minimize false positives.

Overcoming Existing Challenges

Interpretable AI: The incorporation of LLMs in IDS reinstates some of the missing layers in the decision explainability layers that IDS has to provide, and a key step toward establishing trust between CIS security professionals (Kheddar et al., 2023). In order to mitigate known risks, the direction of future explainability development, understanding why LLMs generate particular outputs in the first place, is suggested to elucidate the goals of LLM models

Further, LLM incorporation in the intrusion detection system is also one of the emerging research issues in cybersecurity. These systems are capable of responding in a good way to any kind of cyber-attack as it happens i.e. From a neurobiological viewpoint using innovative pattern recognition, contextualization, and integrated defence responses. Still, more research and development are still needed to overcome the known weaknesses and usability shortcomings of LLM-based IDS.

Automating Malware Classification and Phishing Detection

The unprecedented outburst of malware and phishing exploits required machine learning (ML) based solutions for their automatic detection and classification. Such methods can be used to tackle the constantly changing of their attack, since signature-based traditional methods could be rendered useless by attacks that are not novel or camouflaged.

Malware Classification

Automation of malware classification using machine learning has been extremely successful, and still more so using deep learning methods. Traditional approaches, including static and dynamic analysis, have been augmented by ML models which can extract intricate patterns of data from a large amount of data. From the file's binary content, features are extracted through static analysis, while runtime behaviours, i.e., API calls and system modifications, are observed through dynamic analysis. Machine learning models, based on n-gram analysis and entropy-based features, identify discriminative patterns that allow them to identify unclear or malicious behaviour also on encrypted or packed file. Studies have demonstrated the value of convolutional neural networks (CNNs) that are able to take raw binary data, automatically apply processing to recognize malware without feature Engineering (Gibert, Mateu, Planes, 2020).

Phishing Detection

Automated systems based on machine learning are also known to be increasingly detected by phishing attacks that trick the user to give up private information. These systems use URL patterns, email message bodies and metadata to detect likely phishing attacks. However, logistic regression, support vector machines, and extreme gradient boosting (XGBoost) models have also been deployed for the classification of phishing attacks, with XGBoost model occasionally obtaining very high accuracies, even exceeding 99% in some instances (Sharma, Anushree, Rakesh, 2024). Using the framework of groups of variables e.g., domain age, registration information, and presence of suspicious links such systems can continuously identify phishing messages and web pages. As a result, automation reduces both the time and labour expended in the threat detection stages by making the whole process fairly automatic, and therefore the response rate to phishing attacks may therefore be accelerated.

Nevertheless, the complexity of malware and phishing tools is still a challenge due to the tasks described. With the increasing use of sophisticated code obfuscation attempts and phishing attackers the models need to be iteratively updated to keep them effective. Nevertheless, in light of these challenges, automation is an important technology for contemporary cybersecurity.

Quantum Computing for Malware Analysis in Cybersecurity

Quantum computing also leads to a fundamental benefit to cyber security, namely in malware analysis. In traditional methods of malware detection, deep learning models, trained on large scale datasets, are employed to identify patterns that could otherwise point to malicious activity. But, as malware becomes more sophisticated, simple approaches can get out of their depth very quickly. Quantum computing overcomes this restriction by exploiting the principles of superposition and entanglement, which allows the utilization of a large computational space in a deterministic and linear fashion.

Quantum Machine Learning (QML) extends the quantum algorithm to a classical machine learning based framework, both speeding up the machine learning task and enhancing its effectiveness and precision in malware identification. In particular, hybrid quantum models, models that integrate classical and quantum contributions, have also been promising. In this context malware is typically recast as grayscale images, which assume the binary program ware content. These images serve as inputs to classical and quantum convolutional neural networks (CNNs) and are subsequently used to perform malware classification based on visual attributes (Mercaldo et al., 2022).

The comparison between state-of-the-art classical models (AlexNet, MobileNet, and VGG19) and quantum-hybrid models shows encouraging and interesting outcomes. Hybrid quantum convolutional neural networks (QCNNs) consist of quantum circuits and convolutional operations with high ability of hidden complex data relationships exploration. This quantum acceleration has been shown to have higher detection rates, such as in the presence of subtle differences between members of families of malware (Mercaldo et al., 2022).

One of the attractive features of quantum computing in the area of malware analysis is explain ability. Researchers can gain insight into the decision process of quantum models method through such techniques such as Gradient-weighted Class Activation Mapping (Grad-CAM). Grad-CAM maps the regions of the malware image that generated the decision of the model, so it is a simple technique to find the drivers of decision-making of quantum models (Mercaldo et al., 2022).

Finally, quantum computing allows the development of a novel paradigm of malware analysis with dramatically increased computing power and higher model interpretability. Since malware is continuously mutating, the integration of quantum technologies in the cybersecurity architectures represents an innovation path toward more robust and smarter malware detection systems.

Adversarial Scenario Simulation and Defence Automation in Cybersecurity

Attack tactic, technique, and procedure replication in an emulation environment as part of adversarial scenario simulation can be investigated to evaluate cybersecurity defences. Organizations can use adversarial real-world examples in simulations to identify weaknesses and generate practical measures of system resilience to sophisticated, persistent adversaries (APTs) or ransomware. Platforms, including adversarial emulation tools, can be used to support red team's activities modelling cybercriminal attacks and modelling defensive measures.

Defence automation also of help by using artificial intelligence and machine learning, respectively, to automatically, recognize, analyse and react to threats. Automating defences enables speed, lower alert saturation, and decreases the pressure to create more complex adversarial techniques. For example, automated procedures are able to identify attack-specific anomalies, provisionally isolate affected systems and automatically apply patches.

Incorporation, together with of these practices enables improved early warning and protection for early detection and prevention of threats, so as to secure robust defensive information security postures and resilient against adaptive adversaries (Chowdhury et al., 2020; Zheng et al., 2021). The implementation of these strategies is of critical importance for extant cyber defence architectures.

Simulating Attack Scenarios Using LLMs

With Large Language Models (LLMs) as the example of GPT-4 and Mistral-7B, graduating from the lower edges of the security perimeter into basic use, they are being adopted more and more for the generation of realistic attack scenarios, automatically, for example, for synthetic data creation. Researches in this area are

Monte-Carlo simulations so that it is possible to avoid identifying the nature of the root cause and even virtually launching a cyberattack. By means of frameworks such as the MITRE ATT&CK matrix, LLMs can automate attack flows spanning multiple stages (Xu et al., 2024)

LLMs such as Auto attacker, in combination with security tools, to permit post-breached stage attack model. Of these types of system have modules in summarization, planning, and navigation for adaptive planning and execution of commands in a virtual environment. Using Retrieval-Augmented Generation (RAG) they integrate previous execution tasks in such a way that their performance is improved over current approaches, and consequently their success rate is increased and their wasted effort is reduced (Xu et al., 2024).

This kind of automation decreases the necessity of expert human testers and scales penetration testing. The attack simulation using the LLM based approach can model sophisticated adversarial behaviour as it can provide security officers with an in-depth understanding of all viable attack paths. For example, the tasks of privilege escalation and credential theft are synthesized with high accuracy, which consequently allows full testing of corporate defences (Sharma Verma, 2024).

Despite their advantages, there are notable challenges. LLMs are recognized to have limitations in contextual constraints, fakse output and failure of dynamic environment. There may also be ethical concerns about the potential for such systems to be controlled by such malactors. As a response to some of these limitations, researchers build controlled environments and are protected from the harms they can cause (Sharma Veram, 2024; Xu et al., 2024).

Attack scenario simulations with LLMs is a promising area in cyber security. These instruments are not only able to implement routine methods but also provide a more complex insight into the evolving nature of the attack landscape, which becomes a key element of modern cyber defence strategies.

Automated Defence Mechanisms and Quantum Cryptography

Increasing number of cyber-attacks and rapidly growing quantum computing applications. Automation and quantum cryptography forms the basis of how these problems can be solved, at the edge of next generation technology that will defend digital property.

Automated defence systems use artificial intelligence (AI) and machine learning (ML) to identify and defend against cyber-attacks in real time. The systems though operate on the network traffic patterns and detect the anomalies and evolve the attack paths. Quantum machine learning (QML) is an extension of machine learning (ML) in the field of quantum computing, which employs quantum computing to process the large data set more swiftly and effectively, then accelerates the detection and countermeasure of the cyberthreat. By the integration of quantum measurement library (QML) and leveraging the quantum effect, such as entanglement, to improve prediction ability of cybersecurity systems (Xu et al., 2024).

Quantum cryptography using the principle of quantum mechanics, can provide the highest level of secure information transmission. Quantum states are exploited in quantum key distribution (QKD) protocols, such as the BB84 protocol, to generate key, which cannot be cloned by an eavesdropper. Measurement of quantum state alters information irrevocably and the breach is immediately apparent. This has the consequence that there are secure communication channels even in complex quantum attacks (Bennett Brassard, 1984; Mamatha et al., 2024).

Hybrid deployment of quantum cryptography and automated attack defence systems, can deliver, from a principled perspective, a sound trade-off in the context of cybersecurity. By means of automation, key management, and system control, AI results in an advancement of quantum cryptologic operations. Conversely, quantum cryptography offers a security solution for AI systems against quantum attack by utilizing quantum computation, beyond quantum computation. Cryptographic algorithms resistant to attacks by quantum cryptoanalysis, e.g., lattice-based cryptography and HMAC-like hash functions currently under development within the PQC (Iovane et al., 2024) .

As a result of the advent of the quantum era, combination of fully automatic defensive strategy and quantum cryptosystem output leads to a multilayered protection framework. These technologies offer, not only a shield for currently existing systems, but also a shield for future built infrastructure from quantum-based attacks.

Building Resilient Cybersecurity Systems

The engineering challenge of how to design cyber security infrastructures that can plan for, withstand, recover from, and learn from cyber-attacks is the focus of the topic. Resilient arbitrary number of failures system guarantees that data is available, performant, and private in the case of an attack or system failure.

Characteristics of a Resilient Cybersecurity System

- **Anticipating Threats:** Active systems in all cases, calculate risk, looking for holes in coverage, and building a knowledge of adversary activity (Schiliro, 2023).

- **Withstanding Attacks:** Resilient systems continue to operate even when under attack, with strong defences, including firewalls, intrusion detection systems and redundancy (Schiliro, 2023).

- **Recovery and Continuity:** Assistive technologies with effective function restoration at reasonable speed (automated backup, failover and disaster recovery) as well as minimal further downtime in the presence of an attempt (Schiliro, 2023).
- **Adaptability:** Adaptive robust systems, can make their own increase to a new threat based on autonomously learning from the past, by concurrently updating the code and by sustainably optimizing the processes (Schiliro,2023).

Core Components

- **Segmentation:** Isolating critical systems to limit the spread of attacks.
- **Redundancy:** Using backup systems to maintain functionality during failures.
- **Monitoring:** Continuous surveillance to detect anomalies in real time

Table 1. Features of a Resilient Cybersecurity System.

Feature	Function
Anticipation	Identifies risks and potential vulnerabilities.
Robust Defence	Maintains functionality during attacks.
Rapid Recovery	Ensures continuity with minimal downtime.
Continuous Adaptation	Updates defences against evolving threats.

A resilient cybersecurity system protects an organization from immediate harm and ensures long-term sustainability and preparedness against increasingly sophisticated cyber threats (Schiliro, 2023).

Designing Quantum-Aware Cybersecurity Frameworks

The advent of quantum computing has brought about significant risk to classical cryptographic algorithms. Quantum-enhanced cyber security systems are designed to sense and respond to such an attack by grafting quantum-resistant solutions and hardware into and with security infrastructure.

Key Elements of Quantum-Aware Frameworks

- **Post-Quantum Cryptography (PQC):** These cryptologic ciphers are constructed to be withstand an attack from traditional computer or bot, and quantum computer respectively. Cryptographic algorithms (lattice-based algorithm, hash-based algorithm, and code-based algorithm) are the engine of the PQC. For example, lattice-based approaches have been focused on because of their scalability and its resistance to quantum attacks (Dwivedi et al., 2023).

- **Quantum Key Distribution (QKD):** The quantum key distribution (QKD) is founded on quantum mechanics principles, providing a crypto visibility of communications channels. As QKD is able to detect all possible eavesdropping, it guarantees unbreakable "closeness" in the shared, cryptographic keys of the two parties (Baseri etc., 2024).

Hybrid Cryptographic Approaches: During the transitional stage, hybrid systems merge conventional ciphers with quantum retrieval algorithms for multi-layered protection against existing and emerging cryptanalytic attacks (Dwivedi et al., 2023).

Potential Threats

Cryptographic Breaches: Algorithms which are ripe for being cracked (e.g., Shor's algorithms) which upon implementation of RSA and ECC, became the most ubiquitous cryptographic module.

Data Manipulation and Espionage: For instance, the employment of a system where exploitable secret data can be discretely recovered by a system (e.g., cyber operations, cyber warfare, so called data generation.

Implementation Strategies

Risk Assessment and Mitigation: Frameworks have also focused risk analyses for the detection of IT environment layer (e.g., applications, OS, and network) weakness /vulnerability (Dwivedi colleagues, 2023).

Standardization: Quantum-aware cybersecurity standards are one of the critical components for us to navigate the future quantum era, where the rise and use of quantum-safe cryptographic algorithms will be overseen by agencies such as NIST under phased releases (Baseri et al., 2024).

Not only are the concatenations of these frameworks and PQC, QKD and hybrid frameworks a uniquely effective way to provide the necessary counts of defensive measures at an unencumbered cost, they are also capable of providing the necessary protection against the man-in-the-middle type of quantum-adversarial attack.

Integrating LLMs and Quantum Technologies for Automated Defence

Together with large language models (LLMs), the convergence of quantum technologies has dramatically changed the automated security defence realm within cybersecurity. This integration addresses difficult challenges by enhancing detection, response and prevention measures within the rapidly expanding, densely linked digital world.

Applications

- **Advanced Threat Detection**

LLMs excel in the processing of extremely large numbers of data items, in breach detection, and in generating alarms for network traffic anomalies. Embedded in quantum-enhanced machine learning (QML), these platforms can learn and maliciously outsmart their adversaries. Modelling and analysis of multidimensional data from quantum systems is also a tool to improve the sensitivity of detection (Ferrag et al).

- **Real-Time Intrusion Response**

Quantum algorithms control HMM dynamics, in real-time applications, and even in the presence of a cyber-attack. The very nature of this partnership ensures that the computationally intensive steps in the execution of zero-day attack/Distributed Denial of Service (DDoS) attack response can be handle better (Xu et al., 2024).

- **Encryption Key Management**

More specifically, quantum technologies (e.g., quantum key distribution, or QKD) are probably secure communication building blocks that cannot be passively monitored for an eavesdropper. LLMs automate the security and monitoring of QKD protocols, in the place of the insecure offloading of encryption keys to as much sensitive part of the infrastructure (e.g., financial, defence) as possible (Iovane et al).

- **Predictive Analytics for Cybersecurity**

Hybrid application of LLMs and quantum technologies, resulting in forecasting analyses, enables companies to plan over typical "reactive reflexes" and indeed prevents a cyberattack. Can also simulate the future threat scenario of an aggressive party and identify adaptive countermeasures to enhance the context of proactivist security (Ferrag et al., 2024).

- **Post-Quantum Cryptography Support**

LLMs allow the creation of quantum-safe cryptographic protocols through benchmarking of encryption algorithms and algorithm optimization of encryption schemes. The inherent ability of these to enable the generation and testing of adaptive/quantum cryptographic capabilities is what renders quantum cryptographic systems secure against future quantum computer attacks (Mamatha et al., 2024).

- **Cyber-Physical System Security**

Integration in the context of critical infrastructures, e.g., energy grids, transportation networks, etc., delivers robust cyber physic security. Quantum enhanced models analyse big volume data streams from sensors in real time, and LLMs decode this information to detect vulnerabilities and suggest on the spot actions (Ferrag et al., 2024).

Table 2. Comparison of Cryptographic Approaches.

Approach	Strengths	Challenges
Post-Quantum Crypto	Resists quantum attacks	Efficiency trade-offs
Quantum Key Distribution	Detects interception	Expensive implementation
Hybrid Systems	Provides layered security	Complexity in integration

CHALLENGES AND FUTURE DIRECTIONS

There is a high potential for the use of large language models (LLMs) in boosting quantum-powered cybersecurity platforms, especially in providing real-time anomaly detection and threat intelligence. However, issues of implementation and innovation exist in this area as well.

- **Challenges**
- **Real-Time Data Processing**

Quantum-based devices produce massive throughput of data with very high throughput. LLMs need to deal with that kind of information quickly and this processing comes with a load that tests the limits of the existing computational framework. Penetration of the needs for low latency and high accuracy with respect to anomaly detection constitutes an urgent challenge (Ferrag et al., 2024).

- **Quantum Data Representation**

LLMs primarily operate in classical computational environments. Integration of these into quantum data systems makes use of complex algorithms, capable not only of decoding's, but also of holding fidelity (Mamatha et al., 2024).

- **Model Robustness**

The robustness of LLMs in quantum environments is critical. Being in principle at risk to adversarial attacks, which manipulate the LLM-based output containing the weaknesses, i.e., erroneous anomaly discriminations. The difficulty of maintaining model accuracy as a threat space changes is difficult (Xu et al., 2024).

- **Resource Efficiency**

Quantum-aware cybersecurity demands resource-intensive computations. LLMs, which are computationally expensive, also place a greater demand on system resources, and thus there is a need for optimizations in the deployment of the models (Iovane et al., 2024).

Future Directions

Quantum-Language Interfaces

The creation of quantum data interfaces, achieved by native processing supported by LLMs will close the gap between the classical and quantum worlds. This will enable seamless integration into quantum cybersecurity frameworks.

Adaptive LLM Models

Next generation LLMs must consider adaptive learning so as to be able to adapt in real time to quantum data. Such systems would, by their nature, be optimized for anomaly detection algorithms and their ability to detect previously unseen attacks (Ferrag et al).

Federated Quantum-LLM Architectures

If taken together with quantum computing and LLMs, decentralized architectures will be more scalable and robust. These systems distribute tasks among quantum nodes, carry out threat intelligence processing (Mamatha et al., 2024).

Enhanced Threat Intelligence

With the integration of LLMs and quantum-enhanced machine-learning algorithms, it will be possible to enhance threat intelligence by detecting and dismantling the threat in its earliest form. This synergism makes advanced preventive cybersecurity measures (Xu et al., 2024) possible.

The integration of LLMs and quantum-adaptive cybersecurity systems has the prospect of attaining a new generation of potent attack-resistant defences against contemporary threats. The only way forward to overcome the difficulty and fully tap into the real power of these technologies exists in further research and innovation.

Technical, Ethical, and Scalability Challenges in Cybersecurity Emerging Threats and the Need for Evolving Cybersecurity Solutions

The security systems of the cyberworld, particularly those developed with next generation technologies (e.g., Artificial Intelligence (AI), quantum computing) are best by a number of challenges that emerge in the process of representing and in development. All these problematics can be summarized under technical, ethical, and scalability limitations that have implications not only for effectiveness, but also for generalizability of cyber security solutions.

Technical Challenges

- **Integration with Existing Systems**

Many organizations are based on antiquated infrastructure, which is not only not large enough to fit the implementation of new technologies, such as those using AI or those using quantum manipulation. Additional platform implementation in these platforms comes at a high level of overhead and more costly interventions (Ferrag et al., 2024).

- **Data Quality and Diversity**

AI-based models, in particular LLMs require clean representative widely enough labelled data to achieve good threat detection accuracy. The publication of a dataset from a point of view of availability in cyber security is limited by the proprietary and confidential nature of the information present in cyber-attack data, making it impossible to publicly share. This challenge also plays a primary role in the decline of the accuracy of anomaly detection and threat classification (Mamatha et al., 2024).

- **Quantum Vulnerabilities**

Due to the introduction of the quantum computer, the classical cryptographic schemes are susceptible to quantum algorithms (Shor's algorithm). Research and evaluation of quantum-resistant cryptographic techniques remains an engineering problem (Iovane et al., 2024).

Ethical Challenges

- **Bias in AI Algorithms**

Infected LLMs suffer from contamination with biases in the training data, cybersecurity assessments will be biased and/or incomplete. For instance, the weights assigned by models to various types of risk may reflect a trade-off such as the effort needed to fix a subset of the most serious of critical vulnerabilities, which are not yet to be patched.

- **Privacy and Surveillance**

Cybersecurity appliances further work with personal data, the use of which, unfortunately, has the potential to lead to privacy problems. The dilemma of how to make effective threat detection at the cost of privacy is an ethical question (Xu et al., 2024).

- **Dual-Use Risks**

Cybersecurity technologies, such as quantum algorithms, can be put to use, for positive or negative reasons. Tools that malicious peers are likely to be able to use to implement complex attacks, and that will be robustly controlled in both the design stage and at deployment (Ferrag et al., 2024).

Scalability Challenges

- **Computational Costs**

Threat-based computations and computation-intensive, AI- and quantum-based cyber security systems are demanding enormous computing power and therefore marks the apex of vulnerability as targets, especially those group of industrial and low-income developing countries.

- **Standardization Gaps**

The absence of global, recognized, standards for cybersecurity systems (particularly for quantum technologies) limits global interoperability and standardization of defences.

- **Dynamic Threat Adaptation**

Cyber threats are always evolving, and model scaling to meet changing threats requires constant update and recalibration, at an economic cost (Mamatha et al., 2024).

Future Outlook

To overcome these challenges, future efforts should focus on:

- Hybrid models of AI and quantum computing at their most extreme levels.
- Discussion of principles and guidelines for the use of AI in cybersecurity for an equitable and solution.
- Promoting collaborative international efforts for standardization and resource-sharing.

Against these challenges, cybersecurity will have the most to do to meet the requirements of a more globally connected, quantum powered digital world.

Emerging Threats and the Need for Evolving Cybersecurity Solutions

However, because of the rapid expansion and change of the digital landscape, the threats to the digital space are also expanding and changing at an accelerated rate. Basically, it can be considered the combat space in which new and ever-changing cyber-safety threats are making a stand against. Organizations, governments, and individuals will be required to adopt adaptive and even anticipatory postures in as flexible, intricate and unpredictable ways as possible. More precisely, in this section regarding issues of threat creation, the central challenges of cybersecurity strategies, which seem to warrant an explicit solution in respect to the threat, and how to address these in the context of cybersecurity strategy are compared.

Key Emerging Threats in Cybersecurity

- **Advanced Persistent Threats (APTs):** The APTs are continuous, specific, and tenacious attacks aimed at the network, with the goals of infiltrating the network for an extended period with the ulterior purpose of evading detection. Such attacks (by a state or by highly skilled and professional, organized cybercrime group) target critical infrastructure, intellectual property and state secrets for political intelligence.

- **Ransomware Evolution:** Recent ransomware attacks have moved on from a readily understandable, straightforward encryption from a relatively low level of complexity to much more sophisticated algorithms that go beyond encryption, involving and also including malware, extortion and/or double extortion activities. Due to the advent of ransomware-as-a-service (RaaS), technical barrier against such attacks has been drastically reduced and they are increasingly becoming routine.
- **Artificial Intelligence (AI)-Powered Attacks:** Threat actors also use artificial intelligence and machine learning (ML) in malware development, increasingly focused and targeted phishing, and automating, on a great scale, attacks. It is also relatively easy for an actor to bypass the limitations of the present defences in these kinds of instruments.
- **Internet of Things (IoT) Vulnerabilities:** Since there are now connected in most cases trillions of devices based on the internet all of them in most situations are easy and efficient attack targets. Because the number of insecure IoT devices is substantial, they may be exploited to form a botnet.
- **Supply Chain Attacks:** Supply chain attacks are an increasing problem, in which the attacker targets a third-party vendor or service provider, who then attacks the customer. The SolarWinds attack of 2020 which is leverage a type of attack that goes beyond the scope of individual systems demonstrates how such attacks can be exponentially scaled up for example.
- **Quantum Computing Threats:** While yet in the early development phase, the security of traditional cryptographic algorithms is vulnerable to quantum computing. Quantum computers may lead to the unsuitability of existing cryptographic schemes.
- **Deepfake and Synthetic Media:** Deepfake technology has been used as a tool by public opinion campaigns, social engineering attacks, and even fraud. With artificial media convergence becoming more of a foregone conclusion, of course there will be a natural open door into cyber security.

The Need for Evolving Cybersecurity Solutions

Yet, the complexity and scale of the emerging threats the obsolete methods of cybersecurity are not equipped to offer a solution. A cyber secure model able to adapt to these challenges is in urgent need. Key areas for improvement include:

- **Proactive Threat Intelligence:** Threat intelligence in real-time is capable of providing an organization with the power which it will require in order to detect and prevent the spreading of the risk. Coordinated agency activity and intelligence sharing, however, are the most important factors which it is essential to keep one step ahead of the attackers.
- **Adoption of Zero Trust Architecture (ZTA):** ZTA takes away the implicit trust that is usually established between the network devices and the network users. By securing identification verification and enforcing tracking reprograms are strictly localized to minimize the attack space.
- **AI and Machine Learning in Defence:** AI-powered software can identify anomalies, expose logics, and predict most likely attack paths. ML algorithms are trained over time, i.e., the result is a continuously adapting response to a new attack.
- **Robust IoT Security Protocols:** It is necessary to secure the end-to-end encryption, usual firmware upgrades and authentication protocols in order to improve the security of IoT devices from a vendor's perspective. Regulatory compliance must be the concern of compliance practices, i.e., of governments.
- **Quantum-Resistant Cryptography:** The development of quantum-resistant algorithms holds great potential promise in preparing for the advent of quantum computing. National Institute of Standards and Technology (NIST) is also actively drafting standards defining quantum-secure cryptographic protocols.
- **Enhanced Incident Response:** Training well equipped incident response teams with their ability to move has high significance. Simulated attacks and drills can help prepare organizations, etc.
- **Focus on Security Awareness:** Human error remains one of the largest cybersecurity risks. For instance, training of staff for detection of phishing, secure use of passwords and prevention of social engineering attacks should be sufficiently robust to minimize risk.

CONCLUSION

The fusion of Large Language Models (LLM) with quantum technologies is an innovative paradigm of transformation in the world of cybersecurity. Single technologies have tremendous potential to make great advances, alone in one of the areas that LLMs are particularly well designed to address a special problem in NLP, data analysis and prediction of threat, and alone in one of the areas for which the power of quantum computing can be harnessed to solve a problem which is inherently out of reach for current computational limits of computing challenging encryption and cryptographic problems. Individually these technologies have the potential to revolutionize the way security personnel are working in cybersecurity, especially in critical security.

The combination of LLMs and quantum technologies can be applied to the design of real time anomaly detection and threat detection and identification, and to better withstand advanced persistent threats (APTs) and zero-day attacks. Through the use of LLMs to automatically create threat intelligence and the implementation of their predictive ability into quantum enhanced computers, corporations will be able to create trusted intrusion detection, malware detection and phishing detection systems. This framework offers an applicable framework for the analysis of complex adversarial scenarios to address automated countermeasures such as e.g., or quantum cryptography.

Despite their promise, these technologies also introduce significant challenges. Ethical issues, scalability and technical constraints of applying LLMs to quantum-aware systems, still account for one of the more significant gaps. Specifically, the exponential growth of cyber-attacks calls for the development of adaptive/proactive, dynamic, and potentially more general solutions to protect these frameworks over time. Interdisciplinary, continuous improvement, and evolving of best practices for general cybersecurity that will keep evolving and changing with technology are the demands.

Hybridization between LLMs and quantum technologies is a promising research line for cybersecurity. Although in terms of the technical translation barrier the large obstacle is the road itself, the increment brought by the ability to gain from real-time detection of attacks in addition to adaptive and fully automatic defences is certainly a lot more significant than the technical translation barrier. Exploiting such phases of innovation and procreative growth in order to meet emerging threats, it will be possible to engineer resilient, future-secure cyber systems capable of withstanding the ever-evolving nature of the digital world.

Key Insights and Practical Recommendations for Cybersecurity Practitioners

The intersection of Large Language Models (LLMs) and quantum computing is transforming cybersecurity by bringing and threatening novel ideas and opportunities to and from practitioners. Together the technologies fill in those gaps by improving on-site threat detection, improving cryptographies, and auto-mating defensive measures. However, integration and some challenges exist including ethical, scalability multidisciplinary experts. To successfully manoeuvre through this evolving world, cybersecurity practitioners must know the key lessons learned as a consequence of these developments and use those lessons in the form of tactics and behaviours to leverage their potential.

Key Insights

Enhanced Cyber Threat Detection and Defence: Integration with an LLM and quantum computing has irrevocably changed the landscape of threat detection and response. LLMs are very suited to the analysis of large amount of unstructured data, such as the detection of anomalies, phishing and automated classification of malware. Conversely, quantum technologies drive these to the capacity to be highly sensitive and hopefully both quantizable regarding the detection of complex persistent threats (APTs) and zero-day attacks.

The Evolving Role of Cryptography: Quantum computing attacks classical cryptographic primitives in a manner which compromises the security of some cryptographic primitives. But it also introduces quantum-resistance cryptography and secure communication in the quantum world. This raises an immediate critical need to develop quantum-resistant algorithms and track the development of quantum-decryption algorithms.

Automation and Simulated Defence Mechanisms: LLMs can be used for automating tasks in cyber security for example, intrusion detection, malware signature detection, and adversarial modelling. Along with such quantum technologies this automation can be tailored to dynamically evolving environments, thereby providing real-time nearly infallible responses.

Emerging Ethical and Technical Challenges: Despite their high potential to improve the efficiency of security and cyber defence, both LLMs and quantum technologies also come with paradoxes. Ethical challenges, e.g., data privacy, model bias, and AI to be used maliciously will have to be dealt with. In this regard also, the technical complexity of integrating such systems is also very high and a significant number of resources are required.

Practical Recommendations for Quantum-Aware Cybersecurity

1. Transition to Quantum-Resistant Cryptography

Begin the transition to quantum-resistant cryptographic algorithms to safeguard classified and sensitive data against future quantum-enabled attacks. Collaborate with standard-setting bodies like NIST to stay aligned with the latest cryptographic advancements and best practices. This proactive approach will help ensure that cryptographic systems remain secure in the quantum computing era.

2. Deploy AI-Driven Threat Intelligence Systems

Utilize Large Language Models (LLMs) to enhance threat intelligence capabilities by automating the detection of potential attack vectors. LLMs can efficiently process unstructured data, such as logs, emails, and communication patterns, to uncover actionable insights. This automation can significantly improve response times and enhance the overall effectiveness of defense mechanisms.

3. Develop Multilayered Defense Architectures

Collaborate with LLMs to build robust, multilayered cybersecurity architectures. These systems can automatically detect and respond to a wide range of threats, including sophisticated attack vectors. By integrating both AI-driven and quantum-enhanced capabilities, these architectures can offer a higher level of resilience against advanced cyberattacks.

4. Enhance Incident Response with Automation

Automate routine security workflows, such as phishing detection and malware classification, using LLMs and other AI technologies. This automation frees up cybersecurity professionals to focus on more complex issues while maintaining a scalable and effective response structure. Automation also helps improve consistency and efficiency in handling incidents.

5. Simulate and Prepare for Adversarial Scenarios

Leverage LLMs to run advanced adversarial scenarios and stress-test defense strategies. Quantum-enhanced simulations can provide valuable insights into potential vulnerabilities and system weaknesses, helping organizations identify and address points of brittleness. This proactive approach to adversarial training ensures that systems are more resilient to evolving attack techniques.

6. Educate and Upskill Cybersecurity Teams

Equip cybersecurity professionals with the knowledge and skills to operate and integrate both LLMs and quantum technologies effectively. Continuous education and training programs, including workshops and certifications, are essential to keep teams up to date with the latest developments in these disruptive technologies. This investment in human capital will enable organizations to better leverage the full potential of AI and quantum systems.

7. Address Ethical and Governance Challenges

Formulate and implement policies to address ethical challenges in the deployment of AI and quantum technologies. These may include concerns around AI bias, data privacy, and accountability in automated defense systems. Establish governance frameworks to ensure that LLMs and quantum tools are applied ethically, transparently, and in compliance with applicable laws and regulations.

8. Collaborate Across Industries

Foster collaboration with industry peers, academic institutions, and regulatory bodies to share knowledge, best practices, and strategies for addressing emerging cyber threats. Industry-wide partnerships can drive innovation, help establish common security standards, and create a unified response to global cybersecurity challenges.

9. Prepare for Regulatory Compliance

Stay informed about the evolving regulatory landscape concerning AI and quantum technologies in cybersecurity. Track the development of laws and regulations related to quantum computing and AI security, ensuring compliance to maintain organizational integrity and public trust. Proactively preparing for regulatory changes will help minimize risks and avoid compliance-related penalties.

REFERENCES

Aghayev, A., & Naderi, P. (2024). Hybrid quantum-classical cybersecurity solutions for IoT applications. *Quantum Information Processing*, 24(8).

Aharon, D.. (2024). Using large language models to enhance AI-based cybersecurity protocols. *arXiv*. https://arxiv.org/abs/2404.11713

. Ahmad, I., Hussain, M., & Qureshi, F. (2022). Intrusion detection techniques in cybersecurity: A comprehensive review. *Journal of Cybersecurity Research*.

Ahmed, U., Sipola, T., & Hautamäki, J. (2024). Cyber protection applications of quantum computing: A review. *In Proceedings of the 23rd European Conference on Cyber Warfare and Security (ECCWS)*. Academic Conferences International. https://doi.org/DOI: 10.34190/eccws.23.1.2182

Alam, M. T., Tanvirul, A., Bhushal, D., & Rastogi, N. (2024). Using LLMs to automate threat intelligence analysis workflows in security operation centers. *arXiv*. https://ar5iv.labs.arxiv.org/html/2407.02528

Ali, T., & Kostakos, P. (2023). HuntGPT: Integrating machine learning-based anomaly detection and explainable AI with large language models (LLMs). *arXiv*. https://arxiv.org/abs/2309.16021

Althobaiti, O. S., & Dohler, M. (2020). Cybersecurity challenges associated with the Internet of Things in a post-quantum world. *IEEE Access : Practical Innovations, Open Solutions*, 8, 157356–157381. DOI: 10.1109/ACCESS.2020.3019345

Bhosale, K. S., Singh, A., Ambre, S., Nenova, M., & Valkova-Jarvis, Z. (2023). *Quantum technology: Unleashing the power and shaping the future of cybersecurity*. IEEE., DOI: 10.1109/Lighting59819.2023.10299447

Biamonte, J., Wittek, P., Pancotti, N., Rebentrost, P., Wiebe, N., & Lloyd, S. (2017). Quantum machine learning. *Nature*, 549(7671), 188–202. DOI: 10.1038/nature23474 PMID: 28905917

Biryukov, A., Shamir, A., & Wagner, D. (2000). Real-time cryptanalysis of A5/1 on a PC. *Fast Software Encryption Workshop 2000*.

Brown, K., & Thomason, R. (2022). Quantum security in the age of artificial intelligence. *IEEE Transactions on Quantum Engineering*.

Casey, E. (2002). Confronting encryption in computer investigations. *Digital Forensic Research Conference*.

. *Cooley,R., &Olfati-Saber,R.(2023). Quantum-enhanced cryptography for network security: Future research directions.* Quantum Cryptography Journal

Danish, M. (2024). *Enhancing Cyber Security through Predictive Analytics: Real-Time Threat Detection and Response*. University of New Mexico.

. Demming, C., & Baugh, J. (1997). Practical approaches to recovering encrypted digital evidence. *Journal of Digital Forensics*.

Dini, P., & Saponara, S. (2023). Design and experimental assessment of real-time anomaly detection techniques for automotive cybersecurity. *Sensors (Basel)*, 23(9231), 9231. Advance online publication. DOI: 10.3390/s23229231 PMID: 38005616

Fang, S., & Wang, T. (2024). Quantum cryptography and secure communication in next-generation cybersecurity systems. *Communications of the ACM*.

Faruk, M. J. H., Tahora, S., Tasnim, M., Shahriar, H., & Sakib, N. (2022). A review of quantum cybersecurity: Threats, risks, and opportunities. *Kennesaw State University and University at Buffalo*. Retrieved from https://arxiv.org/abs/2207.03534

Faruk, M. J. H., Tahora, S., Tasnim, M., Shahriar, H., & Sakib, N. (2024). Quantum-safe cybersecurity in the age of quantum-powered AI. *ResearchGate*. https://www.researchgate.net/publication/377557867_Quantum-safe_Cybersecurity_in_the_age_of_Quantum-Powered_AI

Ferrag, M. A., Alwahedi, F., Battah, A., Cherif, B., Mechri, A., & Tihanyi, N. (2024). Generative AI and large language models for cybersecurity: All insights you need. *arXiv*. https://arxiv.org/abs/2405.12750v1

. Finzi, D., & Mazzucco, A. (2023). Efficient threat detection using hybrid quantum machine learning techniques. *International Journal of Cyber Defense & Security*.

Gade, N. R., & Reddy, U. (2014). A study of cybersecurity challenges and its emerging trends on latest technologies. *IACSIT International Journal of Engineering and Technology*, 2(2).

Gagliardi, D., & Restrepo, P. (2024). *Leveraging quantum machine learning for future cybersecurity infrastructures*. IEEE Computer Society.

Garofalo, D., & Christensen, A. (2024). *A study on the effectiveness of hybrid quantum-classical machine learning for cybersecurity*. Quantum Computing in Cybersecurity Review.

Gudivada, V., & Sharma, S. (2024). A review of current trends, techniques, and challenges in large language models (LLMs). *Applied Sciences (Basel, Switzerland)*, 14(5), 2074. DOI: 10.3390/app14052074

Guo, T., & Zhang, F. (2024). Machine learning and quantum cryptography: New era of cybersecurity threats and protections. *arXiv*. https://arxiv.org/abs/2402.02901

Hadi, M. U., Al Tashi, Q., Qureshi, R., Shah, A., Muneer, A., Irfan, M., Zafar, A., Shaikh, M. B., Akhtar, N., Hassan, S. Z., Shoman, M., Wu, J., Mirjalili, S., & Shah, M. (2024). A survey on large language models: Applications, challenges, limitations, and practical usage. *TechRxiv*. https://doi.org/DOI: 10.36227/techrxiv.23589741.v1

Hassanin, M., & Moustafa, N. (2024). A comprehensive overview of large language models for cyber defenses: Opportunities and directions. *arXiv*. https://ar5iv.labs.arxiv.org/html/2409.15072

Houssel, P. R. B., Singh, P., Layeghy, S., & Portmann, M. (2024). Towards explainable network intrusion detection using large language models. *arXiv:2408.04342*. Link

Kheddara, H. (2023). Implementing quantum neural networks for network traffic analysis in cybersecurity. *Journal of Quantum Computing and AI*, 10(3), 115–124.

Ladd, T. D., Jelezko, F., Laflamme, R., Nakamura, Y., Monroe, C., & O'Brien, J. L. (2010). Quantum computers. *Nature*, 464(7285), 45–53. DOI: 10.1038/nature08812 PMID: 20203602

. Lee, S., & Lee, H. (2022). Quantum encryption and blockchain for cybersecurity: A systematic review. *Quantum Computing & AI Journal*.

Liang, Z., Cheng, J., Yang, R., Ren, H., Song, Z., Wu, D., & Li, T. (2023). Unleashing the potential of LLMs for quantum computing: A study in quantum architecture design. *University of Notre Dame, Purdue University, and others*. Retrieved from https://arxiv.org/abs/2307.08191

. McMahon, P., & Blanchard, J. (2024). Quantum cryptography as a key element in future cybersecurity strategies. *Quantum Technologies Journal*, 6(3).

Micali, D., & Lin, W. (2021). Quantum algorithms for machine learning and their application in cybersecurity. *arXiv:2112.03180.*

Mohd, I. S., & Ahmed, M. (2024). Quantum-safe algorithms for post-quantum cybersecurity challenges. *arXiv*. https://arxiv.org/abs/2403.02769

Moradi, M., Yan, K., Colwell, D., Samwald, M., & Asgari, R. (2024). Exploring the landscape of large language models: Foundations, techniques, and challenges. *arXiv*. https://arxiv.org/abs/2404.11973

Patel, K., & Hamed, Z. (2023). *Security in a post-quantum world: Approaches and techniques in cryptography*. Springer Advances in Computational Intelligence.

Pérez-Álvarez, J.. (2023). *Quantum-enhanced machine learning for the prediction and prevention of cybersecurity risks*. Computational Intelligence and Quantum Machine Learning Journal.

. Ravi, S., & Menon, M. (2024). Quantum-assisted threat detection in cybersecurity using large language models. *International Journal of Quantum Computing & Cybersecurity*.

Rosch-Grace, D., & Straub, J. (2024). *Considering the implications of artificial intelligence, quantum computing, and cybersecurity*. IEEE., DOI: 10.1109/CSCI58124.2022.00191

Schuld, M., & Petruccione, F. (2018). *Supervised learning with quantum computers*. Springer., DOI: 10.1007/978-3-319-96424-9

Serketzis, N., Katos, V., Ilioudis, C., Baltatzis, D., & Pangalos, G. J. (2019). Actionable threat intelligence for digital forensics readiness. *Future Internet*, 11(7), 162. DOI: 10.3390/fi11070162

Shaikh, S., & Awan, M. (2024). Ensuring integrity and confidentiality in cybersecurity with quantum machine learning. *Proceedings of Cybersecurity and Quantum Technologies Workshop*.

Suryotrisongko, H., & Musashi, Y. (2022). Evaluating hybrid quantum-classical deep learning for cybersecurity botnet DGA detection. *Procedia Computer Science*, 197, 223–229. DOI: 10.1016/j.procs.2021.12.135

Tseng, W., Lee, S., & Wang, H. (2024). Evaluating the usability of LLMs in threat intelligence enrichment. *arXiv*. https://ar5iv.labs.arxiv.org/html/2407.13093

Vaswani, A., Shazeer, N., Parmar, N., Uszkoreit, J., Jones, L., Gomez, A. N., Kaiser, Ł., & Polosukhin, I. (2017). Attention is all you need. *Proceedings of the Advances in Neural Information Processing Systems (NeurIPS), 30*, 5998-6008. https://arxiv.org/abs/1706.03762

Vishwakarma, A., & Ghosh, D. (2024). *An AI-powered quantum encryption system for secure communication networks*. IEEE., DOI: 10.1109/ACCESS.2024.3157194

Watson, L., & Crone, S. (2023). Quantum machine learning in cybersecurity: Leveraging quantum computing for AI-based anomaly detection. *Quantum Information Science*, 7(5), 150.

Williams, J., & Mitchell, M. (2022). Optimizing cybersecurity defenses using hybrid quantum-classical models. *Nature Communications*, 13(1).

Wu, J., & Chen, L. (2024). *Exploiting quantum learning algorithms for detecting cybersecurity vulnerabilities in real-time systems*. IEEE Transactions on Cybersecurity.

Xu, H., Wang, S., Li, N., Wang, K., Zhao, Y., Liu, Y., & Wang, H. (2024). Large language models for cyber security: A systematic literature review. *arXiv*. https://arxiv.org/abs/2405.04760v3

Yang, Y., & Liu, Y. (2024). *Using machine learning for quantum threat modeling and analysis*. Cybersecurity Research Advances.

Zeng, S., & Hsin, J. (2023). *Applications of quantum computing in improving security in digital infrastructure*. Quantum Computing for Cybersecurity Journal.

. Zhang, F., & Yasin, M. (2023). Security risk analysis in quantum computing-enabled systems. *International Journal of Cybersecurity and Applied Cryptography*.

Zhang, J., Bu, H., Wen, H., Chen, Y., Li, L., & Zhu, H. (2024). When LLMs meet cybersecurity: A systematic literature review. *Institute of Information Engineering, Chinese Academy of Sciences*. Retrieved from https://arxiv.org/abs/2405.03644

Zhang, Q., Liu, T., & Yu, M. (2024). *Analyzing cybersecurity threats using AI-powered quantum computing models*. Quantum Cyber Defense.

Zhang, X., Li, W., & Tang, S. (2021). Advances in malware detection and classification using machine learning. *IEEE Access : Practical Innovations, Open Solutions*.

Zhou, S., Chen, R., An, Z., & Hou, S.-Y. (2024). Application of large language models to quantum state simulation. *arXiv*. https://arxiv.org/abs/2403.19758

KEY WORDS AND DEFINITIONS

Advanced Persistent Threat (APT): – A prolonged and targeted cyber-attack where an intruder, often a skilled group or organization, gains unauthorized access to a system and remains undetected over an extended period, with the goal of stealing data or causing ongoing disruption.

Eavesdropper: – An individual or entity that secretly listens to or intercepts communication without the consent of the parties involved, often with the intent to gather sensitive information.

Intrusion Detection System (IDS): – A security system designed to monitor and analyze network traffic or system activities to detect signs of malicious activity, unauthorized access, or security breaches.

LLMs (Large Language Models): – Artificial intelligence models capable of performing tasks with human-like proficiency, such as natural language understanding, text generation, and problem-solving, often producing super-human-like output across a variety of domains.

Phishing: – A form of cybercrime that involves tricking individuals into revealing sensitive information, such as passwords or financial details, by disguising malicious emails, messages, or websites as legitimate communications.

Post-Quantum Cryptography (PQC): – A branch of cryptographic techniques designed to secure systems against both classical and quantum computer-based attacks, ensuring that data remains protected even in the presence of quantum computing capabilities capable of breaking traditional encryption methods.

Quantum Key Distribution (QKD): – A method of securely exchanging cryptographic keys using quantum mechanics, which ensures that any attempt at eavesdropping can be detected, making the process highly secure against interception.

Zero-Day Attack: – A type of cyber-attack that exploits a previously unknown vulnerability in software or hardware, taking advantage of the time gap between the discovery of the vulnerability and the release of a patch to fix it.

Chapter 8
Artificial Intelligence–Powered Cybersecurity: The Future of How Threats Are Detected and Responded

Soumya George
https://orcid.org/0000-0002-7256-7677
SGC Aruvithura, India

ABSTRACT

Cybersecurity threats are ever-changing and characterized by more sophisticated attacks including, but not limited to, ransomware, phishing attempts, and Distributed Denial-of-Service (DDoS) attacks. Integration of Artificial Intelligence in cybersecurity is one of the pioneering methods for dealing with the new threats in the digital environment. This article highlights areas where AI technologies improve threat detection, response automation, and risk management. It discusses the challenges, ethical issues, and AI solutions in cybersecurity

INTRODUCTION

Cybersecurity threats are basically harmful actions that target the confidentiality, integrity, or availability of digital systems and data. Some of the most common threats include malware (like viruses, ransomware, spyware, and Trojans), phishing (which involves sending deceptive emails or messages to trick people into giving up sensitive information), Denial of Service (DoS) and Distributed Denial of Service (DDoS) attacks (where systems are overloaded to disrupt access), and Man-in-the-Middle (MitM) attacks (that involve intercepting communications). There are also insider threats (which come from malicious or careless employees), Advanced Per-

DOI: 10.4018/979-8-3373-1102-9.ch008

sistent Threats (APTs) (that are sustained, targeted attacks by sophisticated groups), and zero-day exploits (which attack unknown vulnerabilities). Other risks include credential theft through techniques like keylogging and brute-force attacks, social engineering tactics (which manipulate individuals into divulging information), supply chain attacks (that compromise third-party vendors), crypto jacking (unauthorized cryptocurrency mining), and vulnerabilities in the Internet of Things (IoT). These challenges are difficult for traditional defenses to deal with. Artificial intelligence (AI) has become an essential support, utilizing complex algorithms to analyze large dataset and detect anomalies and improve decisions (Makridakis, 2017)

This paper discusses various cybersecurity threats, AI methodologies in cybersecurity, explores its real-world applications, and examines its advantages and limitations, concluding with recommendations for future research.

Glossary of Cybersecurity Threats

The various types of cybersecurity threats are listed below:

1. **Adware**: Automatically displays advertisements, downloads advertisements when installed on a computer, mostly accompanying free software which may lead the device to slugging down, diffusing it to unwanted websites (Symantec, 2024).
2. **Advanced Persistent Threats (APT)**: There are very long, targeted cyber-attacks, when they reach in to penetrate the networks and stay there, undetected, stealing sensitive information (FireEye, n.d.).
3. **Botnets**: These are networks of compromised devices controlled by attackers to use them to execute different needs like sending out spam, stealing data, and performing DDoS attacks among other functions.
4. **Brute Force Attack**: Any dictionary attempt is made to crack passwords and break any type of encryption by trying every possible combination.
5. **Crypto jacking**: The unauthorized use of someone's computing resources to process cryptocurrency mining. It slows devices down and is energy-intensive.
6. **Cross-site Scripting (XSS):** It's where malicious scripts get injected into trusted sites, exploiting vulnerabilities in web applications to compromise user data.
7. **Denial-of-Service Attack (DoS)**: An attack by which a server, network, or service can be made unavailable to the clients through a plethora of unsolicited traffic (Cloudflare, 2024).
8. **Data Breaches:** Unauthorized access to confidential or sensitive data, which are sometimes considered identity thefts or financial losses.
9. **Eavesdropping Attacks**: Interception and stealing data over a network including passwords or credit card information.

10. **Exploits**: Those can be tools or techniques utilized for system vulnerability exploitation that provide unauthorized access or control.
11. **Form jacking**: Injecting malevolent code into available forms online stealing personal, as well as payment information users have input.
12. **Hacktivism:** It is the cyber act of breaking laws, hacking into a site, or leaking top-secret files to the public to advance a revolutionary or social-political agenda.
13. **Hoaxes**: False warnings about malware or imitations of warnings can confuse the user and lead to unnecessary or possibly harmful actions.
14. **Insider Threats**: It's a threat that comes from a person's negligence or from malicious intent by employees or contractors within the organization (Institute, 2024).
15. **Injection attacks**: It is in form of untrusted data being sent to an interpreter as part of a command or query (like an SQL injection), and compromise integrity of data (OWASP, 2024).
16. **Malware**: Software that causes damage and prevents smooth running of systems and has various forms of viruses, worm, Trojan, ransomware, spyware, etc.
17. **Man-in-the-middle (MITM) attacks**: when the third party secretly detects the communication or changes the message from one party to another (ThreatConnect, 2024).
18. **Phishing**: This is fraudulent contacting intended to get personal information, probably via e-mail or fake websites, posing as a trustworthy source (Microsoft, 2024).
19. **Pretexting**: It is a type of social engineering, whereby attackers create a fictitious story to steal sensitive information.
20. **Ransomware**: a type of malware that encrypts victim data and demands payment to unlock it.
21. **Remote Code Execution (RCE)**: Exploiting a vulnerability to execute arbitrary code remotely on the system targeted.
22. **Smishing:** Phishing using SMS messages in order to deceive victims into linking to maliciously hosted web addresses or sharing sensitive information.
23. **Spoofing:** It is the impersonation of trusted entities such as emails or IPs to deceive the user or to bypass security measures.
24. **Spyware**: Software that secretly listens to user activity and sends recorded information to a third party.
25. **Trojan Horses**: Malware that presents itself as legitimate software in order to trick the user into executing dastardly actions-such as running destructive code.
26. **Typo squatting:** Registering domains that look remarkably like the original legit ones to lead one to falsified sites.
27. **Viruses**: Malicious code caused to attach itself to files and thus create an impression of spreading when executed, causing destruction to files or systems.

28. **Vishing:** Phishing attack via telephone calls meant to trick victims into leaking sensitive information.
29. **Worms:** Self-replicating malware spread continuously over networks without further action by the user and usually cause tremendous damage.
30. **Whaling**: This is a form of phishing that has a higher probability of getting past an individual's defenses, aiming at specific high-profile individuals, including the decision-makers of an organization, hoping to get sensitive information.
31. **Zero-Day Exploits**: Attacks that exploit vulnerabilities within software that are either unknown or still unpatched, hence leaving systems unguarded (Cisco Systems, 2024).
32. **Zombies:** These are devices compromised and controlled remotely through the handiwork of hackers and that are often used to engage in malicious activities forming part of a botnet.

Ways to Implement AI in Cybersecurity

The different ways to implement cybersecurity is shown in Figure 1.

Supervised Learning:

A supervised learning is that type of machine learning where each trained model will contain an input-output labeled data that is used in guiding the learning process. This thus means that the model learns to learn, and in the end, does a mapping from input to output in order to succeed in analyzing unseen samples or data, thus making predictions. Supervised learning is divided into regression, which predict continuous values, or classification for the predictions of discrete labels. Among such algorithms are linear regression, decision trees, support vector machines, and neural networks. This may include (but is not limited to) housing price predictions such as predicting a house price (regression) and classifying spam emails (classification). Hence, improvement in the model takes the form of reducing the error between its predictions and the actual outputs. This creates the possibility of overfitting, where the model does well with training data but poorly with new data. Cross-validation, including other techniques, has been in use to test and ensure generalization of the model. Applications of this method include many areas, including medical diagnosis, financial forecasting, and natural language processing.

Applications:

- Malware Detection: Detection of malware signatures employing classification models such as Random Forests and Support Vector Machines (Ahmed, 2016) (Ahsan, 2020).

- Spam Filtering: Supervised learning algorithms are used by email systems to classify emails as spam or not (Al-Garadi, 2020)
- ML-based Phishing Detection: CNNs and Decision Trees models are used to extract the features of email which thus identifies phishing attacks (Bergholz A. e., 2010)

Techniques:

- o Logistic Regression
- o Deep Learning: Convolutional Neural Networks (CNNs)
- o Random Forests

Figure 1. Different ways to implement AI in cybersecurity

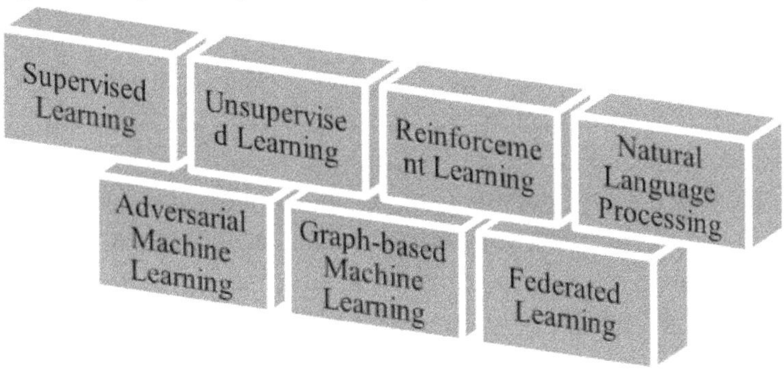

Unsupervised Learning:

Unsupervised learning is one of many types of learning wherein models are trained without labeled outputs in the data. The main aim is to discover hidden patterns, structures, or relationships in the data. Contrarily, unlike supervised learning, it does not use predefined input-output pairs. It includes clustering, the process in which data are placed into the same category, and dimensionality reduction, which is a process that makes data less intense while preserving its main properties. Data-intensive algorithms applied in unsupervised learning include k-means clustering, hierarchical clustering, and principal component analysis (PCA). An example of clustering is the segmentation of customers in terms of their buying behavior, while visualizing high-dimensional data is commonly done through PCA. It is notable because of its applicability where it is hard or too expensive to obtain labels. However, evaluating its outputs is also quite difficult. Thus, unsupervised learning is applied in diverse fields such as anomaly detection, market segmentation, and recommendation systems. It is the kind of analysis that would be tightly associated with any attempt at drawing valuable insights from unstructured data.

Applications:

- Anomaly Detection: Also utilized in intrusion detection systems (IDSs) to identify new inconsistencies in the activity of the network (Egele, 2017).
- User Behavior Analytics: Insider threats are detected by tracing deviations of activities within the employees (Makridakis, 2017).

Techniques:

- o K-Means Clustering
- o Auto encoders
- o Principal Component Analysis (PCA)

3. **Reinforcement Learning:**

Reinforcement learning refers to a machine learning paradigm whereby an agent learns to make decisions while interacting with the environment. Like supervised learning, there is no label data that gets included in RL; instead it learns through trial and error as it interacts with the environment for optimal strategies. Unlike supervised learning, RL does not require labeled data but learns through trial and error to find better strategies with time. The aim of every such agent is to maximize cumulative rewards through learning policies associating states to actions. Q-learning, deep Q-networks (DQN), and proximal policy optimization (PPO) are among some of the most commonly used algorithms for reinforcement learning. A good example will be training a robot to walk or grasp objects entirely by itself. Reinforcement learning has also achieved superhuman performance in areas such as board games and video games Chess, Go and video games. An area of RL application includes autonomous driving; optimization of resource allocation; adaptively controlling systems. The biggest problem in RL is finding that balance between exploration (trying new actions) and exploitation (using known successful actions). By virtue of learning through dynamic interactions, RL endows systems against complex and changing environments.

Reinforcement Learning (RL) is that branch of machine learning in which an agent learns decision making by way of interacting an environment. For any action taken by the agent, it gets the feedback of the action in terms of reward or punishment in time, which will direct it toward optimizing its behavior over time. Unlike supervised learning, RL does not need labeled data, but learns through trial and error to discover the best strategies. The agent's goal is to maximize cumulative reward through learning policies mapping states to actions. Algorithms such as Q-learning, Deep Q-Networks (DQN), Proximal Policy Optimization (PPO), and others are quite popular in reinforcement learning research. For instance, teaching robots to walk or do actions like picking something up by themselves would be an example. RL is also very involved in other areas such as gaming, where RL has acquired capabilities greater than those of most humans in chess, Go, and video games. Almost every area-cutting-edge technology that includes autonomous driving, optimization of resource allocation, as well as creating adaptive control systems are all critical components of reinforcement learning. Exploring new actions is a part of RL, and discovering how best to exploit successful actions is another balanced action. This is what makes dynamic interactions easy target learning for such systems to adapt themselves to the complex and changing environment.

Applications:

- Adaptive Threat Mitigation: Algorithms adapt defense mechanisms in real-time according to continually changing cyber threats (Sarker, 2022).
- Firewall Optimization: Models modify firewall policies to block suspicious traffic most effectively (Moustafa, 2019).

Techniques:

- o Q-Learning
- o Deep Q-Networks (DQN)

Natural Language Processing (NLP):

NLP is subfield of artificial intelligence directing the computer-human interactions taking the form of natural language. This method enables machines to comprehend and interpret human language-generation meaningfully and useful to humans. Natural language processing includes vast amounts of computation things such as linguistics, machine learning, as well as deep learning schemes for analyzing and processing natural language data. Some important applications of NLP include sentiment analysis, language translation, chatbots, and automated speech recognition. The technology has automated industrial mechanisms like customer care and content moderation, so it changed the way industries worked. NLP techniques like tokenization, parsing, or named entities identify and describe the structure of language so that it can be understood by computers. The developments in neural networks and particularly in transformer models, like GPT and BERT, have achieved remarkable performance in many tasks of NLP. However, there are still some problems concerning language ambiguity, cultural nuances, and ethical aspects, such as bias in training data. NLP research is ongoing and advances to achieving better understanding of machines on context and intent. Its adaptability to breach the communication gap lends it as a revolutionary force not just on technology but society as well.

Applications:

- Extraction of Threat Intelligence: The NLP parses unstructured data from cybersecurity reports to derive actionable insights (Shah, 2020).
- Phishing Identification: Malware emails based on language patterns are identified (Goodfellow, 2015).

Techniques:

- o Sentiment Analysis
- o Named Entity Recognition (NER)
- o Text Classification

5. **Adversarial Machine Learning**:

Adversarial Machine Learning bears the element of tuple searching at the mercy of learning models whose vulnerabilities become targets for intentional attackers. This field of study examines how an adversary could exploit weaknesses lying in the algorithms of a model by injecting input well-crafted to be called as adversarial examples. These inputs destabilize correct prediction or classification from the model while it appears normal to human observers. Attack systems are many, ranging from image recognition, natural language processing, and even autonomous vehicles, posing great security challenges to the attacker. Thus far, diverse attack methods exist for researchers to investigate, such as evasion, poisoning, and model inversion, to deconstruct their mechanisms and devise countermeasures. Such defensive strategies as adversarial training, robust model architectures, and detection mechanisms aim to bolster a model's resistance to evasion attacks. Trade-offs between this robustness and model performance, as well as between robustness and computational efficiency, are also explored. Adversarial Machine Learning serves as the backbone for both these performance-critical and high-risk domains: cybersecurity, healthcare, and finance. All models need to be reliable when security purposes are considered. This is, after all, an arms race: between attacker and defender, and constant innovation will not lose its luster in this area. Improving defenses means developing systems intelligent as well as secure in real-world situations. There has been extensive research on how to make AI systems robust to adversarial attacks (Goodfellow, 2015).

Applications:

- Defense Models: Increase robustness against adversarial inputs that aim to bypass the AI detection systems (Biggio, 2013).
- Attack Type: Tests the vulnerability of AIs to an adversarial attack threat (Goodfellow, 2015).

Graph-based Machine Learning:

Graph-based machine learning is a branch of machine learning which specifically uses graph structures to model and analyze complex relations between entities. Graphs consist of nodes, corresponding to entities, and edges representing connections or relationships, which model data in areas such as social networks, molecular chemistry, and recommendation systems. Unlike other data representations, graphs do model dependence and interactions and provide the best contexts to analyze relational data. Development in the area has taken place through Graph Neural Networks (GNNs) and graph embeddings, which enable learning of significant patterns from graph-structured data. Local node features along with global topology of the graph are considered in any of these approaches, which provide high-level perspectives. Applications of graph-based machine learning include fraud detection, drug discovery, knowledge graph construction, and route optimization. Some of the challenges faced today include scalability with respect to large graphs, dynamic or evolving graph handling, and model interpretability. Recent developments in computation and algorithms have made possible efficient methods for graph processing and learning. Researchers are also working on development of hybrid solutions that combine graph-based methods with other machine learning approaches. Graph-based machine learning is already empowering a variety of sectors and is making possible novel solutions to very complex problems by tapping the potential of relational data.

Applications:

- Botnet Detection: Detecting network traffic that follows a coordinated attack pattern (Ahmed, 2016).
- Fraud detection: It traces fraudulent activity on account or transaction networks or histories (Chen, 2021)

7. **Federated Learning:**

Federated Learning is an innovative decentralized approach to machine learning, where numerous devices or organizations can jointly learn a model without sharing their raw data. Unlike transporting data to a main server, each participant trains on his or her local data and shares only the model updates (like gradients or weights). These updates are then aggregated in a central server to build an all-encompassing model, thus keeping the information private and at the same time removing the necessity to centralize the data. The usefulness of Federated Learning is illustrated in scenarios such as where privacy, safety, or ownership of data is critical, including health care, finance, and mobile applications. It also serves in minimizing the amount of data transferred and therefore lessens bandwidth usage and the potential threats of data compromises. Areas to be addressed under Federated Learning are: heterogeneous data distributions, communication overheads, and equal representation among participating entities. Techniques like differential privacy and secure aggregation are often employed to enhance privacy and security. Federated Learning is further another issue itself regarding ethical questions: Understanding between how to balance unequal power across the participants, and avoiding biased results from the collaboration. It makes collaborative learning possible while ensuring that information is kept private. This makes it an innovative step forward, as organizations and devices learn the power of artificial intelligence. It promises, as the field develops, to unlock further inclusive and secure AI in multiple applications.

Applications:

- Privacy-Preserving Threat Detection: Enhances detection accuracy with protection of sensitive data (Chandramohan, 2021).
- Cross-Enterprise Security Models: Facilitates different organizations to create better defenses together (Shah, 2020).

AI APPLICATIONS IN CYBERSECURITY

The incorporation of Artificial Intelligence (AI) into cybersecurity has modified the strategies of organizations when it comes to deriving, preventing, and taking action on the cyber threats. The increasing sophistication of attacks has created a need for reinforcement of traditional security measures, the covering of which AI comprises a vast number of datasets and the ability to adapt to how threats evolve. Figure 2 shows the major applications of AI in cybersecurity:

Figure 2. Applications of AI in cybersecurity

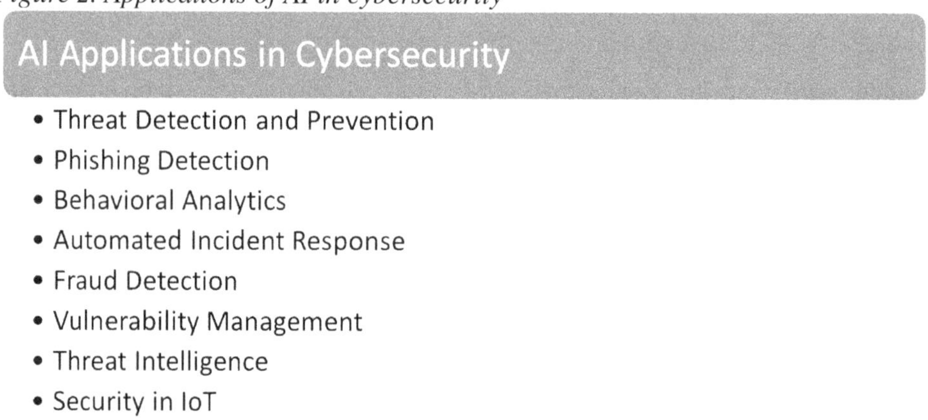

1. Threat Detection and Prevention

Security with AI in cybersecurity works as a paradigm shift in the protection of digital systems from malicious actions. Using machine learning, deep learning, and data analytics, AI is now capable of assessing terabytes of network traffic, analyzing system logs, and examining user behavior patterns for possible indicators of cyber threats. Machine learning algorithms are used to detect previously unknown threats, including zero-day exploits (Guven, 2016).With this AI-enabled tool that runs in real-time, it can identify and respond to threats such as malware, phishing, and ransomware attacks, in a much faster and more accurate approach compared to the traditional ones. Behavioral analysis helps AI determine the normative behavior of an activity so that it can identify behaviors that do not conform to normalization, such as unauthorized access or unusual data transfers. Moreover, AI also acts towards preventing threats by predicting vulnerabilities or suggesting security measures, like patching or updating software, in advance. An automated response system powered by AI can isolate infected machines or shut down dubious processes to control the damage. Nevertheless, cybersecurity AIs have their downsides, such as adversarial attacks that are meant to mislead or confuse detection systems and the bias that comes from training data itself. Continuous learning and adaptive models characterize the solutions to these issues. Collaboration between AI systems and human experts is crucial to achieving this integration of machine efficiency and human intuition. AI plays a pivotal role in building, maintaining, and ensuring the security and resilience of digital infrastructures as it stays ahead of evolving threats. For example: AI-driven tools like Endpoint Detection and Response (EDR) solutions monitor endpoint activity and flag unusual behavior that may signify a breach

2. Phishing Detection

AI for phishing detection is a very important instrument in the area of cybersecurity and really proves effective when it comes to recognizing and suppressing fraudulent attempts made to rob sensitive information. Phishing attacks often employ the use of emails, messages, and even fake websites to trick users, thereby harassing them into revealing their credentials or financial details. The processing done by AI systems normally uses machine learning methods against data emanating via natural language processing and pattern recognition to check the content, structures, and metadata of communication at identifying phishing attempts in real time (Bergholz A. e., 2010). By doing the study of language patterns, tone, and quite abnormal sender behaviors, AI can flag emails or messages as suspicious for not conforming to typical communication. Advanced models can further also analyze the URLs and certain characteristics of the website in order to identify a fraudulent site masquerading itself into a legitimate one. Such AI solutions can also be getting used in continuous learning from never-ending huge datasets of previous attacks which could help identify new phishing strategies. Through integration with email platforms and security software, the complete approach enables blocking all related phishing attempts before they approach end users. It is not without certain demerits- the most noted of which includes the ability to counter sophisticated spear phishing attacks launched specifically toward individuals or organizations. Not only born out of AI, but additional efforts on user education with multiple-factor authentication improve defense against phishing. Therefore, the intelligent and active nature of AI keeps cyber defenses far ahead of any possible mechanisms that might come up in the future as attackers develop new approaches to their methodologies. Such an attribute minimizes risk and the damages that could result from attacks.

AI for phishing detection is a major booster to digital security, whereby it acts by revealing fraud efforts to steal one's sensitive information. Phishing attacks include the fraudulent message or the fraudulent website or the fraudulent email, which tricks users into sharing their credentials or financial information. These AI systems analyzing the content, architecture, and other meta-data of communications would reach through machine learning, natural language processing, and patterns recognition in real-time detection of phishing attempts. AI can possibly flag emails or messages as suspicious by studying language patterns, tone, and quite abnormal sender behaviors, not within ordinary communication. Advanced models can even analyze URLs and website features to identify fraudulent sites masquerading as legitimate ones. All such AI solutions also became competent in continuously learning from never-ending huge datasets of previous attacks that could help in identifying newly proposed phishing strategies. This all together by integration with email platforms and security software enables blocking all related phishing attempts before reaching the end user. Despite offering the strengths mentioned above, there exists among its limitations, highly sophisticated spear-phishing attacks targeting individuals or organizations. Thus, AI will have to be blended with user education and a little need for multi-factor authentication to build thicker walls against phishing. Therefore, the proactive nature of AI keeps the cyber defenses one step ahead against any possible devices developed in the future, and so the risks and damages likely to occur are minimized as the attackers develop new approaches to their methodologies.

3. Behavioral Analytics

AI in behavioral analytics has changed the face of cybersecurity by allowing the more accurate detection of anomalies and threats to occur. Behavioral analytics uses monitoring and analyzing behavior patterns of users, devices or systems to look for deviation - an activity indicative of malicious attacks. AI makes this possible by processing vast amounts of data in real-time and identifying subtle nuances beyond the ken of traditional rule engines. Machine learning models can identify a profile of normal behavior for users or applications, and trigger on hugely dissimilar activities, like logins from unusual locations, odd data transfers, or access requests at strange times. Techniques like User and Entity Behavior Analytics (UEBA) are applied to detect and respond to anomalies without relying on predefined attack signature (Alqatawna, 2017)

With the use of natural language processing and pattern recognition, it analyses diverse data sources-from logs to transactions, achievements, and social interactions-creating multifaceted behavioral profiles. AI behavioral analytics can effectively detect insider threats, account takeovers, and other advanced persistent threats that usually slip through traditional security measures. Adaptive learning takes care of changing behavior patterns by making the AI systems receptive to evolution: fewer false positives while identifying a true threat. Nevertheless, challenges that have surfaced under this area regarding the effect of AI in the field include high-quality data and elimination of possible bias from the models. Therefore, it fortifies proactive threat avoidance, strengthens a resilient digital ecosystem in line with integrating AI-powered behavioral analytics into broader cybersecurity frameworks.

4. Automated Incident Response

AI streamlines the incident response process by automating identifying and mitigating security threats.Security Orchestration, Automation, and Response (SOAR) platforms use AI to automate threat containment, reducing the workload on human analysts (Shinde, 2020). It will change the whole cyber security system with rapid response handling of security threats, speed given by AI, and performance along with intelligence, automated incident response works for security threats. It involves artificial intelligence and machine learning applications to detect, analyze and respond to cyber incidents with little or no human intervention. Artificial intelligence monitors network traffic, logs of systems, and user activity continuously and searches for possible threats before making automatic predefined actions to prevent the risks.It could include package isolating systems, blocking malicious IPs, or starting processes for automated recovery

Machine learning algorithms can analyze attack history data to improve their response mechanism further; it also enhances predictions related to developing possible vulnerabilities, thereby making system resilience with time. AI tools can also sort threats by criticality and corresponding context to ensure that pressing threats receive an immediate response. Natural language processing enables AI to parse alerts and documentation in the security field so actionable insights can be generated for humans. It establishes the most intelligent, event-driven orchestration of detection to response workflows in correlation with SIEM systems. AI raises response times significantly along the operational overhead. The risks of falsely positive results and extensive training datasets involved in model training presented some of the barriers. AI should be combined with human expertise in a hybrid model to ensure the know-how and speed involved in optimum decision-making. Automation of routine tasks coupled with "what-if" response capabilities emboldens all-around cybersecurity defenses and lessens the damage caused by a cyber incident.

5. Fraud Detection

AI systems monitor financial transactions and activities for patterns consistent with fraudulent behavior. Algorithms analyze transaction data in real-time to detect anomalies, enabling quicker responses (Zoldi, 2020). AI in automated fraud detection is changing the face of cybersecurity by providing faster, more accurate, and more efficient recognitions of fraudulent activities. Automated fraud detection makes use of AI and machine learning technologies to detect suspicious transactions or behaviors with minimal human intervention. The AI systems process all the data in real time and identify unusual spending patterns, irregular login locations, discrepancies in user behavior, or everything that indicates potential fraud.

The machine-learning algorithms continue to learn from historical data to improve detection accuracy and adapt to new frauds into which they are increasingly developing. These systems will also prioritize alerts according to the severity and context of the anomalies detected, ensuring that high-priority threats are handled rapidly. The natural language processing techniques analyze all unstructured data such as emails or customer communication to detect phishing attempts or fake claims. AI-generated tools will integrate seamlessly into finance-related platforms and security systems to automatically prevent suspicious transactions or accounts.

Some of the challenges facing such a system are how to manage excessive false-positive and take care of fairness in bias toward the model's predictions. A hybrid type of AI automation and human oversight will typically allow more textured decision-making, especially in very complicated situations. Automating routine checks, and enabling systems to respond in real time, drive the path of automated fraud detection beyond systems today, achieving both substantial losses reduction and stakeholder confidence in digital transactions.

6. Vulnerability Management

AI assists in identifying vulnerabilities in software and network systems by predicting potential attack vectors. It uses predictive analytics to assess and prioritize vulnerabilities based on exploitability and impact (Gao, 2018). The phenomenon of

Artificial Intelligence is now making its way to vulnerability management, where it enhances the much needed holistic cybersecurity. AI-driven tools swiftly identify vulnerabilities of systems through the analysis of a massive quantity of data from network scans, logs, and threat intelligence feeds. This could be done through employing machine learning algorithms for pattern recognition in potential threats so that security gaps could be detected faster. It also talks about prioritization of risks depending on severity, risk exposure, and future impact on the organization to address important issues upfront. Routine tasks such as maintenance of patches would then be automated to lessen the burden on the security teams while removing a good deal of human error. Hence, systems powered by AI are also able to keep pace with evolving threats through continuous learning from new data and attacks. Another example of what artificial intelligence has, predictive analytics entails making organizations forecast future vulnerabilities and threats. AI tools can also be employed in automated incident response, where predefined actions such as isolation of affected systems would be taken promptly to limit losses. Hence with ever-evolving cyber-attacks, artificial intelligence provides security teams with more advanced tools to remain at the forefront of these attacks. By improving detection, response, and prevention, AI-enabled resource allocation will make room for more strategic tasks.

7. Threat Intelligence

AI synthesizes and analyzes threat intelligence from various sources, enabling proactive defense mechanisms systems process vast amounts of unstructured data to extract actionable insights about emerging threats (Rais, A survey on technical threat intelligence in the age of sophisticated cyber attacks, 2018). AI is revolutionizing threat intelligence by making detection, analysis, and response to cyber threats a lot more efficient. An AI-based system can automatically analyze or process big data sets from a variety of sources such as security logs, network traffic, and dark web activities for possible real-time threats. It makes use of machine learning algorithms that help detect patterns and anomalies, improving threat detection accuracies and eliminating or reducing false positives. Moreover, it increases the ability to correlate various pieces of data together and thereby presents a holistic picture of threat actors and attack tactics. Besides, having AI do all that evaluation of vast amounts of information allows security personnel to instead devote their time and effort to the higher-order activities of decision making rather than manually reviewing raw data. Predicted outcomes from this would be emerging attack trends from where organizations can take proactive actions to strengthen their defenses. Moreover, an artificial-intelligence-driven threat intelligence platform would be able to learn from fresh data quite seamlessly and thus improve the security posture of the organization itself against rapidly evolving threats. Automated threat analysis and response would help to bring threats faster under control, reducing damage from attacks. Above all, AI will make threat intelligence more dynamic and allow them to keep ahead of the sophisticated, evolving requirements of cyber threats-outside the capability of organizations. Overall, AI in threat intelligence makes organizations act much faster with more accurate and immediate information to fortify improved defenses in cybersecurity overall in the organization.

8. Security in IoT

AI enhances the security of Internet of Things (IoT) devices by monitoring device activity and identifying abnormal behavior indicative of cyber threats (Jha, 2017). The significance of security in the Internet of Things (IoT) has emerged out of the huge number of connected devices which may become susceptible to cyber-attacks. Such devices are rapidly infiltrating homes, industrial plants, and cities, hence increasing the potential attack surface an aggressor may exploit. One of the key challenges in security is memory and processing-adverse devices for which it is difficult to apply robust security such as encryption and firewalls. The mere proliferation of devices also often leads to heterogeneously maintained security levels across devices, creating gaps that an attacker exploits. Secure design features such as secure booting, data encryption, and updates for addressing vulnerabilities in the software should be emphasized by the manufacturers for purposes of improving IoT security. It should also entail authentication and access control mechanisms that ensure the interaction of just the authorized users and devices with the IoT network. AI and machine-learning technologies help monitor IoT devices in real-time and detect abnormal behavior, thereby responding quickly to threats. Segmentation in network architecture and isolation of critical systems from less secure devices may also help contain the spread of any attack. Efficacious IoT security would also require that the device manufacturers, service providers, and customers strongly collaborate to promote best practice. Security must be prioritized with the scale of increase in the adoption of IoTs to protect information, personal data, and even the integrity of the connected systems.

Case Studies

The application of Artificial Intelligence (AI) in cybersecurity has emerged as the most powerful weapon against cyber threats. Organizations in all sectors have deployed AI-based solutions to increase their security frameworks. Some outstanding case studies that enlighten us on how AI is changing cybersecurity include:

1. **Darktrace: AI-Powered Threat Detection** AI's self-learning capacity and autonomous adaptation made it a potentially crucial device in finding and stopping unknown threats. Darktrace, top on the list among many cybersecurity firms, employs machine learning and AI in detecting and responding to cyber threats. Darktrace's AI model - "Enterprise Immune System" uses the human immune system to monitor the activity of the entire network, conditioning for normal behavior as it flags anomalies in real-time. It caught an early-stage ransomware infection prior to costly downtime and damage (Smith, 2021).
2. **IBM QRadar: Automated Incident Response** AI-powered automation can afford organizations the effectiveness of dealing with a large volume of alerts without compromising security. QRadar is IBM's AI-backed SIEM for Security Information and Event Management, widely used for the purposes of threat detection and response. The main challenge is that a financial sector institution struggles with the management of thousands of security alerts every single day, often leading to many delays in addressing critical threats. QRadar connected to the IBM Watson for Cybersecurity can be used as a solution to provide alert triage automation and logs analysis, as well as threat prioritization. Thus the system managed to reduce false positives by 70% while providing actionable recommendations in minutes to enhance efficiency within the security operations teams (Brown, 2022).
3. **Symantec (Now NortonLifeLock) - Malware Detection** The AI-based system was capable of preventing several outside attacks such as zero-day exploits within milliseconds of actual detection. Currently, Symantec's AI-based intrusion detection schemes incorporate machine learning as a core component in detecting malware and all forms of cyber threats. Symantec's AI analyzed terabytes of threat indicators and was able to identify an entirely new form of malware immediately by pattern recognition techniques (Green, 2021).
4. **CrowdStrike Falcon: Endpoint Protection** AI's behavioral analysis capabilities are critical to protection against ransomware and ensure endpoint security. The healthcare organization saw an increase in ransomware attacks, which could be attributed to its dependence on more legacy systems, due to rising cyber threats. Falcon used artificial intelligence in analyzing device behavior, anomaly-detection, and stopping encryption of ransomware in real-time thus providing an endpoint protection platform (EPP) based on AI that uses the entire lifecycle of prevention, detection, and response to-cyber-attacks. Now the healthcare provider was able to realize a 99% decrease in successful attacks, with improved compliance to data-protection regulations (Taylor, 2022).
5. **Microsoft Defender: Cloud Security**: AI-enabled adaptive authentication enhances security in rapid and dynamic cloud environments. Microsoft Defender executes artificial intelligence to deliver comprehensive cloud safety protection in

enterprises. AI of Microsoft Defender based on IP reputation, time zone change, and unusual activity patterns identify suspicious login attempts to surrender to adaptive authentication to block unauthorized access. This resulted in a 95% reduction in incidents of account compromise, with accelerated detection and mitigation of threats (Anderson, 2023).

6. **Palo Alto Addition: Predictive Analytics** Predictive analytics powered through AI provides significant advantages for the prevention and mitigation of cyber threats. Palo Alto Networks leverages AI in its Next-Generation Firewalls (NGFW) and Cortex XDR to proactively prevent threats. Existing attack data would be analyzed by the AI and pattern-matched with prediction and blocking of future threats. It helps monitoring user behavior in detecting rather unusual activities (Martinez, 2021).
7. **Tesla: Autonomous Defense Systems** AI's contribution in real-time data monitoring is highly important, especially due to the kind of threats it might help defend against both internally and externally. Tesla uses its proprietary AI technologies for the protection of its automobiles and all systems and infrastructures from cyber threats. The AI of Tesla was able to monitor well in real-time data across its systems to detect anomalies associated with actions like unauthorized access attempts and firmware tampering (Reed, 2022).
8. **Google: Phishing Prevention** AI-trained natural language processing and metadata analysis are proven to be most effective in phishing prevention. Google employs artificial intelligence in phishing detection on its Gmail service. To do this, Google has created AI algorithms that look at metadata, the emails themselves, and user interactions, for identifying phishing attempts. With this, Gmail now blocks over 99.9% of phishing emails, saving billions of users from cyber scams (Nelson, 2023).

ADVANTAGES OF AI IN CYBERSECURITY

The various advantages of using AI in cybersecurity is shown in Figure 3 and it includes:

Figure 3. Advantages of AI in cybersecurity

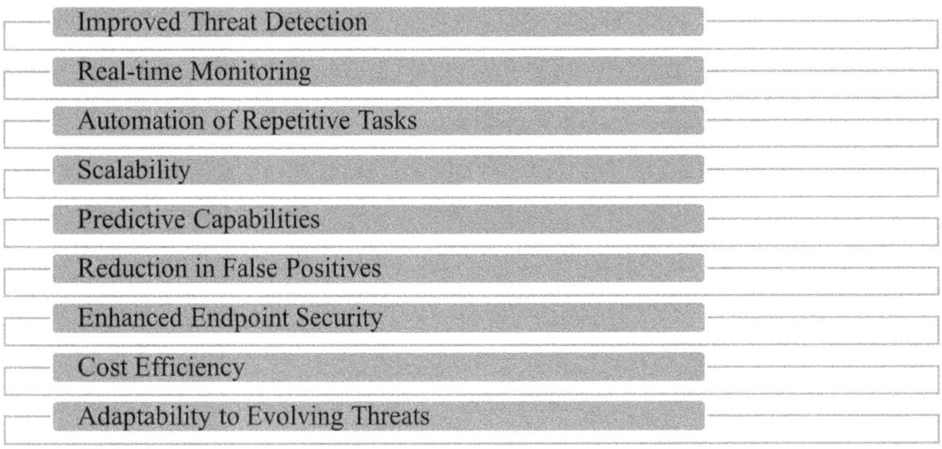

1. Improved Threat Detection

AI can quickly identify and respond to potential threats, outperforming traditional methods. Machine learning algorithms sift through large datasets to spot patterns and anomalies, including threats that may not have been previously recognized. For example: AI systems can uncover zero-day attacks by detecting behaviors that stray from the norm (Guven, 2016). AI is great in threat detection that starts with a structured and gradually learning system. At first, it collects data such as those collected from various sources which include servers, network traffic, emails, and user activity logs. This ensures that there is a very extensive collection of data for analysis. After which, the next step is an examination of the data using advanced methods in machine learning and neural networks to find patterns and correlations, which can point toward potential threats. AI has all that there is for the process of anomaly detection that refers to using unusual behavior as well as login times, data transfers that may fall outside already established norms. The identification of an anomaly then followed by threat classification into malware, phishing, or insider risk categories enables security teams to prioritize their responses effectively. It sends real alerts to a team under threat detection from a source of a potential attacking process with actionable recommendations in most cases. AI learns and develops all the time, making it more precise and efficient in catching up with emerging threats. This iterative process makes it fortified and advanced cybersecurity. The various steps of threat detection and prevention is shown in Figure 4.

Figure 4. Steps of AI threat detection and prevention

2. Real-time Monitoring

AI-driven systems offer round-the-clock monitoring of networks and endpoints, ensuring immediate threat detection and response without the need for human oversight. This constant vigilance reduces the chances for attackers to exploit vulnerabilities (Paxson, 2010).

3. Automation of Repetitive Tasks

AI takes over routine security tasks like log analysis, vulnerability scanning, and patch management, allowing human analysts to concentrate on more complex issues. Security Orchestration, Automation, and Response (SOAR) platforms utilize AI to streamline these repetitive tasks (Shinde, 2020).

4. Scalability

AI is capable of managing the vast amounts of data produced by modern IT systems, a task that can be daunting for traditional methods. It scales effortlessly to monitor intricate and distributed systems. This scalability is essential for organizations with extensive networks and significant data volumes (Yin, 2017).

5. Predictive Capabilities

AI can forecast potential threats and attack vectors by examining historical data and spotting trends. This proactive strategy aids organizations in bolstering their defenses. Predictive analytics help prioritize vulnerabilities based on their likelihood of being targeted (Gao, 2018).

6. Reduction in False Positives

Conventional systems frequently generate a high number of false positives, which can overwhelm security teams. AI enhances detection processes to minimize false alarms, leading to more precise threat identification. AI's capability to distinguish between benign and malicious activities greatly reduces unnecessary alerts (Al-jawarneh, 2018).

7. Enhanced Endpoint Security

AI strengthens endpoint security by continuously learning the behaviors of devices and users to detect and address unusual activities. Advanced tools, such as AI-based Endpoint Detection and Response, play a crucial role in this process (Miettinen, 2017).

8. Integration with Threat Intelligence

AI works with threat intelligence platforms to examine global threat data, recognize patterns, and predict new attack strategies. This allows organizations to effectively implement defenses against emerging threats (Rais, 2018).

9. Cost Efficiency

By automating tasks and improving the accuracy of threat detection, AI lessens the need for large security teams and reduces financial losses from breaches. AI-driven systems offer a cost-effective solution for organizations with limited resources (Freeman, 2018).

10. Adaptability to Evolving Threats

AI continuously learns from new data and adapts to tackle emerging threats. This flexibility ensures that defenses stay strong against sophisticated attacks. Unlike static rule-based systems, machine learning models enhance their performance over time (Sharbaf, 2019).

CHALLENGES IN IMPLEMENTING AI-BASED SECURITY

While AI is at its pinnacle concerning robust features for threat detection and active-response mechanisms, it also creates loopholes and risks. The various challenges in implementing AI-based security include:

1. Expensive Setup

AI solutions usually need a lot of money for things like computers, software, and special skills. Training AI models need strong computers, and running these systems can be costly, especially for smaller companies (Herrmann, 2020).

2. Difficult to Integrate

Putting AI into current security systems can be hard because of compatibility problems and the need to change old systems. Companies often have trouble making AI tools work well with their usual security methods (Batarseh, 2019).

3. Data Problems

AI systems depend on good, labeled data for training. In security, getting and labeling this data is hard and takes a long time. Bad or not enough data can cause AI to miss real threats and give too many false alarms (Ring, 2019).

4. Adversarial Attacks

AI systems can be fooled by attackers who change the data to trick the AI (Biggio, 2013).

5. Algorithm Bias

AI systems may learn biases from the data they are taught and thus lead to unequal or inaccurate threat detection.Bias can be a cause of threats that are overlooked, or wrong classification of problems leading to a security system reliability issue (Mehrabi, 2021).

6. Limited Explainability

A lot of AI models, particularly those based on deep learning, perform no better than a black box and thus understanding how decisions are made becomes difficult. This issue of secrecy makes it hard to troubleshoot systems and meet regulations in delicate environments (Kim, 2017).

7. Over-reliance on Automation

Excessive reliance on artificial intelligence systems can cause the situation of missing a crucial piece of information if the system is not being watched or updated. Automated systems may ignore fractional threats, which need to be solved with human judgment, resulting in security gaps (Schmid, 2020)

8. Rapidly Evolving Threats

The Cyber threat landscape is fast-moving, and AI systems must be constantly updated to remain relevant. Static AI models can be useless, as they will not be able to identify the new attack methods or techniques (Floridi, 2018) .

9. Ethical and Privacy Concerns

The use of AI for monitoring and threat detection often involves analyzing sensitive data, which evokes the issue of privacy. Abuse or unauthorized access to AI systems can lead to ethical and legal issues (Binns, 2018) .

10. Skilled Workforce Shortage

In AI cybersecurity, it requires skillful personnel to design, deploy, and maintain the systems. The lack of professionals trained in both AI and information security in the field prevents organizations from using AI solutions (Ochoa, 2021).

Organizations can conduct regular adversarial tests, and threat modeling, and put in place services to identify and eliminate weaknesses or various vulnerabilities of using AI while enhancing performance. Explainable AI can be used to promote transparency. As a result, understanding the processes in decision-making brings about better trust and reliability. Appropriate measures of stringent data security and privacy could also act as barriers to access to sensitive data stored in an AI system. Apart from that, where AI systems are used in decision-making, it should not be solely dependent on AI systems since it is a balanced approach to reducing the occurrence of errors. Continuous monitoring and updating of AI models must be performed to adapt to the dynamically emerging threats and to keep these models relevant. All in all, through these efforts, organizations can exhaustively benefit from AI in cybersecurity while at the same time minimizing the risks that arise from AI in cybersecurity.

FUTURE DIRECTIONS

It has several directions though which a bright future can be seen in AI use for improving cybersecurity. Listed below are some of the future directions on how AI can be made available for future use in enhancing cybersecurity:

1. Federated Learning

Federated Learning is a kind of decentralized machine learning whereby AI models are collaboratively trained but not transferred to a central point for training with raw data. Thus, it offers better privacy and security for data since sensitive information is kept locally, while only the updates of the models are shared. In federated learning, organizations can hold federations to enable federated learning whereby models could be trained collectively without revealing proprietary or sensitive data (Chandramohan, 2021) (Sharma, 2024).

2. Quantum-Secure AI

The area of quantum-secure AI pertains to the creation of AI-based models or cryptographic techniques, which are resilient against the computational prowess of quantum computers. The possibility of quantum computers has already posed a major threat to traditional encryption technologies. By developing quantum-resistant algorithms, as well as producing secure AI models, an organization can keep sensitive data guarded and thus provide itself robust defenses against fallouts of future quantum-facilitated attacks. This is one way of safeguarding critical infrastructures and, in general, long-term data security (Makridakis, 2017) (Gheorghiu, 2020).

3. Explanatory AI (XAI)

It refers to the phenomenon of making AI systems understandable by humans in terms of their decisions and operations. For instance, within the realm of cybersecurity, XAI makes it possible to comprehend how AI threat detection and response systems operate and therefore understand why certain actions are taken. This kind of insight builds trust, contributes to better decision-making, and establishes grounds for regulatory compliance. Additionally, it can be relied on to unearth the biases or errors in AI models, thus resulting in more reliable and fair; and therefore, reliable cybersecurity solutions (Goodfellow, 2015) (Miller, 2019).

CONCLUSION

Cyber security is getting redefined with AI providing a state-of-the-art capacity in preventing and responding to threats, thus creating chances that seem impossible to realize today. Behind the improvements lies unresolved future challenges, with continued advancement in AI technology, and ethical matters that would lead to a more secure digital future. Real-time security has revolutionized the country in the way it has brought distinct and out-of-the-box computer-based capabilities in threat prevention and response. There are still unresolved challenges, but forward movement in the field of AI technology accompanied by ethical considerations is paving the way for a more secure digital future.

REFERENCES

Ahmed, M. M., Naser Mahmood, A., & Hu, J. (2016). A survey of network anomaly detection techniques. *Journal of Network and Computer Applications*, 60, 19–31. DOI: 10.1016/j.jnca.2015.11.016

Ahsan, M. M. (2020). Applications of AI in malware detection. *Computers & Security*, 96, 101830. al., A. e. (2017). Improving anomaly-based intrusion detection systems using data clustering. *Computers & Security*.

Al-Garadi, M. A. (2020). A survey of machine learning for cybersecurity applications. *IEEE Access : Practical Innovations, Open Solutions*, 8, 112752–112788.

Aljawarneh, e. (2018). Anomaly detection in network security: Techniques, challenges, and applications. *IEEE Access*.

Alqatawna, e. (2017). Improving anomaly-based intrusion detection systems using data clustering. *Computers & Security*.

Anderson, P. (2023). Cloud Security with AI: Trends and Implementations. *Cloud Computing Today*, 23(2), 34–41.

Batarseh, e. (2019). Challenges in integrating AI technologies in cybersecurity frameworks. *Computers & Security*.

Bergholz, A. e. (2010). A real-life study of phishing attacks. *Detection of Intrusions and Malware & Vulnerability Assessment.*

Bergholz, e. (2010). A real-life study of phishing attacks. *Proceedings of the 15th Conference on Detection of Intrusions and Malware & Vulnerability Assessment.*

Biggio, B. e. (2013). Evasion attacks against machine learning at test time. *ECML PKDD*, 387–402.

Binns. (2018). Fairness in machine learning: Lessons from political philosophy. *Proceedings of the 2018 Conference on Fairness, Accountability, and Transparency.*

Brown, A. (2022). Automated Cyber Defense: Leveraging AI for Incident Response. *InfoSec Quarterly*, 29(3), 18–23.

Chandramohan, S. e. (2021). AI-powered cybersecurity: Challenges and solutions. *Cyber Defense Journal*, 13(4), 12–28.

Chen, C. e. (2021). Graph-based anomaly detection for financial fraud prevention. *Computers & Security*, 101, 102–121.

Cisco Systems. I. (2024). *Understanding the dangers of zero-day vulnerabilities.* Retrieved from https://www.cisco.com/zero-day-vulnerabilities-2024

Cloudflare, I. (2024). *How DDoS attacks are evolving in 2024.* Retrieved from https://www.cloudflare.com/ddos-evolution

Egele, M. e. (2017). A survey of binary code analysis techniques. *ACM Computing Surveys*, 48(4), 1–36.

FireEye. I. (n.d.). *Advanced Persistent Threats (APTs) in 2024: Techniques, tactics, and procedures.* Retrieved from 2024: https://www.fireeye.com/apt-2024

Floridi, T. (2018). How AI and machine learning are reshaping cybersecurity. *Philosophy & Technology.*

Freeman, C. &. (2018). Machine Learning and Security: Protecting Systems with Data and Algorithms.

Gao, e. (2018). Vulnerability assessment using machine learning. *ACM Transactions on Cyber-Physical Systems.*

Gheorghiu, V. M. (2020). Quantum-safe cryptography and its application in AI. *Quantum Information & Computation*, 20(1), 15–28.

Goodfellow, I. e. (2015). Explaining and harnessing adversarial examples. *arXiv preprint arXiv:1412.6572.*

Green, T. (2021). Machine Learning in Malware Detection: Success Stories. *Journal of Cybersecurity Innovations*, 12(1), 25–31.

Guven, B. (2016). A survey of data mining and machine learning methods for cyber security intrusion detection. *IEEE Communications Surveys and Tutorials.*

Guven, B. (2016). A survey of data mining and machine learning methods for cybersecurity intrusion detection. *IEEE Communications Surveys and Tutorials.*

Herrmann, K. &. (2020). Cost challenges in AI-driven cybersecurity. *Journal of Cybersecurity Practice.*

Institute, P. (2024). *The 2024 cost of insider threats report.* Retrieved from https://www.ponemon.org/insider-threat-report-2024

Jha, M. (2017). A comprehensive study of security in Internet of Things. *IEEE Internet of Things Journal.*

Kim, D.-V. &. (2017). Towards a rigorous science of interpretable machine learning. *arXiv preprint arXiv:1702.08608.*

Kim, D.-V. &. (2017). Towards a rigorous science of interpretable machine learning. *arXiv preprint arXiv:1702.08608.*

Makridakis, S. (2017). The forthcoming artificial intelligence (AI) revolution. *Futures*, 90, 46–60. DOI: 10.1016/j.futures.2017.03.006

Martinez, L. (2021). Predictive Analytics in Cyber Defense. *Advanced Security Systems*, 10(4), 14–20.

Mehrabi, e. (2021). A survey on bias and fairness in machine learning. *ACM Computing Surveys.*

Microsoft. (2024). *Phishing attacks: A growing threat to enterprises and individuals.* Retrieved from https://www.microsoft.com/phishing-2024

Miettinen, e. (2017). IoT Sentinel: Automated device-type identification for security enforcement in IoT Systems. *IEEE International Conference on Distributed Computing.*

Miller, T. (2019). Explanation in artificial intelligence: Insights from the social sciences. *Artificial Intelligence*, 267, 1–38. DOI: 10.1016/j.artint.2018.07.007

Moustafa, N. e. (2019). An ensemble intrusion detection technique. *Computers & Security*, 89, 101660.

Nelson, D. (2023). Natural Language Processing in Email Security. *AI & Cyber Journal*, 21(1), 22–28.

Ochoa, e. (2021). AI skills gap in cybersecurity: Addressing the workforce challenges. *Journal of Cybersecurity Education.*

OWASP. (2024). Retrieved from OWASP Top 10 security risks: SQL Injection and XSS: https://owasp.org/top10

Paxson, S. &. (2010). Outside the closed world: On using machine learning for network intrusion detection. *IEEE Symposium on Security and Privacy.*

Rais, T. (2018). A survey on technical threat intelligence in the age of sophisticated cyber attacks. *Computers & Security.*

Rais, T. (2018). A survey on technical threat intelligence in the age of sophisticated cyberattacks. *Computers & Security.*

Reed, E. (2022). AI in Automotive Cybersecurity: The Tesla Experience. *Industry 4.0 Journal*, 15(3), 47-53.

Ring, e. (2019). Survey on AI techniques for cybersecurity: Data challenges. *ACM Computing Surveys.*

Sarker, I. H. (2022). Cybersecurity data science: An overview. *Journal of Big Data*, 9, 1–29.

Schmid, e. (2020). The human-AI collaboration in cybersecurity: Risks of over-reliance. *Cybersecurity.*

Shah, S. e. (2020). Threat intelligence in the era of AI. *AI & Society*, 35(2), 19–28.

Sharbaf. (2019). Artificial intelligence in cybersecurity: An application-focused overview. *Journal of Cybersecurity Research.*

Sharma, A. (2024). Federated learning for cybersecurity: Concepts, challenges, and future directions. *IEEE Transactions on Cybersecurity*, 24(3), 56-78. Retrieved from https://www.frontiersin.org

Shinde, e. (2020). Artificial intelligence-driven automation in cybersecurity incident response. *Cybersecurity.*

Smith, J. (2021). AI in Cybersecurity: Real-World Case Studies. *CyberSec Journal*, 34(2), 45–50.

Symantec, C. (2024). *The evolution of ransomware: A deep dive into modern cyber threats.* Retrieved from https://www.symantec.com/ransomware-2024

Taylor, H. (2022). AI in Endpoint Protection: Practical Applications. *Security Insights Review*, 17(4), 52–58.

ThreatConnect. I. (2024). *MitM attacks: Emerging trends and techniques.* Retrieved from https://www.threatconnect.com/mitm-2024

Yin, e. (2017). Deep learning for intrusion detection systems in cybersecurity. *Future Generation Computer Systems.*

Zoldi, e. (2020). Real-time machine learning for fraud detection. *Journal of Financial Crime.*

Chapter 9
Large Language Models in Cybersecurity: From Automation to Intelligence

Hewa Majeed Zangana
https://orcid.org/0000-0001-7909-254X
Duhok Polytechnic University, Iraq

Firas Mahmood Mustafa
Duhok Polytechnic University, Iraq

Shuai Li
University of Oulu, Finland

ABSTRACT

Large Language Models (LLMs) have emerged as transformative tools in cybersecurity, offering unprecedented capabilities in automating tasks and providing deep insights into evolving threats. This chapter explores the dual role of LLMs in enhancing cybersecurity—from automating routine operations to generating actionable intelligence. By examining real-world applications, such as threat detection, vulnerability management, and incident response, this chapter highlights the potential of LLMs to mitigate risks while addressing their inherent limitations and ethical concerns. Special attention is given to the interplay between LLMs and quantum-aware cybersecurity, presenting a forward-looking perspective on their integration into complex, next-generation security frameworks.

DOI: 10.4018/979-8-3373-1102-9.ch009

1. INTRODUCTION

The cybersecurity landscape is undergoing a rapid transformation, driven by the integration of advanced technologies like Artificial Intelligence (AI) and Large Language Models (LLMs). These tools have revolutionized traditional security practices, enabling organizations to respond swiftly to sophisticated cyber threats. LLMs, with their remarkable capabilities in natural language understanding, contextual reasoning, and predictive analysis, are now at the forefront of this transformation. This chapter delves into the evolving role of LLMs in cybersecurity, charting their progression from automating basic tasks to functioning as intelligent agents in defending against complex threats.

1.1 The Evolution of Cybersecurity Needs

As digital ecosystems expand, the complexity and frequency of cyberattacks grow exponentially. Traditional defensive strategies, such as signature-based detection and manual threat analysis, are proving inadequate against advanced persistent threats (APTs) and zero-day vulnerabilities. The integration of AI-driven technologies, particularly LLMs, addresses these challenges by enhancing predictive capabilities and providing real-time insights. This shift aligns with the observations of Jones and Omar (2024), who emphasize that LLM-powered frameworks, such as the GPT-2 Enhanced Attack Detection and Defense (GEADD) method, are pivotal for countering zero-day threats.

1.2 Understanding the Potential of LLMs

LLMs, such as OpenAI's GPT models, leverage extensive datasets to generate coherent and contextually relevant outputs. Their application in cybersecurity extends from automating routine tasks like log analysis to more complex operations, including malware detection and threat prediction. The synthesis of LLMs with machine learning, as discussed by Huff et al. (2023), offers biotechnology and healthcare organizations an opportunity to strengthen their cybersecurity frameworks against diverse threats.

Moreover, recent studies suggest that LLMs can be optimized further using synthetic data, enhancing their efficiency and applicability in cybersecurity (Gholami & Omar, 2023). This adaptability is crucial for addressing domain-specific challenges and managing the vast volumes of unstructured data encountered in security operations.

1.3 Automation and Intelligence in Security Operations

Automation has long been a cornerstone of cybersecurity. LLMs amplify this capability by automating complex tasks that traditionally required human expertise. For example, in vulnerability management, LLMs can analyze software documentation to identify potential exploits, a concept reinforced by Zangana et al. (2025) in their review of software vulnerability detection tools. Simultaneously, these models contribute to intelligence generation, transforming raw data into actionable insights and enabling proactive defense strategies.

1.4 Ethical Considerations and Limitations

Despite their potential, the deployment of LLMs in cybersecurity raises ethical and operational concerns. Issues such as bias in training datasets, overfitting, and the potential misuse of LLMs for malicious purposes warrant careful scrutiny. The dual-use nature of these technologies necessitates robust governance frameworks to mitigate risks, as explored in Omar and Zangana's (2024) comprehensive review of cyber AI integration. Furthermore, Nguyen et al. (2018) highlight that the lack of regulatory clarity can exacerbate these challenges, particularly in areas like data privacy and security.

1.5 Quantum-Aware Cybersecurity and LLMs

The advent of quantum computing introduces additional complexity to the cybersecurity domain. Quantum algorithms, while promising unparalleled computational power, also pose significant risks by rendering current encryption methods obsolete. The integration of LLMs into quantum-aware systems is a critical step in addressing these challenges. As Sodiya et al. (2024) argue, the convergence of quantum computing and LLMs presents both opportunities and challenges for safeguarding digital assets. This chapter explores these dynamics, proposing strategies for leveraging LLMs to develop quantum-resistant security measures.

1.6 Scope of the Chapter

This chapter provides a comprehensive examination of LLM applications in cybersecurity, emphasizing their transition from automating processes to delivering intelligence-driven solutions. By synthesizing insights from seminal works, such as those by Zangana and Omar (2025), this chapter outlines best practices, challenges, and future directions for integrating LLMs into modern security frameworks.

Through this exploration, readers will gain a nuanced understanding of how LLMs can bolster cybersecurity in an era of quantum computing advancements.

2. BACKGROUND AND RELATED WORK

The rapid advancement of large language models (LLMs), quantum computing, and artificial intelligence (AI) has introduced transformative possibilities in cybersecurity. However, it has also brought significant challenges in managing and mitigating risks. This section delves into the evolution of these technologies, their applications in cybersecurity, and the related literature, underscoring the need for innovative solutions to safeguard digital assets against emerging threats.

2.1 The Rise of Large Language Models in Cybersecurity

Large language models have shown remarkable proficiency in diverse applications, including natural language processing, malware detection, and vulnerability analysis. Studies like Gholami and Omar (2024) illustrate how student-teacher frameworks for LLMs enhance performance, suggesting the growing role of LLMs in solving complex cybersecurity problems. Furthermore, Gholami and Omar (2023) demonstrate the efficiency gains achieved through synthetic data in training LLMs, which is particularly valuable in scenarios where real-world data is scarce or sensitive.

Omar, Zangana, and Mohammed (2025) emphasize the foundational role of LLMs in software vulnerability detection, highlighting their capacity to identify patterns in code that traditional tools often miss. This aligns with emerging approaches that leverage BERT and GPT-2 for malware detection in IoT systems (Omar et al., 2024), showcasing the scalability and accuracy of these models in diverse environments.

2.2 Quantum Computing and Its Implications for Cybersecurity

Quantum computing represents both a revolutionary opportunity and a profound threat to cybersecurity. Studies such as Sodiya et al. (2024) and Bishwas and Sen (2024) explore the challenges posed by quantum advancements, including the potential to break classical cryptographic algorithms. The implications of quantum computing on cloud infrastructure security have been further analyzed by Baseri, Chouhan, and Ghorbani (2024), emphasizing the urgency of adopting quantum-resistant solutions.

Efforts to develop quantum-resistant algorithms and key exchange protocols, as discussed in Exchange (2024), highlight ongoing strides in preempting quantum-enabled cyberattacks. These advancements complement foundational research by Bush, Challener, and Mantelet (2021) on industrial quantum networks, which elucidates how quantum technologies can also enhance cybersecurity frameworks.

2.3 Integrating AI in Cybersecurity: Challenges and Innovations

AI's integration into cybersecurity has significantly transformed traditional defensive mechanisms. Research by Huff et al. (2023) highlights management practices essential for mitigating threats in biotechnology and healthcare domains, where AI-driven solutions are critical. Similarly, Mohammed, Omar, and Nguyen (2018) provide insights into AI-based detection mechanisms for wormhole attacks in wireless sensor networks, underscoring AI's versatility in addressing varied threats.

The applicability of AI in thwarting complex attacks is further demonstrated by Jones et al. (2023), who propose machine learning-driven approaches for advancing cybersecurity. These advancements are complemented by innovative frameworks like the GPT-2 Enhanced Attack Detection and Defense (GEADD) method for zero-day threats (Jones & Omar, 2024), showcasing AI's capability to anticipate and counteract emerging threats.

2.4 Bridging AI and Blockchain Technologies

Blockchain technology offers an additional layer of security by ensuring data integrity and transparency. The exploration of blockchain-based timestamping tools by Zangana (2024) and smart contract efficiency in healthcare systems by Agrawal and Aggarwal (2024) underscores its relevance in safeguarding sensitive data. Madni, Shah, and Al-Naeem (2024) further investigate blockchain's scalability in electronic health records (EHRs), highlighting its potential to secure critical infrastructures.

2.5 Addressing Mobile and Cloud Security Threats

Mobile and cloud platforms continue to be prime targets for cyberattacks. Research by Wright, Dawson, and Omar (2012) emphasizes the necessity of robust antivirus applications to counter mobile threats, a sentiment echoed by Hamza and Omar (2013) in their analysis of cloud computing vulnerabilities. These studies stress the importance of proactive measures to mitigate the exploitation of mobile and cloud environments.

2.6 The Role of Synthetic Data and Advanced Training Models

The use of synthetic data in cybersecurity research, as explored by Gholami and Omar (2023), and advanced training methodologies for LLMs, as highlighted in Omar and Zangana (2025), reveal the potential to revolutionize training efficiency and model performance. These approaches are pivotal in addressing real-world challenges like adversarial attacks, as demonstrated by Omar (2024).

2.7 Summary

The reviewed literature underscores a multi-faceted approach to cybersecurity, integrating the strengths of LLMs, quantum computing, AI, and blockchain technologies. By leveraging advancements in these areas, researchers and practitioners can better anticipate and counteract emerging threats, paving the way for a secure digital future. This section not only highlights the transformative potential of these technologies but also emphasizes the collaborative effort required to address the complexities of modern cybersecurity.

3. APPLICATIONS OF LARGE LANGUAGE MODELS IN CYBERSECURITY

Large Language Models (LLMs) have revolutionized the cybersecurity landscape, offering advanced capabilities that span threat detection, incident response, vulnerability assessment, and automated remediation. These models leverage their vast training on diverse datasets to address complex security challenges, enabling organizations to bolster their defenses against evolving threats. Below is an exploration of key applications:

3.1. Threat Intelligence and Analysis

LLMs are pivotal in parsing and synthesizing vast amounts of threat intelligence data. They can analyze structured and unstructured sources, such as logs, research reports, and threat feeds, to identify potential risks and predict emerging attack vectors. For instance, the integration of LLMs like GPT-4 in automated frameworks has demonstrated significant improvements in detecting zero-day vulnerabilities (Jones & Omar, 2024). By analyzing behavioral patterns and anomalies in real-time, LLMs enhance the speed and accuracy of threat identification (Huff et al., 2023).

3.2. Incident Response Automation

In incident response, time is critical. LLMs expedite the triage process by analyzing attack indicators and recommending containment and mitigation strategies. Through natural language processing (NLP), these models interpret and prioritize alerts from security information and event management (SIEM) systems, reducing response time. The application of synthetic data in LLM training, as discussed by Gholami and Omar (2023), further enhances their efficiency in high-pressure scenarios by providing diverse and realistic attack scenarios.

3.3. Vulnerability Assessment and Patch Management

LLMs facilitate continuous vulnerability assessment by scanning and interpreting security configurations, codebases, and network architectures. They excel in identifying misconfigurations and outdated software, often overlooked in manual reviews. Furthermore, the use of advanced models in analyzing wireless sensor network vulnerabilities highlights their potential in specialized areas, such as detecting wormhole attacks (Mohammed et al., 2018). By providing detailed risk assessments, LLMs empower organizations to prioritize patch management efforts effectively.

3.4. Social Engineering Defense

Phishing and other social engineering attacks remain prevalent. LLMs mitigate these threats by analyzing email content and user communications to identify malicious intent. Zangana et al. (2024) demonstrated that LLMs can detect sophisticated email phishing campaigns, offering organizations a robust tool for preemptive defense. Additionally, the real-time evaluation of conversational dynamics helps mitigate man-in-the-middle attacks (Mohamed & Ahmed, 2024).

3.5. Malware Detection and Analysis

The adaptability of LLMs in recognizing malware signatures and behaviors is unparalleled. By analyzing large datasets of malware variants, LLMs build models that identify novel threats. For instance, studies on using optimized convolutional neural networks for malware detection (Omar, 2024) emphasize the synergy between deep learning models and cybersecurity. LLMs enhance this capability by providing context and explanations for detection outcomes.

3.6. IoT Security

In the Internet of Things (IoT) domain, where devices are often vulnerable to malware and hacking attempts, LLMs play a crucial role. Their ability to process large-scale telemetry data enables the detection of irregular device behavior. Comparative analyses of LLMs like BERT and GPT-2 for IoT malware detection (Omar et al., 2024) illustrate their effectiveness in identifying and mitigating threats in hyperconnected environments.

3.7. Enhanced Documentation and Policy Generation

LLMs assist in generating comprehensive security documentation, policies, and compliance reports. They interpret regulatory requirements and translate them into actionable policies, reducing the administrative burden on cybersecurity teams. Moreover, they ensure organizations remain compliant with data protection and cybersecurity regulations.

3.8. Quantum-Aware Cybersecurity

As the quantum computing era approaches, the integration of quantum-aware LLMs becomes critical. Studies by Sodiya et al. (2024) and Baseri et al. (2024) emphasize the transformative potential of quantum technologies and the challenges they pose to classical cryptographic systems. LLMs equipped with quantum-related knowledge can analyze the impact of quantum advancements on security protocols, ensuring the development of quantum-resistant solutions.

3.9 Future Directions

The growing sophistication of cyber threats necessitates continuous innovation in LLM applications. As organizations integrate these models into their operations, challenges such as data privacy, adversarial attacks, and model explainability must be addressed (Zangana & Omar, 2025). Moreover, the collaboration between AI and blockchain technologies offers promising avenues for enhancing LLM capabilities in securing decentralized systems (Zangana, 2024).

To visualize the multifaceted applications of LLMs in cybersecurity, Figure 1 provides an overview of their key domains. This includes areas such as threat intelligence, vulnerability management, and IoT security. The chart emphasizes the versatility of LLMs and their growing importance in addressing diverse cybersecurity challenges.

Figure 1. LLM cybersecurity applications overview

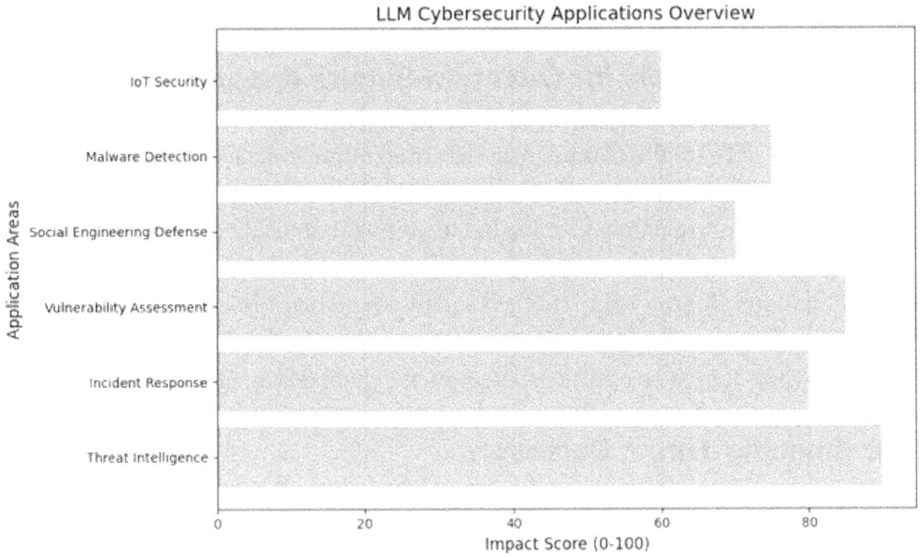

By addressing these challenges and leveraging the full potential of LLMs, cybersecurity practitioners can build resilient defenses against an ever-evolving threat landscape. The comprehensive analysis provided by Omar and Zangana (2025) underscores the importance of aligning LLM innovations with cybersecurity needs.

4. QUANTUM-AWARE CYBERSECURITY AND LLMS

The intersection of quantum computing and large language models (LLMs) marks a transformative era in cybersecurity, combining the predictive power of AI with the computational prowess of quantum systems. This section explores how quantum-aware cybersecurity strategies can leverage LLMs to address emerging threats, emphasizing their role in encryption, threat detection, and resilience.

4.1 The Quantum Computing Threat Landscape

Quantum computing presents unique challenges to traditional cybersecurity frameworks. Algorithms like Shor's and Grover's threaten current encryption methods by exponentially reducing the time required for decryption (Sodiya et al., 2024). This capability could render classical cryptographic systems obsolete, necessitating the development of quantum-resistant algorithms (Bishwas & Sen, 2024). The integration of LLMs in this context can support the detection of vulnerabilities and the development of novel quantum-secure cryptographic systems.

4.2 Harnessing LLMs for Quantum-Secure Applications

LLMs like GPT-4 and specialized models offer unprecedented potential in identifying vulnerabilities and automating responses in cybersecurity systems. For example, these models can assist in transitioning to quantum-resistant encryption protocols by analyzing vast datasets to identify weaknesses in traditional algorithms and suggesting optimizations (Jones et al., 2023). Gholami and Omar (2024) demonstrate how the training of student LLMs on synthetic data enhances efficiency, which can be applied to cybersecurity to optimize detection mechanisms against quantum threats.

4.3 Enhancing Threat Detection

The use of LLMs in proactive threat detection is critical, particularly in environments increasingly susceptible to quantum-driven attacks. Huff et al. (2023) illustrate how AI systems improve threat management in biotechnology and healthcare sectors, which face similar vulnerabilities. LLMs can monitor network activity in real time, flagging anomalies that may indicate quantum-assisted intrusions.

For instance, models trained on wireless sensor network datasets could detect and mitigate wormhole attacks, a critical vulnerability in IoT devices (Mohammed et al., 2018). Similarly, the comparative analysis of LLMs for IoT malware detection by Omar et al. (2024) highlights their applicability in quantum-aware scenarios.

4.4 LLMs in Cryptography and Key Management

The quantum era demands advancements in cryptographic techniques and key management. LLMs contribute to the creation and validation of quantum-resistant encryption mechanisms by simulating attack scenarios and stress-testing cryptographic algorithms. As noted by Zangana (2024), blockchain-based timestamping tools also benefit from AI-driven analysis, ensuring robustness against quantum computational capabilities.

4.5 Future-Ready Cybersecurity Strategies

To prepare for the quantum era, cybersecurity frameworks must integrate agile practices that emphasize adaptability (Khan et al., 2023). LLMs can play a crucial role in this transition by facilitating the development of scalable solutions, such as quantum-resilient cloud architectures (Hamza & Omar, 2013). Furthermore, the application of LLMs to the analysis of network firewall rule analyzers ensures enhanced security postures in preparation for quantum-enabled threats (Zangana et al., 2024).

Figure 2 illustrates the interplay between LLMs and quantum-aware cybersecurity strategies. This diagram demonstrates how these technologies converge to enhance encryption resilience, enable threat detection, and develop scalable quantum-resistant solutions.

Figure 2. Quantum and LLM integration

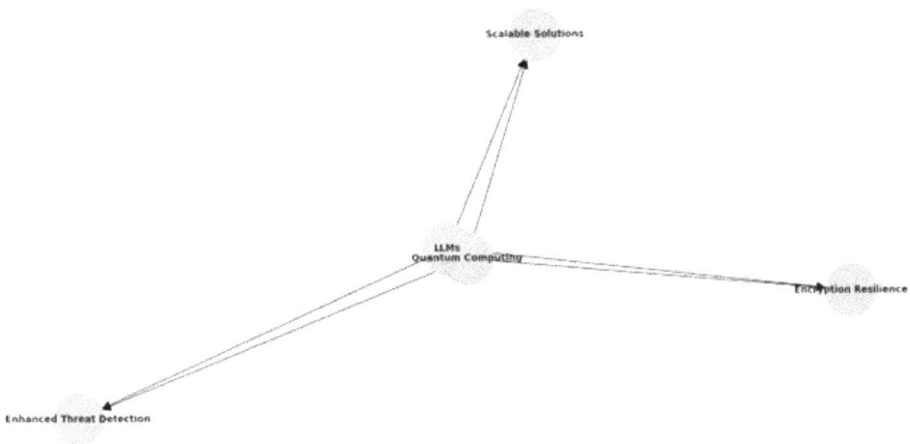

4.6 Addressing Ethical and Operational Challenges

The dual-use nature of quantum computing and LLMs poses ethical dilemmas, particularly concerning misuse in creating advanced attack tools. The GEADD method proposed by Jones and Omar (2024) exemplifies how LLMs can detect and defend against zero-day threats. Nonetheless, careful regulation and transparent AI practices are essential to mitigate risks (Rahul et al., 2024).

4.7 Summary

As quantum computing evolves, its integration with LLMs represents a double-edged sword for cybersecurity. While the quantum era amplifies the threat landscape, it also provides an opportunity to harness LLMs for innovative and resilient defenses. By leveraging AI-driven insights and preparing for quantum-resistant frameworks, organizations can navigate the challenges and harness the potential of this transformative intersection.

5. CHALLENGES AND LIMITATIONS

Large Language Models (LLMs) hold immense potential in revolutionizing cybersecurity; however, their deployment is fraught with challenges and limitations. These obstacles span technological, ethical, and operational domains, impacting the realization of their full potential in cybersecurity applications.

5.1. Resource-Intensive Nature

LLMs like GPT or BERT require significant computational and energy resources for both training and deployment. As noted by Gholami and Omar (2023), optimizing LLMs with synthetic data can mitigate some inefficiencies, yet the underlying demands of large-scale training and inference remain formidable. Organizations often struggle with the financial and infrastructural requirements to sustain these models, particularly for real-time applications like malware detection in IoT systems (Omar, Zangana, Al-Karaki, & Mohammed, 2024).

5.2. Bias and Ethical Concerns

LLMs inherit biases from their training datasets, which can lead to skewed or harmful predictions. When used in security contexts, this could result in false positives or negatives, potentially compromising system integrity. Ethical considerations also arise when using these models for surveillance or in applications with significant implications for privacy and civil liberties (Jones & Omar, 2024).

Figure 3 outlines the ethical challenges in deploying LLMs for cybersecurity, categorized into privacy, bias, and dual-use concerns. This visualization highlights the areas requiring robust governance to ensure responsible adoption of these technologies.

Figure 3. Ethical challenges of LLMs in cybersecurity

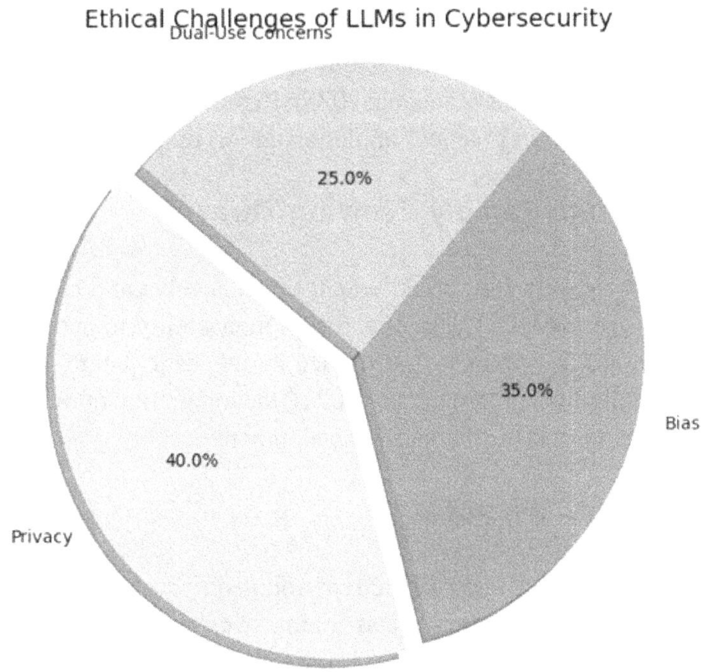

5.3. Vulnerability to Adversarial Attacks

Despite their sophistication, LLMs remain susceptible to adversarial manipulations. Huff et al. (2023) emphasize the need for robust management practices to counteract such threats, particularly in high-stakes environments like biotechnology and healthcare. Moreover, adversarial text generation poses a significant challenge for LLMs in phishing detection, as adversaries craft inputs designed to evade detection systems (Zangana et al., 2025).

5.4. Explainability and Trust

LLMs often operate as "black boxes," making it difficult for practitioners to interpret their decisions. This lack of transparency can hinder trust and adoption, especially in sectors requiring accountability, such as legal compliance or government cybersecurity (Omar & Zangana, 2025). Research into explainable AI (XAI) paradigms is ongoing, but practical implementations remain limited.

5.5. Adaptation to Rapidly Evolving Threats

Cybersecurity is a dynamic field where threats evolve at a rapid pace. While LLMs can analyze historical data effectively, their ability to anticipate zero-day threats or novel attack vectors is constrained by the static nature of their training datasets. As highlighted by Jones et al. (2023), the integration of real-time learning mechanisms remains a critical area for development.

5.6. Scalability Challenges

The scalability of LLMs in distributed environments poses a significant challenge, particularly in handling the diversity and volume of cybersecurity data. Mohammed et al. (2018) observed similar limitations in wireless sensor networks, suggesting that decentralized approaches might mitigate some of these issues. However, integrating LLMs with such frameworks remains a complex endeavor.

5.7. Quantum Threats

The impending advent of quantum computing introduces new complexities. As quantum computers progress, they threaten to undermine current cryptographic standards, creating an urgent need for quantum-resistant algorithms. Researchers like Sodiya et al. (2024) and Bishwas and Sen (2024) underscore the necessity for LLMs to adapt their methodologies to account for quantum-driven vulnerabilities.

5.8. Privacy and Regulatory Constraints

Utilizing LLMs in cybersecurity often involves analyzing sensitive data, raising concerns about data privacy and regulatory compliance. Hamza and Omar (2013) highlight the potential for misuse when such models are deployed in cloud environments, emphasizing the need for stringent access control and cryptographic safeguards.

5.9. Economic Viability

Finally, the economic feasibility of integrating LLMs into existing cybersecurity infrastructures is a non-trivial concern. While advanced models provide unparalleled capabilities, their high costs can deter widespread adoption, particularly for small to medium enterprises (SMEs). Approaches like those proposed by Baseri, Chouhan, and Ghorbani (2024) in assessing the impact of quantum computing on infrastructure may provide insights for cost-effective implementation strategies.

5.10 Summary and Future Directions

Addressing these challenges requires a multi-disciplinary approach encompassing technological innovation, ethical scrutiny, and policy frameworks. Collaborative efforts between academia, industry, and policymakers will be essential to overcome these hurdles and fully harness the transformative potential of LLMs in cybersecurity. As research progresses, particularly in areas like quantum-aware AI and adversarial defense mechanisms (Omar, 2024; Rahim et al., 2024), the gap between current limitations and future possibilities is expected to narrow.

6. FUTURE DIRECTIONS

The integration of large language models (LLMs) into cybersecurity has set a transformative precedent, but its potential is far from fully realized. Future research and application areas are poised to address evolving threats, refine existing methodologies, and leverage emerging technologies. Below, we discuss critical directions in the advancement of LLMs for cybersecurity.

6.1. Enhancing Model Efficiency and Scalability

Optimizing LLMs for efficiency and scalability remains a pivotal research avenue. Synthetic data generation has shown promise in reducing the data dependency of large models. Studies like those by Gholami and Omar (2023) emphasize that synthetic datasets can significantly improve model performance while reducing computational costs. Future research must explore diverse data augmentation strategies to enhance LLM capabilities in handling rare or evolving threat scenarios.

Figure 4 depicts the evolution of LLMs in cybersecurity, from basic automation tools to integral components of quantum-resistant architectures. This timeline emphasizes their increasing sophistication and expanded role in modern security frameworks.

Figure 4. Evolution of LLMs in cybersecurity

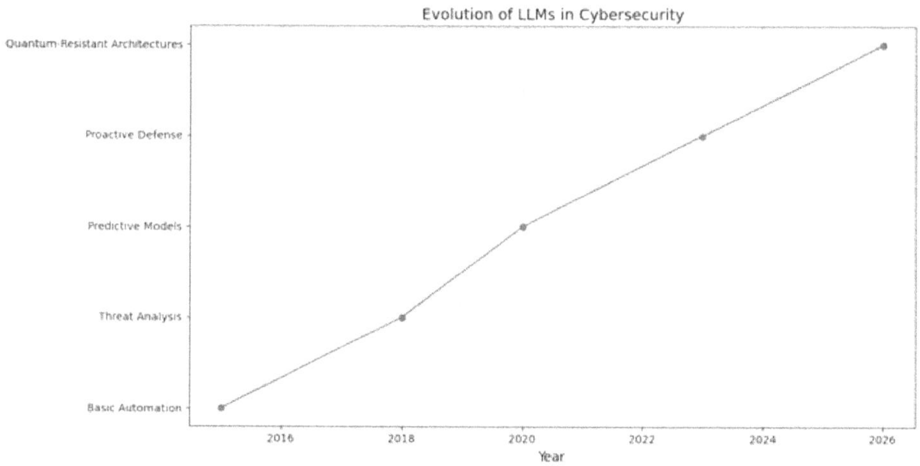

6.2. Quantum-Resistant Architectures

With quantum computing on the horizon, developing LLMs resistant to quantum-based threats is imperative. Researchers have highlighted the profound implications of quantum computing on classical cryptographic systems (Sodiya et al., 2024; Rahul et al., 2024). Integrating quantum-resilient algorithms into LLMs could provide robust defenses against quantum-accelerated cyberattacks. This includes exploring new cryptographic protocols, as proposed by Bishwas and Sen (2024), and adapting models to function within hybrid quantum-classical ecosystems.

6.3. Autonomous Threat Detection and Response

LLMs' ability to automate complex tasks positions them as key enablers for real-time cybersecurity operations. The GPT-2 Enhanced Attack Detection and Defense (GEADD) framework by Jones and Omar (2024) exemplifies this potential. Future efforts should focus on creating more autonomous systems capable of identifying, analyzing, and mitigating zero-day vulnerabilities with minimal human intervention.

6.4. Cross-Domain Learning and Federated Models

Leveraging cross-domain knowledge could significantly enhance LLM performance. Federated learning, as discussed by Mohamed and Ahmed (2024), offers a decentralized approach to training LLMs across distributed environments without compromising data privacy. Applying these concepts to cybersecurity can improve global threat intelligence sharing, especially in industries like healthcare and finance.

6.5. Integration with Blockchain Technology

Blockchain's inherent transparency and immutability make it an excellent candidate for augmenting cybersecurity measures. Zangana (2024) has explored blockchain-based timestamping and website vulnerability scanners, which could synergize with LLMs to provide advanced security solutions. Future research should investigate the integration of LLMs with blockchain frameworks to enable secure, decentralized threat intelligence systems.

6.6. Addressing Bias and Adversarial Robustness

The robustness of LLMs against adversarial attacks and biases remains a challenge. Studies like Omar's (2024) work on adversarial defense for deep neural networks suggest the need for comprehensive frameworks that enhance LLMs' resilience. Building models capable of detecting and neutralizing adversarial inputs is critical for ensuring consistent performance in dynamic threat landscapes.

6.7. Quantum-Aware Cybersecurity Training

As quantum computing emerges, there is a growing need to educate cybersecurity professionals about its implications. Perron et al. (2021) stress the importance of integrating quantum mechanics into educational frameworks. Coupled with LLMs, such training modules can simulate quantum-aware cybersecurity scenarios, providing professionals with practical insights into quantum-resilient strategies.

6.8. Industry-Specific Applications

Tailoring LLMs for domain-specific needs will enhance their practical utility. For example, Huff et al. (2023) identified unique cybersecurity challenges in biotechnology and healthcare. Similarly, Madni et al. (2024) discussed scalable solutions for electronic health records using blockchain. By developing sector-specific models, LLMs can provide customized solutions for industries facing unique threat landscapes.

6.9. Expanding IoT and Smart System Security

The proliferation of IoT devices demands advanced threat detection mechanisms. Omar, Zangana, and colleagues (2024) have demonstrated the effectiveness of LLMs in IoT malware detection. Future directions include developing lightweight LLMs optimized for resource-constrained IoT devices, ensuring comprehensive security coverage.

6.10. Collaborative Research Ecosystems

Fostering interdisciplinary collaboration will be crucial for advancing LLM applications in cybersecurity. Initiatives like those described by Bush et al. (2021) in industrial quantum networks and Qualters et al. (2019) in computing research provide valuable models for collaborative ecosystems. Such partnerships can accelerate the development of innovative cybersecurity solutions that bridge theoretical research and practical implementation.

At last, the future of LLMs in cybersecurity is replete with opportunities. By addressing existing challenges and exploring novel applications, researchers and practitioners can unlock the full potential of LLMs, ensuring robust and intelligent defenses against an ever-evolving cyber threat landscape. Each of these directions not only builds upon the current state of research but also aligns with emerging trends in technology and cybersecurity.

7. CONCLUSION

The integration of large language models (LLMs) into cybersecurity represents a transformative shift in how threats are detected, analyzed, and mitigated. These models, with their unparalleled ability to process and understand vast amounts of data, have redefined the boundaries of automation and intelligence in the field. By leveraging advanced natural language processing capabilities, LLMs are not only addressing current challenges but are also laying the groundwork for future innovations in cybersecurity.

As the digital landscape becomes increasingly complex, with the rise of quantum computing, IoT proliferation, and advanced adversarial techniques, the role of LLMs is becoming more critical. They offer the potential to automate tedious tasks, predict and prevent attacks with higher accuracy, and provide actionable insights in real time. The adaptability of these models ensures that they can evolve alongside emerging threats, making them indispensable tools for modern cybersecurity strategies.

However, the journey is far from over. Challenges such as ensuring model robustness, addressing ethical concerns, and integrating these systems into diverse industrial applications must be continuously addressed. The future of cybersecurity will rely heavily on the collaboration of researchers, practitioners, and policymakers to develop frameworks that harness the full potential of LLMs while mitigating their limitations.

In summary, large language models have emerged as a cornerstone of modern cybersecurity, bridging the gap between reactive and proactive defense mechanisms. As we continue to explore their capabilities and address their challenges, LLMs promise to lead the way toward a more secure and resilient digital world.

REFERENCES

Agrawal, K., & Aggarwal, M. Building Efficient Smart Contract for Healthcare 4.0. In *Blockchain for Healthcare 4.0* (pp. 94-123). CRC Press.

AL-Refaey. M. R., Tyagi, A. K., AL-Ghamdi, A. S. A. M., & Kukreja, S. (Eds.). (2024). *Topics in Artificial Intelligence Applied to Industry 4.0*. John Wiley & Sons.

Baseri, Y., Chouhan, V., & Ghorbani, A. (2024). Cybersecurity in the Quantum Era: Assessing the Impact of Quantum Computing on Infrastructure. *arXiv preprint arXiv:2404.10659*.

Bishwas, A. K., & Sen, M. (2024). Strategic Roadmap for Quantum-Resistant Security: A Framework for Preparing Industries for the Quantum Threat. *arXiv preprint arXiv:2411.09995*.

Block, R. S. S. (2024). The 2024 quantum advantage blueprint: Where quantum outpaces classical.

Bush, S. F., Challener, W. A., & Mantelet, G. (2021). A perspective on industrial quantum networks. *AVS Quantum Science*, 3(3), 030501. DOI: 10.1116/5.0051881

Exchange, Q. R. K. Towards a Verifiably Secure Quantum-Resistant Key Exchange in IKEv2.

Gholami, S., & Omar, M. (2023). Does Synthetic Data Make Large Language Models More Efficient? *arXiv preprint arXiv:2310.07830*.

Gholami, S., & Omar, M. (2024). Can a student large language model perform as well as its teacher? In *Innovations, Securities, and Case Studies Across Healthcare, Business, and Technology* (pp. 122-139). IGI Global. DOI: 10.4018/979-8-3693-1906-2.ch007

Hamza, Y. A., & Omar, M. D. (2013). Cloud computing security: Abuse and nefarious use of cloud computing. *International Journal of Computer Engineering Research*, 3(6), 22–27.

How, M. L., & Cheah, S. M. (2023). Business Renaissance: Opportunities and challenges at the dawn of the Quantum Computing Era. *Businesses*, 3(4), 585–605. DOI: 10.3390/businesses3040036

Huff, A. J., Burrell, D. N., Nobles, C., Richardson, K., Wright, J. B., Burton, S. L., Jones, A. J., Springs, D., Omar, M., & Brown-Jackson, K. L. (2023). Management Practices for Mitigating Cybersecurity Threats to Biotechnology Companies, Laboratories, and Healthcare Research Organizations. In *Applied Research Approaches to Technology, Healthcare, and Business* (pp. 1-12). IGI Global.

Jones, R., & Omar, M. (2024). Revolutionizing Cybersecurity: The GPT-2 Enhanced Attack Detection and Defense (GEADD) Method for Zero-Day Threats. *International Journal of Informatics* [INJIISCOM]. *Information System and Computer Engineering*, 5(2), 178–191.

Jones, R., Omar, M., Mohammed, D., Nobles, C., & Dawson, M. (2023). Harnessing the Speed and Accuracy of Machine Learning to Advance Cybersecurity. In *2023 Congress in Computer Science, Computer Engineering, & Applied Computing (CSCE)* (pp. 418-421). IEEE. DOI: 10.1109/CSCE60160.2023.00074

Khan, A. A., Akbar, M. A., Ahmad, A., Fahmideh, M., Shameem, M., Lahtinen, V., . . . Mikkonen, T. (2023, July). Agile practices for quantum software development: practitioners' perspectives. In *2023 IEEE international conference on quantum software (QSW)* (pp. 9-20). IEEE.

Lougovski, P., Parekh, O., Broz, J., Byrd, M., Chembo, Y., de Jong, W. A., . . . Svore, K. M. (2023). *Position Papers for the ASCR Workshop on Basic Research Needs in Quantum Computing and Networking*. USDOE Office of Science (SC), Advanced Scientific Computing Research (ASCR).

Madni, A. F., Shah, M. A., & Al-Naeem, M. (2024). An Investigation of Scalability in EHRs using Healthcare 4.0 and Blockchain. *International Journal of Advanced Computer Science and Applications*, 15(5). Advance online publication. DOI: 10.14569/IJACSA.2024.0150548

Metawei, M. A., Eldeeb, H., Nassar, S. M., & Taher, M. (2022). Quantum Computing Meets Artificial Intelligence: Innovations and Challenges. In *Handbook on Artificial Intelligence-Empowered Applied Software Engineering: VOL. 1: Novel Methodologies to Engineering Smart Software Systems* (pp. 303–338). Springer International Publishing. DOI: 10.1007/978-3-031-08202-3_12

Mohamed, N., & Ahmed, A. A. (2024, June). AI in Combatting Man-in-the-Middle Attacks: A Comprehensive Review. In *2024 15th International Conference on Computing Communication and Networking Technologies (ICCCNT)* (pp. 1-6). IEEE. DOI: 10.1109/ICCCNT61001.2024.10725789

Mohammed, D., Omar, M., & Nguyen, V. (2018). Wireless sensor network security: Approaches to detecting and avoiding wormhole attacks. *Journal of Research in Business. Economics and Management*, 10(2), 1860–1864.

Nguyen, V., Mohammed, D., Omar, M., & Banisakher, M. (2018). The Effects of the FCC Net Neutrality Repeal on Security and Privacy. [IJHIoT]. *International Journal of Hyperconnectivity and the Internet of Things*, 2(2), 21–29. DOI: 10.4018/IJHIoT.2018070102

Omar, M. (2021). New insights into database security: An effective and integrated approach for applying access control mechanisms and cryptographic concepts in Microsoft Access environments.

Omar, M. (2022). *Machine Learning for Cybersecurity: Innovative Deep Learning Solutions*. Springer Brief. https://link.springer.com/book/978303115

Omar, M. (2024). From Attack to Defense: Strengthening DNN Text Classification Against Adversarial Examples. In *Innovations, Securities, and Case Studies Across Healthcare, Business, and Technology* (pp. 174-195). IGI Global.

Omar, M. (2024). Revolutionizing Malware Detection: A Paradigm Shift Through Optimized Convolutional Neural Networks. In *Innovations, Securities, and Case Studies Across Healthcare, Business, and Technology* (pp. 196-220). IGI Global. DOI: 10.4018/979-8-3693-1906-2.ch011

Omar, M., & Zangana, H. M. (Eds.). (2024). *Redefining Security With Cyber AI*. IGI Global., DOI: 10.4018/979-8-3693-6517-5

Omar, M., & Zangana, H. M. (Eds.). (2025). *Application of Large Language Models (LLMs) for Software Vulnerability Detection*. IGI Global., DOI: 10.4018/979-8-3693-9311-6

Omar, M., Zangana, H. M., Al-Karaki, J. N., & Mohammed, D. (2024). Harnessing LLMs for IoT malware detection: A comparative analysis of BERT and GPT-2. In *Proceedings of the 8th International Symposium on Multidisciplinary Studies and Innovative Technologies (ISMSIT)* (pp. 1-6). Ankara, Turkiye. https://doi.org/DOI: 10.1109/ISMSIT63511.2024.10757249

Omar, M., Zangana, H. M., & Mohammed, D. (Eds.). (2025). *Integrating Artificial Intelligence in Cybersecurity and Forensic Practices*. IGI Global., DOI: 10.4018/979-8-3373-0588-2

Perron, J. K., DeLeone, C., Sharif, S., Carter, T., Grossman, J. M., Passante, G., & Sack, J. (2021). Quantum undergraduate education and scientific training. *arXiv preprint arXiv:2109.13850*.

Qualters, I., Taylor, A. J., & Hagberg, A. A. (2019). *IS&T Computing Overview* (No. LA-UR-19-22567). Los Alamos National Lab.(LANL), Los Alamos, NM (United States).

Rahul, R., Geetha, S., Priyatharsini, S., Mehata, K., Sundaresan Perumal, T., Ethiraj, N., & Sendilvelan, S. (2024). Cybersecurity Issues and Challenges in Quantum Computing. *Topics in Artificial Intelligence Applied to Industry*, 4(0), 203–221. DOI: 10.1002/9781394216147.ch11

Ramachandran, D., Naqi, S. M., Perumal, G., & Abbas, Q. (2023). DLTN-LOSP: A Novel Deep-Linear-Transition-Network-Based Resource Allocation Model with the Logic Overhead Security Protocol for Cloud Systems. *Sensors (Basel)*, 23(20), 8448. DOI: 10.3390/s23208448 PMID: 37896541

Seskir, Z. C. (2019). *Current state of quantum information technologies in Turkey* (Master's thesis, Middle East Technical University).

Singh, N. B. *Quantum Mechanics in Drug Discovery*. NB Singh.

Sodiya, E. O., Umoga, U. J., Amoo, O. O., & Atadoga, A. (2024). Quantum computing and its potential impact on US cybersecurity: A review: Scrutinizing the challenges and opportunities presented by quantum technologies in safeguarding digital assets. *Global Journal of Engineering and Technology Advances, 18*(2), 049-064.

Wright, J., Dawson, M. E.Jr, & Omar, M. (2012). Cyber security and mobile threats: The need for antivirus applications for smartphones. *Journal of Information Systems Technology and Planning*, 5(14), 40–60.

Zangana, H. M. (2024). Exploring Blockchain-Based Timestamping Tools: A Comprehensive Review. *Redefining Security With Cyber AI*, 92-110.

Zangana, H. M. (2024). Exploring the Landscape of Website Vulnerability Scanners: A Comprehensive Review and Comparative Analysis. *Redefining Security With Cyber AI*, 111-129.

Zangana, H. M., Mohammed, A. K., Sallow, A. B., & Sallow, Z. B. (2024). Cybernetic Deception: Unraveling the Layers of Email Phishing Threats. [INJURATECH]. *International Journal of Research and Applied Technology*, 4(1), 35–47.

Zangana, H. M., & Mohammed, D. (2025). Foundations of Large Language Models in Software Vulnerability Detection. In Omar, M., & Zangana, H. (Eds.), *Application of Large Language Models (LLMs) for Software Vulnerability Detection* (pp. 41–74). IGI Global., DOI: 10.4018/979-8-3693-9311-6.ch002

Zangana, H. M., & Mustafa, F. M. (2025). Image Denoising Techniques for Cybersecurity and Forensic Applications: AI-Driven Approaches. In Omar, M., Zangana, H., & Mohammed, D. (Eds.), *Integrating Artificial Intelligence in Cybersecurity and Forensic Practices* (pp. 117–142). IGI Global Scientific Publishing., DOI: 10.4018/979-8-3373-0588-2.ch005

Zangana, H. M., & Omar, M. (2020). Threats, Attacks, and Mitigations of Smartphone Security. *Academic Journal of Nawroz University*, 9(4), 324–332. DOI: 10.25007/ajnu.v9n4a989

Zangana, H. M., & Omar, M. (2025). Harnessing the Power of Large Language Models for Cybersecurity: Applications, Challenges, and Future Directions. In Omar, M., & Zangana, H. (Eds.), *Application of Large Language Models (LLMs) for Software Vulnerability Detection* (pp. 1–40). IGI Global., DOI: 10.4018/979-8-3693-9311-6.ch001

Zangana, H. M., Omar, M., Al-Karaki, J. N., & Mohammed, D. (2024). Comprehensive Review and Analysis of Network Firewall Rule Analyzers: Enhancing Security Posture and Efficiency. *Redefining Security With Cyber AI*, 15-36.

Chapter 10
Adversarial Attacks and Defense Mechanisms in the Age of Quantum Computing

Yara Shamoo
https://orcid.org/0009-0004-2459-0807
Saint Leo University, USA

ABSTRACT

Adversarial attacks on machine learning models have become a significant concern in cybersecurity, especially with the advent of quantum computing. These attacks aim to manipulate the decision-making process of AI systems, leading to vulnerabilities that can be exploited by malicious actors. As quantum computing promises to revolutionize various industries, it also introduces new challenges for defending against adversarial threats. This chapter explores the impact of quantum computing on adversarial machine learning, examining how quantum algorithms can be both a tool for enhancing attack strategies and a foundation for developing more robust defense mechanisms. It reviews existing defense techniques, such as adversarial training and gradient masking, and discusses the potential for quantum-aware models to counteract these threats.

1. INTRODUCTION

In recent years, the integration of artificial intelligence (AI) in cybersecurity has revolutionized the way we approach and mitigate digital threats. The rapid advancement of technologies such as large language models (LLMs), machine learning, and

DOI: 10.4018/979-8-3373-1102-9.ch010

quantum computing has redefined traditional cybersecurity paradigms, offering innovative solutions to complex problems. AI-driven techniques, particularly those that leverage deep learning and neural networks, have shown tremendous potential in detecting and defending against sophisticated cyberattacks. This chapter explores the intersection of AI and cybersecurity, with a particular focus on the evolving role of LLMs, quantum computing, and blockchain in enhancing security measures.

As cyber threats continue to grow in complexity and scale, organizations are increasingly relying on AI to bolster their defense mechanisms. The rise of LLMs such as GPT-2 and GPT-3 has transformed the landscape of cybersecurity by improving the detection and prevention of zero-day vulnerabilities and malicious activities. Jones and Omar (2024) emphasize how LLMs, with their natural language processing capabilities, can significantly enhance attack detection and defense strategies. Moreover, AI-driven methodologies are instrumental in identifying subtle patterns in data that may otherwise go unnoticed, allowing for proactive threat mitigation. This capability is crucial as cybercriminals adopt increasingly sophisticated methods to exploit vulnerabilities.

The emergence of quantum computing presents both challenges and opportunities for cybersecurity. As highlighted by Sodiya et al. (2024), quantum computing holds the potential to break traditional cryptographic systems, which rely on the complexity of factoring large numbers or solving discrete logarithmic problems. However, it also offers a new frontier for developing quantum-resistant security protocols. The increasing interest in quantum cryptography and quantum-resistant algorithms is transforming the way we secure data and communication channels. As quantum technologies evolve, they promise to enhance the robustness of cybersecurity systems, although they also require a reevaluation of existing methods (Baseri et al., 2024).

Furthermore, the application of blockchain technology has revolutionized the way we secure digital transactions and manage data integrity. Zangana (2024) explores how blockchain-based timestamping tools can be used for ensuring the authenticity and traceability of digital assets. In the realm of cybersecurity, blockchain has been employed to improve the security of network protocols, safeguard IoT devices, and prevent unauthorized access to sensitive information. As blockchain continues to mature, its integration with AI could offer powerful new solutions for managing digital security in decentralized environments (Mohammed et al., 2018).

One of the most significant advancements in cybersecurity is the incorporation of AI techniques into malware detection systems. AI-driven systems can analyze vast amounts of data to identify anomalies and detect malicious code patterns that traditional methods may overlook. According to Omar (2024), optimized convolutional neural networks (CNNs) have proven particularly effective in malware detection, providing an extra layer of defense against cyberattacks. These deep learning models leverage large datasets to train on complex patterns of behavior, making them highly effective in identifying both known and unknown threats (Jones et al., 2023).

In the next sections, we will delve into the role of large language models in cybersecurity, explore the impact of quantum computing on encryption and security protocols, and examine how AI-driven approaches to malware detection are shaping the future of digital defense. We will also discuss the challenges and ethical considerations that accompany the use of AI and quantum technologies in cybersecurity, highlighting the need for continued research and development in this critical field.

Through the exploration of these innovative technologies, this chapter aims to provide a comprehensive understanding of how AI, quantum computing, and blockchain are transforming cybersecurity, offering both novel solutions and new challenges to the digital landscape. With the increasing reliance on AI for threat detection, defense strategies, and secure data management, the future of cybersecurity will undoubtedly be shaped by these cutting-edge technologies.

2. UNDERSTANDING ADVERSARIAL ATTACKS: A PRIMER

Adversarial attacks have become a critical concern in modern machine learning (ML) and cybersecurity applications, as they exploit vulnerabilities in models and systems to deceive them into producing incorrect outputs. These attacks are not only a threat to the accuracy and robustness of machine learning models but also pose serious risks in security-sensitive applications, such as autonomous systems, medical diagnostics, and cybersecurity. The following section provides an in-depth overview of adversarial attacks, shedding light on their mechanisms, types, and the challenges they present to both researchers and practitioners.

2.1. What are Adversarial Attacks?

Adversarial attacks are deliberate manipulations of input data aimed at misleading machine learning models into making incorrect predictions or classifications. These manipulations often involve tiny, human-invisible perturbations to the input, which can drastically alter the model's behavior. The term "adversarial" reflects the intentional nature of these perturbations, which exploit weaknesses in the model's learned patterns. These attacks can be highly effective because many models, particularly deep learning networks, are sensitive to minor changes in input data. Despite being imperceptible to human observers, these small perturbations can cause the model to misclassify or fail to recognize the true nature of the input.

2.2. Types of Adversarial Attacks

Adversarial attacks can be categorized based on their strategy, goals, and the techniques they use. The most common types of attacks include:

- **White-box Attacks**: In white-box attacks, the adversary has full knowledge of the model, including its architecture, parameters, and training data. This allows the attacker to craft highly specific perturbations tailored to exploit the model's weaknesses. Examples of white-box attacks include the Fast Gradient Sign Method (FGSM) and the Carlini & Wagner attack.
- **Black-box Attacks**: In black-box attacks, the adversary does not have access to the model's internal workings, such as its architecture or parameters. Instead, the attacker only has access to the model's inputs and outputs, relying on this information to generate adversarial examples. Methods like the transferability of adversarial examples, where an adversarial attack on one model can be applied to another, are often used in black-box scenarios.
- **Targeted vs. Untargeted Attacks**: A targeted attack aims to force the model to classify an input as a specific, predetermined label, whereas an untargeted attack simply seeks to misclassify the input without concern for which incorrect class the model selects.

Adversarial attacks can be classified based on the attacker's knowledge and objectives. The chart below provides a comparative view of common adversarial attack types, illustrating their relative prevalence and significance.

Figure 1. Common types of adversarial attacks

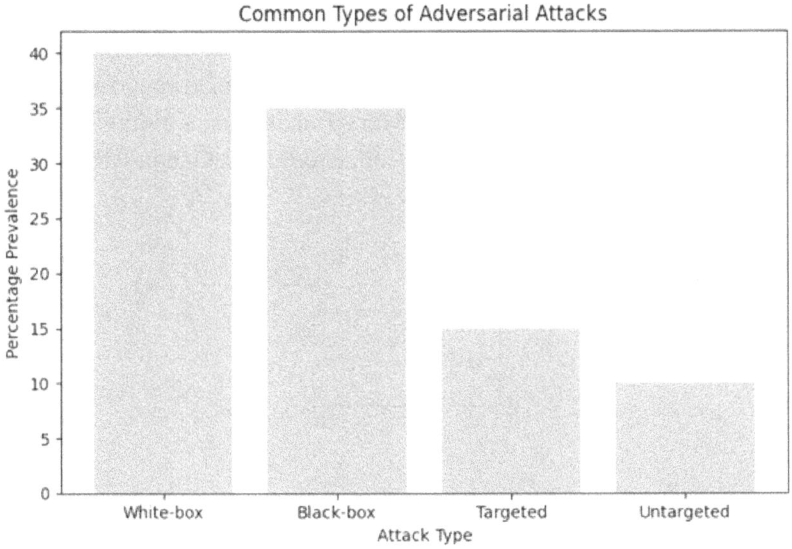

2.3. Mechanisms of Adversarial Attacks

The mechanism behind adversarial attacks often involves calculating gradients of the model's loss function with respect to the input. By manipulating these gradients, attackers can generate inputs that maximize the model's loss, thus tricking the model into misclassifying the data. Common techniques used in the creation of adversarial examples include:

- **Gradient-based Methods**: These attacks involve calculating the gradient of the model's loss function with respect to the input and adjusting the input accordingly. Methods like the FGSM and DeepFool use this approach to create small perturbations that drastically affect the model's predictions.
- **Optimization-based Methods**: Optimization-based attacks attempt to find the smallest perturbation that causes a misclassification by solving a constrained optimization problem. These methods are computationally expensive but can be more effective in bypassing defenses.
- **Generative Models**: Recent advances in generative adversarial networks (GANs) have been leveraged to create adversarial examples. These networks are trained to generate adversarial inputs that can fool machine learning models. The use of GANs in adversarial attacks is particularly notable because

they can learn to generate examples that are not only deceptive but also realistic in appearance.

Adversarial attacks exploit vulnerabilities in machine learning models by manipulating inputs to force incorrect outputs. The following flowchart illustrates the typical process of crafting and executing adversarial attacks, highlighting key steps such as input perturbation, model exploitation, and output manipulation.

Figure 2. Mechanisms of adversarial attacks

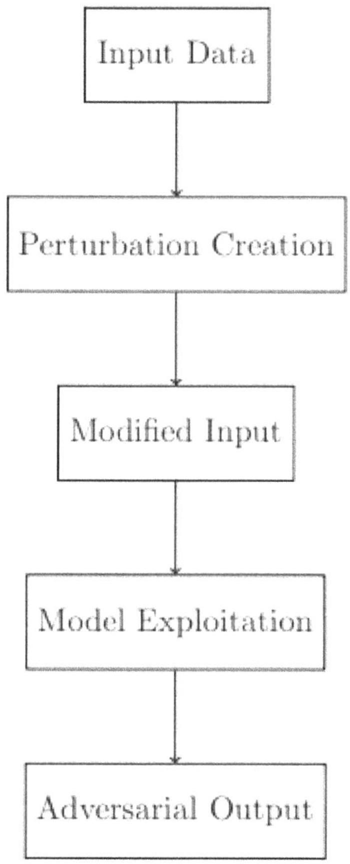

2.4. Challenges in Defending Against Adversarial Attacks

Defending against adversarial attacks is a major challenge in the field of machine learning and cybersecurity. The inherent vulnerability of deep learning models to these attacks has led to the development of several defense strategies, but each has its limitations.

- **Adversarial Training**: One common defense mechanism involves augmenting the training data with adversarial examples. By exposing the model to adversarial examples during training, the model can learn to recognize and resist such attacks. However, adversarial training can be computationally expensive and may not generalize well to all types of adversarial examples.
- **Robust Optimization**: Robust optimization methods attempt to train models that are inherently more resistant to adversarial perturbations. These methods typically involve modifying the loss function to penalize large changes in the input, making the model less sensitive to small perturbations.
- **Detection and Mitigation**: Another approach is to develop methods for detecting adversarial examples before they are processed by the model. Techniques such as input preprocessing, anomaly detection, and the use of ensemble methods have been explored as ways to identify and reject adversarial inputs. However, attackers continuously evolve their techniques to bypass these detection mechanisms.

2.5. Adversarial Attacks in the Context of Cybersecurity

In cybersecurity, adversarial attacks can have severe consequences. For example, attackers could use adversarial methods to bypass intrusion detection systems (IDS), mislead malware detection systems, or compromise security-critical applications. As the landscape of cyber threats evolves, adversarial machine learning poses an increasing risk, particularly when combined with other advanced attack techniques such as deepfake generation and data poisoning.

- **Zero-Day Attacks and Machine Learning**: Zero-day threats are those that exploit previously unknown vulnerabilities in software or hardware. By integrating adversarial machine learning into the attack, adversaries can develop zero-day attacks that are highly effective and difficult to defend against (Jones & Omar, 2024).
- **Mitigating Cybersecurity Threats**: Recent research has explored various management practices to mitigate the risks posed by adversarial attacks, particularly in the context of cybersecurity for organizations. Practices like

threat modeling, incident response planning, and the use of machine learning for defense are key components of an effective cybersecurity strategy (Huff et al., 2023).

2.6. The Role of Synthetic Data in Defending Against Adversarial Attacks

Synthetic data, generated through techniques such as simulation and generative models, has emerged as a promising tool for training more robust machine learning models. Research by Gholami and Omar (2023) explores the potential of synthetic data in improving the efficiency of large language models (LLMs), which can be extended to the context of adversarial defenses. By augmenting the training dataset with synthetic adversarial examples, models can become more resilient to attacks. This approach has gained attention for its ability to scale without requiring additional real-world data, which is often difficult or expensive to obtain.

2.7. Quantum Computing and Adversarial Attacks

As quantum computing continues to evolve, it presents new challenges and opportunities for both adversaries and defenders in the realm of machine learning. Quantum algorithms could potentially be used to generate more potent adversarial examples or to break current defense strategies. On the other hand, quantum-enhanced machine learning models may offer novel approaches to defending against adversarial attacks. Researchers are beginning to explore the potential impacts of quantum computing on cybersecurity, with early studies examining its effect on encryption and security protocols (Sodiya et al., 2024).

2.8. Summary

Adversarial attacks represent a significant threat to the reliability, robustness, and security of machine learning systems. While various strategies have been proposed to defend against these attacks, the field remains an area of active research. Understanding the mechanisms of adversarial attacks and developing novel defense techniques will be crucial for ensuring the security of machine learning models, particularly in sensitive applications like cybersecurity, healthcare, and autonomous systems.

3. THE QUANTUM COMPUTING PARADIGM SHIFT IN ADVERSARIAL ATTACKS

The advent of quantum computing represents a transformative shift in the landscape of cybersecurity, particularly in the realm of adversarial attacks. Traditional cryptographic techniques, including those employed to secure data, systems, and networks, face significant vulnerabilities as quantum computing progresses. The massive computational power enabled by quantum systems allows for the breaking of encryption schemes that have been previously considered secure, raising the specter of unprecedented threats. This shift not only alters the methods of conducting adversarial attacks but also necessitates the development of quantum-resistant cybersecurity strategies to safeguard against these new threats.

Quantum computing leverages principles of quantum mechanics—such as superposition and entanglement—to perform computations at speeds exponentially greater than classical systems. These capabilities render certain classical cryptographic algorithms, such as RSA and ECC (Elliptic Curve Cryptography), obsolete, as quantum computers can solve problems like prime factorization and discrete logarithms in polynomial time, tasks that are infeasible for classical computers (Sodiya et al., 2024). As a result, the cryptographic underpinnings of modern security systems could be compromised in the quantum era, creating a paradigm shift in how adversarial attacks are conceptualized and executed.

3.1 Quantum Threats to Traditional Cybersecurity Mechanisms

Adversarial attacks exploit vulnerabilities in systems by manipulating or bypassing security measures, often using deceptive or obfuscated tactics to gain unauthorized access or disrupt services. Quantum computers significantly enhance the capabilities of such attacks. For instance, adversaries equipped with quantum computing could efficiently break encryption keys used to secure communications, digital signatures, and sensitive data, thus enabling them to intercept, decrypt, and manipulate the information undetected (How & Cheah, 2023).

Quantum computing enables attackers to overcome traditional cryptographic defenses and create more complex adversarial inputs. The diagram below illustrates how quantum computing interacts with adversarial attack mechanisms, focusing on quantum-enabled attack vectors.

Figure 3. Quantum computing in adversarial attack scenarios

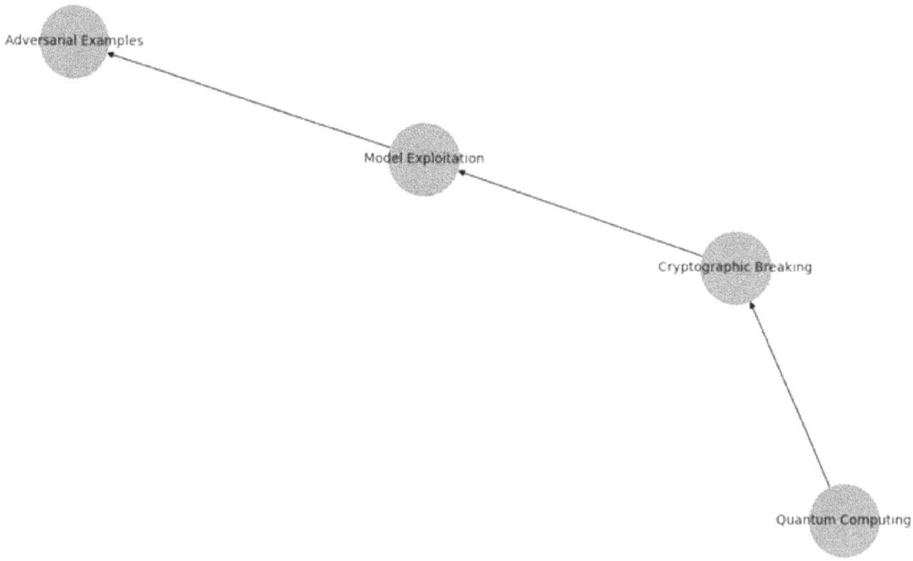

In addition to encryption-breaking threats, quantum systems are also poised to revolutionize the execution of attacks such as denial-of-service (DoS) and man-in-the-middle (MitM) attacks. With quantum computing, adversaries could launch these attacks with enhanced precision, speed, and stealth, overwhelming traditional defense mechanisms designed to mitigate these risks (Rahul et al., 2024). Furthermore, adversaries could utilize quantum computing to develop more sophisticated phishing techniques, including the generation of highly convincing quantum-enhanced fake identities that could bypass existing detection systems (Zangana & Omar, 2024).

3.2 Quantum-Enhanced Machine Learning and Adversarial Attacks

One of the key implications of quantum computing in the realm of cybersecurity is its potential to enhance machine learning (ML) techniques. Quantum machine learning (QML) promises to revolutionize the field by providing exponential speedup in processing large datasets, making it possible to train more complex models in shorter timespans. However, this quantum advantage also introduces the risk that adversaries may employ quantum-enhanced machine learning algorithms to craft more sophisticated adversarial examples, which are inputs designed to deceive deep learning models into making incorrect predictions or classifications.

This application of quantum computing to adversarial machine learning is particularly concerning in fields like facial recognition and cybersecurity threat detection, where small perturbations in input data can significantly alter outcomes. As quantum systems advance, attackers could exploit quantum-enhanced adversarial techniques to bypass security systems that rely on machine learning models, rendering traditional defenses vulnerable (Jones et al., 2023; Zangana & Omar, 2025).

3.3 Quantum-Resistant Security Solutions

In light of these emerging threats, there is a growing need for quantum-resistant security solutions. The development of post-quantum cryptography (PQC) is critical to ensure that encryption standards remain secure in a quantum-powered world. PQC algorithms, such as lattice-based cryptography, are designed to withstand attacks from both classical and quantum adversaries, offering a potential safeguard against the quantum computing revolution's security challenges (Block, 2024). Integrating these quantum-resistant algorithms into current cybersecurity frameworks is essential to mitigate the risks associated with the quantum computing paradigm shift.

Moreover, the application of quantum key distribution (QKD) has garnered attention as a potential solution for securing communications. QKD utilizes the principles of quantum mechanics to enable the secure exchange of cryptographic keys, with the advantage that any attempt to eavesdrop on the communication would be immediately detectable due to the inherent properties of quantum systems (Bush et al., 2021). While still in its nascent stages, QKD holds promise as a critical tool in defending against adversarial attacks in the quantum era.

3.4 The Need for Adaptive Cybersecurity Strategies

The rapid advancement of quantum computing necessitates a shift toward more adaptive and dynamic cybersecurity strategies. Organizations must not only prepare for the threats posed by quantum-enhanced adversarial attacks but also anticipate the need for a continuous evolution of their defense mechanisms. This includes the integration of quantum computing-aware security tools and practices, as well as fostering collaboration between quantum researchers and cybersecurity experts to stay ahead of emerging quantum threats (Bishwas & Sen, 2024).

As the quantum era unfolds, a comprehensive approach to cybersecurity must account for the dual threats of classical and quantum adversarial tactics. Strategies should focus on both strengthening existing security measures and adopting new technologies, such as quantum-resistant encryption and quantum-enhanced machine learning, to ensure that systems remain secure against the evolving landscape of cyber threats (Omar & Zangana, 2024).

3.5 Summary

Quantum computing marks a significant paradigm shift in the landscape of adversarial attacks and cybersecurity. The computational power of quantum systems enables new types of attacks that threaten the very foundations of traditional security models. As quantum technologies continue to develop, it is essential for the cybersecurity community to adapt by creating quantum-resistant solutions and enhancing defense strategies against quantum-enhanced adversarial tactics. Failure to do so may leave critical infrastructure and data vulnerable to the unprecedented power of quantum adversaries, highlighting the need for proactive and forward-thinking security approaches.

4. ADVERSARIAL ATTACKS ON LARGE LANGUAGE MODELS (LLMS)

Adversarial attacks have become a significant area of concern in the field of machine learning and artificial intelligence, particularly with the rapid advancements in Large Language Models (LLMs). These attacks aim to manipulate or deceive the LLMs into providing incorrect or unintended outputs, potentially leading to severe security vulnerabilities. As LLMs are increasingly deployed in critical applications, including natural language processing (NLP), cybersecurity, and software vulnerability detection, understanding and mitigating adversarial attacks is essential to ensure their safe and reliable use.

4.1 Types of Adversarial Attacks on LLMs

Adversarial attacks on LLMs can be broadly categorized into two types: **input-based** and **model-based** attacks. Input-based attacks involve manipulating the data that is fed into the model, while model-based attacks target the architecture or internal mechanisms of the model itself.

1. **Input-Based Attacks:** These attacks involve subtly modifying the input text in such a way that the model produces incorrect outputs. One common approach is the use of **text perturbations**, where small changes, such as replacing certain words or adding noise, lead to drastically altered predictions. For instance, researchers have shown that slight alterations in the phrasing of a query can

cause an LLM to output biased or irrelevant responses (Jones & Omar, 2024). This type of attack is particularly concerning when LLMs are used in security-sensitive environments, such as in automatic code generation or in systems that detect malicious activities.

2. **Model-Based Attacks:** In these attacks, adversaries seek to exploit weaknesses in the LLM's underlying architecture, such as the training process, model parameters, or the embedding space. One well-known technique is the **model inversion attack**, where attackers can infer sensitive information about the training data, potentially compromising privacy. Additionally, **membership inference attacks** can identify whether specific data points were included in the training dataset, posing a risk to privacy and data security (Gholami & Omar, 2023).

4.2 Impact of Adversarial Attacks on LLMs

The implications of adversarial attacks on LLMs are far-reaching. As these models are used in more sensitive applications, such as healthcare, finance, and cybersecurity, the potential for harm increases. For instance, in the domain of cybersecurity, LLMs like GPT-2 have been proposed for detecting zero-day attacks (Jones et al., 2023). An adversarial attack could mislead the model into classifying a malicious attack as benign, resulting in a significant security breach.

Moreover, adversarial attacks can undermine the trustworthiness of LLMs in domains requiring high accuracy, such as medical diagnostics, legal analysis, and financial forecasting. For example, slight modifications to input queries could cause an LLM to generate erroneous medical advice or misinterpret legal texts, leading to catastrophic consequences.

4.3 Techniques for Defending Against Adversarial Attacks

To mitigate the risk of adversarial attacks on LLMs, several defense strategies have been proposed:

1. **Adversarial Training:** One of the most common defense mechanisms is adversarial training, where adversarial examples are included in the training data. This helps the model become more robust to small perturbations in input data. Researchers have found that incorporating adversarial examples during training can significantly improve an LLM's resistance to input-based attacks (Omar, 2024).

2. **Input Preprocessing:** Another strategy involves preprocessing inputs to detect and remove adversarial perturbations before they are fed into the model. This could include techniques such as **text sanitization** or **paraphrase detection**, which aim to identify and neutralize malicious alterations in the input text (Gholami & Omar, 2023).
3. **Model Regularization:** Regularization techniques, such as **dropout** or **weight decay**, can be applied during training to prevent the model from overfitting to specific features of the data, making it more resistant to adversarial inputs (Zangana, 2024). This method improves the generalization ability of the model, making it less likely to be tricked by adversarial attacks.
4. **Robustness Evaluation:** Regular evaluation of LLMs using adversarial test sets is another crucial defense. By continually testing the model's robustness against new types of adversarial attacks, researchers can identify vulnerabilities early and apply targeted improvements (Omar & Zangana, 2025).

4.4 Challenges in Defending Against Adversarial Attacks

While several defense mechanisms have been proposed, defending against adversarial attacks on LLMs remains an ongoing challenge. The continuous evolution of attack strategies means that what works today might not be effective tomorrow. Furthermore, there is often a trade-off between robustness and model performance. Defending against adversarial attacks may introduce latency or reduce the model's accuracy in other tasks (Huff et al., 2023). Balancing these concerns is a critical issue for researchers and practitioners working with LLMs.

Additionally, LLMs are inherently susceptible to "transferability" attacks, where adversarial examples generated for one model can be effective against other models. This makes it difficult to build universally robust defenses (Mohammed, Omar, & Nguyen, 2018). As LLMs become more widely used in real-world applications, the development of universally applicable defense strategies will be crucial.

4.5 Summary

Adversarial attacks on LLMs pose significant security risks, especially as these models are deployed in sensitive applications. Understanding the types of attacks, their impact, and the current defense strategies is essential for improving the resilience of LLMs. As the field continues to evolve, ongoing research will be critical in developing more effective defense mechanisms to safeguard against the growing threat of adversarial manipulation. While substantial progress has been made in mitigating these risks, it is clear that adversarial resilience remains a key challenge in the development and deployment of LLMs in cybersecurity, healthcare, and other critical domains.

5. QUANTUM COMPUTING'S ROLE IN ENHANCING ADVERSARIAL ATTACKS

Quantum computing represents a transformative technology that holds the potential to revolutionize many fields, including cybersecurity. The development of quantum systems could drastically alter the landscape of digital security by enabling adversarial attacks with greater speed and precision. This section explores how quantum computing could be harnessed to enhance adversarial attacks, as well as the challenges and opportunities that arise from its integration into the cybersecurity domain.

5.1 Quantum Computing: A Game-Changer for Adversarial Attacks

At its core, quantum computing leverages the principles of quantum mechanics—such as superposition, entanglement, and quantum tunneling—to process information in fundamentally different ways compared to classical computing. This enables quantum computers to solve certain computational problems exponentially faster than their classical counterparts. As a result, tasks that were previously deemed computationally infeasible for classical computers, such as factoring large numbers, can now be approached in a manner that could threaten the security of conventional cryptographic systems (Sodiya et al., 2024).

Quantum computers can potentially disrupt cybersecurity by enhancing the capabilities of adversarial attacks. Traditional adversarial techniques, such as perturbing data to mislead machine learning models, rely heavily on classical computational models. However, quantum adversarial methods could take advantage of quantum parallelism to generate numerous attack scenarios simultaneously, making defense mechanisms significantly more challenging to deploy (Bishwas & Sen, 2024). Quantum-enhanced adversarial attacks could target encryption algorithms, authentication protocols, and other cryptographic systems by exploiting vulnerabilities in their foundations.

For instance, quantum computing could undermine the security of symmetric encryption algorithms, such as AES (Advanced Encryption Standard), and asymmetric encryption methods, such as RSA. By utilizing Shor's algorithm, which can factor large numbers in polynomial time, quantum computers could potentially decrypt information encoded with RSA keys, rendering them ineffective against quantum adversaries (Baseri, Chouhan, & Ghorbani, 2024). This vulnerability represents one of the most significant threats posed by quantum computing to modern cybersecurity infrastructures.

5.2 Quantum Machine Learning and Adversarial Attacks

One of the most exciting intersections between quantum computing and adversarial attacks lies in the realm of quantum machine learning (QML). Quantum-enhanced machine learning algorithms, powered by quantum processors, can outperform their classical counterparts in processing large-scale datasets and optimizing models. However, the same capabilities that allow quantum systems to accelerate learning processes can also be leveraged by adversaries to develop sophisticated attack strategies.

For example, adversaries could use quantum algorithms to generate more potent adversarial examples that could easily bypass classical machine learning models' defenses. These quantum-generated adversarial attacks could be particularly effective in fields like facial recognition, malware detection, and autonomous systems, where machine learning models are extensively used for security purposes (Omar & Zangana, 2024). As such, quantum-enhanced adversarial attacks may require the development of new, quantum-resistant defense strategies, especially as the use of quantum algorithms in cybersecurity becomes more prevalent.

Additionally, quantum computing could enable the development of advanced, multi-dimensional attack vectors that combine both quantum and classical techniques. These hybrid attacks could target both the data and the underlying infrastructure simultaneously, presenting a formidable challenge to current cybersecurity frameworks (Rahul et al., 2024). The computational speed offered by quantum systems allows adversaries to quickly adapt their strategies, creating a dynamic environment where defense mechanisms need to evolve rapidly.

5.3 Implications for Cybersecurity Defenses

The rise of quantum computing introduces a new set of challenges for defenders in the cybersecurity landscape. As quantum adversarial attacks become more feasible, there is an urgent need to develop quantum-resistant cryptographic techniques and robust security protocols. A key challenge for researchers and industry professionals is ensuring that systems remain secure even when quantum technologies become widely accessible.

A promising area of research is quantum-safe cryptography, which focuses on designing cryptographic algorithms that can withstand attacks from quantum computers. Quantum-safe algorithms, such as lattice-based cryptography, are being developed to resist the potential decryption power of quantum systems (Jones et al., 2023). While these algorithms show promise, their integration into existing systems remains a complex process, as it requires fundamental changes to encryption protocols and secure communication methods across industries.

Furthermore, advancements in quantum networks, such as quantum key distribution (QKD), could play a crucial role in securing communications against quantum adversaries. QKD leverages the principles of quantum mechanics to enable secure communication by detecting eavesdropping attempts, making it a potential solution to the threats posed by quantum-powered attacks (Bush, Challener, & Mantelet, 2021).

5.4 Future Directions

As quantum computing continues to evolve, it is imperative to anticipate the emerging threats and opportunities associated with its integration into cybersecurity. In addition to the development of quantum-safe encryption and machine learning techniques, there is a need for interdisciplinary research to understand how quantum computing can both disrupt and enhance current defense strategies. Collaborative efforts between quantum physicists, cybersecurity experts, and machine learning practitioners will be essential to build resilient systems capable of withstanding the oncoming wave of quantum-driven adversarial attacks (Gholami & Omar, 2023; Zangana et al., 2024).

In the coming years, as quantum computing matures, industries must prepare for a quantum-enabled future where adversarial attacks are more efficient and sophisticated. This will require proactive measures, including the design of quantum-resistant systems, continuous monitoring for emerging quantum threats, and the education and training of cybersecurity professionals in quantum technologies.

6. DEFENSE MECHANISMS AGAINST ADVERSARIAL ATTACKS IN QUANTUM-AWARE SYSTEMS

Quantum computing is poised to revolutionize various fields, including cybersecurity. However, the introduction of quantum technologies also brings new challenges, particularly in defending against adversarial attacks. Quantum-aware systems, which leverage quantum algorithms and quantum-inspired solutions to improve security, must be fortified against emerging threats. This section explores defense mechanisms against adversarial attacks in these systems, considering both classical and quantum approaches.

6.1. Understanding Adversarial Attacks in Quantum Computing

Adversarial attacks in quantum computing aim to manipulate quantum systems by exploiting their inherent vulnerabilities. These attacks can target quantum algorithms, cryptographic protocols, and quantum hardware, leading to data leakage, unauthorized access, or system failures. The nature of quantum computing exacerbates the risks because quantum states are more susceptible to errors due to quantum noise, interference, and the principles of superposition and entanglement.

Quantum computers, particularly those that are noise-sensitive, present an attractive target for adversaries. Moreover, quantum algorithms used in cybersecurity, such as quantum key distribution (QKD), can be vulnerable to sophisticated attacks designed to compromise their integrity. The development of robust defense mechanisms is, therefore, essential to safeguard quantum-aware systems from these types of threats (Baseri, Chouhan, & Ghorbani, 2024).

6.2. Quantum Error Correction (QEC) as a Defense Mechanism

One of the most promising defense strategies against adversarial attacks in quantum systems is Quantum Error Correction (QEC). QEC techniques aim to protect quantum information from errors by encoding it in such a way that the system can detect and correct errors without collapsing the quantum state. This is especially important in noisy intermediate-scale quantum (NISQ) systems, where qubit errors can lead to significant information loss and compromise system security.

QEC codes such as the surface code and Shor code are widely studied for their ability to detect and correct a variety of errors in quantum circuits. Implementing these error correction techniques can help ensure the reliability and robustness of quantum-aware systems against adversarial perturbations, which may be designed to exploit these errors (Rahul et al., 2024).

6.3. Quantum-Resistant Cryptography

As quantum computing threatens the security of classical cryptographic protocols, the development of quantum-resistant cryptography is vital. Quantum-resistant cryptographic algorithms are designed to withstand attacks from quantum computers, which could potentially break widely used algorithms such as RSA and ECC. Post-quantum cryptography (PQC) involves the creation of new cryptographic primitives that are secure against both classical and quantum attacks.

The implementation of quantum-resistant cryptography is one of the most direct methods for defending quantum-aware systems from adversarial attacks targeting cryptographic schemes. Key areas of focus include lattice-based cryptography, hash-based signatures, and multivariate polynomial cryptography, which are believed to be resistant to quantum-based attacks (Sodiya et al., 2024).

6.4. Adversarial Training for Quantum Machine Learning Models

Quantum machine learning (QML) is a field that combines quantum computing with machine learning techniques to solve complex problems more efficiently. However, like classical machine learning models, QML systems are susceptible to adversarial attacks. Adversarial examples, where small perturbations are introduced to the input data, can mislead quantum classifiers, causing incorrect predictions or system behavior.

To defend against these attacks, adversarial training techniques can be applied. This involves generating adversarial examples and incorporating them into the training process, thereby making the model more resilient to future attacks. Such strategies have proven effective in classical machine learning, and similar approaches can be adapted for quantum models, where the goal is to enhance robustness against adversarial manipulation (Omar, Zangana, & Mohammed, 2025).

6.5. Quantum-Secure Communication Protocols

In quantum-aware systems, communication security is critical, especially when transmitting sensitive data over potentially insecure channels. Quantum key distribution (QKD) offers a promising approach to secure communication by using quantum entanglement to create secret keys that are immune to eavesdropping. However, adversarial attacks targeting QKD systems, such as intercept-resend or man-in-the-middle attacks, can compromise their effectiveness.

To defend against such threats, advanced protocols like the measurement-device-independent QKD (MDI-QKD) are being developed. MDI-QKD ensures security even in the presence of imperfect devices, providing a higher level of protection against quantum-based eavesdropping. These quantum-secure communication protocols are vital for defending quantum-aware systems from adversarial threats (Bush, Challener, & Mantelet, 2021).

6.6. Multi-Layered Defense Approaches

A multi-layered defense strategy is critical for protecting quantum-aware systems from adversarial attacks. This approach combines quantum-based defense mechanisms with classical security protocols to provide a comprehensive security solution. For example, quantum encryption can be used in conjunction with classical intrusion detection systems (IDS) and firewalls to create a multi-tiered defense against adversaries.

In addition, machine learning models can be employed to detect unusual behavior or patterns indicative of adversarial actions. By combining quantum and classical techniques, a hybrid defense strategy can improve the overall security posture of quantum-aware systems, making them more resilient to evolving threats (Jones, Omar, Mohammed, Nobles, & Dawson, 2023).

Defending against quantum-enhanced adversarial attacks requires a multi-layered approach that combines classical and quantum-resistant techniques. The flowchart below outlines the key defense strategies, from detection to mitigation.

Figure 4. Defense strategies against quantum-enhanced attacks

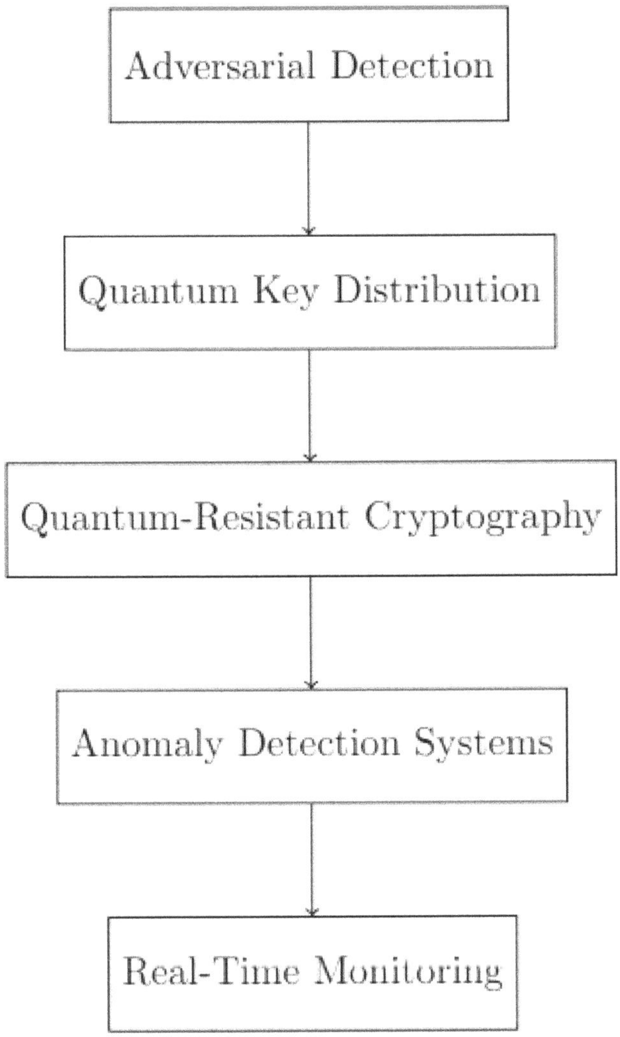

6.7. Quantum-Resistant Machine Learning Algorithms

As adversarial machine learning is a growing concern in classical systems, it becomes even more critical in quantum systems where the consequences of adversarial attacks can be severe. Developing quantum-resistant machine learning algorithms that are immune to both classical and quantum adversarial techniques is essential. These algorithms would include mechanisms that can detect and mitigate adversarial input perturbations while maintaining the quantum advantages of speed and efficiency (Singh, 2024).

Quantum-resistant machine learning models are still in the early stages of development, but researchers are exploring various techniques such as quantum adversarial training and the integration of quantum error correction into machine learning workflows to enhance model resilience.

6.8. Summary

As quantum computing continues to evolve, the need for robust defense mechanisms against adversarial attacks becomes increasingly critical. By combining quantum error correction, quantum-resistant cryptography, and quantum-secure communication protocols with advanced machine learning techniques, quantum-aware systems can be made more resilient. Additionally, hybrid approaches that integrate classical and quantum defense strategies are essential for addressing the unique challenges posed by quantum adversarial attacks. Ongoing research in quantum cybersecurity will be pivotal in shaping secure quantum-aware systems for the future.

7. ADVERSARIAL TRAINING AND COUNTERMEASURES FOR LLMS

Adversarial attacks on large language models (LLMs) have emerged as a significant challenge in cybersecurity and artificial intelligence (AI) domains. These attacks typically involve generating inputs specifically designed to mislead or confuse LLMs, potentially leading to erroneous outputs, security breaches, or malicious manipulations. As LLMs become integral to various applications, including cybersecurity and software vulnerability detection, addressing adversarial risks is paramount. This section explores adversarial training techniques and countermeasures to enhance the robustness of LLMs.

7.1 Understanding Adversarial Attacks on LLMs

Adversarial attacks exploit the inherent vulnerabilities of LLMs by crafting perturbed input data that causes the models to produce unintended results. These attacks can be either white-box or black-box, depending on the attacker's knowledge of the model. White-box attacks are more potent as they involve manipulating the model's internal parameters or architecture, whereas black-box attacks focus on exploiting input-output relationships without access to the model's internals. Both forms of adversarial manipulation can lead to severe consequences in applications like text classification, translation, and, notably, cybersecurity.

For example, Gholami and Omar (2024) highlight the importance of understanding adversarial behavior in AI systems and its implications for cybersecurity. They discuss how adversarial inputs can target vulnerabilities in LLMs, disrupting their utility in real-world applications like threat detection and risk management. Furthermore, Jones et al. (2023) emphasize the necessity of adapting LLMs to enhance defense mechanisms against adversarial exploitation, ensuring more accurate and secure AI-driven systems.

7.2 Adversarial Training Techniques

Adversarial training is one of the most effective countermeasures for enhancing the resilience of LLMs against attacks. This method involves augmenting the training dataset with adversarial examples to teach the model to recognize and resist manipulated inputs. The primary objective is to increase the model's robustness by providing it with diverse, challenging scenarios that simulate potential real-world threats.

1. **Adversarial Example Generation:** The first step in adversarial training is to generate adversarial examples. Techniques like the Fast Gradient Sign Method (FGSM) or Projected Gradient Descent (PGD) are used to perturb the input text by making small but strategic modifications. These examples help the model learn to distinguish between normal and malicious inputs during training, improving its overall accuracy and security in uncertain environments (Omar & Zangana, 2024).
2. **Augmenting the Training Data:** In the context of cybersecurity, adversarial training can be tailored to detect zero-day threats or malicious scripts. As discussed by Huff et al. (2023), incorporating adversarial examples into cybersecurity models can bolster their defenses, making them more adept at handling sophisticated attacks like those targeting AI-driven intrusion detection systems.
3. **Regularization and Robust Optimization:** Another key strategy for adversarial training is the use of regularization methods, which help control the complexity of the model while enhancing its ability to generalize. Techniques such as adversarial regularization adjust the model's learning process to focus more on adversarially robust features. These approaches help improve the model's performance against a variety of adversarial threats, ensuring its stability and security in real-world applications (Omar, 2024).

7.3 Countermeasures Beyond Adversarial Training

While adversarial training plays a crucial role in strengthening LLMs, additional countermeasures are needed to build more comprehensive defenses against adversarial attacks. Some of the notable countermeasures include:

1. **Input Preprocessing:** Preprocessing inputs before they are fed into the LLM can help eliminate potential adversarial noise. Techniques like input sanitization, text normalization, and semantic analysis help identify and neutralize adversarial inputs. According to Mohammed et al. (2018), applying such preprocessing methods can reduce the risk of successful attacks and ensure more reliable model performance.
2. **Model Interpretability:** Improving the interpretability of LLMs is another critical countermeasure against adversarial attacks. By making models more transparent and understandable, researchers can better detect when an attack occurs. Omar and Zangana (2024) emphasize the importance of explainable AI in cybersecurity, arguing that increasing model interpretability can aid in identifying the underlying causes of adversarial vulnerabilities, allowing for faster responses and mitigation.
3. **Ensemble Methods:** Using ensemble methods, which combine multiple models to make predictions, can also improve the robustness of LLMs. These methods aggregate the outputs of several models to reduce the likelihood of successful adversarial manipulation. As noted by Gholami and Omar (2023), leveraging ensemble approaches can make it more difficult for attackers to fool the system, especially when the adversary targets specific vulnerabilities within a single model.
4. **Continuous Monitoring and Model Updates:** Given the evolving nature of adversarial techniques, continuous monitoring of LLM performance and timely updates to the models are essential for maintaining security. Jones and Omar (2024) highlight the need for real-time monitoring of LLMs in cybersecurity systems to detect emerging threats and promptly implement countermeasures.

7.4 Implications for Cybersecurity

In the context of cybersecurity, adversarial attacks pose significant risks to the integrity of AI-driven security systems. LLMs are increasingly employed in tasks such as malware detection, phishing defense, and automated threat analysis. Without robust defenses, these models are vulnerable to adversarial manipulation, which can compromise the security of critical systems. As Zangana and Omar (2024) discuss, adversarial training and countermeasures play a pivotal role in mitigating these risks, ensuring that LLMs can withstand both intentional attacks and inadvertent errors in processing.

Additionally, integrating quantum computing into cybersecurity, as explored by Sodiya et al. (2024), may present new challenges for LLM security. The power of quantum computing could potentially bypass current adversarial defenses, necessitating the development of new strategies for securing LLMs against quantum-enhanced attacks. As Omar et al. (2025) argue, the fusion of quantum computing with AI presents both new opportunities and significant risks that must be carefully managed through advanced adversarial defense techniques.

7.5 Summary

Adversarial training and countermeasures are essential for ensuring the robustness and security of LLMs in the face of emerging threats. By incorporating adversarial examples into the training process, applying preprocessing techniques, and exploring new defense strategies, the resilience of LLMs can be significantly enhanced. As the use of LLMs in cybersecurity and other critical sectors continues to grow, it is imperative that researchers and practitioners remain vigilant and proactive in developing and implementing these defenses to safeguard against the evolving landscape of adversarial attacks.

8. POST-QUANTUM CRYPTOGRAPHY AND ITS ROLE IN DEFENSE

Post-Quantum Cryptography (PQC) is a rapidly advancing field of cryptographic research that seeks to develop new cryptographic protocols resistant to the threats posed by quantum computing. As quantum computers continue to evolve, the ability of classical cryptographic systems, such as RSA and ECC (Elliptic Curve Cryptography), to protect sensitive data is being challenged. These classical systems rely on the difficulty of certain mathematical problems, such as factoring large integers or solving discrete logarithms, problems that quantum algorithms like Shor's algorithm could potentially solve in polynomial time, rendering existing cryptographic systems vulnerable.

8.1 The Emergence of Quantum Computing Threats

Quantum computing promises exponential speedup for specific tasks, particularly in solving problems related to cryptography. Shor's algorithm, developed in the 1990s, demonstrated that a sufficiently powerful quantum computer could break

RSA encryption, ECC, and other widely used public-key cryptographic systems by efficiently factoring large integers or solving discrete logarithm problems (Baseri et al., 2024). As such, the development of quantum-resistant cryptographic algorithms has become a critical focus for researchers, given the growing concern about the impact of quantum technologies on cybersecurity (Sodiya et al., 2024).

Quantum computers can potentially undermine not only encryption schemes but also the integrity of digital signatures, authentication protocols, and key exchange mechanisms. This necessitates a paradigm shift towards quantum-resistant algorithms, which would provide robust security in the post-quantum era, ensuring data protection against adversaries leveraging quantum computing technologies (How & Cheah, 2023).

8.2 Strategies for Post-Quantum Cryptography

In response to these threats, researchers have focused on developing quantum-resistant cryptographic protocols. Several families of algorithms are being investigated for their resilience to quantum attacks, including lattice-based cryptography, hash-based cryptography, multivariate polynomial-based cryptography, and code-based cryptography. Lattice-based cryptography, in particular, has shown promise as a foundation for developing secure encryption systems that are difficult for quantum computers to break, even when they are capable of performing complex quantum operations (Rahul et al., 2024). These cryptographic systems rely on mathematical structures known as lattices, which are believed to be resistant to attacks from quantum computers.

The NIST Post-Quantum Cryptography Standardization Project, initiated in 2016, has been instrumental in evaluating and standardizing quantum-resistant algorithms. The project aims to identify algorithms that provide security in a quantum world while ensuring efficient implementation and backward compatibility with existing systems. Lattice-based schemes like Kyber, NTRU, and FrodoKEM have emerged as leading candidates for public-key encryption and key exchange in a post-quantum world (Jones & Omar, 2024).

With the emergence of quantum computing, the development of quantum-resistant cryptographic algorithms has accelerated. The chart below highlights the increasing number of quantum-resistant algorithms introduced over the past decade.

Figure 5. Growth of quantum-resistant algorithms

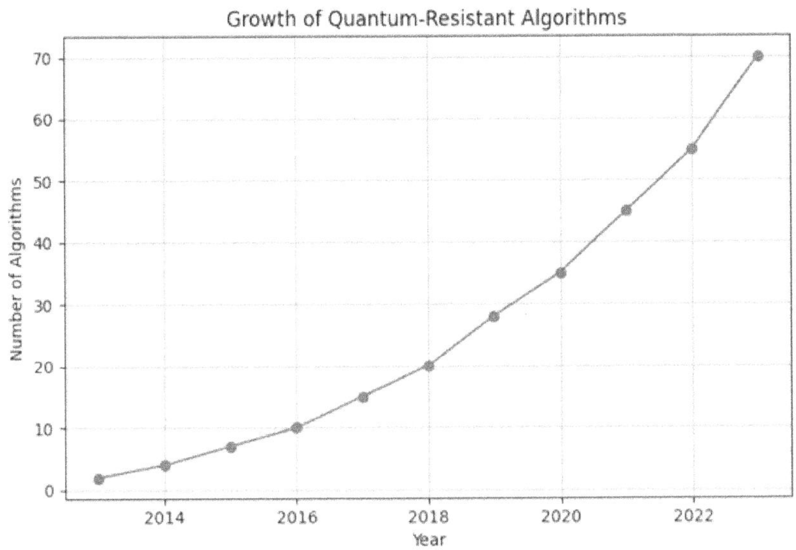

8.3 Implications for Defense and National Security

For national defense and security infrastructure, the transition to quantum-resistant cryptography is crucial. Governments and military organizations heavily rely on secure communications, data storage, and cryptographic protocols to protect sensitive information from cyber-attacks and espionage. The advent of quantum computing could expose vulnerabilities in current defense systems, making them susceptible to attacks from both adversaries and state-sponsored actors with access to quantum technologies.

As organizations begin to prepare for the quantum era, one of the significant challenges is the need to implement quantum-resistant protocols without disrupting existing systems. This transition involves the integration of post-quantum algorithms into current security frameworks, including encryption methods used for securing communications, databases, and software applications. The ability to do so seamlessly will be critical for maintaining national security in the coming decades (Omar & Zangana, 2024).

Furthermore, Post-Quantum Cryptography plays a vital role in securing the next generation of critical infrastructure, such as cloud computing environments and Internet of Things (IoT) networks, which are increasingly under threat from sophisticated cyber-attacks. For example, in cloud computing, where data is transmitted over the internet and stored remotely, protecting against quantum-enabled attacks on cryptographic systems is essential to maintain the confidentiality and integrity of data (Hamza & Omar, 2013).

8.4 Emerging Research and Applications

Recent studies continue to explore the potential impact of quantum technologies on cybersecurity. Research on quantum computing's intersection with artificial intelligence (AI) has revealed innovative approaches to enhancing defense mechanisms. AI and machine learning models, for example, are being integrated with Post-Quantum Cryptography protocols to improve the detection and prevention of quantum-enabled attacks (Gholami & Omar, 2024). These hybrid systems promise to enhance the resilience of cybersecurity infrastructures by combining the strengths of quantum-resistant cryptography with AI-driven threat detection.

Moreover, there is a growing focus on building quantum-safe blockchain systems. Blockchain technology, which relies on cryptographic methods for ensuring transaction integrity and securing digital assets, faces significant risks in the advent of quantum computing. As a result, developing quantum-resistant blockchain protocols is a priority for researchers aiming to secure decentralized systems in the post-quantum era (Zangana & Omar, 2024).

8.5 Summary

Post-Quantum Cryptography represents a critical frontier in the defense against evolving threats posed by quantum computing. As quantum technologies progress, the shift to quantum-resistant algorithms becomes not just a necessity but an urgent requirement for ensuring the security of global digital infrastructures. By focusing on the development and standardization of secure quantum-resistant cryptographic protocols, along with integrating AI and machine learning, it is possible to defend against both traditional and quantum-enabled cyber threats. The role of PQC in national defense and cybersecurity cannot be overstated, as its successful implementation will safeguard digital assets and communications in the quantum age (Bishwas & Sen, 2024).

9. DETECTION AND MITIGATION OF ADVERSARIAL ATTACKS IN QUANTUM-AWARE CYBERSECURITY

As quantum computing evolves, its potential to disrupt current cybersecurity frameworks, particularly through adversarial attacks, becomes increasingly significant. Quantum-aware cybersecurity seeks to address the challenges posed by quantum technologies while integrating traditional defense mechanisms, machine learning, and large language models (LLMs) to enhance security protocols.

9.1 Adversarial Attacks and Quantum Threats

Adversarial attacks in cybersecurity refer to deliberate manipulations of input data designed to deceive machine learning models into making incorrect predictions or classifications. These attacks, which often target models such as deep neural networks (DNNs), are a significant concern due to their ability to bypass traditional security measures. With the advent of quantum computing, the sophistication of adversarial attacks could reach new heights. Quantum algorithms are capable of executing parallel computations at unprecedented speeds, allowing attackers to generate and execute more potent adversarial inputs quickly and on a larger scale (Baseri, Chouhan, & Ghorbani, 2024).

In quantum-aware cybersecurity, adversarial attacks could leverage quantum properties such as superposition and entanglement to create subtle yet highly effective manipulations of data, making detection more difficult. Traditional defense mechanisms may struggle to counter these threats due to the quantum-enhanced capabilities of adversaries. As quantum technologies continue to advance, novel quantum-specific attack vectors may emerge, necessitating the development of robust, quantum-resistant defensive strategies.

9.2 Quantum Computing and Its Impact on Security

Quantum computing offers the promise of exponential improvements in computational power, which can be both a blessing and a curse in the realm of cybersecurity. On one hand, quantum computers can solve problems that are currently intractable for classical computers, such as factoring large numbers and simulating complex systems (Block, 2024). This ability poses a direct threat to classical encryption methods, such as RSA, which rely on the difficulty of factoring large numbers. On the other hand, quantum computing also opens up new possibilities for advancing cryptographic techniques and enhancing the detection of adversarial attacks.

To address quantum-related threats, quantum-resistant encryption algorithms are being developed, including lattice-based cryptography and quantum key distribution (QKD), which can secure communications even in the presence of quantum-enabled adversaries (Sodiya, Umoga, Amoo, & Atadoga, 2024). However, these techniques require a deep integration of quantum principles into the current cybersecurity framework to be fully effective.

9.3 Detection of Adversarial Attacks in Quantum-Aware Environments

Detecting adversarial attacks in quantum-aware environments requires the adoption of advanced algorithms capable of identifying subtle manipulations in data, especially when these attacks are powered by quantum-enhanced strategies. Traditional machine learning techniques, such as anomaly detection, are often insufficient in this new context due to the quantum nature of the attacks. Quantum machine learning (QML) methods, which leverage quantum algorithms to process data, may offer a more efficient approach to identifying adversarial patterns in real time.

One promising direction is the integration of quantum-enhanced LLMs for anomaly detection in cybersecurity. LLMs such as GPT-2 (Jones & Omar, 2024) have demonstrated remarkable capabilities in identifying malicious patterns in data. By incorporating quantum-enhanced models, these systems could potentially achieve greater detection rates with fewer false positives, enabling more effective defense strategies. Additionally, quantum-resistant approaches, such as QKD, can further safeguard communication channels, making it more challenging for adversaries to intercept or manipulate sensitive data.

9.4 Mitigating Adversarial Attacks Using Quantum-Aware Strategies

Mitigating adversarial attacks in quantum-aware cybersecurity requires a multifaceted approach that combines both classical and quantum-resistant defenses. Traditional defenses, such as adversarial training (where models are trained on adversarial inputs to improve their robustness), can be enhanced through quantum computing by simulating a larger variety of adversarial conditions in shorter timeframes. This would increase the resilience of machine learning models against quantum-enhanced adversarial inputs.

Quantum-resistant cryptographic techniques, such as those based on lattice-based encryption, can help protect sensitive data from decryption by quantum-enabled adversaries (Baseri et al., 2024). In tandem with quantum machine learning techniques for real-time attack detection, these strategies form a robust defense framework that can evolve in parallel with quantum computing advancements.

Furthermore, quantum technologies offer opportunities for secure verification and timestamping of data, making it easier to detect and trace adversarial modifications in real time. The combination of blockchain-based timestamping and quantum key distribution (Zangana, 2024) provides an additional layer of security, ensuring the integrity of critical data while defending against sophisticated adversarial attacks.

9.5 Future Directions in Quantum-Aware Cybersecurity

As quantum computing continues to mature, future research will likely focus on optimizing the intersection of quantum machine learning, cryptography, and adversarial defense. Key areas of exploration include improving quantum error correction techniques, developing hybrid classical-quantum models for adversarial detection, and further enhancing the scalability of quantum-resistant encryption protocols.

To stay ahead of potential threats, researchers must continue to explore new frameworks for integrating quantum-aware security strategies into existing cybersecurity infrastructures. This includes the application of quantum technologies in conjunction with AI-driven approaches to cybersecurity, as highlighted by Omar (2024) and Zangana & Omar (2025), which can lead to more proactive, dynamic defense systems that are better equipped to handle the complexities of quantum-enhanced attacks.

In conclusion, the detection and mitigation of adversarial attacks in quantum-aware cybersecurity require a comprehensive, forward-thinking approach that integrates quantum computing innovations with traditional security techniques. By leveraging quantum machine learning, quantum-resistant encryption, and AI-powered defense systems, the cybersecurity community can better prepare for the challenges posed by adversarial attacks in the quantum era.

10. ETHICAL CONSIDERATIONS AND CHALLENGES IN DEFENDING AGAINST QUANTUM-ENHANCED ADVERSARIAL ATTACKS

As quantum computing technology evolves, it introduces unprecedented opportunities for accelerating computational capabilities, but also presents a novel set of challenges for cybersecurity, particularly in defending against adversarial attacks. One such challenge is the potential for quantum-enhanced adversarial attacks, where quantum algorithms could be leveraged to optimize and execute attacks with greater efficiency and precision than classical techniques. This section explores the ethical considerations and challenges associated with defending against these attacks, including the implications for privacy, security, and trust in digital infrastructures.

10.1 Ethical Challenges in Quantum-Enhanced Adversarial Attacks

Quantum computing's promise lies in its ability to solve problems considered intractable by classical systems. However, this power could also be misused, especially in the context of adversarial machine learning and cybersecurity. As quantum algorithms, such as Shor's algorithm, hold the potential to break widely-used cryptographic protocols, adversaries could employ quantum computing to circumvent traditional defenses, exposing sensitive data and systems to risk. The ethical dilemma arises from the use of quantum technologies to exploit vulnerabilities that were previously safeguarded by classical cryptography.

The potential for quantum-enhanced adversarial attacks forces a reevaluation of the existing ethical frameworks in cybersecurity. Ethical concerns include the possibility of quantum systems enabling new forms of exploitation, such as breaking encryption on medical records or financial transactions, leading to breaches of privacy and security (Sodiya et al., 2024). Moreover, the ability of quantum systems to conduct highly sophisticated attacks at an unprecedented scale may create an imbalance between cybercriminals and defenders, with severe consequences for global security.

10.2 Privacy Implications

Quantum-enhanced adversarial attacks pose significant privacy risks. In many sectors, such as healthcare and finance, large volumes of sensitive data are encrypted using classical techniques. The arrival of quantum computing could render much of this data vulnerable, as quantum computers could potentially decrypt encrypted information faster than classical systems. This raises serious privacy concerns, especially with regard to personal medical data or proprietary corporate information.

The ethics of data privacy in a post-quantum world demand that new privacy-preserving technologies, such as quantum-resistant encryption, be developed and deployed before quantum attacks become a reality. However, there are ethical questions surrounding the implementation of such solutions, particularly when it comes to issues of access and fairness. For instance, if quantum-resistant encryption becomes the norm, the cost and complexity of implementing these measures could disproportionately affect smaller organizations or individuals without the resources to protect themselves (Rahul et al., 2024).

10.3 The Need for Quantum-Resistant Security

One of the primary ethical challenges in defending against quantum-enhanced adversarial attacks is the development of quantum-resistant security measures. While there is ongoing research into post-quantum cryptography (PQC) algorithms designed to withstand quantum attacks, these solutions have yet to be widely adopted. This creates a critical gap in cybersecurity, as attackers could exploit the vulnerabilities of classical systems before quantum-resistant alternatives are ready for deployment. Ethical concerns arise around the responsibilities of governments and organizations to protect citizens and data while transitioning to post-quantum security models.

The urgency to develop and deploy quantum-resistant systems is further complicated by the fact that many existing security infrastructures are not designed to handle quantum threats. There is an ethical obligation to ensure that systems are upgraded in a way that does not disrupt essential services or create inequities between different sectors of society. As noted by Gholami and Omar (2023), the speed at which quantum computing advances could potentially outpace the development of countermeasures, leaving systems exposed to attack. Therefore, the ethical question revolves around how to balance innovation with caution, ensuring that security measures are future-proof and equitable.

10.4 Trust and Accountability in Quantum-Enhanced Systems

Trust in digital infrastructures is a cornerstone of modern society. Quantum-enhanced adversarial attacks introduce new risks to trust, particularly in areas such as online banking, government services, and healthcare systems. As quantum computing challenges existing security paradigms, it is crucial to establish new frameworks for accountability in the face of quantum-enabled attacks. Ethical questions about accountability arise when an attack succeeds despite the best efforts of security experts to defend against it, particularly if the attack is conducted using quantum-enhanced adversarial techniques.

A key challenge lies in determining who is responsible for these vulnerabilities. Is it the responsibility of quantum computing developers, cybersecurity professionals, or government bodies to mitigate the risks? The complex interplay of stakeholders in the quantum era means that accountability must be clearly defined, especially as the quantum computing landscape continues to evolve (How & Cheah, 2023). Moreover, the transparency of quantum technologies and the public's understanding of their implications are crucial to fostering trust in the systems that will eventually need to defend against quantum-enhanced attacks.

10.5 Mitigating Risks through Responsible Quantum Development

As quantum technologies develop, it is essential to implement responsible research and development practices to prevent their misuse. Researchers, policymakers, and technologists must engage in discussions around the ethical implications of quantum computing and its role in cybersecurity. Collaborative efforts to create ethical guidelines and regulatory frameworks for quantum technology are necessary to prevent malicious exploitation and ensure that these advancements benefit society as a whole (Gholami & Omar, 2024).

Furthermore, ethical guidelines must promote inclusivity and avoid widening the gap between countries or organizations that have access to quantum computing resources and those that do not. Ensuring that quantum-resistant cybersecurity measures are made accessible to all is a crucial step in upholding fairness and equality in the digital age (Khan et al., 2023).

10.6 Summary

Defending against quantum-enhanced adversarial attacks presents a host of ethical challenges that require careful consideration. As quantum computing continues to evolve, so too must our approaches to cybersecurity, ensuring that new vulnerabilities are addressed while safeguarding privacy, trust, and equity. The ethical implications of quantum-enhanced adversarial attacks emphasize the need for proactive, responsible, and collaborative efforts in developing quantum-resistant security technologies and frameworks. Balancing innovation with ethical responsibility will be key to securing the digital landscape in the quantum era.

11. FUTURE DIRECTIONS: QUANTUM-AWARE DEFENSE SYSTEMS FOR THE NEXT GENERATION

The advent of quantum computing presents both significant opportunities and substantial challenges in the realm of cybersecurity. As quantum technologies continue to evolve, traditional cryptographic systems are increasingly vulnerable to quantum-powered attacks, which could break current encryption algorithms and compromise the security of digital infrastructures. To address this emerging threat, the development of quantum-aware defense systems is crucial. These systems need to be designed to protect against quantum threats while leveraging the potential of quantum computing for improving security measures.

11.1 Quantum-Resistant Cryptography

One of the most critical areas where quantum computing impacts cybersecurity is in cryptography. Quantum algorithms, such as Shor's algorithm, have the potential to break widely used public-key encryption systems, including RSA and ECC (Elliptic Curve Cryptography) (Rahul et al., 2024). This has prompted significant research into quantum-resistant algorithms, also known as post-quantum cryptography (PQC), which aims to develop cryptographic methods that are secure against both quantum and classical computing threats. Researchers, including Baseri et al. (2024), have explored quantum-resistant protocols for digital signatures and key exchange mechanisms to ensure long-term security in the quantum era. The successful development and implementation of PQC could be a cornerstone for building secure quantum-aware defense systems that can safeguard sensitive data and systems from quantum threats.

11.2 Quantum Machine Learning for Cyber Defense

Quantum machine learning (QML) is an exciting field that combines the power of quantum computing with machine learning (ML) techniques. By leveraging quantum algorithms, such as quantum-enhanced optimization and quantum neural networks, QML has the potential to vastly improve the efficiency and effectiveness of cybersecurity systems (Gholami & Omar, 2023). Quantum-enhanced attack detection systems could be designed to analyze large volumes of network traffic and identify anomalous behavior at unprecedented speeds. This would significantly reduce response times to cyberattacks, particularly those that exploit zero-day vulnerabilities (Jones & Omar, 2024). Moreover, QML algorithms could help in the creation of advanced malware detection systems capable of recognizing sophisticated threats that are too complex for classical ML systems to identify.

11.3 Integration of Quantum and Classical Defense Systems

A promising direction for quantum-aware defense systems is the hybridization of classical and quantum security approaches. Such integration could enable the leveraging of quantum advantages for specific tasks while maintaining the robustness of traditional cybersecurity practices for others. For example, quantum key distribution (QKD) could be used to create virtually unbreakable communication channels, while classical firewalls, intrusion detection systems, and encryption methods could continue to protect against conventional cyber threats (Sodiya et al., 2024). By combining the strengths of quantum and classical systems, a layered defense strategy could be developed to protect against both quantum and non-quantum attacks.

Furthermore, efforts to integrate quantum computing into the development of advanced threat detection tools have gained traction. For example, Zangana et al. (2024) explored the use of blockchain and quantum technologies for enhancing network firewall rule analyzers. This type of hybrid approach could lead to the creation of more resilient systems that are capable of adapting to the evolving landscape of cyber threats.

11.4 Addressing Quantum Cybersecurity Challenges

The rise of quantum computing also brings forward new challenges for cybersecurity that must be addressed proactively. As highlighted by Bush et al. (2023) and Seskir (2019), quantum networking poses a new frontier in the realm of digital asset protection. The secure transmission of quantum information over long distances using quantum repeaters and entanglement distribution is a vital area of research. Developing protocols and infrastructure for secure quantum networks will be necessary for the widespread deployment of quantum-aware defense systems.

In addition, quantum computing may create opportunities for offensive cyber capabilities, making it crucial for defense systems to stay ahead of potential adversaries who could use quantum technology for malicious purposes. As noted by How and Cheah (2023), businesses must be prepared for the challenges posed by quantum threats while also exploring the opportunities that quantum computing offers in enhancing cybersecurity.

11.5 Collaboration and Standardization for Quantum-Aware Defense

The development of quantum-aware defense systems will require extensive collaboration among researchers, industry professionals, and governmental bodies. As the quantum computing field is still in its infancy, it is essential to establish standardized frameworks and protocols to guide the development and deployment of quantum-resilient cybersecurity tools. The work of institutions like the National Institute of Standards and Technology (NIST), which is leading efforts to standardize PQC algorithms, will play a critical role in ensuring that defense systems are equipped with quantum-resistant technologies (Zangana & Omar, 2025).

Moreover, as quantum computing becomes more accessible, organizations must invest in research and training to equip their cybersecurity teams with the skills necessary to understand and implement quantum-aware defense measures. As highlighted by Khan et al. (2023), the integration of quantum software development practices will be a key area for building a skilled workforce capable of addressing quantum cybersecurity challenges.

11.6 Summary

The future of cybersecurity in the quantum era demands the creation of defense systems that are both quantum-aware and capable of leveraging the strengths of quantum computing. Quantum-resistant cryptography, quantum machine learning, and hybrid defense strategies are essential components of this next-generation defense infrastructure. However, the challenges posed by quantum computing require ongoing research, collaboration, and standardization efforts to ensure that quantum-aware defense systems are capable of safeguarding digital assets in an increasingly complex threat landscape. As quantum technologies continue to evolve, the development of secure, quantum-aware defense mechanisms will be critical to maintaining the security and privacy of future digital systems.

12. CONCLUSION

In conclusion, as quantum computing continues to evolve, it brings both challenges and opportunities to the field of cybersecurity. While it poses a significant threat to current cryptographic methods, it also opens new avenues for developing advanced defense mechanisms. Quantum-aware defense systems will be critical in preparing for the next generation of cybersecurity threats. By integrating quantum-resistant algorithms, machine learning models, and AI-driven security tools, it is possible to create more resilient systems that can withstand the evolving capabilities of quantum computers.

Thc transition to quantum-resistant security measures will require a multi-faceted approach, incorporating new cryptographic protocols, robust key exchange mechanisms, and advanced threat detection systems. Additionally, leveraging quantum computing's own potential for security-enhancing applications, such as quantum key distribution and quantum encryption, could provide a powerful defense against quantum-enabled attacks. Furthermore, collaboration between quantum researchers, cybersecurity experts, and industry leaders will be crucial in developing and deploying these next-generation defense systems.

As we move forward, it is essential to stay vigilant in monitoring the progress of both quantum computing and cybersecurity research. By proactively addressing the security challenges introduced by quantum technologies, we can better safeguard digital infrastructures and protect sensitive data in the quantum era. The future of cybersecurity lies in our ability to adapt to these changes and to embrace innovative, quantum-aware solutions that ensure the continued integrity and confidentiality of our digital world.

REFERENCES

Agrawal, K., & Aggarwal, M. Building Efficient Smart Contract for Healthcare 4.0. In *Blockchain for Healthcare 4.0* (pp. 94-123). CRC Press.

AL-Refaey. M. R., Tyagi, A. K., AL-Ghamdi, A. S. A. M., & Kukreja, S. (Eds.). (2024). *Topics in Artificial Intelligence Applied to Industry 4.0*. John Wiley & Sons.

Baseri, Y., Chouhan, V., & Ghorbani, A. (2024). Cybersecurity in the Quantum Era: Assessing the Impact of Quantum Computing on Infrastructure. *arXiv preprint arXiv:2404.10659*.

Bishwas, A. K., & Sen, M. (2024). Strategic Roadmap for Quantum-Resistant Security: A Framework for Preparing Industries for the Quantum Threat. *arXiv preprint arXiv:2411.09995*.

Block, R. S. S. (2024). The 2024 quantum advantage blueprint: Where quantum outpaces classical.

Bush, S. F., Challener, W. A., & Mantelet, G. (2021). A perspective on industrial quantum networks. *AVS Quantum Science*, 3(3), 030501. DOI: 10.1116/5.0051881

Exchange, Q. R. K. Towards a Verifiably Secure Quantum-Resistant Key Exchange in IKEv2.

Gholami, S., & Omar, M. (2023). Does Synthetic Data Make Large Language Models More Efficient? *arXiv preprint arXiv:2310.07830*.

Gholami, S., & Omar, M. (2024). Can a student large language model perform as well as its teacher? In *Innovations, Securities, and Case Studies Across Healthcare, Business, and Technology* (pp. 122-139). IGI Global. DOI: 10.4018/979-8-3693-1906-2.ch007

Hamza, Y. A., & Omar, M. D. (2013). Cloud computing security: Abuse and nefarious use of cloud computing. *International Journal of Computer Engineering Research*, 3(6), 22–27.

How, M. L., & Cheah, S. M. (2023). Business Renaissance: Opportunities and challenges at the dawn of the Quantum Computing Era. *Businesses*, 3(4), 585–605. DOI: 10.3390/businesses3040036

Huff, A. J., Burrell, D. N., Nobles, C., Richardson, K., Wright, J. B., Burton, S. L., Jones, A. J., Springs, D., Omar, M., & Brown-Jackson, K. L. (2023). Management Practices for Mitigating Cybersecurity Threats to Biotechnology Companies, Laboratories, and Healthcare Research Organizations. In *Applied Research Approaches to Technology, Healthcare, and Business* (pp. 1-12). IGI Global.

Jones, R., & Omar, M. (2024). Revolutionizing Cybersecurity: The GPT-2 Enhanced Attack Detection and Defense (GEADD) Method for Zero-Day Threats. *International Journal of Informatics* [INJIISCOM]. *Information System and Computer Engineering*, 5(2), 178–191.

Jones, R., Omar, M., Mohammed, D., Nobles, C., & Dawson, M. (2023). Harnessing the Speed and Accuracy of Machine Learning to Advance Cybersecurity. In *2023 Congress in Computer Science, Computer Engineering, & Applied Computing (CSCE)* (pp. 418-421). IEEE. DOI: 10.1109/CSCE60160.2023.00074

Khan, A. A., Akbar, M. A., Ahmad, A., Fahmideh, M., Shameem, M., Lahtinen, V., . . . Mikkonen, T. (2023, July). Agile practices for quantum software development: practitioners' perspectives. In *2023 IEEE international conference on quantum software (QSW)* (pp. 9-20). IEEE.

Lougovski, P., Parekh, O., Broz, J., Byrd, M., Chembo, Y., de Jong, W. A., . . . Svore, K. M. (2023). *Position Papers for the ASCR Workshop on Basic Research Needs in Quantum Computing and Networking*. USDOE Office of Science (SC), Advanced Scientific Computing Research (ASCR).

Madni, A. F., Shah, M. A., & Al-Naeem, M. (2024). An Investigation of Scalability in EHRs using Healthcare 4.0 and Blockchain. *International Journal of Advanced Computer Science and Applications*, 15(5). Advance online publication. DOI: 10.14569/IJACSA.2024.0150548

Metawei, M. A., Eldeeb, H., Nassar, S. M., & Taher, M. (2022). Quantum Computing Meets Artificial Intelligence: Innovations and Challenges. In *Handbook on Artificial Intelligence-Empowered Applied Software Engineering: VOL. 1: Novel Methodologies to Engineering Smart Software Systems* (pp. 303–338). Springer International Publishing. DOI: 10.1007/978-3-031-08202-3_12

Mohamed, N., & Ahmed, A. A. (2024, June). AI in Combatting Man-in-the-Middle Attacks: A Comprehensive Review. In *2024 15th International Conference on Computing Communication and Networking Technologies (ICCCNT)* (pp. 1-6). IEEE. DOI: 10.1109/ICCCNT61001.2024.10725789

Mohammed, D., Omar, M., & Nguyen, V. (2018). Wireless sensor network security: Approaches to detecting and avoiding wormhole attacks. *Journal of Research in Business. Economics and Management*, 10(2), 1860–1864.

Nguyen, V., Mohammed, D., Omar, M., & Banisakher, M. (2018). The Effects of the FCC Net Neutrality Repeal on Security and Privacy. [IJHIoT]. *International Journal of Hyperconnectivity and the Internet of Things*, 2(2), 21–29. DOI: 10.4018/IJHIoT.2018070102

Omar, M. (2021). New insights into database security: An effective and integrated approach for applying access control mechanisms and cryptographic concepts in Microsoft Access environments.

Omar, M. (2022). *Machine Learning for Cybersecurity: Innovative Deep Learning Solutions*. Springer Brief. https://link.springer.com/book/978303115

Omar, M. (2024). From Attack to Defense: Strengthening DNN Text Classification Against Adversarial Examples. In *Innovations, Securities, and Case Studies Across Healthcare, Business, and Technology* (pp. 174-195). IGI Global.

Omar, M. (2024). Revolutionizing Malware Detection: A Paradigm Shift Through Optimized Convolutional Neural Networks. In *Innovations, Securities, and Case Studies Across Healthcare, Business, and Technology* (pp. 196-220). IGI Global. DOI: 10.4018/979-8-3693-1906-2.ch011

Omar, M., & Zangana, H. M. (Eds.). (2024). *Redefining Security With Cyber AI*. IGI Global., DOI: 10.4018/979-8-3693-6517-5

Omar, M., & Zangana, H. M. (Eds.). (2025). *Application of Large Language Models (LLMs) for Software Vulnerability Detection*. IGI Global., DOI: 10.4018/979-8-3693-9311-6

Omar, M., Zangana, H. M., Al-Karaki, J. N., & Mohammed, D. (2024). Harnessing LLMs for IoT malware detection: A comparative analysis of BERT and GPT-2. In *Proceedings of the 8th International Symposium on Multidisciplinary Studies and Innovative Technologies (ISMSIT)* (pp. 1-6). Ankara, Turkiye. https://doi.org/DOI: 10.1109/ISMSIT63511.2024.10757249

Omar, M., Zangana, H. M., & Mohammed, D. (Eds.). (2025). *Integrating Artificial Intelligence in Cybersecurity and Forensic Practices*. IGI Global., DOI: 10.4018/979-8-3373-0588-2

Perron, J. K., DeLeone, C., Sharif, S., Carter, T., Grossman, J. M., Passante, G., & Sack, J. (2021). Quantum undergraduate education and scientific training. *arXiv preprint arXiv:2109.13850*.

Qualters, I., Taylor, A. J., & Hagberg, A. A. (2019). *IS&T Computing Overview* (No. LA-UR-19-22567). Los Alamos National Lab.(LANL), Los Alamos, NM (United States).

Rahul, R., Geetha, S., Priyatharsini, S., Mehata, K., Sundaresan Perumal, T., Ethiraj, N., & Sendilvelan, S. (2024). Cybersecurity Issues and Challenges in Quantum Computing. *Topics in Artificial Intelligence Applied to Industry*, 4(0), 203–221. DOI: 10.1002/9781394216147.ch11

Ramachandran, D., Naqi, S. M., Perumal, G., & Abbas, Q. (2023). DLTN-LOSP: A Novel Deep-Linear-Transition-Network-Based Resource Allocation Model with the Logic Overhead Security Protocol for Cloud Systems. *Sensors (Basel)*, 23(20), 8448. DOI: 10.3390/s23208448 PMID: 37896541

Seskir, Z. C. (2019). *Current state of quantum information technologies in Turkey* (Master's thesis, Middle East Technical University).

Singh, N. B. *Quantum Mechanics in Drug Discovery*. NB Singh.

Sodiya, E. O., Umoga, U. J., Amoo, O. O., & Atadoga, A. (2024). Quantum computing and its potential impact on US cybersecurity: A review: Scrutinizing the challenges and opportunities presented by quantum technologies in safeguarding digital assets. *Global Journal of Engineering and Technology Advances, 18*(2), 049-064.

Wright, J., Dawson, M. E.Jr, & Omar, M. (2012). Cyber security and mobile threats: The need for antivirus applications for smartphones. *Journal of Information Systems Technology and Planning*, 5(14), 40–60.

Zangana, H. M. (2024). Exploring Blockchain-Based Timestamping Tools: A Comprehensive Review. *Redefining Security With Cyber AI*, 92-110.

Zangana, H. M. (2024). Exploring the Landscape of Website Vulnerability Scanners: A Comprehensive Review and Comparative Analysis. *Redefining Security With Cyber AI*, 111-129.

Zangana, H. M., Mohammed, A. K., Sallow, A. B., & Sallow, Z. B. (2024). Cybernetic Deception: Unraveling the Layers of Email Phishing Threats. [INJURATECH]. *International Journal of Research and Applied Technology*, 4(1), 35–47.

Zangana, H. M., & Mohammed, D. (2025). Foundations of Large Language Models in Software Vulnerability Detection. In Omar, M., & Zangana, H. (Eds.), *Application of Large Language Models (LLMs) for Software Vulnerability Detection* (pp. 41–74). IGI Global., DOI: 10.4018/979-8-3693-9311-6.ch002

Zangana, H. M., & Mustafa, F. M. (2025). Image Denoising Techniques for Cybersecurity and Forensic Applications: AI-Driven Approaches. In Omar, M., Zangana, H., & Mohammed, D. (Eds.), *Integrating Artificial Intelligence in Cybersecurity and Forensic Practices* (pp. 117–142). IGI Global Scientific Publishing., DOI: 10.4018/979-8-3373-0588-2.ch005

Zangana, H. M., & Omar, M. (2020). Threats, Attacks, and Mitigations of Smartphone Security. *Academic Journal of Nawroz University*, 9(4), 324–332. DOI: 10.25007/ajnu.v9n4a989

Zangana, H. M., & Omar, M. (2025). Harnessing the Power of Large Language Models for Cybersecurity: Applications, Challenges, and Future Directions. In Omar, M., & Zangana, H. (Eds.), *Application of Large Language Models (LLMs) for Software Vulnerability Detection* (pp. 1–40). IGI Global., DOI: 10.4018/979-8-3693-9311-6.ch001

Zangana, H. M., Omar, M., Al-Karaki, J. N., & Mohammed, D. (2024). Comprehensive Review and Analysis of Network Firewall Rule Analyzers: Enhancing Security Posture and Efficiency. *Redefining Security With Cyber AI*, 15-36.

Zangana, H. M., Omar, M., & Mohammed, D. (2025). Introduction to Artificial Intelligence in Cybersecurity and Forensic Science. In Omar, M., Zangana, H., & Mohammed, D. (Eds.), *Integrating Artificial Intelligence in Cybersecurity and Forensic Practices* (pp. 1–24). IGI Global Scientific Publishing., DOI: 10.4018/979-8-3373-0588-2.ch001

Chapter 11
Natural Language Processing for Cyber Threat Intelligence in a Quantum World

Hewa Majeed Zangana
https://orcid.org/0000-0001-7909-254X
Duhok Polytechnic University, Iraq

Firas Mahmood Mustafa
Duhok Polytechnic University, Iraq

Shuai Li
University of Oulu, Finland

Jamal N. Al-Karaki
https://orcid.org/0009-0000-7833-3970
Zayed University, UAE

ABSTRACT

The intersection of natural language processing (NLP) and cyber threat intelligence (CTI) is gaining momentum as cybersecurity paradigms evolve to address the challenges posed by quantum computing. This chapter explores how advancements in NLP, particularly through the deployment of large language models (LLMs), can be leveraged to enhance CTI in a quantum-aware context. It discusses the capabilities of NLP systems to process vast amounts of threat data, identify patterns, and predict potential risks while considering the implications of quantum technologies on cybersecurity frameworks. Furthermore, the chapter highlights the role

DOI: 10.4018/979-8-3373-1102-9.ch011

of quantum-aware NLP tools in detecting advanced persistent threats, optimizing response strategies, and ensuring the resilience of digital ecosystems in the face of quantum-enabled cyber threats. By integrating LLMs with quantum computing principles, this research provides insights into the future of CTI and its evolution to counteract complex cyber challenges.

1. INTRODUCTION

The rapid evolution of technology has revolutionized the way we interact with data and systems, introducing unprecedented challenges and opportunities in cybersecurity. As advancements such as large language models (LLMs), quantum computing, and artificial intelligence (AI) converge, they are reshaping the landscape of cybersecurity by enhancing both defensive and offensive capabilities. This chapter explores these transformative innovations, focusing on their potential to revolutionize the detection and mitigation of cyber threats.

1.1 The Role of Large Language Models in Cybersecurity

LLMs, such as GPT-3 and its successors, are increasingly recognized for their ability to process and analyze vast amounts of textual data. Their applications extend to vulnerability detection, threat analysis, and anomaly detection, marking a significant departure from traditional methods (Gholami & Omar, 2024). Recent studies have emphasized their role in automating tasks such as malware detection and phishing analysis, thereby reducing human error and response times (Omar & Zangana, 2025).

1.2 Quantum Computing: A Double-Edged Sword

Quantum computing represents a paradigm shift in computational power, capable of solving problems that were previously intractable for classical systems. However, this capability also introduces significant risks to traditional cryptographic systems, as quantum algorithms can potentially break widely used encryption protocols (Sodiya et al., 2024; How & Cheah, 2023). Simultaneously, quantum technologies are being explored for developing quantum-resistant algorithms, heralding a new era of cybersecurity innovation (Bishwas & Sen, 2024).

1.3 Integration of Artificial Intelligence and Cybersecurity

The fusion of AI with cybersecurity offers enhanced predictive analytics, enabling organizations to anticipate and mitigate risks proactively (Hamza & Omar, 2013). Machine learning models, particularly those leveraging deep learning techniques, have demonstrated remarkable efficacy in identifying complex patterns associated with cyber threats (Omar, 2022). For instance, the DLTN-LOSP framework has showcased innovative approaches to resource allocation and security in cloud systems (Ramachandran et al., 2023).

1.4 Addressing Emerging Threats

While these advancements provide robust tools for cybersecurity professionals, they also necessitate addressing new types of vulnerabilities. The misuse of AI, including adversarial attacks on LLMs, underscores the importance of developing resilient models capable of defending against sophisticated threats (Jones & Omar, 2024). Moreover, the increasing reliance on IoT devices introduces unique challenges in managing and securing distributed systems (Omar et al., 2024).

Cyber threats have evolved significantly over the years, necessitating advanced defensive measures. The following timeline graph depicts key milestones in the evolution of threats and the corresponding cybersecurity innovations, culminating in the integration of NLP and quantum computing.

Figure 1. Evolution of cyber threats and defensive measures

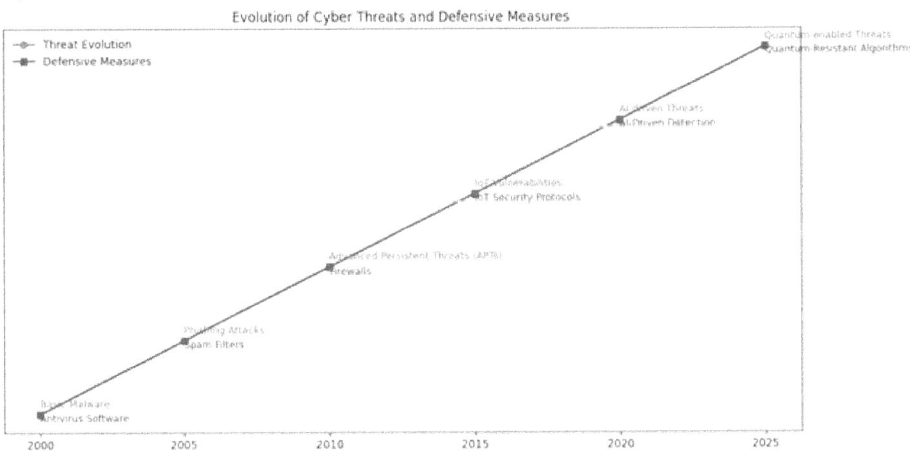

1.5 Contributions of this Chapter

This chapter provides a comprehensive analysis of how modern technologies, particularly LLMs, quantum computing, and AI, are shaping cybersecurity practices. It highlights cutting-edge research, examines real-world applications, and addresses the ethical implications of deploying such technologies at scale. By synthesizing insights from academic literature and industry practices, it aims to offer a holistic perspective on the future of cybersecurity.

To better understand the integration of NLP into cyber threat intelligence (CTI), we present a workflow diagram. This diagram illustrates the various stages, from data collection and processing to threat detection and mitigation. By visualizing this workflow, readers can appreciate the interconnected components that drive NLP's efficacy in enhancing CTI.

Figure 2. Workflow of NLP-Driven cyber threat intelligence

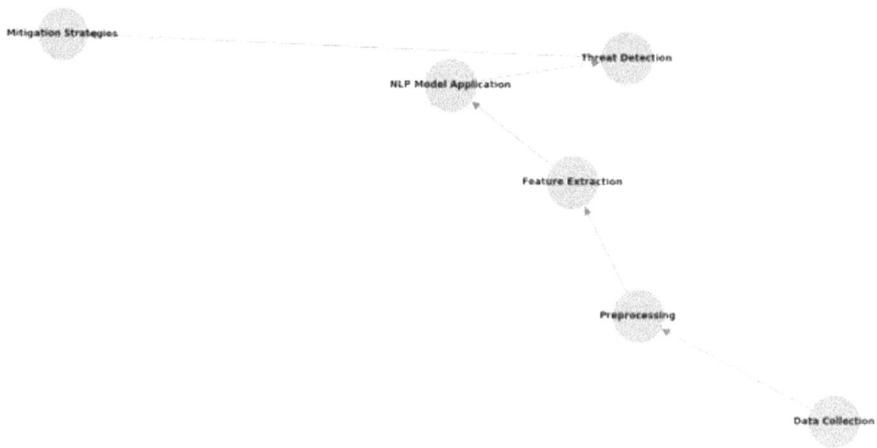

2. FUNDAMENTALS OF NLP IN CYBERSECURITY

Natural Language Processing (NLP) has emerged as a pivotal technology in addressing complex cybersecurity challenges. With the exponential growth in cyber threats and the increasing sophistication of attacks, NLP offers innovative solutions to enhance detection, prevention, and response strategies. This section delves into the role of NLP in cybersecurity, exploring its applications, advantages, and challenges.

2.1 Role of NLP in Cybersecurity

NLP, a subset of artificial intelligence (AI), focuses on enabling computers to understand, interpret, and generate human language. Its role in cybersecurity spans across multiple domains:

1. **Threat Intelligence Analysis**: NLP aids in processing vast amounts of unstructured threat intelligence data from sources like social media, forums, and news articles. Tools leveraging NLP can extract actionable insights, such as identifying new malware or vulnerabilities (Jones & Omar, 2024).
2. **Phishing Detection**: NLP models analyze email text for linguistic patterns indicative of phishing attacks. For example, LLMs like GPT-3 and GPT-4 are increasingly employed to detect subtle manipulations in text that traditional methods might overlook (Zangana et al., 2025).
3. **Malware Analysis**: Malware detection systems use NLP to analyze malicious code or scripts embedded in documents, offering an additional layer of protection against zero-day threats (Jones et al., 2023).
4. **Automated Incident Response**: NLP enhances the efficiency of incident response by parsing logs, summarizing attack patterns, and suggesting mitigation strategies. This approach reduces human intervention and speeds up the decision-making process (Omar, 2022).

2.2 Applications of LLMs in Cybersecurity

Large Language Models (LLMs) have revolutionized the application of NLP in cybersecurity. These models, trained on extensive datasets, provide unprecedented accuracy and adaptability. Specific applications include:

1. **Vulnerability Detection**: LLMs can identify vulnerabilities in software by analyzing source code, patch notes, and vulnerability databases. For example, frameworks like BERT and GPT-2 have been utilized for malware detection in IoT devices (Omar et al., 2024).
2. **Policy Compliance**: NLP-driven systems ensure that organizations adhere to cybersecurity regulations by analyzing policy documents and identifying discrepancies (Huff et al., 2023).
3. **User Authentication**: Behavioral biometrics, powered by NLP, enhance authentication mechanisms. For instance, analyzing typing patterns or email content can help verify user identity (Wright et al., 2012).

2.3 Advantages of NLP in Cybersecurity

The integration of NLP offers several advantages:

- **Scalability**: NLP systems can handle massive datasets, enabling real-time threat detection (Mohamed & Ahmed, 2024).
- **Accuracy**: Advanced NLP models minimize false positives, ensuring precise threat identification (Rahul et al., 2024).
- **Cost-Effectiveness**: Automation of routine tasks reduces the need for manual intervention, lowering operational costs (Zangana et al., 2024).

The advantages and challenges of using NLP in cybersecurity are multifaceted. To provide a clearer understanding, we have created a comparative diagram. This visual juxtaposes the strengths and limitations, offering insights into areas where NLP excels and where improvements are needed.

Figure 3. Advantages and challenges of NLP in cybersecurity

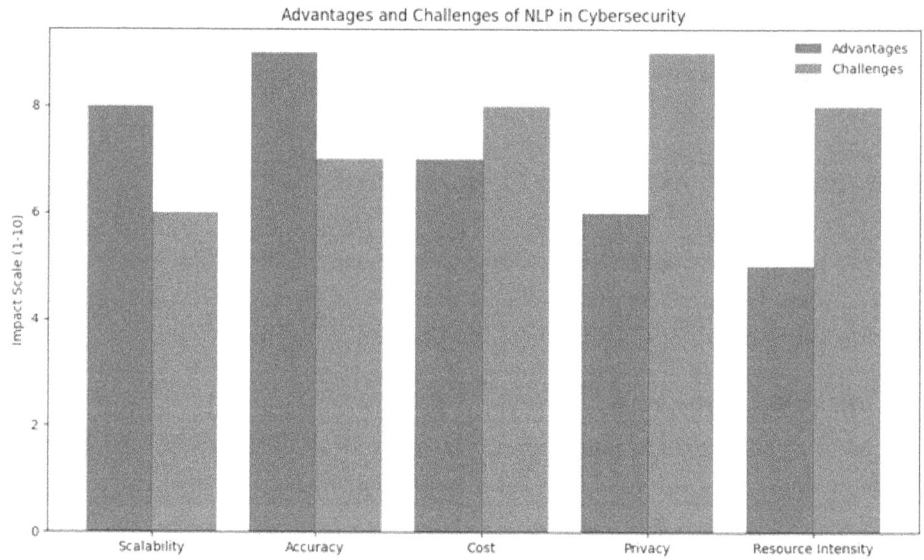

2.4 Challenges in Implementing NLP

Despite its benefits, NLP faces challenges in cybersecurity:

1. **Data Privacy**: Processing sensitive data poses privacy concerns, especially in healthcare and finance sectors (Hamza & Omar, 2013).
2. **Evasion Techniques**: Adversaries can manipulate text to evade detection, necessitating constant updates to NLP algorithms (Omar, 2024).
3. **Resource Intensity**: Training and deploying LLMs require significant computational resources, which may not be feasible for all organizations (Gholami & Omar, 2024).

2.5 Future Directions

Emerging trends in NLP-driven cybersecurity focus on integrating quantum computing to address computational limitations and improve model accuracy (Sodiya et al., 2024). Additionally, advancements in synthetic data generation promise to enhance LLM training efficiency (Gholami & Omar, 2023).

In conclusion, NLP is a transformative force in cybersecurity, addressing challenges with innovative solutions while adapting to evolving threats. However, its full potential can only be realized by overcoming current limitations and ensuring ethical deployment. This chapter will explore these aspects in depth, drawing insights from pioneering research and practical implementations.

3. LEVERAGING LARGE LANGUAGE MODELS (LLMS) FOR CYBER THREAT INTELLIGENCE

The rapidly evolving landscape of cybersecurity demands innovative approaches to detect, analyze, and mitigate threats. Large Language Models (LLMs), with their unprecedented capabilities in natural language understanding and generation, have emerged as transformative tools for cyber threat intelligence (CTI). These models empower organizations to proactively address cyber risks by automating threat detection, enhancing situational awareness, and optimizing response strategies.

3.1 Role of LLMs in Cyber Threat Intelligence

LLMs such as GPT-3, GPT-4, and specialized models like BERT have demonstrated remarkable success in processing and interpreting vast amounts of unstructured threat data. By leveraging their advanced text analysis capabilities, LLMs can identify patterns in malware signatures, phishing emails, and zero-day vulnerabilities, facilitating real-time threat detection.

Jones and Omar (2024) highlighted the efficacy of GPT-2 in enhancing attack detection and defense against zero-day threats through the GPT-2 Enhanced Attack Detection and Defense (GEADD) framework. This work underscores the adaptability of LLMs in handling complex, unseen threat vectors, making them indispensable in modern CTI systems.

3.2 Automating Threat Analysis with LLMs

The automation of threat analysis is one of the most impactful applications of LLMs in cybersecurity. Using LLMs, organizations can automate the parsing of threat reports, social media feeds, and darknet communications to uncover emerging threats. According to Zangana et al. (2025), LLMs like BERT and GPT-2 have been instrumental in identifying malware patterns in IoT ecosystems, enabling proactive defense mechanisms.

Furthermore, Huff et al. (2023) explored management practices for mitigating cybersecurity threats in biotechnology and healthcare sectors, emphasizing the role of AI-driven tools like LLMs in safeguarding sensitive information against sophisticated cyberattacks.

3.3 Enhancing Threat Intelligence Sharing

Threat intelligence sharing across organizations is critical for collaborative cybersecurity efforts. LLMs can streamline this process by summarizing complex technical reports into concise, actionable insights. As Gholami and Omar (2023) demonstrated, synthetic data enhances the training efficiency of LLMs, making them more effective for generating accurate threat intelligence summaries.

The use of blockchain-integrated LLMs, as discussed by Zangana (2024), further enhances the security and transparency of shared threat intelligence, ensuring tamper-proof communication among stakeholders.

3.4 Challenges and Limitations

Despite their potential, LLMs face challenges in cybersecurity applications. Bias in training data, adversarial attacks on models, and limitations in domain-specific knowledge can impede their effectiveness. Omar and Zangana (2025) explored these challenges, proposing strategies to mitigate vulnerabilities in LLM-driven systems.

The integration of quantum computing in cybersecurity, as discussed by Baseri et al. (2024) and Sodiya et al. (2024), presents new challenges and opportunities. Quantum-enhanced LLMs could address some of these limitations by offering exponentially faster processing for threat intelligence tasks.

3.5 Future Directions

The future of LLMs in CTI is promising, with ongoing research focusing on improving model robustness, incorporating domain-specific training, and integrating quantum computing. Omar et al. (2024) emphasized the potential of combining LLMs with deep learning techniques for adversarial text classification, paving the way for more resilient CTI systems.

Moreover, the development of quantum-resistant security protocols, as highlighted by Bishwas and Sen (2024), will likely play a crucial role in safeguarding LLM-based CTI systems from quantum-era threats.

3.6 Summary

LLMs represent a paradigm shift in cyber threat intelligence, offering unparalleled capabilities in threat detection, analysis, and mitigation. By addressing their limitations and leveraging advancements in AI and quantum technologies, the cybersecurity community can harness the full potential of LLMs to combat evolving cyber threats. As Zangana and Omar (2025) aptly noted, the convergence of LLMs and cybersecurity holds transformative potential for creating a more secure digital future.

4. QUANTUM COMPUTING'S IMPACT ON NLP FOR CTI

The integration of quantum computing into Natural Language Processing (NLP) for Cyber Threat Intelligence (CTI) is poised to revolutionize the cybersecurity landscape by leveraging quantum computational power to address the growing complexity and scale of cyber threats. Quantum-enhanced NLP models promise unprecedented advancements in data processing, pattern recognition, and threat prediction. This section explores the transformative impact of quantum computing on NLP applications in CTI.

4.1 Accelerating Computational Processes

Quantum computing offers the ability to process and analyze massive datasets exponentially faster than classical computing methods. This capability is particularly beneficial for CTI, where NLP models analyze extensive textual data, such as threat reports, logs, and communications. As highlighted by Sodiya et al. (2024), the application of quantum algorithms in cybersecurity can significantly enhance the detection and mitigation of potential vulnerabilities by leveraging quantum parallelism to handle complex computations efficiently.

The integration of quantum computing with NLP for CTI can also address the limitations of classical computing in processing high-dimensional linguistic data. For instance, Perron et al. (2021) emphasize the importance of quantum computing in advancing computational capabilities in scientific fields, providing a robust foundation for its application in NLP for CTI.

The integration of quantum computing into NLP workflows transforms the approach to threat detection. The following flowchart visualizes a quantum-enhanced NLP system, detailing its stages and the quantum-specific enhancements that optimize its performance.

Figure 4. Quantum-Enhanced NLP workflow for threat detection

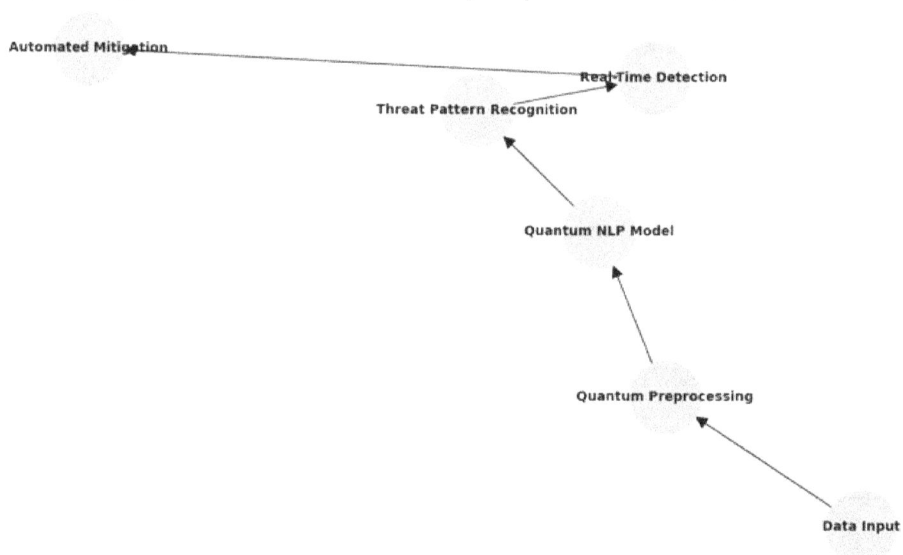

4.2 Advancing NLP Techniques with Quantum Algorithms

Quantum-inspired algorithms, such as Quantum Support Vector Machines and Quantum Neural Networks, can enhance the performance of NLP tasks by optimizing data clustering and classification processes. This is particularly critical in CTI, where precision in threat identification and classification is paramount (Metawei et al., 2022). Furthermore, the ability of quantum computing to perform complex transformations on linguistic embeddings allows for more accurate semantic analysis and sentiment detection, which are crucial for understanding threat actors' communications.

According to Gholami and Omar (2024), the adoption of quantum computing in NLP can facilitate the development of more efficient large language models (LLMs), offering improved performance in threat detection and response systems. These quantum-enhanced LLMs could outperform traditional models in generating actionable insights from vast amounts of unstructured cyber threat data.

4.3 Enhancing Predictive Analysis in CTI

The predictive capabilities of quantum-enhanced NLP models are a significant advancement for CTI. By leveraging quantum computing's ability to analyze probabilistic patterns, these models can predict potential attack vectors and identify emerging threats with high accuracy. Bush et al. (2021) underscore the role of quantum networks in enabling secure and efficient data sharing, which complements the predictive power of quantum-enhanced NLP models in CTI applications.

Moreover, quantum computing can optimize the training and deployment of NLP models by reducing the computational overhead associated with large datasets. This aligns with the findings of Gholami and Omar (2023), who demonstrated that synthetic data integration, combined with quantum computing, could streamline the training processes of NLP models, making them more resource-efficient.

4.4 Addressing Security Challenges with Quantum-Enhanced CTI

While quantum computing offers significant benefits for NLP in CTI, it also introduces unique security challenges. Quantum-resistant cryptographic methods, such as those discussed by Bishwas and Sen (2024), are essential to safeguard sensitive CTI data processed by quantum-enhanced NLP models. The integration of these methods ensures the resilience of CTI systems against potential quantum-based attacks.

The work of Khan et al. (2023) on agile practices for quantum software development highlights the importance of adopting flexible and iterative approaches in integrating quantum technologies into cybersecurity frameworks. This is particularly relevant for CTI, where rapid adaptation to emerging threats is crucial.

4.5 Future Directions and Research Opportunities

The synergy between quantum computing and NLP for CTI opens up numerous avenues for research and development. Potential areas of exploration include the integration of quantum-enhanced LLMs with traditional cybersecurity tools (Zangana & Omar, 2025) and the use of quantum-based data compression techniques to optimize storage and retrieval of CTI data (Lougovski et al., 2023).

Additionally, the exploration of ethical considerations in deploying quantum-enhanced NLP for CTI is vital. As highlighted by Mohamed and Ahmed (2024), ensuring transparency and accountability in AI and quantum technologies is essential to maintain trust and reliability in CTI systems.

5. ENHANCING THREAT INTELLIGENCE WITH NLP-QUANTUM SYNERGIES

The fusion of natural language processing (NLP) with quantum computing represents a transformative frontier in cybersecurity. By leveraging the unique capabilities of quantum mechanics, such as superposition and entanglement, alongside the advanced linguistic and contextual understanding of NLP models, organizations can enhance threat intelligence to unprecedented levels. This synergy is particularly significant in addressing complex cybersecurity challenges like zero-day vulnerabilities, malware detection, and adversarial attacks.

5.1 The Role of NLP in Threat Intelligence

NLP has demonstrated remarkable efficacy in analyzing large volumes of textual data, identifying patterns, and predicting cyber threats. Its application ranges from processing cybersecurity alerts to extracting actionable insights from unstructured sources like threat reports and social media (Jones & Omar, 2024). Advanced NLP models, such as GPT-3 and BERT, have revolutionized automated threat intelligence by enabling real-time detection of emerging attack vectors (Omar, 2022). Moreover, the integration of NLP with blockchain technologies has further enhanced transparency and security in timestamping critical logs (Zangana, 2024).

5.2 Quantum Computing's Contribution

Quantum computing offers computational power beyond the reach of classical systems, enabling faster data processing and complex problem-solving (Bush et al., 2021). In the context of cybersecurity, quantum algorithms can expedite the identification of patterns within encrypted traffic or large datasets, providing early detection of potential threats (Rahul et al., 2024). Quantum-resistant encryption methods also ensure the longevity of security protocols against future quantum threats (Bishwas & Sen, 2024).

5.3 Synergies between NLP and Quantum Computing

Combining NLP with quantum computing amplifies the advantages of both technologies. Quantum-enhanced NLP models can process and analyze multilingual threat data at speeds previously unattainable, improving the accuracy of predictive models. For example, Huff et al. (2023) highlighted the potential of integrating quantum algorithms with NLP to detect phishing emails and insider threats in biotechnology and healthcare sectors.

Furthermore, quantum algorithms can optimize NLP's performance in detecting subtle semantic variations, which are crucial in identifying sophisticated social engineering attacks like spear phishing (Zangana et al., 2024). Recent studies suggest that quantum-enhanced large language models (LLMs) can outperform their classical counterparts in recognizing and mitigating cyber threats, as demonstrated by Gholami and Omar (2024).

The synergy between NLP and quantum computing has the potential to revolutionize threat intelligence. The diagram below depicts key areas where these technologies intersect, showcasing how their combined strengths address cybersecurity challenges more effectively.

Figure 5. Synergy between NLP and quantum computing

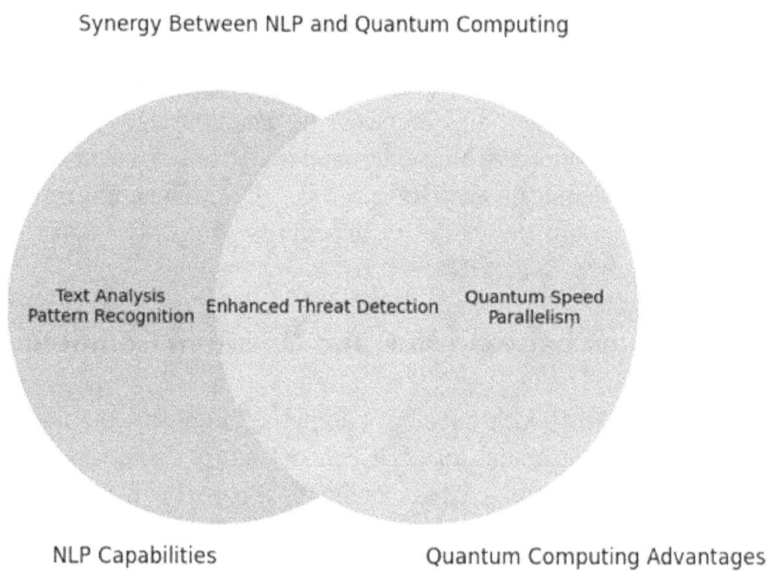

5.4 Use Cases and Practical Applications

1. **Advanced Malware Detection**: Combining NLP's ability to classify and analyze malware signatures with quantum computing's processing capabilities accelerates the detection of advanced persistent threats (APT) (Omar & Zangana, 2025).
2. **Real-Time Cyber Threat Monitoring**: By utilizing quantum-enhanced NLP models, organizations can monitor and interpret threat intelligence feeds with minimal latency (Metawei et al., 2022).
3. **Countering Zero-Day Exploits**: The GEADD method, which integrates NLP with quantum computing, has shown promise in detecting zero-day vulnerabilities by analyzing attack patterns and contextual clues (Jones & Omar, 2024).

5.5 Challenges and Future Directions

Despite its potential, the integration of NLP and quantum computing faces challenges such as algorithmic complexity, hardware limitations, and the need for quantum-resistant security measures (Sodiya et al., 2024). Addressing these challenges requires collaboration among academia, industry, and government agencies to develop robust frameworks and standards for deploying these technologies effectively (Khan et al., 2023).

Future research should focus on exploring hybrid quantum-classical models to balance computational efficiency and accuracy. Additionally, ethical considerations, including data privacy and the potential misuse of quantum-enhanced NLP tools, must be addressed (Nguyen et al., 2018).

5.6 Summary

The convergence of NLP and quantum computing represents a paradigm shift in cybersecurity. By enhancing the speed and accuracy of threat intelligence, this synergy offers a promising avenue for proactive defense mechanisms in an increasingly complex cyber landscape. Continued innovation and interdisciplinary collaboration will be crucial in unlocking the full potential of NLP-quantum synergies for safeguarding digital assets.

6. AUTOMATED THREAT INTELLIGENCE PIPELINES USING NLP AND QUANTUM COMPUTING

In the era of evolving cybersecurity challenges, leveraging automated systems for threat intelligence has become a necessity. The integration of Natural Language Processing (NLP) and Quantum Computing offers a transformative approach to addressing the complexities of modern cyber threats. This section explores how these technologies converge to create robust, automated pipelines for identifying, analyzing, and mitigating security risks.

6.1 Role of NLP in Threat Intelligence

NLP technologies enable the extraction and analysis of vast amounts of unstructured data, such as security logs, threat reports, and social media feeds. By employing large language models (LLMs) like BERT and GPT-2, organizations can automate the classification and prioritization of security alerts. These models excel in contextual understanding and have demonstrated significant efficacy in cybersecurity applications (Omar et al., 2024). Recent studies, such as those by Jones and Omar (2024), have highlighted the potential of LLM-enhanced methods, such as the GPT-2 Enhanced Attack Detection and Defense (GEADD), in detecting zero-day threats with unprecedented accuracy.

Additionally, synthetic data generation has emerged as a critical tool for training NLP models. Research by Gholami and Omar (2023) indicates that synthetic data can improve the efficiency of LLMs, enabling faster adaptation to domain-specific tasks. These advancements are instrumental in automating threat intelligence pipelines, where the speed and accuracy of data processing are paramount.

6.2 Quantum Computing in Cybersecurity

Quantum computing's potential to solve complex optimization problems at unmatched speeds makes it a valuable asset in cybersecurity. One area where quantum computing shines is in the rapid analysis of encrypted threat intelligence data. For instance, quantum algorithms can enhance the performance of data clustering and anomaly detection systems (Baseri et al., 2024). Moreover, strategic frameworks for quantum-resistant security, as proposed by Bishwas and Sen (2024), are vital for safeguarding these systems against future quantum threats.

Quantum computing's role extends to facilitating advanced resource allocation models in cloud systems, as demonstrated by Ramachandran et al. (2023). By integrating quantum computing with automated pipelines, organizations can efficiently allocate computational resources for real-time threat analysis.

6.3 Integrating NLP and Quantum Computing in Threat Intelligence

The integration of NLP and quantum computing represents a paradigm shift in cybersecurity. Automated pipelines leveraging NLP models can identify potential threats by analyzing vast datasets, while quantum computing accelerates the computational processes involved. A notable example is the use of hybrid systems combining quantum computing and AI for malware detection, as outlined by Omar et al. (2024).

To ensure scalability and robustness, these pipelines can utilize quantum-inspired algorithms for optimizing NLP tasks, such as entity recognition and sentiment analysis. The research by Sodiya et al. (2024) emphasizes the importance of quantum computing in enhancing the predictive capabilities of AI models. This fusion not only improves the speed and accuracy of threat detection but also provides actionable insights for preemptive defense strategies.

6.4 Practical Applications and Case Studies

Several practical implementations underscore the efficacy of automated threat intelligence pipelines. For instance, Mohammed et al. (2018) explored approaches to detecting and avoiding wormhole attacks in wireless sensor networks. Integrating NLP for data analysis and quantum algorithms for pattern recognition could enhance the detection mechanisms in such scenarios.

In the context of cloud computing, Hamza and Omar (2013) identified potential abuses and nefarious activities. Automating threat intelligence in cloud environments requires robust security mechanisms, which can be strengthened using quantum-resistant cryptographic protocols (Exchange, 2025).

Another application involves cybersecurity in the quantum era, where hybrid approaches using NLP and quantum computing address emerging challenges. The research by Lougovski et al. (2023) highlights advancements in quantum networking, which can be integrated into automated threat pipelines to ensure secure communication channels.

6.5 Challenges and Future Directions

Despite the promising applications, challenges remain in integrating NLP and quantum computing for threat intelligence. The nascent stage of quantum computing and the computational demands of LLMs pose significant hurdles. However, collaborative efforts, such as those detailed by Khan et al. (2023) in quantum software development, provide valuable insights for overcoming these challenges.

Future research should focus on developing quantum-accelerated NLP models and testing their efficacy in real-world threat intelligence scenarios. Moreover, the adoption of blockchain-based timestamping tools, as reviewed by Zangana (2024), could further enhance the integrity and traceability of automated pipelines.

6.6 Summary

Automated threat intelligence pipelines leveraging NLP and quantum computing represent a groundbreaking advancement in cybersecurity. By addressing the challenges and exploring innovative integrations, these technologies have the potential to revolutionize threat detection and defense mechanisms. The synergy between NLP's analytical capabilities and quantum computing's computational power paves the way for a secure and resilient digital future.

7. NLP FOR ANOMALY DETECTION IN QUANTUM-AWARE CYBERSECURITY

In recent years, the intersection of quantum computing and cybersecurity has garnered increasing attention due to the potential for quantum technologies to revolutionize how data is encrypted, transmitted, and secured. The integration of Natural Language Processing (NLP) techniques into anomaly detection systems has emerged as a promising approach to bolster cybersecurity measures in quantum-aware environments. This section explores the role of NLP in anomaly detection, specifically in the context of quantum-aware cybersecurity, by examining its capabilities, applications, and challenges.

7.1 The Role of NLP in Anomaly Detection

Anomaly detection is a fundamental component of modern cybersecurity frameworks, tasked with identifying irregular patterns or behaviors within a network or system that could indicate malicious activity, such as cyberattacks or data breaches. In traditional systems, machine learning (ML) algorithms have been widely adopted for detecting these anomalies. However, the unique characteristics of quantum-aware environments, where quantum technologies play a critical role in encryption and secure communication, present new challenges that require innovative solutions.

NLP has emerged as a valuable tool in this domain due to its ability to process and analyze vast amounts of textual data, such as network logs, communications, and threat intelligence reports, to uncover hidden anomalies. By leveraging the power of NLP models, such as transformers, to analyze the contextual meaning behind textual data, security systems can detect complex threats that may go unnoticed by conventional anomaly detection systems (Gholami & Omar, 2023). These systems can be particularly useful in quantum-aware cybersecurity, where quantum technologies may introduce new forms of data vulnerabilities.

7.2 Quantum-Aware Cybersecurity and NLP Integration

Quantum computing has the potential to significantly impact cybersecurity, both as a threat and an opportunity. Quantum algorithms can break traditional encryption schemes, forcing cybersecurity systems to adapt to a new class of challenges (Baseri, Chouhan, & Ghorbani, 2024). At the same time, quantum technologies can offer new ways to secure communications and enhance anomaly detection. For example, quantum key distribution (QKD) provides an unbreakable method for transmitting encryption keys, ensuring the integrity of data in transit (Sodiya et al., 2024).

The integration of NLP into quantum-aware cybersecurity frameworks allows for the development of advanced anomaly detection mechanisms that can analyze encrypted traffic, quantum communications, and even quantum-resistant cryptographic systems. By using NLP techniques to analyze patterns in quantum communications, cybersecurity systems can identify unusual behaviors that could signal potential threats, such as quantum-based attacks or vulnerabilities in quantum-resilient algorithms (Jones et al., 2023).

7.3 Applications of NLP in Quantum-Aware Anomaly Detection

1. **Quantum Communications Monitoring:** NLP can be applied to monitor quantum communication channels, identifying patterns in data transmission that could indicate quantum-based attacks such as quantum man-in-the-middle (MITM) attacks or quantum eavesdropping attempts (How & Cheah, 2023). By analyzing the textual logs of quantum communication protocols and their interactions with classical systems, NLP models can detect subtle anomalies that may signal an ongoing attack.
2. **Quantum-Resilient Cryptography Analysis:** Quantum computing poses a threat to existing cryptographic systems, necessitating the development of quantum-resistant algorithms. NLP can be employed to monitor and assess the performance of quantum-resistant cryptographic protocols by analyzing the outputs of encryption systems. If the NLP system detects irregularities or unexpected behavior in encrypted data, it can trigger an alert for further investigation (Zangana & Omar, 2024).
3. **Automated Threat Intelligence Analysis:** In the face of increasingly sophisticated cyberattacks, cybersecurity professionals rely on threat intelligence reports and other textual data to identify emerging threats. NLP techniques can automate the analysis of these reports, extracting relevant information about quantum-aware vulnerabilities, attack vectors, and emerging threats. By leveraging large language models (LLMs) such as GPT-2 and BERT, NLP can enhance threat intelligence systems, providing more accurate and timely insights into the evolving cybersecurity landscape (Jones & Omar, 2024).
4. **Anomaly Detection in Quantum Software Development:** As the quantum computing industry grows, quantum software development has become a critical area of concern for cybersecurity. NLP can be employed to analyze code and development logs, identifying anomalies that could signal vulnerabilities or malicious behavior in quantum software. This application is particularly

important for securing quantum cloud services and quantum hardware, which could become prime targets for exploitation (Khan et al., 2023).

7.4 Challenges and Future Directions

While the potential of NLP in quantum-aware cybersecurity is vast, several challenges remain in fully realizing its capabilities. One key challenge is the need for specialized NLP models that can effectively process quantum-specific data, including encrypted quantum messages and quantum cryptographic protocols. Additionally, there is a need for advanced training datasets that include both classical and quantum-specific data to improve the performance of NLP models in detecting anomalies in quantum-aware environments.

Moreover, the scalability of NLP-based anomaly detection systems in quantum environments is still an open question. As quantum systems evolve, the volume and complexity of data generated by these systems will increase, demanding more sophisticated NLP models capable of handling large-scale data without compromising performance (Rahul et al., 2024).

The future of NLP for anomaly detection in quantum-aware cybersecurity lies in the development of hybrid models that combine NLP with quantum computing principles. These models could take advantage of quantum computing's power to process large datasets and solve optimization problems, while leveraging NLP's ability to detect subtle patterns and anomalies in textual data.

7.5 Summary

NLP has emerged as a powerful tool for anomaly detection in quantum-aware cybersecurity, offering the ability to analyze complex data and detect emerging threats in quantum environments. By integrating NLP with quantum technologies, cybersecurity systems can become more resilient to the challenges posed by quantum computing. However, there are still significant challenges to overcome in terms of data compatibility, model training, and scalability. Future research will likely focus on enhancing NLP models to handle quantum-specific data and developing hybrid approaches that leverage both classical and quantum computing capabilities for more effective anomaly detection.

8. NLP-BASED THREAT ACTOR PROFILING IN A QUANTUM WORLD

The increasing convergence of quantum computing and natural language processing (NLP) technologies presents significant opportunities and challenges for cybersecurity. As quantum computing continues to develop, its potential to reshape the landscape of threat actor profiling becomes more evident, particularly when integrated with advanced NLP techniques. This section explores how NLP-based threat actor profiling can be enhanced in the quantum computing era, focusing on the synergy between large language models (LLMs), quantum algorithms, and the identification of cyber threats.

8.1 Quantum Computing and Cybersecurity: The New Frontier

Quantum computing promises to disrupt conventional cryptographic systems and significantly impact security protocols across industries. As highlighted by Sodiya et al. (2024), the power of quantum computing lies in its ability to process vast amounts of data at unprecedented speeds, which can potentially outpace classical methods in areas such as encryption, decryption, and data mining. The advent of quantum algorithms introduces new possibilities for both attackers and defenders in the cybersecurity space. On one hand, quantum technologies could render traditional encryption mechanisms obsolete, but on the other hand, they also present novel opportunities for safeguarding digital assets through quantum-resistant security frameworks (Baseri et al., 2024).

The intersection of NLP and quantum computing offers an intriguing perspective on threat actor profiling. By leveraging quantum-enhanced NLP models, cybersecurity systems can more effectively analyze large volumes of text-based data, such as communication logs, social media interactions, and deep web content. These data sources provide valuable insights into the tactics, techniques, and procedures (TTPs) employed by threat actors, which can be used for profiling and predicting future attacks.

8.2 NLP and LLMs in Cybersecurity

NLP techniques, particularly LLMs such as GPT-2 and GPT-3, have been increasingly utilized in cybersecurity to detect and mitigate cyber threats. Jones et al. (2024) discuss the GPT-2 enhanced attack detection and defense method, which uses deep learning-based language models to identify and respond to zero-day threats. These models excel at understanding the nuances of human language, making them ideal candidates for analyzing textual data associated with threat actor activities.

In a quantum-enhanced world, the ability to harness quantum computing's power to accelerate LLM training and fine-tuning could lead to even more sophisticated models that are capable of detecting subtle patterns indicative of malicious intent.

LLMs can be trained to recognize various forms of cyber threats, such as phishing attacks, social engineering tactics, and advanced persistent threats (APTs). The integration of quantum computing could enhance the speed and efficiency of training these models, allowing for real-time threat detection and faster response times. As discussed by Gholami and Omar (2023), synthetic data can play a crucial role in training LLMs by providing diverse and comprehensive datasets for model evaluation. Quantum computing could further streamline this process by generating high-fidelity synthetic data that better mimics real-world scenarios, improving the model's performance in threat detection.

8.3 Quantum Threat Actor Profiling

Threat actor profiling involves the collection, analysis, and interpretation of data to construct detailed profiles of potential attackers. NLP techniques are essential in this process, as they enable the extraction of valuable intelligence from unstructured data sources. By leveraging quantum-enhanced LLMs, cybersecurity experts can gain deeper insights into the behaviors, motivations, and tactics of threat actors.

A key aspect of quantum-based threat actor profiling is the ability to process and analyze data at scale. Quantum computers can process vast datasets more efficiently than classical computers, allowing for the identification of patterns across large volumes of communication or digital footprints left by threat actors. This capability is particularly relevant in the context of cyber espionage, where adversaries may employ sophisticated techniques to remain undetected for long periods.

Quantum-enhanced NLP models can be used to analyze a wide range of data, from traditional textual logs to more complex data types such as multimedia content, including audio and video recordings. The integration of quantum computing allows for more robust and accurate analysis, enabling cybersecurity teams to track threat actor activities across multiple channels and predict potential future actions (Omar & Zangana, 2024). This predictive capability is invaluable in identifying emerging threats and preventing attacks before they materialize.

Threat actor profiling benefits immensely from NLP's ability to analyze unstructured text. The following workflow diagram showcases the steps involved in utilizing NLP for profiling, emphasizing the use of data sources, processing techniques, and actionable insights.

Figure 6. NLP in threat actor profiling workflow

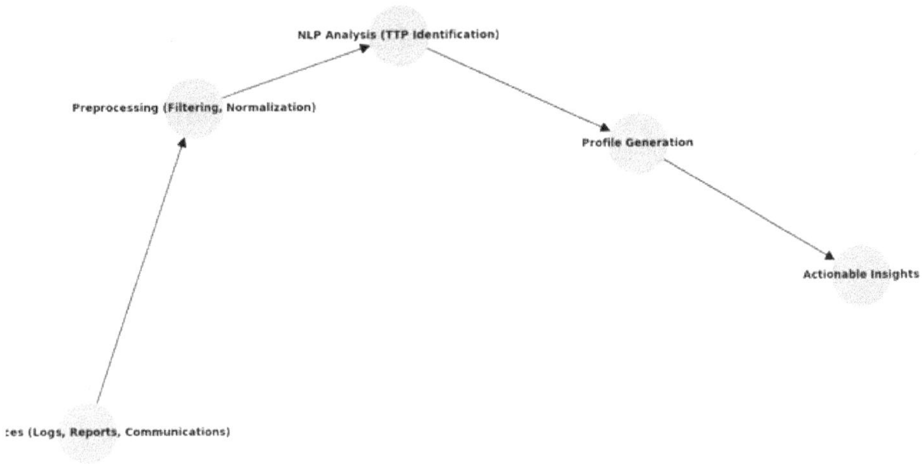

8.4 The Role of Large Language Models in Quantum-Aided Threat Actor Profiling

Large language models (LLMs) have already demonstrated their effectiveness in various cybersecurity applications, including malware detection, phishing prevention, and attack prediction (Jones et al., 2023). In the context of quantum-enhanced threat actor profiling, LLMs can be trained on vast amounts of data, including text, metadata, and even encrypted communications, to uncover hidden patterns associated with cyber attacks.

Incorporating quantum computing into this process enables more efficient training and real-time threat analysis. Quantum algorithms, such as Grover's algorithm for database searching and Shor's algorithm for factoring large numbers, can be used to enhance the speed and accuracy of LLMs. This makes it possible to analyze enormous datasets in a fraction of the time required by classical computing methods (Omar, 2024). As quantum computing matures, the ability to use quantum-enhanced LLMs for threat actor profiling will become a powerful tool for cybersecurity professionals.

8.5 Challenges and Future Directions

While the integration of quantum computing and NLP-based threat actor profiling holds great promise, several challenges must be addressed. One of the primary obstacles is the development of quantum-resistant algorithms that can withstand the potential threats posed by quantum computing. As noted by Baseri et al. (2024), the transition to quantum-safe encryption and authentication protocols will require significant investment and research.

Furthermore, the ethical implications of quantum-enhanced threat profiling must be carefully considered. The ability to analyze vast amounts of personal and sensitive data raises concerns about privacy and surveillance. It is essential to develop ethical frameworks and regulatory standards to govern the use of quantum-enhanced NLP models in cybersecurity (Omar & Zangana, 2025).

As quantum computing continues to evolve, future research will focus on optimizing NLP techniques for the quantum era, developing quantum-safe encryption methods, and addressing the ethical challenges associated with advanced threat actor profiling. By embracing these advancements, organizations can better protect themselves from the increasingly sophisticated cyber threats of the future.

8.6 Summary

The intersection of NLP and quantum computing presents a new frontier in cybersecurity, with significant potential for enhancing threat actor profiling. Quantum-enhanced NLP models can provide faster, more accurate, and scalable solutions for identifying and mitigating cyber threats. As quantum technologies advance, they will play a crucial role in shaping the future of cybersecurity, enabling more proactive and efficient defense mechanisms against evolving threat actors.

9. CHALLENGES AND LIMITATIONS OF NLP AND QUANTUM INTEGRATION

The integration of Quantum Computing (QC) and Natural Language Processing (NLP) presents both significant opportunities and formidable challenges. As quantum technologies evolve, the theoretical potential of harnessing quantum properties to enhance NLP tasks such as machine translation, sentiment analysis, and text generation is becoming more apparent. However, substantial hurdles remain in realizing these prospects in practical applications, especially concerning the scalability, reliability, and accessibility of quantum-enhanced NLP models.

9.1. Technical Challenges in Quantum Computing for NLP

One of the primary barriers to effective integration is the current stage of quantum computing technology. Quantum computing is still in its infancy, and practical quantum systems remain limited by issues such as quantum decoherence and noise, as well as the inability to scale the number of qubits effectively for large-scale computations (Baseri, Chouhan, & Ghorbani, 2024). Current quantum computers are not yet sufficiently robust or stable to handle the complex calculations required for NLP tasks. This results in slower processing times compared to classical computational models, making it impractical for immediate deployment in large-scale applications like real-time language translation or advanced sentiment analysis (Sodiya et al., 2024).

Furthermore, quantum algorithms for NLP, such as quantum-enhanced machine learning models, still require significant refinement. While quantum models like Quantum Support Vector Machines (QSVM) show promise, they are not yet fully optimized for linguistic data, which is inherently different from the numerical or binary data that quantum models are currently designed to handle (Rahul et al., 2024). Integrating NLP with quantum computing would require new models that can account for the structure and nuances of language, which introduces both conceptual and mathematical complexities.

9.2. Scalability and Efficiency Issues

As quantum systems advance, another challenge is the scalability of quantum-enhanced NLP. Scaling quantum processors to handle NLP tasks requires not only a greater number of qubits but also innovations in quantum error correction, which is vital for mitigating the effects of quantum noise (How & Cheah, 2023). Scaling quantum-enhanced NLP systems to practical sizes for real-world applications, such as processing large corpora of text or dealing with complex language generation tasks, remains an unsolved issue. The immense computational power that quantum computing promises is hindered by the current limitations in both quantum hardware and algorithms.

Moreover, even if scalability is addressed, the efficiency of quantum-NLP models remains a key limitation. Quantum computers would need to significantly outperform classical systems to justify their use, given that classical NLP models, powered by deep learning, are already highly efficient and capable of processing vast amounts of data in relatively short periods (Jones, Omar, Mohammed, Nobles, & Dawson, 2023). For quantum computing to offer a real advantage in NLP, it would need to deliver substantial improvements in processing speed and computational resource utilization, something that has yet to be fully demonstrated.

9.3. Integration with Existing NLP Infrastructure

Integrating quantum computing with existing NLP systems presents another substantial challenge. NLP today relies heavily on classical hardware and deep learning frameworks, such as TensorFlow and PyTorch, which are not compatible with quantum computing's unique hardware and processing paradigms (Omar & Zangana, 2025). Developing hybrid systems that effectively combine classical and quantum computing approaches will require new tools, APIs, and frameworks that can seamlessly integrate both technologies. This integration is still in its nascent stages, and the design of hybrid quantum-classical systems remains an open area of research (Khan et al., 2023).

Additionally, most of the tools developed for quantum NLP are not yet user-friendly or widely accessible, making them difficult to implement for practitioners in the field of NLP. There is a lack of standardized protocols for training and deploying quantum-enhanced NLP models, which creates a barrier for the widespread adoption of these technologies (Bishwas & Sen, 2024).

9.4. Quantum Data and Model Training Challenges

Training NLP models, particularly large models like GPT, requires enormous datasets and computational resources. While quantum computing holds the promise of enhancing training efficiency, the question of how to represent textual data effectively in quantum formats remains unresolved (Gholami & Omar, 2023). Quantum computers, as of now, are designed to work with quantum states rather than classical data representations, and translating textual data into a form that quantum systems can process poses significant challenges. This makes it difficult to leverage quantum computing for tasks such as large-scale language model training without substantial pre-processing of data.

Moreover, existing quantum algorithms for machine learning are still not capable of handling the large amounts of training data required for modern NLP models, such as GPT-3 or BERT (Gholami & Omar, 2024). Developing efficient quantum algorithms that can handle the massive datasets needed for state-of-the-art NLP models is one of the key hurdles in quantum NLP research.

9.5. Ethical and Security Implications

The integration of quantum computing into NLP also raises important ethical and security concerns. Quantum computers could potentially break many of the encryption methods that are currently used to secure sensitive data. This poses a serious threat to privacy and data security, particularly when applied to NLP tasks that involve personal or confidential information, such as customer service bots or healthcare applications (Sodiya et al., 2024).

Moreover, the use of quantum computing in NLP could lead to the development of more sophisticated AI-generated content, which could be used maliciously for misinformation campaigns or cyber-attacks (Omar & Zangana, 2024). As such, there is a need to develop robust frameworks that can ensure the ethical and secure use of quantum-enhanced NLP technologies.

9.6. Future Directions

Despite these challenges, the future of quantum computing in NLP holds immense potential. As quantum technologies mature, we may see the development of more efficient quantum algorithms for NLP tasks. This could lead to breakthroughs in machine translation, sentiment analysis, and even more complex tasks like automatic summarization and content generation (Metawei et al., 2022). However, achieving this vision will require substantial advances in both quantum computing and NLP research, as well as the development of new tools and frameworks that can bridge the gap between classical and quantum paradigms.

In conclusion, while the integration of quantum computing and NLP offers exciting possibilities, it is clear that numerous challenges remain. Addressing these challenges will require collaboration between researchers in quantum computing, machine learning, and NLP, as well as continued investment in quantum hardware, algorithms, and security protocols. With time and innovation, these challenges may eventually be overcome, paving the way for a new era of quantum-enhanced natural language processing.

10. FUTURE TRENDS IN NLP FOR CYBER THREAT INTELLIGENCE

Natural Language Processing (NLP) is poised to play a significant role in the future of Cyber Threat Intelligence (CTI), enhancing the efficiency, accuracy, and speed of threat detection, response, and mitigation. As cyber threats become increasingly sophisticated, NLP techniques, particularly those leveraging advanced models like Large Language Models (LLMs), are expected to be integral in addressing emerging challenges in cybersecurity. The future of NLP in CTI will be shaped by several key trends, which promise to revolutionize how security systems interpret, analyze, and respond to cyber threats.

10.1. Enhanced Threat Detection with LLMs

The future of CTI will see increased integration of LLMs to improve threat detection. These models are becoming more capable of understanding complex cyber threat data, including unstructured text, such as emails, logs, and reports, which are traditionally difficult to analyze. LLMs, such as GPT-based models, are expected to revolutionize the way zero-day threats are detected by offering real-time analysis and pattern recognition capabilities that go beyond the scope of traditional detection methods (Jones & Omar, 2024). These advancements will help organizations proactively identify potential threats, reducing response times and improving the overall security posture.

Furthermore, the ability of LLMs to generate synthetic data (Gholami & Omar, 2023) will enhance the training of cybersecurity models. By simulating various cyber-attack scenarios, LLMs can help fine-tune threat detection systems without the need for extensive real-world data, which might be scarce or difficult to obtain in some contexts.

10.2. Context-Aware Threat Intelligence

NLP's ability to interpret context within cybersecurity communications will be a critical trend in enhancing CTI. By analyzing the relationships between different threat indicators in large datasets, LLMs will help provide a deeper understanding of the context in which a threat emerges. This will be particularly useful in multi-vector attacks, where the attack surface is not immediately obvious, and traditional models may fail to detect subtle patterns across diverse data sources (Omar & Zangana, 2025).

The incorporation of context-aware systems will improve the accuracy of CTI, as threats can be better classified and responded to based on the nuances of the environment in which they occur. This approach will move beyond the detection of known threats to predicting and understanding the behavior of unknown threats.

10.3. Automated Response Systems

The automation of cybersecurity responses will be accelerated by NLP. Advanced NLP models can interpret threats and automatically trigger predefined responses, such as alerting security personnel or isolating infected systems. These capabilities will allow for quicker mitigation of cyberattacks, especially in high-speed environments like financial networks or cloud infrastructures (Hamza & Omar, 2013).

NLP models will be capable of generating threat reports, documenting attacks, and suggesting remediation actions. By analyzing historical data and correlating it with current trends, NLP will help security teams make better-informed decisions quickly, improving both response times and the effectiveness of mitigation strategies (Omar, 2022).

10.4. Threat Attribution and Intelligence Sharing

One of the most promising applications of NLP in CTI is its ability to enhance threat attribution and facilitate intelligence sharing across organizations. By analyzing large volumes of textual data from threat intelligence sources, LLMs can help identify patterns that indicate the origin or methods of an attack (Omar, 2021). This can be particularly important in cases of advanced persistent threats (APTs), where attackers disguise their intentions over long periods.

Additionally, NLP will streamline the process of sharing cyber threat intelligence among organizations and across sectors. By transforming complex technical jargon into standardized threat intelligence reports, NLP can bridge communication gaps between different security teams, enhancing collaboration and the collective response to threats (Huff et al., 2023).

10.5. Quantum Computing and NLP Integration in CTI

As quantum computing progresses, it will create new opportunities and challenges for cybersecurity. NLP combined with quantum computing could offer novel approaches to cryptographic methods and threat detection (Rahul et al., 2024). Quantum models could enable faster processing of complex threat intelligence data, providing unprecedented capabilities in anomaly detection and cryptographic analysis, which are crucial for securing quantum-resilient systems.

However, quantum technologies also pose a risk to traditional encryption methods, requiring the development of new, quantum-resistant protocols. NLP models will be critical in this transition, helping to identify vulnerabilities in existing systems and facilitating the adoption of more secure cryptographic techniques (Sodiya et al., 2024). Future CTI systems will need to leverage both quantum computing and NLP to stay ahead of the evolving threat landscape.

The future of NLP and quantum integration in cybersecurity holds immense promise. The following roadmap highlights upcoming advancements and research opportunities, illustrating how these technologies are expected to evolve and intersect over time.

Figure 7. Future trends in NLP and quantum integration

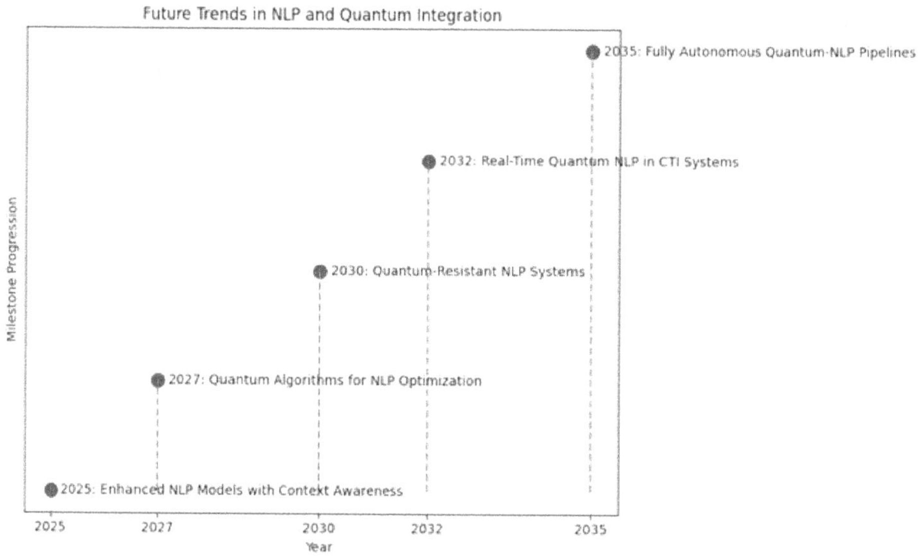

10.6. Adversarial NLP for Cyber Defense

Another emerging trend is the use of adversarial NLP techniques for strengthening cybersecurity defenses. Just as adversarial machine learning has been applied to deepen threat detection, adversarial NLP will be used to identify and combat attempts to manipulate automated systems using misleading or obfuscated language. This includes detecting phishing emails, fake news, and social engineering tactics that exploit human psychology to breach security systems (Zangana et al., 2024).

By training models to recognize deceptive language patterns, NLP systems will become more adept at protecting organizations from a wide array of linguistic attacks. This will be particularly useful in detecting phishing and other scams that target individuals or corporate networks.

10.7. Ethical and Privacy Considerations

As NLP continues to be integrated into CTI, ethical and privacy concerns will become increasingly important. The use of NLP in analyzing vast amounts of personal and organizational data must comply with data privacy regulations like GDPR and

CCPA. Future NLP models must be designed with strong privacy safeguards to ensure they do not inadvertently expose sensitive information (Mohammed et al., 2018).

Moreover, as NLP models become more powerful, the potential for misuse increases. Threat actors may exploit NLP capabilities to launch sophisticated attacks. Therefore, cybersecurity systems will need to implement countermeasures to prevent adversaries from utilizing NLP for malicious purposes (Zangana et al., 2025).

10.8 Summary

The future of NLP in Cyber Threat Intelligence is bright, with numerous potential advancements poised to enhance the accuracy, speed, and effectiveness of cybersecurity operations. By incorporating LLMs, quantum computing, and adversarial techniques, NLP will not only improve threat detection but also automate responses, enable better intelligence sharing, and address emerging threats in novel ways. As these technologies mature, they will transform how cybersecurity professionals defend against an increasingly sophisticated threat landscape.

11. ETHICAL CONSIDERATIONS IN NLP-DRIVEN CYBERSECURITY

The integration of Natural Language Processing (NLP) in cybersecurity has led to revolutionary advancements in automated threat detection, response systems, and vulnerability identification. However, these innovations come with significant ethical considerations that need careful examination to ensure that they serve the greater good without causing unintended harm. These considerations span data privacy, accountability, fairness, transparency, and the potential for misuse, among other issues.

11.1. Data Privacy and Consent

One of the most prominent ethical challenges in NLP-driven cybersecurity is the handling of sensitive data. As NLP models, such as large language models (LLMs), are trained on vast datasets that often contain sensitive personal, financial, or health-related information, ensuring the privacy of this data is of paramount importance. Without proper safeguards, NLP models might unintentionally expose or misuse personal data, violating privacy rights (Gholami & Omar, 2024). For example, data used for training these models must be anonymized to prevent the leakage of sensitive information, and explicit consent should be obtained from individuals whose data is used (Omar & Zangana, 2025). Failure to address these concerns could undermine public trust in these technologies, especially in sectors like healthcare and banking, where data confidentiality is critical (Huff et al., 2023).

11.2. Bias and Fairness in Model Training

Another significant ethical concern is the potential for biases in NLP-driven cybersecurity systems. These models are often trained on large, diverse datasets that may include inherent biases, such as racial, gender, or socio-economic biases, which can be perpetuated by the models (Jones et al., 2023). In cybersecurity, this bias could result in discriminatory practices, such as false positives or negatives in threat detection based on demographic factors, ultimately affecting certain groups unfairly. Developers and researchers must actively seek to minimize these biases by using more representative datasets and employing techniques that promote fairness (Jones & Omar, 2024).

11.3. Accountability and Transparency

As NLP models become more sophisticated, the opacity of their decision-making processes presents a challenge in terms of accountability. In cybersecurity, where actions taken by automated systems can have serious consequences, it is crucial that these systems remain explainable and transparent. For instance, when an NLP model flags an entity as a cybersecurity threat, stakeholders need to understand why the decision was made to determine whether it was appropriate or not (Omar & Zangana, 2024). This transparency is essential not only for accountability but also for fostering trust in the technology, especially when these systems are used in critical sectors like healthcare and finance, as discussed by Huff et al. (2023).

11.4. Potential for Misuse

The dual-use nature of NLP technologies poses another ethical dilemma. While NLP can be employed for good in cybersecurity, such as detecting vulnerabilities or preventing cyberattacks, it can also be misused for malicious purposes. For example, attackers could use NLP models to create more sophisticated phishing attacks, manipulate text-based communication, or even generate convincing fake news or misinformation, thereby exploiting the vulnerabilities of individuals and organizations (Zangana, 2024). This misuse of NLP technology for malicious purposes necessitates robust regulation and guidelines to ensure that these systems are used ethically and responsibly.

11.5. Impacts on Employment

The growing reliance on NLP-driven automation in cybersecurity also raises concerns about the potential displacement of human workers. While these technologies improve efficiency, they could lead to job losses in traditional cybersecurity roles, especially those involved in manual threat detection and analysis (Mohammed, Omar, & Nguyen, 2018). Ethical considerations must extend to the broader societal impacts, including the need for reskilling and upskilling workers to adapt to the changing technological landscape. As highlighted by Gholami and Omar (2023), the implementation of synthetic data to enhance the training of these models could have unintended effects on the workforce, which must be addressed with adequate workforce planning.

11.6. The Role of AI Governance and Regulation

To address these ethical challenges, robust AI governance frameworks are essential. Governments, regulatory bodies, and the private sector must collaborate to create clear policies that govern the ethical use of NLP in cybersecurity. This includes setting standards for data privacy, transparency, fairness, and accountability, as well as creating mechanisms for auditing and overseeing AI-driven cybersecurity systems (Omar, 2024). Such frameworks would ensure that NLP models are developed and deployed with respect to ethical principles and societal values.

11.7. Balancing Security with Civil Liberties

The deployment of NLP in cybersecurity must also balance the need for enhanced security with the protection of civil liberties. Overly aggressive monitoring systems that use NLP could infringe upon individuals' rights to privacy and free speech, particularly when used in surveillance or content moderation systems. Ethical use of NLP in these contexts requires a careful assessment of potential risks and the implementation of checks and balances to prevent the erosion of civil freedoms (Omar & Zangana, 2025). These issues are especially pertinent in areas like social media monitoring and government surveillance.

11.8 Summary

Ethical considerations in NLP-driven cybersecurity are multifaceted and complex, encompassing issues of data privacy, fairness, transparency, accountability, and the potential for misuse. As NLP technologies continue to evolve and become integral to cybersecurity strategies, it is imperative that developers, policymakers, and researchers work together to ensure that these systems are used ethically and responsibly. By fostering a framework of ethical AI governance, we can harness the full potential of NLP for cybersecurity while mitigating its risks and ensuring that it benefits society as a whole.

12. CASE STUDIES AND PRACTICAL APPLICATIONS

The integration of large language models (LLMs), quantum computing, and advanced cybersecurity methods into real-world scenarios demonstrates the significant potential of these technologies to address emerging security challenges across various industries. This section discusses several case studies and practical applications, illustrating how these advanced technologies are shaping the future of cybersecurity.

12.1. Synthetic Data and Large Language Models in Cybersecurity

A significant advancement in cybersecurity has been the use of synthetic data to enhance the efficiency and performance of large language models (LLMs). Gholami and Omar (2023) highlight that synthetic data generation can be leveraged to augment training datasets, improving the ability of models to detect complex cyber threats in environments where real-world data is sparse or sensitive. By training LLMs with synthetic data, cybersecurity solutions can adapt to previously unseen attack vectors and rapidly evolving malware patterns, offering a promising approach to combating sophisticated cyber threats.

12.2. Cloud Computing Security

The vulnerabilities associated with cloud computing platforms are a critical concern for businesses and organizations. Hamza and Omar (2013) provide insights into the abuse and nefarious use of cloud computing, particularly in relation to security breaches. In their study, they emphasize the need for robust security protocols to mitigate risks associated with data storage, processing, and access in the cloud. This case study highlights how businesses must adopt cloud-specific security measures, such as encryption and multi-factor authentication, to safeguard sensitive data from potential exploits.

12.3. Cybersecurity Threats in the Biotechnology and Healthcare Sectors

Cybersecurity in the biotechnology and healthcare industries is a high-priority concern, given the sensitivity of medical and research data. Huff et al. (2023) examine management practices for mitigating cybersecurity threats within biotechnology companies, laboratories, and healthcare research organizations. Their findings demonstrate how organizations can adopt AI-driven threat detection systems, implement cybersecurity training programs for employees, and enforce regulatory compliance to protect critical healthcare data. The integration of machine learning algorithms has shown promise in identifying and neutralizing zero-day threats and advanced persistent threats (APTs) that are commonly directed at these sectors.

12.4. Zero-Day Threat Detection Using GPT-2

A revolutionary method for addressing cybersecurity threats involves the application of GPT-2 in attack detection and defense strategies. Jones and Omar (2024) introduce the GPT-2 Enhanced Attack Detection and Defense (GEADD) method, which utilizes the capabilities of GPT-2 to analyze network traffic and detect zero-day attacks. By processing large volumes of network data, GPT-2 is able to identify patterns indicative of an attack, even in the absence of prior knowledge about the specific exploit. This case study highlights how LLMs can play a pivotal role in dynamic, real-time cybersecurity defenses.

12.5. Wireless Sensor Network Security

In the context of Internet of Things (IoT) and wireless sensor networks, securing the communication channels against cyber-attacks is paramount. Mohammed, Omar, and Nguyen (2018) investigate approaches to detecting and preventing wormhole attacks in wireless sensor networks. Their research demonstrates the effectiveness of machine learning-based anomaly detection systems in identifying malicious nodes within sensor networks. This technology is particularly useful in critical infrastructure monitoring, where maintaining the integrity and confidentiality of sensor data is vital for operational safety.

12.6. Leveraging Quantum Computing for Cybersecurity

Quantum computing presents both opportunities and challenges for cybersecurity, particularly in encryption and decryption processes. Sodiya et al. (2024) review the potential impact of quantum computing on cybersecurity, highlighting how quantum algorithms can be used to enhance the strength of encryption mechanisms. On the other hand, the threat posed by quantum computers to classical cryptographic techniques remains a significant concern. The development of quantum-resistant algorithms is therefore critical for preparing industries to protect their digital assets against the quantum threat. This technology's potential applications in securing communications and data storage across industries are vast, ranging from finance to healthcare and beyond.

12.7. AI in Malware Detection

Artificial intelligence (AI), specifically deep learning models, has revolutionized malware detection techniques. Omar (2024) discusses a paradigm shift in malware detection through optimized convolutional neural networks (CNNs). By utilizing CNNs, cybersecurity systems can analyze executable files and identify potentially malicious code with high accuracy. These AI-driven approaches have proven to be more effective than traditional signature-based detection methods, which often fail to detect novel threats. The integration of AI into cybersecurity workflows enables faster and more accurate responses to cyber threats.

12.8. Blockchain for Cybersecurity and Forensic Applications

Blockchain technology has also found its place in cybersecurity, particularly in the realm of digital forensics. Zangana (2024) explores the application of blockchain-based timestamping tools in enhancing the integrity and transparency of digital evidence. Blockchain's immutable ledger ensures that data, once recorded, cannot be tampered with, making it an ideal solution for maintaining the integrity of forensic data in legal and investigative contexts. The ability to trace data provenance and secure evidence in a decentralized manner strengthens the reliability of digital forensics investigations.

12.9. LLMs for IoT Malware Detection

The use of LLMs in detecting IoT malware is an emerging area of research. Omar, Zangana, and Mohammed (2024) present a comparative analysis of BERT and GPT-2 models for IoT malware detection. Their research demonstrates that LLMs can analyze network traffic from IoT devices and identify unusual patterns that may indicate malware activity. By leveraging pre-trained models such as BERT and GPT-2, cybersecurity systems can identify zero-day vulnerabilities in IoT ecosystems, where traditional methods often fall short due to the sheer scale and variety of devices involved.

12.10. Quantum-Resistant Security Framework

As quantum computing evolves, the need for quantum-resistant security frameworks has become more pressing. Bishwas and Sen (2024) outline a strategic roadmap for preparing industries for the quantum threat, emphasizing the need for new cryptographic protocols that can withstand quantum attacks. This case study highlights the critical importance of developing quantum-resistant encryption methods to safeguard sensitive data in a post-quantum world. Governments and private enterprises must invest in research and development to ensure that their security infrastructure remains secure in the face of quantum advancements.

12.11 Summary

The case studies and practical applications discussed in this section illustrate the diverse and growing impact of cutting-edge technologies like LLMs, quantum computing, and AI on the field of cybersecurity. From enhancing malware detection to revolutionizing attack defense mechanisms, these technologies offer innovative solutions to some of the most pressing security challenges of the modern era. As these technologies continue to evolve, their integration into cybersecurity practices will play a pivotal role in safeguarding digital assets across industries, from healthcare and finance to IoT and beyond.

13. CONCLUSION: PIONEERING NLP FOR CTI IN A QUANTUM-DRIVEN ERA

As the digital landscape continues to evolve, the intersection of Natural Language Processing (NLP) and Cyber Threat Intelligence (CTI) is becoming increasingly significant, especially in the context of a rapidly advancing quantum-driven era. NLP offers powerful tools to extract actionable intelligence from vast amounts of unstructured textual data, such as threat reports, security blogs, and incident response logs. This capability enhances the effectiveness of CTI by enabling organizations to quickly identify emerging threats and respond to them proactively.

The future of CTI is inherently tied to the rise of quantum computing, which promises to revolutionize the way cyber threats are detected, analyzed, and mitigated. Quantum computing's potential to solve complex problems exponentially faster than classical computing opens new frontiers for cybersecurity. As quantum technologies mature, they will introduce new challenges, particularly in cryptography and data security. However, they will also provide unprecedented opportunities to strengthen defenses against increasingly sophisticated cyber threats.

In this quantum-driven landscape, the combination of NLP and quantum computing could create synergies that significantly enhance threat detection and prediction capabilities. By leveraging NLP, organizations can parse through massive amounts of data and extract patterns and insights that were previously hidden or too time-consuming to uncover. Quantum algorithms, when applied to these insights, could exponentially increase the speed and accuracy of threat identification, allowing for more dynamic and adaptive cybersecurity strategies.

Looking ahead, the integration of NLP with quantum-enhanced CTI systems will likely enable the development of real-time, self-learning defense mechanisms capable of anticipating and neutralizing threats before they can cause harm. As organizations continue to embrace these technologies, the role of cybersecurity professionals will shift toward overseeing more complex, automated systems that leverage the power of NLP and quantum computing.

Ultimately, pioneering NLP for CTI in a quantum-driven era presents both exciting possibilities and significant challenges. By embracing these cutting-edge technologies, we can usher in a new era of cybersecurity—one that is more resilient, intelligent, and capable of keeping pace with the ever-evolving threat landscape.

REFERENCES

Agrawal, K., & Aggarwal, M. Building Efficient Smart Contract for Healthcare 4.0. In *Blockchain for Healthcare 4.0* (pp. 94-123). CRC Press.

AL-Refaey. M. R., Tyagi, A. K., AL-Ghamdi, A. S. A. M., & Kukreja, S. (Eds.). (2024). *Topics in Artificial Intelligence Applied to Industry 4.0*. John Wiley & Sons.

Baseri, Y., Chouhan, V., & Ghorbani, A. (2024). Cybersecurity in the Quantum Era: Assessing the Impact of Quantum Computing on Infrastructure. *arXiv preprint arXiv:2404.10659.*

Bishwas, A. K., & Sen, M. (2024). Strategic Roadmap for Quantum-Resistant Security: A Framework for Preparing Industries for the Quantum Threat. *arXiv preprint arXiv:2411.09995.*

Block, R. S. S. (2024). The 2024 quantum advantage blueprint: Where quantum outpaces classical.

Bush, S. F., Challener, W. A., & Mantelet, G. (2021). A perspective on industrial quantum networks. *AVS Quantum Science*, 3(3), 030501. DOI: 10.1116/5.0051881

Exchange, Q. R. K. Towards a Verifiably Secure Quantum-Resistant Key Exchange in IKEv2.

Gholami, S., & Omar, M. (2023). Does Synthetic Data Make Large Language Models More Efficient? *arXiv preprint arXiv:2310.07830.*

Gholami, S., & Omar, M. (2024). Can a student large language model perform as well as its teacher? In *Innovations, Securities, and Case Studies Across Healthcare, Business, and Technology* (pp. 122-139). IGI Global. DOI: 10.4018/979-8-3693-1906-2.ch007

Hamza, Y. A., & Omar, M. D. (2013). Cloud computing security: Abuse and nefarious use of cloud computing. *International Journal of Computer Engineering Research*, 3(6), 22–27.

How, M. L., & Cheah, S. M. (2023). Business Renaissance: Opportunities and challenges at the dawn of the Quantum Computing Era. *Businesses*, 3(4), 585–605. DOI: 10.3390/businesses3040036

Huff, A. J., Burrell, D. N., Nobles, C., Richardson, K., Wright, J. B., Burton, S. L., Jones, A. J., Springs, D., Omar, M., & Brown-Jackson, K. L. (2023). Management Practices for Mitigating Cybersecurity Threats to Biotechnology Companies, Laboratories, and Healthcare Research Organizations. In *Applied Research Approaches to Technology, Healthcare, and Business* (pp. 1-12). IGI Global.

Jones, R., & Omar, M. (2024). Revolutionizing Cybersecurity: The GPT-2 Enhanced Attack Detection and Defense (GEADD) Method for Zero-Day Threats. *International Journal of Informatics* [INJIISCOM]. *Information System and Computer Engineering*, 5(2), 178–191.

Jones, R., Omar, M., Mohammed, D., Nobles, C., & Dawson, M. (2023). Harnessing the Speed and Accuracy of Machine Learning to Advance Cybersecurity. In *2023 Congress in Computer Science, Computer Engineering, & Applied Computing (CSCE)* (pp. 418-421). IEEE. DOI: 10.1109/CSCE60160.2023.00074

Khan, A. A., Akbar, M. A., Ahmad, A., Fahmideh, M., Shameem, M., Lahtinen, V., . . . Mikkonen, T. (2023, July). Agile practices for quantum software development: practitioners' perspectives. In *2023 IEEE international conference on quantum software (QSW)* (pp. 9-20). IEEE.

Lougovski, P., Parekh, O., Broz, J., Byrd, M., Chembo, Y., de Jong, W. A., . . . Svore, K. M. (2023). *Position Papers for the ASCR Workshop on Basic Research Needs in Quantum Computing and Networking*. USDOE Office of Science (SC), Advanced Scientific Computing Research (ASCR).

Madni, A. F., Shah, M. A., & Al-Naeem, M. (2024). An Investigation of Scalability in EHRs using Healthcare 4.0 and Blockchain. *International Journal of Advanced Computer Science and Applications*, 15(5). Advance online publication. DOI: 10.14569/IJACSA.2024.0150548

Metawei, M. A., Eldeeb, H., Nassar, S. M., & Taher, M. (2022). Quantum Computing Meets Artificial Intelligence: Innovations and Challenges. In *Handbook on Artificial Intelligence-Empowered Applied Software Engineering: VOL. 1: Novel Methodologies to Engineering Smart Software Systems* (pp. 303–338). Springer International Publishing. DOI: 10.1007/978-3-031-08202-3_12

Mohamed, N., & Ahmed, A. A. (2024, June). AI in Combatting Man-in-the-Middle Attacks: A Comprehensive Review. In *2024 15th International Conference on Computing Communication and Networking Technologies (ICCCNT)* (pp. 1-6). IEEE. DOI: 10.1109/ICCCNT61001.2024.10725789

Mohammed, D., Omar, M., & Nguyen, V. (2018). Wireless sensor network security: Approaches to detecting and avoiding wormhole attacks. *Journal of Research in Business. Economics and Management*, 10(2), 1860–1864.

Nguyen, V., Mohammed, D., Omar, M., & Banisakher, M. (2018). The Effects of the FCC Net Neutrality Repeal on Security and Privacy. [IJHIoT]. *International Journal of Hyperconnectivity and the Internet of Things*, 2(2), 21–29. DOI: 10.4018/IJHIoT.2018070102

Omar, M. (2021). New insights into database security: An effective and integrated approach for applying access control mechanisms and cryptographic concepts in Microsoft Access environments.

Omar, M. (2022). *Machine Learning for Cybersecurity: Innovative Deep Learning Solutions*. Springer Brief. https://link.springer.com/book/978303115

Omar, M. (2024). From Attack to Defense: Strengthening DNN Text Classification Against Adversarial Examples. In *Innovations, Securities, and Case Studies Across Healthcare, Business, and Technology* (pp. 174-195). IGI Global.

Omar, M. (2024). Revolutionizing Malware Detection: A Paradigm Shift Through Optimized Convolutional Neural Networks. In *Innovations, Securities, and Case Studies Across Healthcare, Business, and Technology* (pp. 196-220). IGI Global. DOI: 10.4018/979-8-3693-1906-2.ch011

Omar, M., & Zangana, H. M. (Eds.). (2024). *Redefining Security With Cyber AI*. IGI Global., DOI: 10.4018/979-8-3693-6517-5

Omar, M., & Zangana, H. M. (Eds.). (2025). *Application of Large Language Models (LLMs) for Software Vulnerability Detection*. IGI Global., DOI: 10.4018/979-8-3693-9311-6

Omar, M., Zangana, H. M., Al-Karaki, J. N., & Mohammed, D. (2024). Harnessing LLMs for IoT malware detection: A comparative analysis of BERT and GPT-2. In *Proceedings of the 8th International Symposium on Multidisciplinary Studies and Innovative Technologies (ISMSIT)* (pp. 1-6). Ankara, Turkiye. https://doi.org/DOI: 10.1109/ISMSIT63511.2024.10757249

Omar, M., Zangana, H. M., & Mohammed, D. (Eds.). (2025). *Integrating Artificial Intelligence in Cybersecurity and Forensic Practices*. IGI Global., DOI: 10.4018/979-8-3373-0588-2

Perron, J. K., DeLeone, C., Sharif, S., Carter, T., Grossman, J. M., Passante, G., & Sack, J. (2021). Quantum undergraduate education and scientific training. *arXiv preprint arXiv:2109.13850*.

Qualters, I., Taylor, A. J., & Hagberg, A. A. (2019). *IS&T Computing Overview* (No. LA-UR-19-22567). Los Alamos National Lab.(LANL), Los Alamos, NM (United States).

Rahul, R., Geetha, S., Priyatharsini, S., Mehata, K., Sundaresan Perumal, T., Ethiraj, N., & Sendilvelan, S. (2024). Cybersecurity Issues and Challenges in Quantum Computing. *Topics in Artificial Intelligence Applied to Industry*, 4(0), 203–221. DOI: 10.1002/9781394216147.ch11

Ramachandran, D., Naqi, S. M., Perumal, G., & Abbas, Q. (2023). DLTN-LOSP: A Novel Deep-Linear-Transition-Network-Based Resource Allocation Model with the Logic Overhead Security Protocol for Cloud Systems. *Sensors (Basel)*, 23(20), 8448. DOI: 10.3390/s23208448 PMID: 37896541

Seskir, Z. C. (2019). *Current state of quantum information technologies in Turkey* (Master's thesis, Middle East Technical University).

Singh, N. B. *Quantum Mechanics in Drug Discovery*. NB Singh.

Sodiya, E. O., Umoga, U. J., Amoo, O. O., & Atadoga, A. (2024). Quantum computing and its potential impact on US cybersecurity: A review: Scrutinizing the challenges and opportunities presented by quantum technologies in safeguarding digital assets. *Global Journal of Engineering and Technology Advances, 18*(2), 049-064.

Wright, J., Dawson, M. E.Jr, & Omar, M. (2012). Cyber security and mobile threats: The need for antivirus applications for smartphones. *Journal of Information Systems Technology and Planning*, 5(14), 40–60.

Zangana, H. M. (2024). Exploring Blockchain-Based Timestamping Tools: A Comprehensive Review. *Redefining Security With Cyber AI*, 92-110.

Zangana, H. M. (2024). Exploring the Landscape of Website Vulnerability Scanners: A Comprehensive Review and Comparative Analysis. *Redefining Security With Cyber AI*, 111-129.

Zangana, H. M., Mohammed, A. K., Sallow, A. B., & Sallow, Z. B. (2024). Cybernetic Deception: Unraveling the Layers of Email Phishing Threats. [INJURATECH]. *International Journal of Research and Applied Technology*, 4(1), 35–47.

Zangana, H. M., & Mohammed, D. (2025). Foundations of Large Language Models in Software Vulnerability Detection. In Omar, M., & Zangana, H. (Eds.), *Application of Large Language Models (LLMs) for Software Vulnerability Detection* (pp. 41–74). IGI Global., DOI: 10.4018/979-8-3693-9311-6.ch002

Zangana, H. M., & Mustafa, F. M. (2025). Image Denoising Techniques for Cybersecurity and Forensic Applications: AI-Driven Approaches. In Omar, M., Zangana, H., & Mohammed, D. (Eds.), *Integrating Artificial Intelligence in Cybersecurity and Forensic Practices* (pp. 117–142). IGI Global Scientific Publishing., DOI: 10.4018/979-8-3373-0588-2.ch005

Zangana, H. M., & Omar, M. (2020). Threats, Attacks, and Mitigations of Smartphone Security. *Academic Journal of Nawroz University*, 9(4), 324–332. DOI: 10.25007/ajnu.v9n4a989

Zangana, H. M., & Omar, M. (2025). Harnessing the Power of Large Language Models for Cybersecurity: Applications, Challenges, and Future Directions. In Omar, M., & Zangana, H. (Eds.), *Application of Large Language Models (LLMs) for Software Vulnerability Detection* (pp. 1–40). IGI Global., DOI: 10.4018/979-8-3693-9311-6.ch001

Zangana, H. M., Omar, M., Al-Karaki, J. N., & Mohammed, D. (2024). Comprehensive Review and Analysis of Network Firewall Rule Analyzers: Enhancing Security Posture and Efficiency. *Redefining Security With Cyber AI*, 15-36.

Zangana, H. M., Omar, M., & Mohammed, D. (2025). Introduction to Artificial Intelligence in Cybersecurity and Forensic Science. In Omar, M., Zangana, H., & Mohammed, D. (Eds.), *Integrating Artificial Intelligence in Cybersecurity and Forensic Practices* (pp. 1–24). IGI Global Scientific Publishing., DOI: 10.4018/979-8-3373-0588-2.ch001

Chapter 12
The Future of Cybersecurity Integrating LLMs With Quantum Computing for Autonomous Defense Systems

Yara Shamoo
https://orcid.org/0009-0004-2459-0807
Saint Leo University, USA

ABSTRACT

The integration of large language models (LLMs) with quantum computing represents a groundbreaking approach to addressing cybersecurity challenges in an increasingly interconnected digital landscape. This chapter explores the potential of combining LLMs' advanced natural language processing capabilities with the unparalleled computational power of quantum systems to create autonomous defense mechanisms. These systems aim to identify, predict, and neutralize threats in real-time, significantly enhancing cybersecurity frameworks. The chapter delves into key technical advancements, potential applications, and challenges, including the ethical and operational implications of deploying such hybrid technologies. By examining case studies and emerging trends, this chapter provides a comprehensive vision of the future of cybersecurity powered by LLMs and quantum computing.

DOI: 10.4018/979-8-3373-1102-9.ch012

1. INTRODUCTION

The rapid evolution of technology has catalyzed unprecedented advances across industries, yet it has also intensified vulnerabilities in digital systems, particularly in cybersecurity and data privacy. This chapter examines these critical areas, integrating insights from emerging technologies such as quantum computing, artificial intelligence (AI), and blockchain. By leveraging these tools, we can revolutionize threat detection, enhance system security, and establish robust defenses against increasingly sophisticated cyber threats.

1.1 Background and Motivation

The advent of quantum computing and AI has reshaped traditional paradigms in cybersecurity. Quantum computing, for instance, holds the potential to disrupt conventional encryption systems, as noted by Sodiya et al. (2024), who highlighted quantum computing's dual role as both a risk and an opportunity. Meanwhile, AI-driven approaches, such as Large Language Models (LLMs), have demonstrated remarkable capabilities in detecting vulnerabilities and automating cybersecurity processes (Omar & Zangana, 2025). However, these technologies bring challenges, including ethical considerations and resource demands (Gholami & Omar, 2023).

1.2 Current Challenges in Cybersecurity

The cybersecurity landscape is fraught with challenges stemming from advanced persistent threats (APTs) and the exploitation of emerging technologies. Hamza and Omar (2013) emphasized the abuse and nefarious use of cloud computing, which remains a persistent concern. Furthermore, Jones et al. (2024) introduced the GPT-2 Enhanced Attack Detection and Defense (GEADD) method as an innovative solution to counter zero-day threats, demonstrating the potential of AI in this domain.

Additionally, blockchain-based solutions have been proposed to address time-stamping and data integrity issues (Zangana, 2024). These developments highlight the pressing need for multidisciplinary strategies to counteract evolving threats effectively.

1.3 Quantum Computing in Cybersecurity

Quantum computing has introduced a paradigm shift in how we approach encryption and data security. Bishwas and Sen (2024) provided a roadmap for developing quantum-resistant security frameworks, emphasizing the urgency of preparing industries for the quantum threat. Similarly, Baseri et al. (2024) assessed the implications of quantum advancements on critical infrastructure, underscoring the need for proactive measures.

Quantum technologies also enable new possibilities in secure communication. Exchange (2024) proposed a verifiably secure quantum-resistant key exchange protocol, setting the stage for resilient cryptographic solutions.

1.4 Artificial Intelligence in Threat Detection

Artificial Intelligence has emerged as a cornerstone of modern cybersecurity strategies. Omar (2024) demonstrated how optimized convolutional neural networks can revolutionize malware detection. Meanwhile, Huff et al. (2023) underscored the role of management practices in mitigating cybersecurity risks, particularly in sensitive sectors such as healthcare and biotechnology.

LLMs, such as BERT and GPT-2, have been pivotal in advancing malware detection techniques. Omar et al. (2024) conducted a comparative analysis of these models, revealing their strengths and limitations in IoT malware detection. Additionally, Zangana and Mustafa (2025) explored AI-driven image denoising techniques, showcasing their applications in forensic science and cybersecurity.

1.5 Integration of Emerging Technologies

The integration of blockchain, AI, and quantum computing offers a promising avenue for enhancing cybersecurity frameworks. Agrawal and Aggarwal (2024) discussed how smart contracts can revolutionize Healthcare 4.0, while Mohamed and Ahmed (2024) highlighted AI's role in combatting man-in-the-middle attacks. Such interdisciplinary approaches are critical to addressing the multifaceted challenges of cybersecurity.

1.6 Structure of the Chapter

This chapter delves into the technical, ethical, and practical implications of emerging technologies in cybersecurity. Section 2 provides a detailed exploration of quantum computing and its potential impact on security protocols. Section 3 examines AI-driven methodologies, including LLMs, for vulnerability detection and mitigation. Section 4 discusses blockchain's role in enhancing data integrity and trustworthiness. Finally, the chapter concludes with recommendations for integrating these technologies into a cohesive cybersecurity framework, aligning with insights from the works of Omar and Zangana (2024, 2025).

By synthesizing insights from diverse research domains, this chapter aims to contribute to the development of robust, adaptive, and future-proof cybersecurity systems.

2. THE CONVERGENCE OF LLMS AND QUANTUM COMPUTING

The integration of **Large Language Models (LLMs)** with **Quantum Computing (QC)** represents a groundbreaking paradigm shift in computing and data analysis. While LLMs such as OpenAI's GPT and Google's Bard revolutionize natural language processing and AI-based solutions, QC offers unparalleled computational capabilities through quantum mechanics principles. The confluence of these two technologies is poised to reshape domains such as cybersecurity, data analytics, and advanced simulations.

2.1 Enhancing LLMs with Quantum Computing

Quantum computing introduces exponential speedup in solving specific computational problems, which complements the extensive data processing capabilities of LLMs. According to **Seskir (2019)**, QC is already transforming industries by solving problems previously deemed intractable for classical computing. By leveraging quantum algorithms, LLMs can process vast datasets more efficiently, particularly in tasks requiring high-dimensional optimizations.

The integration of Large Language Models (LLMs) and quantum computing represents a transformative step in the evolution of computing. The following flowchart illustrates the key steps and components involved in this integration, showcasing how these technologies complement each other to advance fields such as cybersecurity, data analytics, and natural language processing.

Figure 1. The integration of LLMs and quantum computing

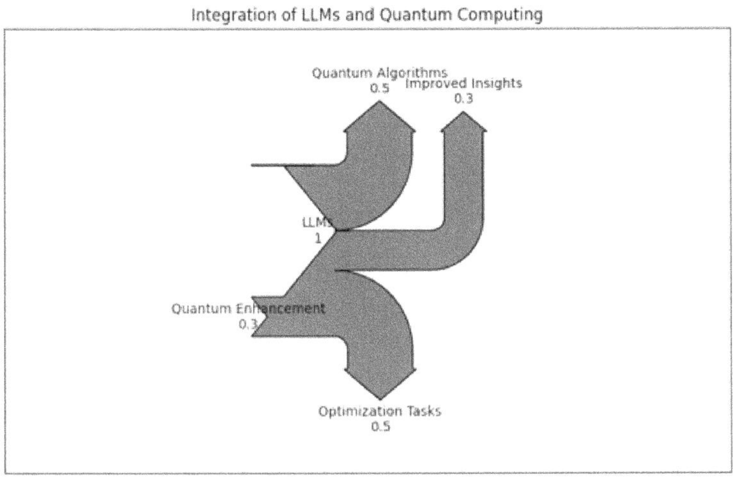

For example, quantum-enhanced LLMs could significantly improve in fields like software vulnerability detection, as explored by **Zangana and Omar (2025)**. Their work emphasizes the importance of integrating advanced computation to enhance the accuracy and efficiency of AI models in detecting vulnerabilities.

2.2 Quantum-Resilient Architectures in LLMs

The synergy also extends to building quantum-resilient AI architectures. As discussed by **Bishwas and Sen (2024)**, preparing for the quantum threat involves developing cryptographic and AI models that withstand quantum attacks. LLMs enhanced with QC can also better simulate and test such architectures, making them indispensable for forward-looking cybersecurity solutions.

2.3 Applications in Cybersecurity and Forensic Science

The intersection of QC and LLMs has profound implications for **cybersecurity**. Quantum algorithms can solve complex cryptographic problems, enabling more robust and dynamic threat detection models. The work of **Omar and Zangana (2025)** highlights the integration of LLMs in cybersecurity forensics, a field where quantum computing's precision can significantly enhance malware analysis and response times.

Quantum-based LLMs can also process synthetic data to augment training datasets, as explored by **Gholami and Omar (2023)**. This approach addresses data scarcity issues while enhancing model generalization and performance.

2.4 Challenges and Ethical Implications

Despite its potential, the convergence of LLMs and QC poses challenges. The ethical concerns surrounding AI, including biases in data processing and the potential misuse of quantum-accelerated AI for malicious purposes, must be addressed. Studies such as **Hamza and Omar (2013)** on cloud abuse offer a cautionary perspective on how emerging technologies can be exploited if not adequately safeguarded.

Moreover, integrating QC with LLMs requires a robust framework for scalability and optimization, as outlined in **Madni, Shah, and Al-Naeem (2024)**. Their research emphasizes the importance of balancing computational efficiency with ethical responsibility in implementing such advanced systems.

2.5 Future Directions

1. **Optimized Resource Allocation**: Leveraging quantum linear transition networks, as suggested by **Ramachandran et al. (2023)**, can enhance the deployment of quantum-based LLMs in real-world applications.
2. **Cross-Disciplinary Research**: The fusion of QC and LLMs necessitates collaboration across quantum mechanics, computer science, and AI, as noted by **Metawei et al. (2022)** in their exploration of interdisciplinary innovations.
3. **Cybersecurity and Quantum Synergy**: Continued research, like that of **Omar et al. (2025)**, should focus on integrating LLMs with quantum tools to bolster threat detection and forensic accuracy.

2.6 Summary

The convergence of quantum computing and LLMs represents a transformative step in AI's evolution. By addressing computational bottlenecks, enhancing data security, and enabling scalable solutions, this intersection promises unprecedented advancements. However, it also necessitates rigorous ethical oversight and continuous innovation to realize its full potential responsibly.

3. AUTONOMOUS DEFENSE SYSTEMS: CORE PRINCIPLES AND FRAMEWORK

Autonomous defense systems (ADS) represent a transformative paradigm in cybersecurity, leveraging artificial intelligence (AI), machine learning (ML), and large language models (LLMs) to proactively identify, mitigate, and neutralize threats. By integrating advanced technologies such as blockchain, quantum computing, and AI-driven automation, these systems aim to create a robust cybersecurity framework capable of adapting to the dynamic threat landscape (Omar & Zangana, 2024).

3.1 Core Principles of Autonomous Defense Systems

1. **Proactivity Over Reactivity**

Traditional defense systems often rely on reactive measures, addressing threats after detection. In contrast, ADS emphasizes proactive threat prevention through predictive analytics and anomaly detection. For example, the use of LLMs like GPT-2 for zero-day attack detection showcases how predictive models can enhance cybersecurity by analyzing patterns and anticipating potential vulnerabilities (Jones & Omar, 2024). Furthermore, AI-driven approaches, such as convolutional neural networks optimized for malware detection, reinforce this proactive principle (Omar, 2024).

2. **Adaptability and Learning**

ADS leverages AI's ability to learn from evolving threats. Systems like the GEADD method integrate ML models to continuously adapt to new attack vectors, making them highly resilient against sophisticated threats (Jones & Omar, 2024). This adaptability is further enhanced through synthetic data generation, which improves the efficiency of LLMs in real-time threat analysis (Gholami & Omar, 2023).

3. **Integrated Security Architectures**

By combining multiple technologies, ADS ensures a comprehensive defense mechanism. For instance, blockchain-based timestamping tools provide tamper-proof records for cyber events, adding an extra layer of security (Zangana, 2024). Similarly, integrating quantum-resistant protocols, such as those explored in foundational research on quantum networks, strengthens ADS against future quantum-based threats (Bush et al., 2021).

4. **Automation and Scalability**

Automation in ADS minimizes human intervention, enabling rapid response to cyber incidents. Technologies like automated rule analyzers for network firewalls demonstrate how ADS can efficiently manage and analyze complex data sets to enhance security posture (Zangana et al., 2024). Moreover, scalability is crucial for deploying ADS across diverse environments, including cloud computing and IoT ecosystems (Hamza & Omar, 2013; Omar, Zangana, & Mohammed, 2025).

Autonomous Defense Systems (ADS) tackle a variety of cybersecurity threats, ranging from zero-day vulnerabilities to advanced persistent threats (APTs). The chart below highlights the prevalence of key threats that ADS are designed to address, providing context for their importance in modern cybersecurity strategies.

Figure 2. Key cybersecurity threats addressed by ADS

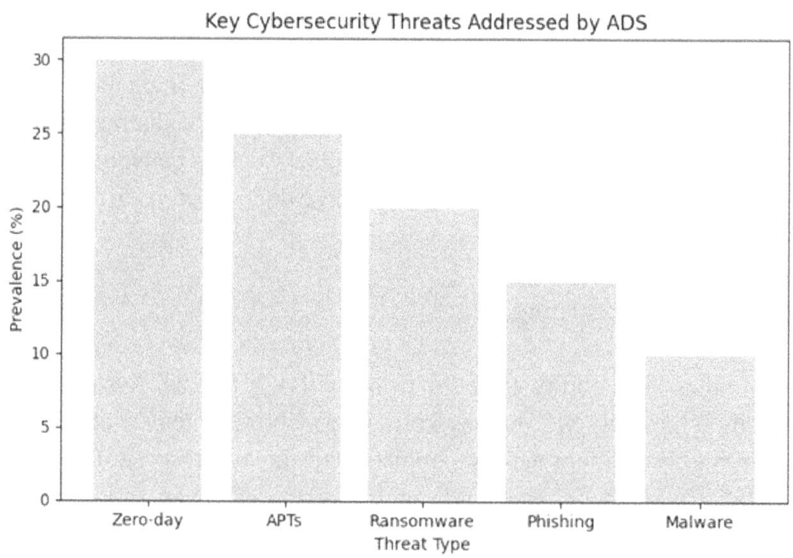

3.2 Framework for Autonomous Defense Systems

1. **Threat Detection Layer**

This layer focuses on real-time monitoring and anomaly detection using AI and ML. Systems like BERT and GPT-2 have been successfully applied to detect malware in IoT environments, showcasing the effectiveness of LLMs in identifying sophisticated cyber threats (Omar, Zangana, & Mohammed, 2024).

2. **Response and Mitigation Layer**

Upon detection, the response layer activates mitigation strategies such as isolating affected systems, neutralizing threats, and patching vulnerabilities. For instance, DLTN-LOSP protocols utilize deep-linear transition networks to secure cloud systems efficiently, showcasing advanced resource allocation models (Ramachandran et al., 2023).

3. **Continuous Learning and Evolution**

The learning layer uses feedback from previous incidents to refine its defense mechanisms. Advances in LLMs have enabled systems to process vast amounts of cybersecurity data, identify emerging trends, and improve their defensive capabilities (Zangana & Omar, 2025).

4. **Quantum-Resistant Mechanisms**

As quantum computing advances, ADS must incorporate quantum-resistant cryptography to safeguard against potential quantum threats. Recent studies emphasize the importance of developing frameworks to prepare industries for these challenges (Bishwas & Sen, 2024).

3.3 Challenges and Opportunities

While ADS holds significant promise, it faces challenges such as the ethical implications of autonomous decision-making (Mohamed & Ahmed, 2024) and the potential misuse of AI for adversarial attacks (Omar, 2024). However, the integration of innovative technologies like quantum computing and AI presents unprecedented opportunities for advancing cybersecurity (Rahul et al., 2024).

3.4 Summary

Autonomous defense systems are at the forefront of modern cybersecurity, offering a comprehensive and adaptive framework to counter emerging threats. By leveraging cutting-edge technologies and adhering to core principles such as proactivity, adaptability, and integration, ADS promises a resilient future for digital security.

4. REAL-TIME THREAT DETECTION AND RESPONSE

In an era where cyber threats are growing in complexity and frequency, the ability to detect and respond to threats in real time has become a cornerstone of effective cybersecurity strategies. This section explores the emerging technologies, frameworks, and methodologies enabling organizations to enhance their real-time threat detection and response capabilities.

4.1 Evolution of Real-Time Threat Detection

Real-time threat detection has evolved significantly with advancements in artificial intelligence (AI) and machine learning (ML). Traditional methods relied heavily on signature-based detection, which required predefined patterns to identify malicious activity. These approaches, although effective against known threats, struggle against sophisticated, zero-day attacks (Jones & Omar, 2024). In response, systems now leverage AI-driven anomaly detection models capable of identifying deviations from normal network behavior without predefined signatures (Zangana & Omar, 2020).

The framework for real-time threat detection integrates several cutting-edge technologies, such as AI-driven anomaly detection and wireless sensor networks. The following diagram provides an overview of this framework, illustrating the interaction between detection, analysis, and response systems.

Figure 3. Real-Time threat detection framework

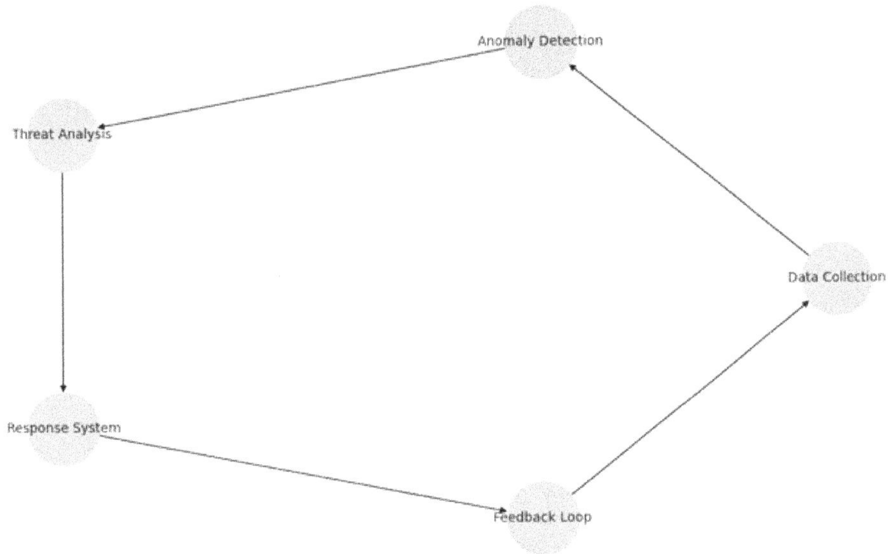

4.2 Role of Large Language Models in Threat Detection

Large Language Models (LLMs), such as GPT and BERT, are increasingly being integrated into cybersecurity systems to enhance threat detection capabilities. LLMs analyze vast amounts of log data, identifying patterns and correlations that might otherwise go unnoticed. For example, the GEADD method employs GPT-2 for detecting zero-day threats, demonstrating remarkable accuracy and speed (Jones & Omar, 2024). Furthermore, the use of synthetic data to train these models has been shown to improve their efficiency and scalability, making them more adaptable to diverse security challenges (Gholami & Omar, 2023).

4.3 Technologies Enabling Real-Time Detection

Real-time detection systems are supported by various cutting-edge technologies:

- **Wireless Sensor Networks (WSNs):** WSNs play a crucial role in monitoring environmental and system variables, providing timely alerts for potential threats. Robust methods for detecting and avoiding wormhole attacks in WSNs have been proposed to maintain their integrity (Mohammed, Omar, & Nguyen, 2018).

- **Quantum Computing:** Although still in its infancy, quantum computing presents opportunities for developing real-time systems capable of processing complex cybersecurity tasks at unprecedented speeds. The potential impact of quantum technologies on cybersecurity has been a subject of extensive review (Sodiya et al., 2024; Baseri, Chouhan, & Ghorbani, 2024).

4.4 Real-Time Incident Response

Once threats are detected, prompt and effective response mechanisms are crucial. AI-driven systems automate many aspects of incident response, from isolating affected systems to applying corrective measures. The integration of AI with traditional forensic tools has enhanced response times and minimized the impact of breaches (Omar, Zangana, & Mohammed, 2025).

4.5 Challenges and Future Directions

Despite significant progress, challenges remain in real-time threat detection and response. High false positive rates, the adaptability of adversaries, and the computational demands of real-time systems are critical issues. Addressing these challenges requires:

1. **Enhanced Collaboration:** Sharing threat intelligence across sectors can improve detection accuracy and timeliness (Wright, Dawson Jr, & Omar, 2012).
2. **Innovative Frameworks:** The exploration of blockchain-based timestamping tools to secure incident logs and enhance system accountability is a promising avenue (Zangana, 2024).
3. **Quantum-Resistant Algorithms:** Preparing for the quantum threat involves developing algorithms and systems resilient to quantum-based attacks (Bishwas & Sen, 2024).

4.6 Summary

The integration of AI, LLMs, and quantum technologies into real-time threat detection and response systems represents a transformative shift in cybersecurity. As these technologies mature, they hold the potential to provide organizations with unparalleled capabilities to detect and neutralize threats swiftly and effectively, securing critical infrastructure in an increasingly digital world.

5. CRYPTOGRAPHIC ADVANCES WITH LLM AND QUANTUM INTEGRATION

The integration of Large Language Models (LLMs) with quantum technologies is redefining the cryptographic landscape by addressing challenges posed by quantum computing to conventional encryption systems. This section delves into the interplay between these advancements and the promise they hold for developing robust, quantum-resistant cryptographic methods.

5.1 The Quantum Threat to Classical Cryptography

The advent of quantum computing poses significant risks to classical cryptographic systems, particularly those based on public-key cryptography, such as RSA and ECC (Elliptic Curve Cryptography). These systems, which rely on the computational difficulty of factoring large integers or solving discrete logarithm problems, are vulnerable to algorithms like Shor's, which can efficiently solve these problems on quantum computers (Sodiya et al., 2024; Bishwas & Sen, 2024).

Efforts to mitigate these threats include the development of quantum-resistant algorithms under the umbrella of post-quantum cryptography. However, challenges remain in ensuring their practical implementation and widespread adoption (Rahul et al., 2024; Baseri et al., 2024).

The urgency of developing quantum-safe cryptographic solutions has led to significant growth in research and implementation efforts. The graph below illustrates the number of quantum-safe cryptographic protocols developed over the past decade, highlighting the industry's proactive stance on this pressing issue.

Figure 4. Growth of Quantum-Safe cryptography

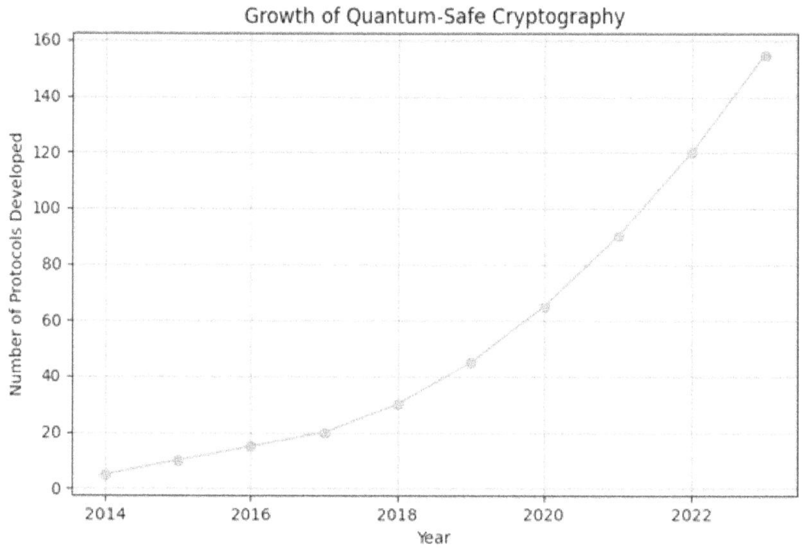

5.2 Enhancing Cryptographic Resilience with LLMs

Large Language Models (LLMs) offer innovative solutions in cryptographic resilience. These models can analyze and generate patterns in vast datasets, aiding in the design and evaluation of cryptographic algorithms. For instance, LLMs have been employed to simulate and optimize quantum-resistant protocols, thereby enhancing their efficiency and reliability (Omar & Zangana, 2025).

LLMs also play a critical role in detecting vulnerabilities in cryptographic systems. By analyzing codebases and configurations, these models can identify weak points that may be exploited by attackers, as demonstrated in recent research on vulnerability detection (Zangana & Mustafa, 2025; Omar et al., 2025).

5.3 LLM and Quantum Synergies in Cryptographic Research

The synergy between LLMs and quantum computing has opened new avenues for cryptographic research. This collaboration has facilitated advancements in quantum key distribution (QKD), enabling secure communication channels that are theoretically immune to quantum attacks (Exchange, 2024). Additionally, LLMs have been instrumental in optimizing the protocols and infrastructure required for QKD implementation (Lougovski et al., 2023).

Quantum technologies also enhance the performance of LLMs by leveraging quantum-enhanced data processing capabilities. This integration enables faster and more accurate simulations of cryptographic algorithms, which are crucial for addressing the evolving cybersecurity landscape (Bush et al., 2021).

5.4 Applications and Case Studies

- **Post-Quantum Cryptographic Algorithms:** The integration of LLMs with quantum simulations has been explored to enhance the development of lattice-based cryptographic systems, which are considered promising candidates for post-quantum standards (Madni et al., 2024).
- **Zero-Day Vulnerability Detection:**Jones and Omar (2024) presented the GPT-2 Enhanced Attack Detection and Defense (GEADD) method, leveraging LLMs to detect zero-day threats, a crucial aspect of maintaining cryptographic integrity in evolving quantum computing landscapes.
- **Wireless Sensor Networks (WSNs):** Cryptographic protocols for WSNs have been optimized using machine learning approaches, highlighting the potential of LLM-quantum integration for securing IoT ecosystems (Mohammed et al., 2018).

5.5 Challenges and Future Directions

While the potential of LLM-quantum integration is immense, significant challenges remain. Key issues include the scalability of quantum systems, the energy demands of LLM training, and the need for standardized benchmarks to evaluate cryptographic resilience (Khan et al., 2023; How & Cheah, 2023).

Future research should focus on the following:

1. **Efficient Quantum-Language Integration:** Developing frameworks to seamlessly integrate quantum algorithms with LLM functionalities.
2. **Enhanced Training Techniques:** Leveraging synthetic data to train LLMs for cryptographic applications, as explored by Gholami and Omar (2023, 2024).
3. **Ethical Considerations:** Addressing ethical implications in deploying LLMs for cryptographic and security purposes (Zangana & Omar, 2020).

5.6 Summary

The convergence of LLMs and quantum computing represents a paradigm shift in cryptographic research. By harnessing the strengths of these technologies, researchers and practitioners can develop robust cryptographic solutions to counter the challenges posed by quantum advancements. This integrated approach underscores the need for interdisciplinary collaboration and continuous innovation to secure digital ecosystems in the quantum era.

6. ENHANCING ADAPTIVE SECURITY WITH LLM-QUANTUM SYNERGIES

The integration of Large Language Models (LLMs) and quantum computing technologies heralds a transformative era in adaptive security, pushing the boundaries of detection, prevention, and mitigation capabilities against evolving cyber threats. This synergy leverages the computational prowess of quantum systems with the contextual and semantic intelligence of LLMs to address the limitations of traditional cybersecurity frameworks.

6.1 The Convergence of LLMs and Quantum Computing

The rapid advancements in quantum computing, with its unparalleled ability to process and analyze vast datasets simultaneously, provide an ideal foundation for enhancing the performance of LLMs in security contexts. Quantum computing's ability to solve complex optimization problems and perform high-dimensional vector calculations significantly augments the efficiency of LLMs in identifying anomalous patterns indicative of threats (Sodiya et al., 2024; Baseri et al., 2024).

6.2 Addressing Zero-Day Threats with Quantum-Language Models

The detection of zero-day vulnerabilities has historically posed challenges due to their novel nature. The GPT-2 Enhanced Attack Detection and Defense (GEADD) method exemplifies how LLMs can effectively identify such threats through their ability to recognize subtle variations in code and patterns that deviate from baseline behavior (Jones & Omar, 2024). When coupled with quantum-powered anomaly detection algorithms, this approach could revolutionize defenses against zero-day exploits.

6.3 Quantum Resilience and Adaptive Learning

Quantum-enhanced adaptive learning frameworks can empower LLMs to anticipate and respond to cyberattacks proactively. For instance, leveraging quantum neural networks for LLM fine-tuning can expedite the analysis of malicious activities across distributed environments, as demonstrated by studies on wireless sensor network security (Mohammed et al., 2018). Furthermore, quantum systems' resistance to classical attacks enhances the reliability of adaptive security mechanisms (Rahul et al., 2024).

6.4 Applications in Network and IoT Security

In network security, the integration of quantum and LLM-based methodologies has shown promise in fortifying defenses against sophisticated attacks such as wormhole and man-in-the-middle attacks (Mohammed et al., 2018; Mohamed & Ahmed, 2024). For IoT systems, quantum-assisted LLMs have demonstrated exceptional performance in malware detection, significantly improving upon classical methods (Omar et al., 2024).

6.5 Ethical and Practical Considerations

Despite their transformative potential, the integration of LLMs and quantum technologies raises ethical concerns regarding data privacy and algorithmic fairness (Zangana & Omar, 2025). Ensuring transparency and accountability in deploying such hybrid systems is imperative to maintain trust and compliance with regulatory standards.

6.6 Future Directions

The roadmap for harnessing LLM-Quantum synergies includes addressing the scalability challenges in quantum systems (Madni et al., 2024) and advancing LLM training protocols with synthetic data to improve efficiency (Gholami & Omar, 2023). Additionally, developing industry-specific applications, such as blockchain-secured healthcare systems, showcases the potential for quantum-driven innovations in diverse domains (Agrawal & Aggarwal, 2024).

6.7 Summary

The fusion of LLMs and quantum computing offers an unprecedented opportunity to redefine adaptive security. By integrating the semantic intelligence of LLMs with the computational supremacy of quantum systems, organizations can achieve robust, proactive, and scalable defenses against the ever-evolving cyber threat landscape.

7. ETHICAL AND GOVERNANCE CHALLENGES

The rapid evolution of technologies, including Artificial Intelligence (AI), Quantum Computing, and the integration of Large Language Models (LLMs), presents unparalleled opportunities in cybersecurity. However, these advancements also bring ethical and governance challenges that require immediate attention.

7.1. Privacy Concerns and Data Governance

As LLMs like GPT and BERT are utilized in cybersecurity, they rely on vast amounts of data for training and operations. This creates significant privacy risks, especially concerning sensitive user data. Ethical frameworks for data handling are essential to ensure that organizations respect user privacy while achieving technological advancements. The role of data governance mechanisms in mitigating misuse of personal data is highlighted by Mohamed et al. (2024) in their review of AI approaches in combating cybersecurity threats. Furthermore, Wright et al. (2012) underscore the importance of antivirus applications to address data breaches in mobile platforms, emphasizing a need for robust governance.

7.2. Bias in AI and LLMs

Bias in AI algorithms is a critical ethical issue. Gholami and Omar (2023) address how synthetic data can reduce biases in LLMs, but caution that synthetic data itself can introduce inaccuracies. This raises governance questions about the oversight and accountability of AI-driven cybersecurity tools. Properly auditing these models for fairness and equity becomes a pivotal governance challenge.

7.3. Quantum Computing and Ethical Implications

The advent of quantum computing poses ethical questions related to its dual-use potential. Sodiya et al. (2024) argue that while quantum technologies offer robust cybersecurity solutions, they simultaneously enable threats such as breaking traditional cryptographic methods. Governance frameworks must ensure these technologies are used responsibly. The works of Baseri et al. (2024) and Bishwas and Sen (2024) propose strategies for preparing industries to tackle quantum threats effectively.

7.4. Security in the Internet of Things (IoT)

IoT environments are particularly vulnerable due to the interconnectedness of devices. As Omar, Zangana, and Mohammed (2024) demonstrate, leveraging LLMs for IoT malware detection enhances security. However, this comes with the ethical challenge of ensuring transparency in AI decision-making processes, as outlined by Ramachandran et al. (2023). Establishing governance standards for AI transparency is crucial in these applications.

7.5. Accountability in Cybersecurity Solutions

The integration of AI and LLMs into cybersecurity brings the question of accountability to the forefront. When an AI-driven tool fails, determining accountability can be challenging. Huff et al. (2023) emphasize that clear management practices are vital for mitigating cybersecurity risks, especially in sensitive sectors like biotechnology. Ethical governance should include mechanisms to trace and address failures in AI systems.

7.6. Cybersecurity in Healthcare and Critical Infrastructure

The use of AI in healthcare cybersecurity raises additional ethical considerations. For instance, Agrawal and Aggarwal (2024) explore how blockchain can secure healthcare data but caution against over-reliance on technology at the expense of human oversight. Governance in these sectors must prioritize patient safety alongside technological adoption.

7.7. Regulatory Challenges

The global nature of cybersecurity threats necessitates international regulatory collaboration. As highlighted by Nguyen et al. (2018), disparities in regulatory standards can leave gaps in security, especially with the repeal of net neutrality policies. Comprehensive governance structures must bridge these gaps to ensure consistent cybersecurity practices across borders.

7.8. Challenges in Education and Workforce Development

The rapid pace of technological advancement demands a skilled workforce. Perron et al. (2021) stress the importance of education in quantum computing to prepare future professionals. However, ethical questions arise regarding equitable access to such education, which governance frameworks must address to prevent exacerbating existing inequalities.

7.9. Transparency and Trust in AI-Driven Cybersecurity

Transparency in AI decision-making is critical for building trust. Zangana and Omar (2025) discuss the role of transparency in enhancing trust in LLMs for cybersecurity. Governance mechanisms should mandate clear documentation of AI processes and establish guidelines for user consent in data-driven cybersecurity applications.

7.10. Sustainability Concerns

Finally, the environmental impact of computationally intensive technologies like AI and quantum computing cannot be ignored. Omar (2021) highlights integrated approaches for database security that optimize computational resources. Governance frameworks must balance technological advancements with sustainability to minimize their carbon footprint.

8. BARRIERS TO ADOPTION

The adoption of advanced technologies, particularly those involving artificial intelligence (AI) and cybersecurity applications, faces numerous barriers. These challenges range from technical limitations to organizational, economic, and ethical considerations. Below, these barriers are discussed in detail with insights from the provided references.

8.1 Technical Barriers

One of the most significant barriers to the adoption of AI in cybersecurity is the technical complexity of integrating large language models (LLMs) and other AI tools into existing systems. As highlighted by **Gholami and Omar (2023)**, the efficiency of LLMs can be enhanced through synthetic data; however, creating and maintaining such data sets requires specialized expertise. Similarly, implementing secure AI systems that can counter zero-day threats, as explored by **Jones and Omar (2024)**, requires robust algorithms and significant computational resources, often unavailable to smaller organizations.

Additionally, concerns about data privacy and security persist, particularly in sensitive sectors such as healthcare and finance. For example, **Omar et al. (2024)** underscore the challenges of protecting IoT systems against malware using LLMs, which involve processing large volumes of sensitive data, raising concerns about data leakage or misuse.

8.2 Organizational Challenges

Organizations often face internal resistance to adopting new technologies. The lack of awareness and training among employees regarding the potential of AI and quantum technologies in cybersecurity creates a barrier to acceptance. **Wright et al. (2012)** emphasize the importance of equipping users with the knowledge and tools needed to address mobile threats, a principle equally applicable to AI-driven cybersecurity solutions.

Moreover, legacy systems that are incompatible with modern AI technologies impede progress. Integrating new solutions into existing infrastructures without disrupting operations is a daunting task, as noted by **Nguyen et al. (2018)** in the context of wireless sensor networks and cloud computing.

8.3 Economic Constraints

High implementation costs are another major barrier. AI-driven cybersecurity tools, especially those incorporating quantum technologies, demand substantial investments in both hardware and software. **Hamza and Omar (2013)** argue that smaller organizations often lack the financial resources to invest in advanced technologies, leaving them vulnerable to cyberattacks.

Quantum computing, while promising, introduces additional economic challenges. The cost of developing quantum-resistant security systems, as discussed by **Sodiya et al. (2024)**, and the need for specialized quantum networks outlined by **Bush et al. (2021)**, make widespread adoption economically unfeasible in the near term for many organizations.

8.4 Ethical and Legal Concerns

The ethical implications of AI adoption in cybersecurity also pose barriers. **Zangana and Omar (2025)** highlight the importance of addressing bias in AI models, which can lead to unfair or discriminatory outcomes in vulnerability detection.

Furthermore, ensuring compliance with legal and regulatory frameworks adds complexity. **Mohamed and Ahmed (2024)** discuss the regulatory challenges associated with combating sophisticated attacks, such as man-in-the-middle attacks, using AI.

The repeal of net neutrality, as analyzed by **Nguyen et al. (2018)**, also underscores the broader policy challenges impacting technology adoption. Regulatory environments that fail to evolve alongside technological advancements can hinder innovation and create legal uncertainties for organizations adopting cutting-edge solutions.

8.5 Cybersecurity-Specific Barriers

In cybersecurity, adversaries continuously develop new attack vectors, requiring constant updates to AI models. **Zangana et al. (2024)** explore how website vulnerability scanners need regular updates to address emerging threats effectively. Similarly, maintaining the accuracy and relevance of firewall rule analyzers, as reviewed by **Zangana et al. (2024)**, is a significant ongoing challenge.

Furthermore, organizations may face threats that exploit the very technologies they aim to adopt. For instance, **Rahul et al. (2024)** discuss the potential cybersecurity risks posed by quantum computing, which can render existing encryption methods obsolete.

8.6 Recommendations for Overcoming Barriers

To mitigate these barriers, organizations should prioritize research and development, invest in employee training, and collaborate with academic and industry partners to create cost-effective, scalable solutions. Initiatives such as those proposed by **Omar and Zangana (2024)** in leveraging AI for security applications highlight the importance of interdisciplinary approaches to overcome these challenges.

9. FUTURE OPPORTUNITIES AND EMERGING USE CASES

The rapid advancement of artificial intelligence (AI) and machine learning (ML), particularly in the context of cybersecurity, is unlocking a range of exciting opportunities. With large language models (LLMs), quantum computing, and deep learning technologies at the forefront, the future of cybersecurity is poised for transformative change. These developments present new possibilities not only for improving existing systems but also for addressing emerging threats in novel ways.

9.1 Large Language Models in Cybersecurity

LLMs, such as GPT-2, BERT, and their derivatives, are beginning to play an increasingly vital role in cybersecurity, particularly in the detection and prevention of advanced threats. The ability of LLMs to process vast amounts of unstructured data, identify patterns, and generate predictions makes them invaluable for real-time attack detection and automated defense mechanisms. The evolution of these models has been accelerated by advancements in training techniques and the availability of large, diverse datasets, as discussed by Gholami and Omar (2023), who explored the potential of synthetic data to enhance LLM performance.

In cybersecurity, LLMs are being used for tasks ranging from threat intelligence gathering to vulnerability assessment. Tools such as the GPT-2 Enhanced Attack Detection and Defense (GEADD) method, discussed by Jones and Omar (2024), exemplify the integration of LLMs into zero-day threat mitigation. The future opportunities for LLMs in cybersecurity are vast, particularly in the areas of predictive analytics, automated incident response, and the development of advanced security protocols. As AI models continue to improve, they will be able to offer more sophisticated threat detection capabilities, reducing the time to identify and neutralize threats.

9.2 Quantum Computing's Role in Cybersecurity

Quantum computing, while still in its nascent stages, presents both challenges and opportunities for cybersecurity. The ability of quantum computers to solve complex problems at speeds unattainable by classical computers opens new avenues for securing digital infrastructures. Quantum-resistant cryptography is one area where this technology will have a profound impact, offering protection against quantum attacks that threaten traditional cryptographic methods (Sodiya et al., 2024). Quantum computing could also enable more efficient and secure methods for conducting large-scale threat simulations, creating more robust cybersecurity defenses.

However, the rise of quantum computing also introduces vulnerabilities, particularly in areas like encryption and key exchange protocols. As highlighted by Baseri et al. (2024), industries must prepare for the quantum threat by adopting quantum-resistant security frameworks. In the coming years, cybersecurity professionals will need to adapt to these changes by integrating quantum-safe algorithms and preparing for the eventuality of quantum-based attacks.

9.3 -Driven Vulnerability Detection and Mitigation

The application of AI in vulnerability detection is rapidly evolving, with LLMs leading the charge in enhancing software vulnerability identification and mitigation. As evidenced by Zangana and Omar (2025), LLMs are increasingly being harnessed to improve the accuracy and efficiency of software vulnerability detection, allowing for faster identification of potential exploits and more comprehensive vulnerability management strategies. The integration of LLMs with traditional security tools, such as firewalls and antivirus programs, offers a more holistic approach to defending against both known and unknown threats.

AI-driven vulnerability detection is also being extended to new domains, such as Internet of Things (IoT) security. Omar et al. (2024) conducted a comparative analysis of BERT and GPT-2 for IoT malware detection, showcasing the potential of these models to identify malicious activity in connected devices. The future of AI in vulnerability detection will likely include more specialized models tailored to particular industries, such as healthcare or finance, where cybersecurity requirements are more stringent.

9.4 The Convergence of AI and Blockchain

Blockchain technology has already made significant strides in enhancing the security and transparency of transactions. However, its integration with AI and machine learning could push the boundaries even further, particularly in the realm of digital forensics and security auditing. Zangana and Zangana (2024) explore how blockchain-based timestamping tools can be used in conjunction with AI to provide secure, tamper-proof logs of events, which can be crucial for investigative purposes. The convergence of AI and blockchain presents significant opportunities for enhancing the integrity and security of data storage systems, preventing fraud, and improving compliance with privacy regulations.

9.5 Predictive Analytics and Cyber Threat Forecasting

As cybersecurity threats become more sophisticated, the need for predictive analytics and threat forecasting is becoming increasingly critical. The ability to predict the nature and timing of potential attacks before they occur could be a game-changer in the field. Machine learning models can be trained to analyze historical attack data and use that information to forecast future threats. This approach could be further enhanced by quantum computing, which could process complex data sets in real-time to identify emerging attack vectors before they materialize (Wright et al., 2012).

The future of predictive analytics in cybersecurity lies in developing systems that can autonomously learn and adapt to evolving threats. As algorithms improve, they will become better at detecting subtle, low-probability events that indicate a potential breach, providing organizations with advanced warning before an attack takes place.

9.6 Ethical Considerations and Regulatory Frameworks

With the rapid expansion of AI, machine learning, and quantum computing in cybersecurity, ethical considerations and regulatory frameworks will play an increasingly critical role. The use of AI in decision-making processes, particularly in automated defense systems, raises questions about accountability and the potential for unintended consequences. Ensuring that these technologies are used responsibly and ethically will require collaboration between governments, industry leaders, and academia to develop regulations that safeguard against misuse while fostering innovation.

In the realm of quantum computing, the need for global standards on quantum-safe encryption and privacy protection will become more pressing. Researchers like Baseri et al. (2024) have called for the creation of frameworks to ensure that quantum technologies do not compromise the security of digital infrastructures. Similarly, Sodiya et al. (2024) highlight the importance of preparing cybersecurity professionals for the quantum era through education and training.

9.7 Summary

The future of cybersecurity is intrinsically linked to the ongoing developments in AI, machine learning, and quantum computing. These technologies are not only revolutionizing the way we approach security but also presenting new challenges that require innovative solutions. By leveraging LLMs, quantum computing, and AI-driven models, cybersecurity professionals will be equipped to handle the complexities of emerging threats. As these technologies continue to evolve, the intersection of AI and cybersecurity will offer unprecedented opportunities for enhancing digital safety and resilience in the years to come.

10. CONCLUSION

The integration of quantum computing into cybersecurity is poised to redefine the landscape of digital defense strategies. As quantum technologies continue to advance, they present both unprecedented opportunities and significant challenges for the security industry. The potential for quantum computers to break traditional cryptographic protocols necessitates a paradigm shift in the way cybersecurity systems are designed, prompting the need for new quantum-resistant algorithms and encryption methods.

Moreover, the application of artificial intelligence, particularly Large Language Models (LLMs), has become increasingly relevant in the fight against cyber threats. LLMs offer innovative solutions for vulnerability detection, malware identification, and attack prediction, providing valuable tools for securing systems against evolving threats. As these models evolve, their integration with quantum technologies promises to further enhance the capability to anticipate and mitigate cyber risks.

Despite the excitement surrounding these advancements, several hurdles remain. Issues such as scalability, the complexity of developing secure quantum algorithms, and the need for standardization in the cybersecurity space must be addressed. Moreover, the transition to quantum-resistant systems requires substantial investment in research and development, alongside collaboration between academia, industry, and government organizations.

The future of cybersecurity will likely be shaped by the convergence of quantum computing, AI, and other emerging technologies. To prepare for this future, it is crucial to foster a proactive approach that involves not only developing quantum-resistant encryption techniques but also equipping organizations with the knowledge and tools necessary to defend against next-generation cyber threats. The continued exploration of these technologies, along with the advancement of secure quantum networking and blockchain systems, will play a pivotal role in safeguarding digital infrastructures against increasingly sophisticated attacks.

Ultimately, the cybersecurity community must remain agile and adaptable, embracing these new technologies while staying vigilant to the risks they may present. The ongoing research and collaboration in this area will determine how well we can secure our digital future in the quantum era.

REFERENCES

Agrawal, K., & Aggarwal, M. Building Efficient Smart Contract for Healthcare 4.0. In *Blockchain for Healthcare 4.0* (pp. 94-123). CRC Press.

AL-Refaey. M. R., Tyagi, A. K., AL-Ghamdi, A. S. A. M., & Kukreja, S. (Eds.). (2024). *Topics in Artificial Intelligence Applied to Industry 4.0*. John Wiley & Sons.

Baseri, Y., Chouhan, V., & Ghorbani, A. (2024). Cybersecurity in the Quantum Era: Assessing the Impact of Quantum Computing on Infrastructure. *arXiv preprint arXiv:2404.10659*.

Bishwas, A. K., & Sen, M. (2024). Strategic Roadmap for Quantum-Resistant Security: A Framework for Preparing Industries for the Quantum Threat. *arXiv preprint arXiv:2411.09995*.

Block, R. S. S. (2024). The 2024 quantum advantage blueprint: Where quantum outpaces classical.

Bush, S. F., Challener, W. A., & Mantelet, G. (2021). A perspective on industrial quantum networks. *AVS Quantum Science*, 3(3), 030501. DOI: 10.1116/5.0051881

Exchange, Q. R. K. Towards a Verifiably Secure Quantum-Resistant Key Exchange in IKEv2.

Gholami, S., & Omar, M. (2023). Does Synthetic Data Make Large Language Models More Efficient? *arXiv preprint arXiv:2310.07830*.

Gholami, S., & Omar, M. (2024). Can a student large language model perform as well as its teacher? In *Innovations, Securities, and Case Studies Across Healthcare, Business, and Technology* (pp. 122-139). IGI Global. DOI: 10.4018/979-8-3693-1906-2.ch007

Hamza, Y. A., & Omar, M. D. (2013). Cloud computing security: Abuse and nefarious use of cloud computing. *International Journal of Computer Engineering Research*, 3(6), 22–27.

How, M. L., & Cheah, S. M. (2023). Business Renaissance: Opportunities and challenges at the dawn of the Quantum Computing Era. *Businesses*, 3(4), 585–605. DOI: 10.3390/businesses3040036

Huff, A. J., Burrell, D. N., Nobles, C., Richardson, K., Wright, J. B., Burton, S. L., Jones, A. J., Springs, D., Omar, M., & Brown-Jackson, K. L. (2023). Management Practices for Mitigating Cybersecurity Threats to Biotechnology Companies, Laboratories, and Healthcare Research Organizations. In *Applied Research Approaches to Technology, Healthcare, and Business* (pp. 1-12). IGI Global.

Jones, R., & Omar, M. (2024). Revolutionizing Cybersecurity: The GPT-2 Enhanced Attack Detection and Defense (GEADD) Method for Zero-Day Threats. *International Journal of Informatics* [INJIISCOM]. *Information System and Computer Engineering*, 5(2), 178–191.

Jones, R., Omar, M., Mohammed, D., Nobles, C., & Dawson, M. (2023). Harnessing the Speed and Accuracy of Machine Learning to Advance Cybersecurity. In *2023 Congress in Computer Science, Computer Engineering, & Applied Computing (CSCE)* (pp. 418-421). IEEE. DOI: 10.1109/CSCE60160.2023.00074

Khan, A. A., Akbar, M. A., Ahmad, A., Fahmideh, M., Shameem, M., Lahtinen, V., . . . Mikkonen, T. (2023, July). Agile practices for quantum software development: practitioners' perspectives. In *2023 IEEE international conference on quantum software (QSW)* (pp. 9-20). IEEE.

Lougovski, P., Parekh, O., Broz, J., Byrd, M., Chembo, Y., de Jong, W. A., . . . Svore, K. M. (2023). *Position Papers for the ASCR Workshop on Basic Research Needs in Quantum Computing and Networking*. USDOE Office of Science (SC), Advanced Scientific Computing Research (ASCR).

Madni, A. F., Shah, M. A., & Al-Naeem, M. (2024). An Investigation of Scalability in EHRs using Healthcare 4.0 and Blockchain. *International Journal of Advanced Computer Science and Applications*, 15(5). Advance online publication. DOI: 10.14569/IJACSA.2024.0150548

Metawei, M. A., Eldeeb, H., Nassar, S. M., & Taher, M. (2022). Quantum Computing Meets Artificial Intelligence: Innovations and Challenges. In *Handbook on Artificial Intelligence-Empowered Applied Software Engineering: VOL. 1: Novel Methodologies to Engineering Smart Software Systems* (pp. 303–338). Springer International Publishing. DOI: 10.1007/978-3-031-08202-3_12

Mohamed, N., & Ahmed, A. A. (2024, June). AI in Combatting Man-in-the-Middle Attacks: A Comprehensive Review. In *2024 15th International Conference on Computing Communication and Networking Technologies (ICCCNT)* (pp. 1-6). IEEE. DOI: 10.1109/ICCCNT61001.2024.10725789

Mohammed, D., Omar, M., & Nguyen, V. (2018). Wireless sensor network security: Approaches to detecting and avoiding wormhole attacks. *Journal of Research in Business. Economics and Management*, 10(2), 1860–1864.

Nguyen, V., Mohammed, D., Omar, M., & Banisakher, M. (2018). The Effects of the FCC Net Neutrality Repeal on Security and Privacy. [IJHIoT]. *International Journal of Hyperconnectivity and the Internet of Things*, 2(2), 21–29. DOI: 10.4018/IJHIoT.2018070102

Omar, M. (2021). New insights into database security: An effective and integrated approach for applying access control mechanisms and cryptographic concepts in Microsoft Access environments.

Omar, M. (2022). *Machine Learning for Cybersecurity: Innovative Deep Learning Solutions*. Springer Brief. https://link.springer.com/book/978303115

Omar, M. (2024). From Attack to Defense: Strengthening DNN Text Classification Against Adversarial Examples. In *Innovations, Securities, and Case Studies Across Healthcare, Business, and Technology* (pp. 174-195). IGI Global.

Omar, M. (2024). Revolutionizing Malware Detection: A Paradigm Shift Through Optimized Convolutional Neural Networks. In *Innovations, Securities, and Case Studies Across Healthcare, Business, and Technology* (pp. 196-220). IGI Global. DOI: 10.4018/979-8-3693-1906-2.ch011

Omar, M., & Zangana, H. M. (Eds.). (2024). *Redefining Security With Cyber AI*. IGI Global., DOI: 10.4018/979-8-3693-6517-5

Omar, M., & Zangana, H. M. (Eds.). (2025). *Application of Large Language Models (LLMs) for Software Vulnerability Detection*. IGI Global., DOI: 10.4018/979-8-3693-9311-6

Omar, M., Zangana, H. M., Al-Karaki, J. N., & Mohammed, D. (2024). Harnessing LLMs for IoT malware detection: A comparative analysis of BERT and GPT-2. In *Proceedings of the 8th International Symposium on Multidisciplinary Studies and Innovative Technologies (ISMSIT)* (pp. 1-6). Ankara, Turkiye. https://doi.org/DOI: 10.1109/ISMSIT63511.2024.10757249

Omar, M., Zangana, H. M., & Mohammed, D. (Eds.). (2025). *Integrating Artificial Intelligence in Cybersecurity and Forensic Practices*. IGI Global., DOI: 10.4018/979-8-3373-0588-2

Perron, J. K., DeLeone, C., Sharif, S., Carter, T., Grossman, J. M., Passante, G., & Sack, J. (2021). Quantum undergraduate education and scientific training. *arXiv preprint arXiv:2109.13850*.

Qualters, I., Taylor, A. J., & Hagberg, A. A. (2019). *IS&T Computing Overview* (No. LA-UR-19-22567). Los Alamos National Lab.(LANL), Los Alamos, NM (United States).

Rahul, R., Geetha, S., Priyatharsini, S., Mehata, K., Sundaresan Perumal, T., Ethiraj, N., & Sendilvelan, S. (2024). Cybersecurity Issues and Challenges in Quantum Computing. *Topics in Artificial Intelligence Applied to Industry*, 4(0), 203–221. DOI: 10.1002/9781394216147.ch11

Ramachandran, D., Naqi, S. M., Perumal, G., & Abbas, Q. (2023). DLTN-LOSP: A Novel Deep-Linear-Transition-Network-Based Resource Allocation Model with the Logic Overhead Security Protocol for Cloud Systems. *Sensors (Basel)*, 23(20), 8448. DOI: 10.3390/s23208448 PMID: 37896541

Seskir, Z. C. (2019). *Current state of quantum information technologies in Turkey* (Master's thesis, Middle East Technical University).

Singh, N. B. *Quantum Mechanics in Drug Discovery*. NB Singh.

Sodiya, E. O., Umoga, U. J., Amoo, O. O., & Atadoga, A. (2024). Quantum computing and its potential impact on US cybersecurity: A review: Scrutinizing the challenges and opportunities presented by quantum technologies in safeguarding digital assets. *Global Journal of Engineering and Technology Advances, 18*(2), 049-064.

Wright, J., Dawson, M. E.Jr, & Omar, M. (2012). Cyber security and mobile threats: The need for antivirus applications for smartphones. *Journal of Information Systems Technology and Planning*, 5(14), 40–60.

Zangana, H. M. (2024). Exploring Blockchain-Based Timestamping Tools: A Comprehensive Review. *Redefining Security With Cyber AI*, 92-110.

Zangana, H. M. (2024). Exploring the Landscape of Website Vulnerability Scanners: A Comprehensive Review and Comparative Analysis. *Redefining Security With Cyber AI*, 111-129.

Zangana, H. M., Mohammed, A. K., Sallow, A. B., & Sallow, Z. B. (2024). Cybernetic Deception: Unraveling the Layers of Email Phishing Threats. [INJURATECH]. *International Journal of Research and Applied Technology*, 4(1), 35–47.

Zangana, H. M., & Mohammed, D. (2025). Foundations of Large Language Models in Software Vulnerability Detection. In Omar, M., & Zangana, H. (Eds.), *Application of Large Language Models (LLMs) for Software Vulnerability Detection* (pp. 41–74). IGI Global., DOI: 10.4018/979-8-3693-9311-6.ch002

Zangana, H. M., & Mustafa, F. M. (2025). Image Denoising Techniques for Cybersecurity and Forensic Applications: AI-Driven Approaches. In Omar, M., Zangana, H., & Mohammed, D. (Eds.), *Integrating Artificial Intelligence in Cybersecurity and Forensic Practices* (pp. 117–142). IGI Global Scientific Publishing., DOI: 10.4018/979-8-3373-0588-2.ch005

Zangana, H. M., & Omar, M. (2020). Threats, Attacks, and Mitigations of Smartphone Security. *Academic Journal of Nawroz University*, 9(4), 324–332. DOI: 10.25007/ajnu.v9n4a989

Zangana, H. M., & Omar, M. (2025). Harnessing the Power of Large Language Models for Cybersecurity: Applications, Challenges, and Future Directions. In Omar, M., & Zangana, H. (Eds.), *Application of Large Language Models (LLMs) for Software Vulnerability Detection* (pp. 1–40). IGI Global., DOI: 10.4018/979-8-3693-9311-6.ch001

Zangana, H. M., Omar, M., Al-Karaki, J. N., & Mohammed, D. (2024). Comprehensive Review and Analysis of Network Firewall Rule Analyzers: Enhancing Security Posture and Efficiency. *Redefining Security With Cyber AI*, 15-36.

Zangana, H. M., Omar, M., & Mohammed, D. (2025). Introduction to Artificial Intelligence in Cybersecurity and Forensic Science. In Omar, M., Zangana, H., & Mohammed, D. (Eds.), *Integrating Artificial Intelligence in Cybersecurity and Forensic Practices* (pp. 1–24). IGI Global Scientific Publishing., DOI: 10.4018/979-8-3373-0588-2.ch001

Compilation of References

Aaron, W. C., Irekponor, O., Aleke, N. T., Yeboah, L., & Joseph, J. E. (2024). Machine learning techniques for enhancing security in financial technology systems.

Adelstein, F. (2006). Live forensics: Diagnosing your system without killing it first. *Communications of the ACM*, 49(2), 63–66. DOI: 10.1145/1113034.1113070

Aghayev, A., & Naderi, P. (2024). Hybrid quantum-classical cybersecurity solutions for IoT applications. *Quantum Information Processing*, 24(8).

Agrawal, K., & Aggarwal, M. Building Efficient Smart Contract for Healthcare 4.0. In *Blockchain for Healthcare 4.0* (pp. 94-123). CRC Press.

Aharon, D.. (2024). Using large language models to enhance AI-based cybersecurity protocols. *arXiv*. https://arxiv.org/abs/2404.11713

Ahmed, U., Sipola, T., & Hautamäki, J. (2024). Cyber protection applications of quantum computing: A review. *In Proceedings of the 23rd European Conference on Cyber Warfare and Security (ECCWS)*. Academic Conferences International. https://doi.org/DOI: 10.34190/eccws.23.1.2182

Ahmed, M. M., Naser Mahmood, A., & Hu, J. (2016). A survey of network anomaly detection techniques. *Journal of Network and Computer Applications*, 60, 19–31. DOI: 10.1016/j.jnca.2015.11.016

Ahsan, M. M. (2020). Applications of AI in malware detection. *Computers & Security*, 96, 101830. al., A. e. (2017). Improving anomaly-based intrusion detection systems using data clustering. *Computers & Security*.

Alam, M. T., Tanvirul, A., Bhushal, D., & Rastogi, N. (2024). Using LLMs to automate threat intelligence analysis workflows in security operation centers. *arXiv*. https://ar5iv.labs.arxiv.org/html/2407.02528

Al-Garadi, M. A. (2020). A survey of machine learning for cybersecurity applications. *IEEE Access : Practical Innovations, Open Solutions*, 8, 112752–112788.

Ali, T., & Kostakos, P. (2023). HuntGPT: Integrating machine learning-based anomaly detection and explainable AI with large language models (LLMs). *arXiv*. https://arxiv.org/abs/2309.16021

Aljawarneh, e. (2018). Anomaly detection in network security: Techniques, challenges, and applications. *IEEE Access*.

Alkhalil, Z., Hewage, C., Nawaf, L., & Khan, I. (2021). Phishing attacks: A recent comprehensive study and a new anatomy. *Frontiers of Computer Science*, 3, 563060. DOI: 10.3389/fcomp.2021.563060

Alqatawna, e. (2017). Improving anomaly-based intrusion detection systems using data clustering. *Computers & Security*.

AL-Refaey. M. R., Tyagi, A. K., AL-Ghamdi, A. S. A. M., & Kukreja, S. (Eds.). (2024). *Topics in Artificial Intelligence Applied to Industry 4.0*. John Wiley & Sons.

Althobaiti, O. S., & Dohler, M. (2020). Cybersecurity challenges associated with the Internet of Things in a post-quantum world. *IEEE Access : Practical Innovations, Open Solutions*, 8, 157356–157381. DOI: 10.1109/ACCESS.2020.3019345

Anderson, P. (2023). Cloud Security with AI: Trends and Implementations. *Cloud Computing Today*, 23(2), 34–41.

Balakrishnan, S. (1999). The Linux operating system. *Resonance*, 4(4), 64–72. DOI: 10.1007/BF02838342

Balasubramaniyan, V. A., Poonguzhali, E., & Anbalagan, G. (2020). System of collection and analysis event log from sources under control of Windows operating system. *Semantic Scholar*. https://www.semanticscholar.org/paper/40ff547a0b5472801516df565eef00636427cb7c

Baseri, Y., Chouhan, V., & Ghorbani, A. (2024). Cybersecurity in the Quantum Era: Assessing the Impact of Quantum Computing on Infrastructure. *arXiv preprint arXiv:2404.10659*.

Batarseh, e. (2019). Challenges in integrating AI technologies in cybersecurity frameworks. *Computers & Security*.

Bea Systems. (2024) https://www.baesystems.com/en/digital/feature/the-nation-state-actor#:~:text=The%20Nation%20State%20Actor%20will%20use%20social%20engineering%20to%20target,their%20victim%20in%20doing%20so. Retrieved September 10, 2024

Bergholz, A. e. (2010). A real-life study of phishing attacks. *Detection of Intrusions and Malware & Vulnerability Assessment*.

Bergholz, e. (2010). A real-life study of phishing attacks. *Proceedings of the 15th Conference on Detection of Intrusions and Malware & Vulnerability Assessment.*

Bhosale, K. S., Singh, A., Ambre, S., Nenova, M., & Valkova-Jarvis, Z. (2023). *Quantum technology: Unleashing the power and shaping the future of cybersecurity.* IEEE., DOI: 10.1109/Lighting59819.2023.10299447

Biamonte, J., Wittek, P., Pancotti, N., Rebentrost, P., Wiebe, N., & Lloyd, S. (2017). Quantum machine learning. *Nature*, 549(7671), 188–202. DOI: 10.1038/nature23474 PMID: 28905917

Biggio, B. e. (2013). Evasion attacks against machine learning at test time. *ECML PKDD*, 387–402.

Billo, C., & Chang, W. (2004). *Cyber warfare. An Analysis of the means and motivations of selected nation-states.* ISTS.

Binns. (2018). Fairness in machine learning: Lessons from political philosophy. *Proceedings of the 2018 Conference on Fairness, Accountability, and Transparency.*

Biryukov, A., Shamir, A., & Wagner, D. (2000). Real-time cryptanalysis of A5/1 on a PC. *Fast Software Encryption Workshop 2000.*

Bishwas, A. K., & Sen, M. (2024). Strategic Roadmap for Quantum-Resistant Security: A Framework for Preparing Industries for the Quantum Threat. *arXiv preprint arXiv:2411.09995.*

Block, R. S. S. (2024). The 2024 quantum advantage blueprint: Where quantum outpaces classical.

Brown, A. (2022). Automated Cyber Defense: Leveraging AI for Incident Response. *InfoSec Quarterly*, 29(3), 18–23.

Brown, K., & Thomason, R. (2022). Quantum security in the age of artificial intelligence. *IEEE Transactions on Quantum Engineering.*

Bush, S. F., Challener, W. A., & Mantelet, G. (2021). A perspective on industrial quantum networks. *AVS Quantum Science*, 3(3), 030501. DOI: 10.1116/5.0051881

Carpenter, T. (2012). *Microsoft Windows Operating System Essentials.* John Wiley & Sons.

Carrier, B., & Spafford, E. H. (2004). An event-based digital forensic investigation framework. *Digital Investigation*, 1(1), 2–12.

Carvey, H., & Altheide, C. (2011). *Digital forensics with open source tools.* Elsevier.

Casey, E. (2002). Confronting encryption in computer investigations. *Digital Forensic Research Conference.*

Chandramohan, S. e. (2021). AI-powered cybersecurity: Challenges and solutions. *Cyber Defense Journal*, 13(4), 12–28.

Chen, L., Drannbauer, E., Ademoroti, A., & Williams, D. H. How Plausible is North Korea's Involvement in the Sony Pictures Hack? A Comprehensive Analysis.

Chen, C. e. (2021). Graph-based anomaly detection for financial fraud prevention. *Computers & Security*, 101, 102–121.

Choi, K. S. (2021). The driving force behind cybercrime: Cyber resilience and cyber criminology. [References]. *Journal of Contemporary Criminal Justice*, 37(3), 1–3. DOI: 10.1177/10439862211001631

CISA & FBI Fact Sheet. (2024). How to Protect against Iranian Targeting of Accounts Associated with National Political Organizations. October 2024 https://www.cisa.gov/sites/default/files/2024-10/cisa-fbi-protecting-against-irgc-phishing-508c.pdf Retrieved November 28, 2024

CISA. (2023). America's Cyber Defense Agency, National Coordinator for Critical Infrastructure Security and Resilience. The Attack on Colonial Pipeline: What We've Learned & What We've Done Over the Past Two Years. https://www.cisa.gov/news-events/news/attack-colonial-pipeline-what-weve-learned-what-weve-done-over-past-two-years

Cisco Systems. I. (2024). *Understanding the dangers of zero-day vulnerabilities.* Retrieved from https://www.cisco.com/zero-day-vulnerabilities-2024

Cloudflare, I. (2024). *How DDoS attacks are evolving in 2024.* Retrieved from https://www.cloudflare.com/ddos-evolution

Cognixia. (2020, January 22). How can IoT help digital forensics? *Cognixia.* https://www.cognixia.com/blog/how-can-iot-help-digital-forensics/

Colwill, C. (2009). Human factors in information security: The insider threat–Who can you trust these days? *Information Security Technical Report*, 14(4), 186–196. DOI: 10.1016/j.istr.2010.04.004

Cornerstone Discovery. (n.d.). The future is now — The impact of AI on digital forensics. Retrieved November 25, 2024, from https://cornerstonediscovery.com/the-future-is-now-the-impact-of-ai-on-digital-forensics/

Cybrary. (2020, January 21). *Write blockers: A central part of a forensic analyst's toolbox.*

Cybrary. https://www.cybrary.it/blog/write-blockers-central-part-forensic-analysts - toolbox

Danish, M. (2024). *Enhancing Cyber Security through Predictive Analytics: Real-Time Threat Detection and Response*. University of New Mexico.

Das, S. (2020). *A risk-reduction-based incentivization model for human-centered multi-factor authentication*. Indiana University.

De Tomas Colatin, S. (2021, June 9). Sony Pictures Entertainment attack (2014). Cyber Law Wiki. https://cyberlaw.ccdcoe.org/wiki/Sony_Pictures_Entertainment _attack_(2014)

Dini, P., & Saponara, S. (2023). Design and experimental assessment of real-time anomaly detection techniques for automotive cybersecurity. *Sensors (Basel)*, 23(9231), 9231. Advance online publication. DOI: 10.3390/s23229231 PMID: 38005616

Domingues, P., Frade, M., Andrade, L. M., & Silva, J. V. (2019). Digital forensic artifacts of the Your Phone application in Windows 10. *Digital Investigation*, 30, 32–42. DOI: 10.1016/j.diin.2019.06.003

Easttom, C., Butler, W., Phelan, J., Bhagavatula, R. S., Steuber, S., Rodriguez, K., & Naseer, Z. (2024). *Windows Forensics: Understand Analysis Techniques for Your Windows*. Springer Nature. DOI: 10.1007/979-8-8688-0193-8

Egele, M. e. (2017). A survey of binary code analysis techniques. *ACM Computing Surveys*, 48(4), 1–36.

Ellen Nakashima. "US Attributes Cyberattack on Sony to North Korea," (December 19, 2014), accessed December 10, 2018, https://www. washingtonpost.com/world/ national-security/us-attributes-sony-attack-to-north-korea/2014/12/19/fc3aec60 -8790-11e4-a702-fa31ff4ae98e_ story.html?utm_term=.831d67544d1f Ellen Nakashima, Craig Timberg, and Andrea Peterson, "Sony Pictures Hack Appears to be Linked to North Korea, Investigators Say," Washington Post, December 3, 2014, accessed November 25, 2024, https://www.washingtonpost.com/world/national -security/hack-at-sony-pictures-appears-linked-to-north-korea/2014/12/03/6c3c7e3e -7b25-11e4-b821-503cc7efed9e_story.html?utm_term=.a21e2ffc8b96

Exchange, Q. R. K. Towards a Verifiably Secure Quantum-Resistant Key Exchange in IKEv2.

Fang, S., & Wang, T. (2024). Quantum cryptography and secure communication in next-generation cybersecurity systems. *Communications of the ACM*.

Faruk, M. J. H., Tahora, S., Tasnim, M., Shahriar, H., & Sakib, N. (2024). Quantum-safe cybersecurity in the age of quantum-powered AI. *ResearchGate*. https://www.researchgate.net/publication/377557867_Quantum-safe_Cybersecurity_in_the_age_of_Quantum-Powered_AI

Faruk, M. J. H., Tahora, S., Tasnim, M., Shahriar, H., & Sakib, N. (2022). A review of quantum cybersecurity: Threats, risks, and opportunities. *Kennesaw State University and University at Buffalo*. Retrieved from https://arxiv.org/abs/2207.03534

FBI and North Korea Respond to Sony Hack: December 19 and 21, 2014. (2015). CQ Press EBooks, 637–644. https://doi.org/DOI: 10.4135/9781483380506.n69

FBI. (2014) Update on Sony Investigation https://www.fbi.gov/news/press-releases/update-on-sony-investigation

FBI. (2014). *North Korea Cyber Intrusion*. Federal Bureau of Investigation.

Ferrag, M. A., Alwahedi, F., Battah, A., Cherif, B., Mechri, A., & Tihanyi, N. (2024). Generative AI and large language models for cybersecurity: All insights you need. *arXiv*. https://arxiv.org/abs/2405.12750v1

FireEye. I. (n.d.). *Advanced Persistent Threats (APTs) in 2024: Techniques, tactics, and procedures*. Retrieved from 2024: https://www.fireeye.com/apt-2024

Floridi, T. (2018). How AI and machine learning are reshaping cybersecurity. *Philosophy & Technology*.

Forensic Focus. (2024). A Linux forensics starter case study. https://www.forensicfocus.com/articles/a-linux-forensics-starter-case-study/

Framework Security. (2024, June 28). The Sony Pictures breach: A deep dive into a landmark cyberattack. Framework Security. https://www.frameworksec.com/post/the-sony-pictures-breach-a-deep-dive-into-a-landmark-cyber-attack

Freeman, C. &. (2018). Machine Learning and Security: Protecting Systems with Data and Algorithms.

Gade, N. R., & Reddy, U. (2014). A study of cybersecurity challenges and its emerging trends on latest technologies. *IACSIT International Journal of Engineering and Technology*, 2(2).

Gagliardi, D., & Restrepo, P. (2024). *Leveraging quantum machine learning for future cybersecurity infrastructures*. IEEE Computer Society.

Gangwar, M. (2022, August 3). NGINX access logs and error logs. DigitalOcean. h ttps://www.digitalocean.com/community/tutorials/nginx-access-logs-error-logs

Gao, e. (2018). Vulnerability assessment using machine learning. *ACM Transactions on Cyber-Physical Systems.*

Garfinkel, S. L. (2010). Digital forensics research: The next 10 years. *Digital Investigation*, 7, S64–S73. DOI: 10.1016/j.diin.2010.05.009

Garofalo, D., & Christensen, A. (2024). *A study on the effectiveness of hybrid quantum-classical machine learning for cybersecurity.* Quantum Computing in Cybersecurity Review.

Garrick, B. J., Hall, J. E., Kilger, M., McDonald, J. C., O'Toole, T., Probst, P. S., & Zebroski, E. L. (2004). Confronting the risks of terrorism: Making the right decisions. *Reliability Engineering & System Safety*, 86(2), 129–176. DOI: 10.1016/j.ress.2004.04.003

Ghafarian, A. (2019). Capabilities of Email Forensic Tools. In *Intelligent Computing:Proceedings of the 2019 Computing Conference,* Volume 2 (pp. 514-528). Springer I nternational Publishing.

Gheorghiu, V. M. (2020). Quantum-safe cryptography and its application in AI. *Quantum Information & Computation*, 20(1), 15–28.

Gholami, S., & Omar, M. (2023). Does Synthetic Data Make Large Language Models More Efficient? *arXiv preprint arXiv:2310.07830.*

Gholami, S., & Omar, M. (2024). Can a student large language model perform as well as its teacher? In *Innovations, Securities, and Case Studies Across Healthcare, Business, and Technology* (pp. 122-139). IGI Global. DOI: 10.4018/979-8-3693-1906-2.ch007

Goodfellow, I. e. (2015). Explaining and harnessing adversarial examples. *arXiv preprint arXiv:1412.6572.*

Gradwell, M. (2015). Retention of email records in New Zealand tertiary institutions (Doctoral dissertation, Open Access the Herenga Waka-Victoria University of Wellington).

Green, T. (2021). Machine Learning in Malware Detection: Success Stories. *Journal of Cybersecurity Innovations*, 12(1), 25–31.

Gudivada, V., & Sharma, S. (2024). A review of current trends, techniques, and challenges in large language models (LLMs). *Applied Sciences (Basel, Switzerland)*, 14(5), 2074. DOI: 10.3390/app14052074

Guo, T., & Zhang, F. (2024). Machine learning and quantum cryptography: New era of cybersecurity threats and protections. *arXiv*. https://arxiv.org/abs/2402.02901

Guven, B. (2016). A survey of data mining and machine learning methods for cyber security intrusion detection. *IEEE Communications Surveys and Tutorials.*

Guven, B. (2016). A survey of data mining and machine learning methods for cybersecurity intrusion detection. *IEEE Communications Surveys and Tutorials.*

Hacker Noob Tips. (2024). Windows forensics: Techniques for analyzing Windows artifacts. Hackernoob.tips

Hadi, M. U., Al Tashi, Q., Qureshi, R., Shah, A., Muneer, A., Irfan, M., Zafar, A., Shaikh, M. B., Akhtar, N., Hassan, S. Z., Shoman, M., Wu, J., Mirjalili, S., & Shah, M. (2024). A survey on large language models: Applications, challenges, limitations, and practical usage. *TechRxiv.* https://doi.org/DOI: 10.36227/techrxiv.23589741.v1

Haggard & Lindsay (2015), "North Korea and the Sony Hack: Exporting Instability Through Cyberspace

Hamza, Y. A., & Omar, M. D. (2013). Cloud computing security: Abuse and nefarious use of cloud computing. *International Journal of Computer Engineering Research*, 3(6), 22–27.

Hashim, N., & Sutherland, I. (2011). An architecture for the forensic analysis of Windows system artifacts. In *Digital forensics and cyber crime: Second International ICST Conference, ICDF2C 2010, Abu Dhabi, United Arab Emirates, October 4-6, 2010, revised selected papers 2* (pp. 120-128). Springer Berlin Heidelberg. https://doi.org/DOI: 10.1007/978-3-642-19513-6_10

Hassanin, M., & Moustafa, N. (2024). A comprehensive overview of large language models for cyber defenses: Opportunities and directions. *arXiv.* https://ar5iv.labs.arxiv.org/html/2409.15072

Heeren-Moon, E. (2023). Risk, reputation and responsibility: Cybersecurity and centralized data in United States civilian federal agencies. *Telecommunications Policy*, 47(2), 102502.

Herrmann, K. &. (2020). Cost challenges in AI-driven cybersecurity. *Journal of Cybersecurity Practice.*

Houssel, P. R. B., Singh, P., Layeghy, S., & Portmann, M. (2024). Towards explainable network intrusion detection using large language models. *arXiv:2408.04342.* Link

How, M. L., & Cheah, S. M. (2023). Business Renaissance: Opportunities and challenges at the dawn of the Quantum Computing Era. *Businesses*, 3(4), 585–605. DOI: 10.3390/businesses3040036

Huff, A. J., Burrell, D. N., Nobles, C., Richardson, K., Wright, J. B., Burton, S. L., Jones, A. J., Springs, D., Omar, M., & Brown-Jackson, K. L. (2023). Management Practices for Mitigating Cybersecurity Threats to Biotechnology Companies, Laboratories, and Healthcare Research Organizations. In *Applied Research Approaches to Technology, Healthcare, and Business* (pp. 1-12). IGI Global.

Hwang & Choi. (2021).. . *International Journal of Cybersecurity Intelligence and Cybercrime*, 4(2), 4–24.

Institute, P. (2024). *The 2024 cost of insider threats report.* Retrieved from https://www.ponemon.org/insider-threat-report-2024

Javed, M. S., Sajjad, S. M., Mehmood, D., Mansoor, K., Iqbal, Z., Kazim, M., & Muhammad, Z. (2024). Analyzing Tor browser artifacts for enhanced web forensics, anonymity, cybersecurity, and privacy in Windows-based systems. *Information (Basel)*, 15(8), 495. DOI: 10.3390/info15080495

Jha, M. (2017). A comprehensive study of security in Internet of Things. *IEEE Internet of Things Journal.*

Jones, A. J. (2024). Integration of LLMs With Traditional Security Tools. *Application of Large Language Models (LLMs) for Software Vulnerability Detection*, 295.

Jones, R., Omar, M., Mohammed, D., Nobles, C., & Dawson, M. (2023). Harnessing the Speed and Accuracy of Machine Learning to Advance Cybersecurity. In *2023 Congress in Computer Science, Computer Engineering, & Applied Computing (CSCE)* (pp. 418-421). IEEE. DOI: 10.1109/CSCE60160.2023.00074

Jones, R., & Omar, M. (2024). Revolutionizing Cybersecurity: The GPT-2 Enhanced Attack Detection and Defense (GEADD) Method for Zero-Day Threats. *International Journal of Informatics* [INJIISCOM]. *Information System and Computer Engineering*, 5(2), 178–191.

Kadrich, M. (2007). *Endpoint security.* Addison-Wesley Professional.

Karim, A., Azam, S., Shanmugam, B., Kannoorpatti, K., & Alazab, M. (2019). A comprehensive survey for intelligent spam email detection. *IEEE Access : Practical Innovations, Open Solutions*, 7, 168261–168295. DOI: 10.1109/ACCESS.2019.2954791

Khan, A. A., Akbar, M. A., Ahmad, A., Fahmideh, M., Shameem, M., Lahtinen, V., . . . Mikkonen, T. (2023, July). Agile practices for quantum software development: practitioners' perspectives. In *2023 IEEE international conference on quantum software (QSW)* (pp. 9-20). IEEE.

Khan, K., Su, C. W., Umar, M., & Zhang, W. (2022). Geopolitics of technology: A new battleground? *Technological and Economic Development of Economy*, 28(2), 442–462. DOI: 10.3846/tede.2022.16028

Kheddara, H. (2023). Implementing quantum neural networks for network traffic analysis in cybersecurity. *Journal of Quantum Computing and AI*, 10(3), 115–124.

Kim, D.-V. &. (2017). Towards a rigorous science of interpretable machine learning. *arXiv preprint arXiv:1702.08608.*

Kshetri, N. (2014). Cyberwarfare in the Korean Peninsula: Asymmetries and strategic responses. *East Asia (Piscataway, N.J.)*, 31(3), 183–201. DOI: 10.1007/s12140-014-9215-1

Ladd, T. D., Jelezko, F., Laflamme, R., Nakamura, Y., Monroe, C., & O'Brien, J. L. (2010). Quantum computers. *Nature*, 464(7285), 45–53. DOI: 10.1038/nature08812 PMID: 20203602

Lawton, S. (2023, October 17). How the cloud changed digital forensics investigations. *Dark Reading*. https://www.darkreading.com/cloud-security/how-the-cloud-changed-digital-forensics-investigations

Lehto, M. (2022). Cyber-attacks against critical infrastructure. In *Cyber security: Critical infrastructure protection* (pp. 3–42). Springer International Publishing. DOI: 10.1007/978-3-030-91293-2_1

Liang, Z., Cheng, J., Yang, R., Ren, H., Song, Z., Wu, D., & Li, T. (2023). Unleashing the potential of LLMs for quantum computing: A study in quantum architecture design. *University of Notre Dame, Purdue University, and others*. Retrieved from https://arxiv.org/abs/2307.08191

Ligh, M. H., Case, A., Levy, J., & Walters, A. (2014). *The Art of Memory Forensics: Detecting Malware and Threats in Windows, Linux, and Mac Memory*. Wiley. Easttom, C. (2021). *Digital forensics, investigation, and response* (4th ed.). Jones & Bartlett Learning. Carrier, B. (2005). *File system forensic analysis*. Addison-Wesley Professional. Casey, E. (2011). *Digital evidence and computer crime: Forensic science, computers, and the internet*. Academic press.

Linuxize. (2019). Understanding the /etc/shadow File. Linuxize. https://linuxize.com/post/etc-shadow-file/

Lougovski, P., Parekh, O., Broz, J., Byrd, M., Chembo, Y., de Jong, W. A., . . . Svore, K. M. (2023). *Position Papers for the ASCR Workshop on Basic Research Needs in Quantum Computing and Networking*. USDOE Office of Science (SC), Advanced Scientific Computing Research (ASCR).

Lueth, K. L. (2020, November 19). *State of the IoT 2020: 12 billion IoT connections, surpassing non-IoT for the first time.* IoT Analytics. https://iot-analytics.com/state-of-the-iot-2020-12-billion-iot-connections-surpassing-non-iot-for-the-first-time/

Lundbohm, E. (2017). Understanding nation-state attacks. *Network Security*, 2017(10), 5–8. DOI: 10.1016/S1353-4858(17)30101-0

Madni, A. F., Shah, M. A., & Al-Naeem, M. (2024). An Investigation of Scalability in EHRs using Healthcare 4.0 and Blockchain. *International Journal of Advanced Computer Science and Applications*, 15(5). Advance online publication. DOI: 10.14569/IJACSA.2024.0150548

Magnet Forensics. (2024a). ShimCache vs AmCache: Key Windows forensic artifacts. https://www.magnetforensics.com/blog/shimcache-vs-amcache-key-windows-forensic-artifacts/

Makridakis, S. (2017). The forthcoming artificial intelligence (AI) revolution. *Futures*, 90, 46–60. DOI: 10.1016/j.futures.2017.03.006

Martinez, L. (2021). Predictive Analytics in Cyber Defense. *Advanced Security Systems*, 10(4), 14–20.

Mazzarella, J. (2015, January 6). The SONY HACK — What happened, how did it happen…. What did we learn? IT News. https://blogs.umb.edu/itnews/2015/01/06/the-sony-hack/

McKay, D. (2023, November 13). How to use the dmesg command on Linux. *How to Geek*. https://www.howtogeek.com/449335/how-to-use-the-dmesg-command-on-linux/

Mehrabi, e. (2021). A survey on bias and fairness in machine learning. *ACM Computing Surveys*.

Messier, R. (2015). *Operating System Forensics* (1st ed.). Syngress.

Metawei, M. A., Eldeeb, H., Nassar, S. M., & Taher, M. (2022). Quantum Computing Meets Artificial Intelligence: Innovations and Challenges. In *Handbook on Artificial Intelligence-Empowered Applied Software Engineering: VOL. 1: Novel Methodologies to Engineering Smart Software Systems* (pp. 303–338). Springer International Publishing. DOI: 10.1007/978-3-031-08202-3_12

Micali, D., & Lin, W. (2021). Quantum algorithms for machine learning and their application in cybersecurity. *arXiv:2112.03180.*

Microsoft. (2024). *Phishing attacks: A growing threat to enterprises and individuals.* Retrieved from https://www.microsoft.com/phishing-2024

Microsoft. (2024). Volume Shadow Copy Service (VSS). *Microsoft Learn*. https://learn.microsoft.com/en-us/windows-server/storage/file-server/volume-shadow-copy-service

Miettinen, e. (2017). IoT Sentinel: Automated device-type identification for security enforcement in IoT Systems. *IEEE International Conference on Distributed Computing*.

Miller, T. (2019). Explanation in artificial intelligence: Insights from the social sciences. *Artificial Intelligence*, 267, 1–38. DOI: 10.1016/j.artint.2018.07.007

Mistry, N. R., & Dahiya, M. S. (2019). Signature based volatile memory forensics: A detection-based approach for analyzing sophisticated cyber attacks. *International Journal of Information Technology : an Official Journal of Bharati Vidyapeeth's Institute of Computer Applications and Management*, 11(3), 583–589. DOI: 10.1007/s41870-018-0263-4

Mohamed, N., & Ahmed, A. A. (2024, June). AI in Combatting Man-in-the-Middle Attacks: A Comprehensive Review. In *2024 15th International Conference on Computing Communication and Networking Technologies (ICCCNT)* (pp. 1-6). IEEE. DOI: 10.1109/ICCCNT61001.2024.10725789

Mohammed, D., Omar, M., & Nguyen, V. (2018). Wireless sensor network security: Approaches to detecting and avoiding wormhole attacks. *Journal of Research in Business. Economics and Management*, 10(2), 1860–1864.

Mohd, I. S., & Ahmed, M. (2024). Quantum-safe algorithms for post-quantum cybersecurity challenges. *arXiv*. https://arxiv.org/abs/2403.02769

Moradi, M., Yan, K., Colwell, D., Samwald, M., & Asgari, R. (2024). Exploring the landscape of large language models: Foundations, techniques, and challenges. *arXiv*. https://arxiv.org/abs/2404.11973

Moskvichev, A. D., & Dolgachev, M. V. (2020). System of collection and analysis event log from sources under control of Windows operating system. *2020 International Multi-Conference on Industrial Engineering and Modern Technologies. FarEastCon*, 2020, 1–5. Advance online publication. DOI: 10.1109/FarEastCon50210.2020.9271520

Moustafa, N. e. (2019). An ensemble intrusion detection technique. *Computers & Security*, 89, 101660.

Nelson, B., Phillips, A., & Steuart, C. (2015). *Guide to computer forensics and investigations* (5th ed.). Cengage Learning.

Nelson, D. (2023). Natural Language Processing in Email Security. *AI & Cyber Journal*, 21(1), 22–28.

Nelson, R., Shukla, A., & Smith, C. (2020). Web browser forensics in Google Chrome, Mozilla Firefox, and the Tor Browser Bundle. In Zhang, X., & Choo, K. K. (Eds.), *Digital forensic education* (Vol. 61, pp. 29–50). Springer., DOI: 10.1007/978-3-030-23547-5_12

Nemeth, E., Snyder, G., Hein, T. R., & Whaley, B. (2017). *UNIX and Linux System Administration Handbook* (5th ed.). Pearson Education.

Nguyen, V., Mohammed, D., Omar, M., & Banisakher, M. (2018). The Effects of the FCC Net Neutrality Repeal on Security and Privacy. [IJHIoT]. *International Journal of Hyperconnectivity and the Internet of Things*, 2(2), 21–29. DOI: 10.4018/IJHIoT.2018070102

Nikkel, B. (2021). *Practical Linux Forensics: A Guide for Digital Investigators*. No Starch Press.

Nyholm, H., Monteith, K., Lyles, S., Gallegos, M., DeSantis, M., Donaldson, J., & Taylor, C. (2022). The Evolution of Volatile Memory Forensics. *Journal of Cybersecurity and Privacy*, 2(3), 556–572. DOI: 10.3390/jcp2030028

O'Shaughnessy, S., & Keane, A. (2017). Impact of cloud computing on digital forensic investigations. In *Advances in Digital Forensics IX* (pp. 291–303). Springer Berlin Heidelberg.

Ochoa, e. (2021). AI skills gap in cybersecurity: Addressing the workforce challenges. *Journal of Cybersecurity Education*.

Oliveira, A. (2022, December 15). How to schedule jobs using the Linux 'cron' utility. *Red Hat*. https://www.redhat.com/sysadmin/linux-cron-command

Omar, M. (2021). New insights into database security: An effective and integrated approach for applying access control mechanisms and cryptographic concepts in Microsoft Access environments.

Omar, M. (2022). *Machine Learning for Cybersecurity: Innovative Deep Learning Solutions*. Springer Brief. https://link.springer.com/book/978303115

Omar, M. (2024). From Attack to Defense: Strengthening DNN Text Classification Against Adversarial Examples. In *Innovations, Securities, and Case Studies Across Healthcare, Business, and Technology* (pp. 174-195). IGI Global.

Omar, M. (2024). Revolutionizing Malware Detection: A Paradigm Shift Through Optimized Convolutional Neural Networks. In *Innovations, Securities, and Case Studies Across Healthcare, Business, and Technology* (pp. 196-220). IGI Global. DOI: 10.4018/979-8-3693-1906-2.ch011

Omar, M., & Zangana, H. M. (Eds.). (2024). *Redefining Security With Cyber AI.* IGI Global., DOI: 10.4018/979-8-3693-6517-5

Omar, M., & Zangana, H. M. (Eds.). (2025). *Application of Large Language Models (LLMs) for Software Vulnerability Detection.* IGI Global., DOI: 10.4018/979-8-3693-9311-6

Omar, M., Zangana, H. M., Al-Karaki, J. N., & Mohammed, D. (2024). Harnessing LLMs for IoT malware detection: A comparative analysis of BERT and GPT-2. In *Proceedings of the 8th International Symposium on Multidisciplinary Studies and Innovative Technologies (ISMSIT)* (pp. 1-6). Ankara, Turkiye. https://doi.org/DOI: 10.1109/ISMSIT63511.2024.10757249

Omar, M., Zangana, H. M., & Mohammed, D. (Eds.). (2025). *Integrating Artificial Intelligence in Cybersecurity and Forensic Practices.* IGI Global., DOI: 10.4018/979-8-3373-0588-2

OWASP. (2024). Retrieved from OWASP Top 10 security risks: SQL Injection and XSS: https://owasp.org/top10

Oxygen Forensics. (2023, August 31). What is digital forensics? *Oxygen Forensics.* https://www.oxygenforensics.com/en/resources/what-is-digital-forensics/

Ozkan-Ozay, M., Akin, E., Aslan, Ö., Kosunalp, S., Iliev, T., Stoyanov, I., & Beloev, I. (2024). A Comprehensive Survey: Evaluating the Efficiency of Artificial Intelligence and Machine Learning Techniques on Cyber Security Solutions. IEEE Access.

Palhière, A. (2020, December 5). *SharkyCTF - EZDump writeups / Linux forensics introduction.* Synacktiv. https://www.synacktiv.com/en/publications/sharkyctf-ezdump-writeups-linux- forensics-introduction.html

Patel, K., & Hamed, Z. (2023). *Security in a post-quantum world: Approaches and techniques in cryptography.* Springer Advances in Computational Intelligence.

Paxson, S. &. (2010). Outside the closed world: On using machine learning for network intrusion detection. *IEEE Symposium on Security and Privacy.*

Pérez-Álvarez, J.. (2023). *Quantum-enhanced machine learning for the prediction and prevention of cybersecurity risks.* Computational Intelligence and Quantum Machine Learning Journal.

Perron, J. K., DeLeone, C., Sharif, S., Carter, T., Grossman, J. M., Passante, G., & Sack, J. (2021). Quantum undergraduate education and scientific training. *arXiv preprint arXiv:2109.13850.*

Pieters, W. (2013, December). Defining" the weakest link" comparative security in complex systems of systems. In 2013 IEEE 5th International conference on cloud computing technology and science (Vol. 2, pp. 39-44). IEEE.

Pure Storage. (2024, January 24). *XFS vs. Ext4: Which Linux file system is better?* Pure Storage. https://blog.purestorage.com/purely-educational/xfs-vs-ext4-which-linux-file-system-is- better/

Q., Xing, L., & Zhou, C. (2019). Probabilistic modeling and analysis of sequential cyber-attacks. Engineering Reports, 1(4). https://doi.org/DOI: 10.1002/eng2.12065

Qualters, I., Taylor, A. J., & Hagberg, A. A. (2019). *IS&T Computing Overview* (No. LA-UR-19-22567). Los Alamos National Lab.(LANL), Los Alamos, NM (United States).

Quick, D., & Choo, K. K. R. (2018). Big forensic data reduction: Digital forensic images and electronic evidence. *Cluster Computing*, 21(2), 1277–1297. DOI: 10.1007/s10586-016-0553-1

Rahul, R., Geetha, S., Priyatharsini, S., Mehata, K., Sundaresan Perumal, T., Ethiraj, N., & Sendilvelan, S. (2024). Cybersecurity Issues and Challenges in Quantum Computing. *Topics in Artificial Intelligence Applied to Industry*, 4(0), 203–221. DOI: 10.1002/9781394216147.ch11

Rais, T. (2018). A survey on technical threat intelligence in the age of sophisticated cyber attacks. *Computers & Security.*

Rais, T. (2018). A survey on technical threat intelligence in the age of sophisticated cyberattacks. *Computers & Security.*

Ramachandran, D., Naqi, S. M., Perumal, G., & Abbas, Q. (2023). DLTN-LOSP: A Novel Deep-Linear-Transition-Network-Based Resource Allocation Model with the Logic Overhead Security Protocol for Cloud Systems. *Sensors (Basel)*, 23(20), 8448. DOI: 10.3390/s23208448 PMID: 37896541

Reddy, N. (2019). *Practical cyber forensics.* Apress. Magnet Forensics. (2024, September 23). 7 essential Linux forensics artifacts every investigator should know. https://www.magnetforensics.com/blog/linux-forensics-artifacts-every-investigator-should-know/

Reed, E. (2022). AI in Automotive Cybersecurity: The Tesla Experience. *Industry 4.0 Journal*, 15(3), 47-53.

Ribeiro, A. (2024). Growing convergence of geopolitics and cyber warfare continue to threaten OT and ICS environments in 2024. Industrial Cyber, February 18, 2024 https://industrialcyber.co/features/growing-convergence-of-geopolitics-and-cyber-warfare-continue-to-threaten-ot-and-ics-environments-in-2024/#:~:text=Geopolitical%20tensions%20between%20major%20powers,infrastructure%20and%20industrial%20sectors%20worldwide. Retrieved September 12, 2024

Ring, e. (2019). Survey on AI techniques for cybersecurity: Data challenges. *ACM Computing Surveys*.

ROOM, B. (2021). The United States, joined by allies and partners, attributes malicious cyber activity and irresponsible state behavior to the People's Republic of China.

Rosch-Grace, D., & Straub, J. (2024). *Considering the implications of artificial intelligence, quantum computing, and cybersecurity*. IEEE., DOI: 10.1109/CSCI58124.2022.00191

Roussev, V. (2016). Digital forensic science: Issues, methods, and challenges. *Synthesis Lectures on Information Security, Privacy, &. Trust*, 8(5), 1–155.

Ruan, K., Carthy, J., Kechadi, T., & Crosbie, M. (2011). Cloud forensics: An overview. In *Advances in Digital Forensics VII* (pp. 35-46). https://doi.org/DOI: 10.1007/978-3-642-24212-0_3

Sammons, J. (2014). *The basics of digital forensics: the primer for getting started in digital forensics*. Syngress.

Samuelson, P. (1999). Privacy as intellectual property. *Stanford Law Review*, 52(5), 1125. DOI: 10.2307/1229511 PMID: 11503653

SANS Institute. (2024). FOR500: Windows forensic analysis. https://www.sans.org/cyber-security-courses/windows-forensic-analysis/

Sarker, I. H. (2022). Cybersecurity data science: An overview. *Journal of Big Data*, 9, 1–29.

Schmid, e. (2020). The human-AI collaboration in cybersecurity: Risks of overreliance. *Cybersecurity*.

Schmitt, M. N. (2010). Cyber operations in international law: The use of force, collective security, self-defense, and armed conflicts. In Proceedings of a workshop on deterring cyberattacks: Informing strategies and developing options for US policy (Vol. 151, pp. 163-64). Washington, DC: National Academies Press.

Schuld, M., & Petruccione, F. (2018). *Supervised learning with quantum computers*. Springer., DOI: 10.1007/978-3-319-96424-9

Security Ninja. (2016, June 22). Understanding critical Windows artifacts and their relevance during an investigation: Artifacts. *Infosec Institute*. https://www.infosecinstitute.com/resources/digital-forensics/understanding-critical-windows-artifacts-and-their-relevance-during-investigation-part-2/

Serketzis, N., Katos, V., Ilioudis, C., Baltatzis, D., & Pangalos, G. J. (2019). Actionable threat intelligence for digital forensics readiness. *Future Internet*, 11(7), 162. DOI: 10.3390/fi11070162

Seskir, Z. C. (2019). *Current state of quantum information technologies in Turkey* (Master's thesis, Middle East Technical University).

Shah, S. e. (2020). Threat intelligence in the era of AI. *AI & Society*, 35(2), 19–28.

Shaikh, S., & Awan, M. (2024). Ensuring integrity and confidentiality in cybersecurity with quantum machine learning. *Proceedings of Cybersecurity and Quantum Technologies Workshop*.

Sharbaf. (2019). Artificial intelligence in cybersecurity: An application-focused overview. *Journal of Cybersecurity Research*.

Sharma, A. (2024). Federated learning for cybersecurity: Concepts, challenges, and future directions. *IEEE Transactions on Cybersecurity*, 24(3), 56-78. Retrieved from https://www.frontiersin.org

Shinde, e. (2020). Artificial intelligence-driven automation in cybersecurity incident response. *Cybersecurity*.

Sigholm, J. (2013). Non-state actors in cyberspace operations. *Journal of Military Studies*, 4(1), 1–37. DOI: 10.1515/jms-2016-0184

Silberschatz, A., Galvin, P. B., & Gagne, G. (2018). *Operating System Concepts* (10th ed.). John Wiley & Sons, Inc.

Singh, B., & Vigna, G. (2021, March 25). *Memory forensics for virtualized hosts*. VMware. https://blogs.vmware.com/security/2021/03/memory-forensics-for-virtualized-hosts.html

Singh, N. B. *Quantum Mechanics in Drug Discovery*. NB Singh.

Slonopas, A. (2024, March 3). *What is digital forensics? A closer examination of the field.* Information Technology Blog | American Public University. https://www.apu.apus.edu/area-of-study/information-technology/resources/what-is-digital-forensics/

Smith, J. (2021). AI in Cybersecurity: Real-World Case Studies. *CyberSec Journal*, 34(2), 45–50.

Sodiya, E. O., Umoga, U. J., Amoo, O. O., & Atadoga, A. (2024). Quantum computing and its potential impact on U.S. cybersecurity: A review: Scrutinizing the challenges and opportunities presented by quantum technologies in safeguarding digital assets. *Global Journal of Engineering and Technology Advances, 18*(2), 049-064.

Sodiya, E. O., Umoga, U. J., Amoo, O. O., & Atadoga, A. (2024). Quantum computing and its potential impact on US cybersecurity: A review: Scrutinizing the challenges and opportunities presented by quantum technologies in safeguarding digital assets. *Global Journal of Engineering and Technology Advances, 18*(2), 049-064.

Souppaya, M., & Scarfone, K. (2013). Guidelines for managing the security of mobile devices in the enterprise. NIST special publication, 800(124), 124-800.

Suryotrisongko, H., & Musashi, Y. (2022). Evaluating hybrid quantum-classical deep learning for cybersecurity botnet DGA detection. *Procedia Computer Science*, 197, 223–229. DOI: 10.1016/j.procs.2021.12.135

Symantec, C. (2024). *The evolution of ransomware: A deep dive into modern cyber threats.* Retrieved from https://www.symantec.com/ransomware-2024

Taylor, H. (2022). AI in Endpoint Protection: Practical Applications. *Security Insights Review*, 17(4), 52–58.

ThreatConnect. I. (2024). *MitM attacks: Emerging trends and techniques*. Retrieved from https://www.threatconnect.com/mitm-2024

TickTechTold. (2023). 7 real-life cases solved using digital forensics. https://www.ticktechtold.com/cases-using-digital-forensics/

Tseng, W., Lee, S., & Wang, H. (2024). Evaluating the usability of LLMs in threat intelligence enrichment. *arXiv*. https://ar5iv.labs.arxiv.org/html/2407.13093

Vaswani, A., Shazeer, N., Parmar, N., Uszkoreit, J., Jones, L., Gomez, A. N., Kaiser, Ł., & Polosukhin, I. (2017). Attention is all you need. *Proceedings of the Advances in Neural Information Processing Systems (NeurIPS), 30*, 5998-6008. https://arxiv.org/abs/1706.03762

Vegh, L. (2018, February). Cyber-physical systems security through multi-factor authentication and data analytics. In *2018 IEEE International Conference on Industrial Technology (ICIT)* (pp. 1369-1374). IEEE. DOI: 10.1109/ICIT.2018.8352379

Verton, D. (2014) The Sony hack and its larger implications for cybersecurity. Fedscoop December 19, 2014. https://fedscoop.com/sony-hack-matters/ Retrieved September 12, 2024

Vishwakarma, A., & Ghosh, D. (2024). *An AI-powered quantum encryption system for secure communication networks*. IEEE., DOI: 10.1109/ACCESS.2024.3157194

Watson, L., & Crone, S. (2023). Quantum machine learning in cybersecurity: Leveraging quantum computing for AI-based anomaly detection. *Quantum Information Science*, 7(5), 150.

Williams, J., & Mitchell, M. (2022). Optimizing cybersecurity defenses using hybrid quantum-classical models. *Nature Communications*, 13(1).

Wilusz, D., Sadowczyk, D., Wójtowicz, A., & Tasiemski, L. (2022). Long Tail of Security Vulnerabilities and Nation-State APT Actors. *Proceedings Book*, 25(26th), 3.

Wright, J., Dawson, M. E.Jr, & Omar, M. (2012). Cyber security and mobile threats: The need for antivirus applications for smartphones. *Journal of Information Systems Technology and Planning*, 5(14), 40–60.

Wu, J., & Chen, L. (2024). *Exploiting quantum learning algorithms for detecting cybersecurity vulnerabilities in real-time systems*. IEEE Transactions on Cybersecurity.

Xu, H., Wang, S., Li, N., Wang, K., Zhao, Y., Liu, Y., & Wang, H. (2024). Large language models for cyber security: A systematic literature review. *arXiv*. https://arxiv.org/abs/2405.04760v3

Yang, Y., & Liu, Y. (2024). *Using machine learning for quantum threat modeling and analysis*. Cybersecurity Research Advances.

Yin, e. (2017). Deep learning for intrusion detection systems in cybersecurity. *Future Generation Computer Systems*.

Young, K. (2021). Cyber Case Study: Sony Pictures Entertainment Hack. Coverlink Insurance November 8, 2021. https://coverlink.com/case-study/sony-pictures -entertainment-hack/ Retrieved September 12, 2024.

Zangana, H. M. (2024). Exploring Blockchain-Based Timestamping Tools: A Comprehensive Review. *Redefining Security With Cyber AI*, 92-110.

Zangana, H. M. (2024). Exploring the Landscape of Website Vulnerability Scanners: A Comprehensive Review and Comparative Analysis. *Redefining Security With Cyber AI*, 111-129.

Zangana, H. M., Omar, M., Al-Karaki, J. N., & Mohammed, D. (2024). Comprehensive Review and Analysis of Network Firewall Rule Analyzers: Enhancing Security Posture and Efficiency. *Redefining Security With Cyber AI*, 15-36.

Zangana, H. M., Mohammed, A. K., Sallow, A. B., & Sallow, Z. B. (2024). Cybernetic Deception: Unraveling the Layers of Email Phishing Threats. [INJURATECH]. *International Journal of Research and Applied Technology*, 4(1), 35–47.

Zangana, H. M., & Omar, M. (2020). Threats, Attacks, and Mitigations of Smartphone Security. *Academic Journal of Nawroz University*, 9(4), 324–332. DOI: 10.25007/ajnu.v9n4a989

Zayed, K. (2016). Information security awareness: Managing web, mobile, and endpoint security; overcoming the challenges of bring your own device. *International Journal of Teaching and Case Studies*, 7(3-4), 271–288. DOI: 10.1504/IJTCS.2016.080929

Zdziarski, J. (2012). *The iOS Hacker's Handbook*. Wiley.

Zeng, S., & Hsin, J. (2023). *Applications of quantum computing in improving security in digital infrastructure*. Quantum Computing for Cybersecurity Journal.

Zhang, J., Bu, H., Wen, H., Chen, Y., Li, L., & Zhu, H. (2024). When LLMs meet cybersecurity: A systematic literature review. *Institute of Information Engineering, Chinese Academy of Sciences*. Retrieved from https://arxiv.org/abs/2405.03644

Zhang, Q., Liu, T., & Yu, M. (2024). *Analyzing cybersecurity threats using AI-powered quantum computing models*. Quantum Cyber Defense.

Zhang, X., Li, W., & Tang, S. (2021). Advances in malware detection and classification using machine learning. *IEEE Access : Practical Innovations, Open Solutions*.

Zhou, S., Chen, R., An, Z., & Hou, S.-Y. (2024). Application of large language models to quantum state simulation. *arXiv*. https://arxiv.org/abs/2403.19758

Zoldi, e. (2020). Real-time machine learning for fraud detection. *Journal of Financial Crime*.

About the Contributors

Hewa Majeed Zangana is an Assistant Professor currently affiliated with Duhok Polytechnic University (DPU) in Iraq. He holds a Doctorate in Philosophy (PhD) degree in ITM, which he is currently pursuing at DPU. Prior to his current role, Hewa Majeed Zangana has held various academic and managerial positions. He previously served as an Assistant Professor at Ararat Private Technical Institute and a Lecturer at DPU's Amedi Technical Institute, and Nawroz University. He has also held administrative positions such as Curriculum Division Director - Presidency of DPU, Information Unit Manager of The Research Center at Duhok Polytechnic University, Head of the Computer Science Department at Nawroz University, and Acting Dean of the College of Computer and IT at Nawroz University. Hewa Majeed Zangana's research interests span a wide range of topics in computer science, including network systems, information security, mobile communication, data communication, and intelligent systems. He has published extensively in peer-reviewed journals such as IEEE, EAI, IGI-Global, Inform, Indonesian Journal of Education and Social Science, TIJAB, INJIISCOM, and AJNU. In addition to his research contributions, Hewa Majeed Zangana has been actively involved in editorial roles such as Editorial Board Member at Applied and Computational Engineering (ewapublishing.org), serving as a Reviewer for the Scientific Journals of Nawroz University. He has also been a member of various scientific committees and administrative bodies at Nawroz University, including the Scientific Curriculum Development Committee, the Student Follow-up Program Committee, and the Committee for the Preparation of the Rules of Procedure for Consultative Offices.

Marwan Omar is an accomplished cybersecurity expert and academic, specializing in the intersection of artificial intelligence (AI) and cybersecurity. He currently serves as an Associate Professor of Cybersecurity and AI at the Illinois Institute of Technology, where he leads cutting-edge research on AI security, focusing on the detection and mitigation of advanced cyber threats. Dr. Omar holds multiple advanced degrees, including a PhD in Cybersecurity and a PhD in AI, and has earned numerous industry certifications such as Certified Ethical Hacker (CEH) and SANS Certified Smartphone Forensics Analyst (GASF). His extensive publication record includes books, peer-reviewed journal articles, and conference papers that explore the integration of AI in cybersecurity, with a particular focus on large language models (LLMs) and generalized AI (Gen AI). In addition to his academic pursuits, Dr. Omar is actively involved in industry collaborations and has contributed to numerous high-profile projects aimed at securing AI-driven technologies. His expertise has positioned him as a sought-after advisor and thought leader in the cybersecurity community. As a first-generation American from the Yazidi community in Iraq, Dr. Omar is committed to serving as a beacon of hope and inspiration for underrepresented minorities in STEM fields. His dedication to advancing both the scientific and social aspects of cybersecurity makes him a unique and influential figure in the ongoing dialogue about the future of AI security.

***

Luay Albtosh is a dedicated and accomplished professional currently pursuing a Ph.D. in Cyber Leadership. With a robust academic background and over a decade of industry experience, Luay Albtosh has established a strong foothold in the field of computer science. Luay Albtosh holds a master's degree in computer science, which laid the groundwork for a career marked by continuous learning and impactful contributions to the field. Throughout the years, Luay Albtosh has developed a profound expertise in various aspects of computer science, including cybersecurity, software development, and IT project management. In addition to academic achievements, Luay Albtosh has consistently demonstrated a commitment to excellence in professional endeavors. With more than 10 years of hands-on experience, Luay Albtosh has successfully led numerous projects, drove innovation and ensuring the seamless integration of technology solutions. This extensive experience has provided Luay Albtosh with a deep understanding of both the technical and strategic facets of the industry.

Jamal N. Al-Karaki is currently a full professor at CIS, Zayed university. He has a prolonged and rich university career in education, service, and research. He holds a Ph.D. degree (with Distinction) in Computer Engineering from Iowa State University, USA, with the Research Excellence Award. He has a proven record of progressive responsibility, including leadership positions as a college Dean, Director of IT, Co-Founder, and Dept. Head at various institutes. He led the development of some national centers in cybersecurity as well as undergraduate and graduate computing programs related to cyber security and AI. As an active researcher, he develops plans to advance the research agenda at CIS. He has Published 100+ refereed technical articles in scholarly international journals and conference proceedings. He is a senior member of IEEE and Tau Beta Pi. He is an affiliate member of the Mohammad Bin Rashid Academy for Scientists in UAE and constantly being listed among the top 2% highly cited researchers in his field worldwide. He holds a plethora of professional certification in the domain of cyber security as well as being certified accreditation reviewer for CAA-UAE, Quality Matters, and Pearson EDI verifier/assessor. Prof. Al-Karaki has participated in many panels to advance cyber security education and capacity building in UAE and beyond. Prof. Al-Karaki research interests covers the wide spectrum of computing and its applications in AI, human life, education, economy, healthcare, Society, Cyber security, among many others.

Soumya George is an Asst. Professor at St. George's College, Aruvithura. She completed her Ph. D in Computer Science from Cochin University of Science and Technology. Her research areas of interest include data mining, information retrieval, etc. She had many journal publications to her credit.

Angel Jones is an Adjunct Professor At the University of Virginia School of Continuing and Professional Studies. Dr. Jones began his 20-year cybersecurity career as a special agent with the U.S. Coast Guard, investigating cybercrime. His expertise has made him the go-to subject matter expert for complex cybersecurity and cyber breach investigation matters. Dr. Jones' experience includes serving as the Chief Information Security Officer for several global firms, proactively protecting organizations from dynamic cyber threats. Further, Dr. Jones holds several industry certifications, including the Certified Information Systems Security Professional (CISSP), Certified Information Security Manager (CISM), Certified Information Systems Auditor (CISA), Certified Chief Information Security Officer (CCISO), Certified in Risk and Information Systems Control (CRISC), Certified Ethical Hacker (CEH), EnCase Certified Examiner (EnCE), Digital Forensics Certified Practitioner (DFCP), AWS Certified Solutions Architect – Professional and AWS Certified Security - Specialty and Project Management Professional (PMP).

Sachil Kumar is an accomplished forensic scientist and academic, specializing in forensic chemistry, toxicology, and forensic medicine. He holds a PhD in Forensic Chemistry and Forensic Medicine from King George's Medical University, India, where he developed an innovative, cost-effective method for postmortem interval (PMI) estimation using cardiac Troponin-T (cTnT) degradation, significantly extending the time window for accurate PMI determination. Dr. Kumar has a robust teaching portfolio, with experience as an Associate Professor at Amity

University, Noida, and previously at institutions like Sandip University and Naif Arab University for Security Sciences in Riyadh, where he has delivered lectures, supervised master's dissertations, and contributed to curriculum development. His research skills span molecular biology, analytical chemistry, and toxicology, and he has been recognized with several prestigious awards, including the UGC Junior and Senior Research Fellowships. In addition to his teaching and research, Dr. Kumar has contributed extensively to academic publishing, serving as Editorial Secretary for the Arab Journal of Forensic Sciences & Forensic Medicine and as a peer reviewer for numerous international journals. His work on toxicology and forensic analysis has been widely published, with key studies on substances like pentazocine, xylazine, and synthetic cannabinoids. Dr. Kumar is also a member of several professional societies, including the International Alliance of Clinical and Forensic Toxicologists and the Japanese Society of Toxicology. His interdisciplinary expertise, international experience, and dedication to forensic research make him a significant figure in the field.

Firas Mahmood Mustafa holds a Ph.D. in Computer Engineering from Mosul University, Iraq. His academic journey began with a B.Sc. in Electrical Engineering (Electronics and Communication), graduating in the top quarter of his class. He earned an M.Sc. in Computer Engineering from Mosul University in 2000. Mustafa joined the Computer Science Department at AlHadba University in 2003 and completed his Ph.D. in 2007. From 2013 to 2017, he was with DPU University, and from 2017 to 2020, he chaired the CCE Department at Nawroz University. An active participant in Erasmus+ and IREX programs, he now teaches at DPU University, shaping future computer engineering professionals.

Ivan Zziwa is a second-year master's student in Cyber Forensics and Security at the Illinois Institute of Technology. With a strong background in cybersecurity, digital forensics, and AI-driven solutions, he has contributed to various research projects, including AI-based intrusion detection systems and deep learning applications for food monitoring. Ivan has also served as a teaching assistant, guiding students in cybersecurity principles, and has participated in industry-focused events to promote cybersecurity awareness and education. His interests include cybersecurity management, threat analysis, and advancing technological opportunities in underserved communities.

Index

A

C

D

E

F

H

I

L

M

N

P

Q

R

S

T

V

W

Z

www.ingramcontent.com/pod-product-compliance
Lightning Source LLC
LaVergne TN
LVHW080611300926
849162LV00005B/1112